ISBN 978-1-334-23717-1
PIBN 10758127

1 MONTH OF
FREE
READING

at
www.ForgottenBooks.com

By purchasing this book you are eligible for one month membership to ForgottenBooks.com, giving you unlimited access to our entire collection of over 700,000 titles via our web site and mobile apps.

To claim your free month visit:

www.forgottenbooks.com/free758127

English
Français
Deutsche
Italiano
Español
Português

www.forgottenbooks.com

Mythology Photography **Fiction**
Fishing Christianity **Art** Cooking
Essays Buddhism Freemasonry
Medicine **Biology** Music **Ancient
Egypt** Evolution Carpentry Physics
Dance Geology **Mathematics** Fitness
Shakespeare **Folklore** Yoga Marketing
Confidence Immortality Biographies
Poetry **Psychology** Witchcraft
Electronics Chemistry History **Law**
Accounting **Philosophy** Anthropology
Alchemy Drama Quantum Mechanics
Atheism Sexual Health **Ancient History**
Entrepreneurship Languages Sport
Paleontology Needlework Islam
Metaphysics Investment Archaeology
Parenting Statistics Criminology
Motivational

TO

ADAM CLARKE,

D.D. L.L.D. F.R.S. F.A.S. and A.S.S.

SIR.

FORASMUCH as many have taken in hand, to set forth in order, a declaration of those things, which are most surely believed among us, even as they delivered them unto us, who, from the beginning, were *strangers*, and *ignorant* of the word:

It seemeth good to me, also, having had perfect understanding of all things, from the very first, to write unto thee, in order, most excellent ADAM CLARKE, that thou mightest know the *un*certainty of those things, wherein thou has been instructed. (Luke i. 1. and 4.)

Being about to commence a Review of the Nativity, Life, Death, and Resurrection of Jesus, called the Christ, recorded in those books which are now attributed to Matthew, Mark, Luke, and John, I have selected you from the body of Theological Professors, as being most competent, by your superior and extensive knowledge, to appreciate my conclusions, and correct my errors : because, from your deep researches, and elaborate commentaries, on those books, you have attained to a degree of notoriety, far beyond that acquired by any of your brethren.

The CRISIS has now arrived, in which it becomes an imperative duty for every man to come forward boldly and assist in extirpating that system of fraud and delusion, which, for ages past, has shackled and enslaved the minds of so many human beings.

> " To see the sufferings, of my fellow-creatures,
> And own myself a man ! to see our senators
> Cheat the deluded people with a show
> Of Liberty, which, yet, they ne'er must taste of:
>
> ————whom they please they lay in basest bonds ;
> Bring whom they please to infamy and sorrow :
>
> All that bear this, are villains ; and I one,
> Not to rouse up at the great call of nature,
> And check the growth of these domestic spoilers,
> That makes us slaves, and tell us 'tis our charter."

It is true, that we have not that stimulus, which is extorted from the pockets of the poor, to call forth the energies of our minds and bodies. But, we have others, which, to the mind, is more consoling: one of which, is a peaceful and delightful reflection, assuring us, that we have contributed our mite towards the welfare and happiness of mankind ; by our endeavours to teach the ignorant, and our efforts to release them, from those groundless terrors and deceptive arts, with which their imprisoned senses have so long been bound by that FAITH, which is

> " The Priest's strong chain,
> And prop of the
> DIVINITY."

It is this consolation which buoys us up, while passing through the waters of tribulation: and, though the flood-gates of persecution, may be opened wide, yet, it will not overflow us: even whilst walking through the fire of our enemies, we shall not be consumed ; neither shall the flame of their malignant tongues, kindle upon us.

I have made thus bold, Sir, to address myself to you, knowing you to be a defender of that system which I am compelled to look upon as nothing more than a "fancied vision." Having made the Old and New Testaments my particular study, during these last four years, in the hope of finding some internal evidence of their authenticity, I have at length discovered that there is none ; and that to build upon them, is like resting on a "thing of nought." I shall, therefore, henceforth, *fix my dependance*, not on doctrines, which are made and unmade at pleasure; but upon a pure, uncontaminated, stable, system of morality; which is founded on *Reason*, and has for its object, general utility. For those doctrines and ceremonies, which are only founded upon things not seen, and things *hoped* for, can only be beneficial to those individuals, who, in submitting thereto, find it an easy and profitable profession. Thus the priests, taking advantage of the credulity of the ignorant, soon found themselves secure, and ruled over them as they pleased; and who, notwithstanding the increase of knowledge, still continue to claim, through the force of custom, that as a right, which was first obtained by subtilty, and now sanctioned by antiquity. But the age has now arrived in which their dogmas shall no longer be held sacred. Men will not tamely submit, to the customs and authority of their credulous fore-fathers; because they find that they have been founded only in ignorance and fraud. Therefore, if I do not obtain some better evidence than I now possess, concerning the utility and veracity of the dogmas of the Christian Religion, I must speedily renounce the name of Christianity, and adopt some other that is more allied to virtue: where the principle of " doing to others, as we would wish them to do to us," is less talked of, and more practised.

It is said, that Man, by reason, may controul every propensity; then surely, that which has only existed in opinion, may, by the force of reason, be effectually removed, when found to be erroneous. It is the knowledge of this, which raises the venom of the priesthood against reason. It is carnal, they say. It is at variance with God. It is unable to comprehend the things which are spiritual. But, Sir, do you not affirm that reason is the gift of God? If this be true, where is his wisdom and justice displayed, in giving to us that which is incompatible with our wants and welfare? For, if our reason be the gift of God, it is our greatest evil; seeing that by it we are drawn aside from that faith, which is so necessary for our salvation, and without which you, moreover, tell us we cannot be saved.

It not only deprives us of those inestimable blessings, held forth to us in those books, but it draws us, imperceptibly, to the brink of a dangerous precipice, whence, if what you say be true, we can have no chance of escaping, but a sure and certain doom of falling headlong into an abyss of endless torment; as it is written, that, *he that believeth not, shall be damned.*[1] But, if this reason be carnal, and unable to comprehend the things which are spiritual, why does your spiritual God invite us to come and reason with him,[2] and to bring forth all our *strong reasons*,[3] if he knew that the reasoning powers which we possess, were not sufficient to comprehend him?

The Priests, we find, although they make pretensions of holding familar intercourse with their God, and ascribe to him certain attributes and qualities, which they pretend to expound, by the aid and assistance of his *holy* spirit, nevertheless cannot agree among themselves, in any one of their dogmas. Yet they will all concur, in drawing their subsistence from the labour of the poor. How is this? Are they not composed of the same elements, and organized like ourselves? Are they not, likewise, subject to the same calamities, and infirmities, even the dissolution of their bodies, as other men? What natural claim can they have, then, to the fruits of our labour? Is it to their abstemious and moral conduct, that we are to ascribe their "right divine?" No; we find them, in general, the most lascivious and voluptuous, whenever the veil of reverence is drawn aside, and all their "hidden man" exposed. To what purpose, then, are they employed? Is it to expound the word and will of a God of infinite wisdom, as though he were not competent to make himself understood, without an interpreter? If so, which, among them all, are we to believe, seeing, that so many different explanations of it are given by them? And, if this be the word of God, cannot we read it and judge for ourselves, without employing another to do it for us? Surely, it is time, then, that they were driven to some more useful employment than that of decorating their persons with long robes, in which, for a show, they make long prayers,[4] telling us that only, which we might easily know by ourselves. That time, I trust, is fast approaching. The eye of reason, having detected the imposition, and discovered their utter uselessness, the " Age of Reason" is now exposing them. The spell of superstition is broken. The walls are tottering. And though the "powers that be," aided by prejudice and interest, are endeavouring to support them, yet, having no other foundation, but sophistry and ignorance, fall they must before the "unsophisticated voice of Reason." We see that the "gangs," which have been raised in their behalf, are now scattered ; and those who have conducted their numerous prosecutions have experienced little else than shame and disgrace—still, should they have the temerity to proceed further, they will find, when too late for them, that their conduct has only hastened, the downfall of superstition.

I have been induced to say thus much, by way of introduction ; in order that I might be perfectly understood, before I commence with the body of the work that I have proposed to examine. My intention is to show you that the internal evidence of those books, called Old and New Testaments, will not warrant our assent to their genuineness and authenticity. Also, that their style and composition prove them, instead of emanating from an all wise and perfect being, to have been the production of the most ignorant and depraved of all civilised human beings. In so doing, I shall endeavour, as much as possible, to confine myself to the books themselves ; and draw from them my conclusions. As it is written, "by thy words thou shalt be justified, and by thy words thou shalt be condemned."[5]

JOHN CLARKE.

CHAP. I.

Verse 1. " The book of the generation of Jesus Christ, the son of David, the son of Abraham."

Prithee, Doctor, what would you think of that historian, who, whilst writing the genealogy of King George, should say " George, the son of James the first, the son of Henry the seventh ?" Here, you see, is only a hop, and then a jump to the top! But the next verse, we shall find bringing him down again, step by step.

Verse 2. " Abraham begat Isaac ; and Isaac begat Jacob ; and Jacob begat Judas and his brethren."

I cannot see, why the *brethren* of Judas should be introduced, into this genealogy of Jesus, more than the brethren of David, Solomon, and the rest. Were they such an honour to the *holy child*, Jesu ? No, surely; for we find, that they were all a gang of murderers. Read Gen. xxxvii. 5. and you will there learn, that they *hated* their brother Joseph, whom they attempted to destroy; and you know, that John says, he that *hateth* his brother is a *murderer.*[6] Even while they were mere boys, some of them thought nothing of slaying all the men in the city, in the most treacherous and barbarous manner.[7] And I would also ask you, who are so well acquainted with history, whether you ever heard of a more unfeeling and despotic monster, than Joseph is represented to have been ? When but a child, he was continually sowing discord among his brethren, by telling them his idle dreams; which conduct, Solomon says, is an abomination to the Lord.[8] When a servant, he disturbed the peace of the family, by his misogyny and vanity, because, forsooth! he was a goodly person and well favoured.[9] While in prison, he made his fellow prisoners miserable, through his pretensions *to fortune-telling.*[10] And, after having ingratiated himself into favour with the King of Egypt, he disturbed the peace of the whole nation, by predicting a seven years of famine;[11] a circumstance which could not possibly occur, without making God a liar : for he had formerly promised, that, while the earth remained, seed-time and harvest should not cease;[12] which was impossible for him to have forgotten, because he set his bow in the cloud, to remind him of it![13] Again, observe the manner in which this Joseph sported with the feelings of his brethren and parent.[14] And, it is moreover, evident, that if they had not come to him, he would never have sent for them; although he had had the command of the whole land of Egypt, for seven years prior to their coming. Besides, what greater tyranny could ever be practised by the most execrable tyrant that ever existed, than by this monster; who, not satisfied with monopolizing all their money, their cattle, and their lands, must exact the fifth part of the future produce of their labour for ever?[15]

Verse. 3. "And Judas begat Phares and Zara of Thamar."

If you suppose, that any person were ever inspired, by an "all wise," and "all powerful God," to communicate these words to men, would it not, necessarily, have followed, that the words, so communicated, would have been written in a language, understood by all mankind, if he willeth that *all* men should be saved, and come to the knowledge of the truth?[16] Or should we admit, that the foolishness of God[17] once confounded the language of all men,[18] still it would be necessary that the words, so communicated, if required to be translated for the benefit and salvation of all men, should be attended by the same *divine* inspiration and teaching, in order to prevent any error or inaccuracy, which unavoidably happens, through the fallibility of men translating one language into another. Would it not be also requisite, and absolutely necessary, that every transcriber, and printer, with all their assistants, even the very *devil*,* should be divinely inspired, so

* Printer's Devil.

that there should be no need of altering, revising and
correcting the words of this God, which are so essential to be made known and understood? We read that
he has done such things, when it was far less important
or necessary than in the present case. Has he not *Inspired* men to cut and carve timber and stones, and to
do all sorts of cunning workmanship, such as making
of lamps, candlesticks, and snuffers?[19] Isaiah says,
that he, moreover, condescended to instruct the plough-
man and farmer.[20] Yet this book, in which we are
told to search for eternal life, [21] needs correcting in
every page, and in almost every verse; besides, being
full of contradictions, and of things incomprehensible to
every human being. But I cannot discover wherein
this book (the Bible) layeth claim to the title of being
called the word of God. Neither does its matter
require that it should be so denominated; as it contains the history, chronology, words, actions, and
dreams of men, as well as the supposed messages from
God; which, alone, would convince every reflecting
being, that it could not have been written by *divine*
inspiration. For why should God trouble himself to
inform us that Paul had a cloak and some parchment,
which he left at Troas, along with Carpus?[22] We
are none the better for his cloak: neither does it concern us, whether Samson slept upon the knees or breast
of Delilah, while he was being shaved![23] So that
when the nature of the book is so clearly seen, we can
no longer hesitate in saying, that it was written, not by
men inspired with any degree of superior wisdom, but
by some of the most illiterate and depraved of the
human species; whose design was to sport with the
credulity of their fellow creatures, and subsist upon the
fruits of their labour.

I grant that the mistake of a letter, in the name of
a man, is not sufficient authority to warrant the condemnation of any book; but when we find it in almost
every name, some having two, three, four, and
more letters, omitted, inserted and transposed, no confidence can be placed in any name, place, or words of

more importance, which this book may contain. For instance; how can I be assured, but that the "Holy Ghost" means the "Holy Priest?" which is more consistent with our understanding than the other: for what do we know about ghosts or invisible things, if they cannot be seen? What idea can we have of them? yet Paul says they are *clearly seen!*[24] If they were, why should so many of the learned deny their existence?

Now if you will take the trouble to look in Gen. xxxviii, 29, 30, you will find it written thus: Tamar, Zarah, and Pharez. But Mr. Matthew has taken the letter *h* out of Zarah, and put it into Tamar; besides exchanging the letter *z* for the letter *s* in Pharez: although we find, in Rev. xxii. 18, 19, that a severe punishment is denounced against any man, who shall attempt to add or diminish ought to or from that which is written in this book. And who were those aforesaid persons? Why Tamar, we find, was daughter-in-law to Judas; who, after she had enveigled her father-in-law into an adulterous connexion with her, the Lord was graciously pleased to favour in an especial manner by ordaining (for all things were known to God from the beginning[25]) that the holy and immaculate Jesus should spring from the fruit of this incestuous amour!

This "Phares begat Esrom; and Esrom begat Aram," Matthew says; but if we look into those scriptures, which you say were written by divine inspiration, we shall find it written, Hezron and Ram.[26]

Verse 4. "And Aram begat Aminadab; and Aminadab begat Naasson; and Naasson begat Salmon."

The same words are quoted by Luke, iii. 32, 33; but in Ruth, iv. 20. we find it written, Aminadab and Nahshon; and in 1 Chron. ii. 11. Salma. These errors, I grant, are but trifling, and very common in the writings of *uninspired* men; but in those *divinely* inspired every word should be perfect and consistent. However if we find none greater than those, we will not dispute its *divine* authority; it being probable that God, not expecting his writings to be criticised in this manner, grew weary of his job; he being oftentimes subject to weariness! Isaiah i. 14, and xliii. 24. Jer. xv. 6. Mal. ii. 17. &c.

Verse 5. " And Salmon begat Booz of Rachab; and Booz begat Obed of Ruth; and Obed begat Jesse."

This Rachab you acknowledge to have been her who is called Rachab the harlot; who entertained two of God's chosen people at a brothel in Jericho.[27] But you say she was not an harlot, only an innkeeper, who got her bread honestly, by, keeping an house of entertainment for strangers! Really, Doctor, if you take it upon yourself to pervert words, which are so plain and evident, you had far better make a fresh Bible altogether. For if the word "harlot" means an "innkeeper," perhaps the word sinner means a pot-boy! as we oftentimes find the word sinners annexed to publicans.[28] Do you not think that both Paul and James knew what she was as well as you? and they both say she was an harlot.[29] This woman, then, you tell us, was " actually married to Salmon, a Jewish prince." And is it probable, you moreover ask, " that a prince of Judah would have taken her to wife, if she had been such a person, as our text represents?" Why, Doctor, you would almost make one suppose, that you had never read the Bible thoroughly, or you could never have so far forgot yourself. In the first place, you have no authority for asserting that Salmon was a prince of Judah. His son Boaz, is only described as being a man of wealth:[30] and his great-grand-son, Jesse, the father of David, is represented as having been a plain man, a Bethlehemite.[31] Yet, admitting that he was a prince, was it uncommon for princes to take whores or concubines? Witness Solomon, who had 300![32] Neither was it impracticable for a prince to take to wife one who had been an harlot, when we find that David himself took to wife Bathsheba. It is, therefore more probable that she was only a whore to Salmon, instead of his wife; because they were strictly forbidden to take to them wives from any of these nations.[33]

And who was Ruth? We find that she was a Moabiteess,[34] (one of the descendants of Lot's eldest daughter, when she got herself with child, by her own father![35]) that lived in the time of the Judges in Israel; when the Israelites, having a famine in their own land flowing with milk and honey,[36] were obliged to go and sojourn in the land of Moab. This Ruth, the Moabitess, who sprang from the incestuous intercourse of drunken Lot with his daughter, (that just and righteous man, whose soul was vexed from day to day with the unlawful deeds and filthy conversation of the wicked,[37]) in imitation of her ingenious ancestor, Lot's daughter, coveted the embraces of a near kinsman.[38] Therefore, she, also, as well as Rachab the harlot, was considered worthy of being the fore-mother to God's only son, Jesus!

Verse 6. "And Jesse begat David the King; and David begat Solomon of her, that had been the wife of Urias."

This David, we are told, was a man of God;[39] after his own heart:[40] that is, he was full of mercy and goodness; abounding therewith more than any of the chosen people of God. For if required, as a favour, to go and slay one hundred men, he would, to display the mercy and loving kindness of God, go and butcher two hundred![41] And, moreover, so very modest and obliging, that he would stoop to cut of all their *foreskins,* to make a present, perhaps, a necklace, for Michal, the daughter of Saul! Further, to convince us of the sure mercies of David,[42] we have only to read the tender regard that he had for those creatures, whose souls were in the hand of the Lord,[43] when he caused them to pass through *brick-kilns,* and put them under harrows of iron, under saws, and axes of iron.[44] He not only possessed those exemplary virtues, but displayed a greatness of mind above all his countrymen: for he dare stand, boldly, before the Priest of God, and tell him a brazen lie to his face;[45] knowing, at the same time,[46] that not only the Priests of God, to the number of eighty five, would be all put to death in consequence thereof, but that all the men, women, children, and sucklings, in the city, would, in like manner, be barbarously slain.[47] And, so tenacious was he of his honour, that he would not suffer the husband of any woman to live after he had seduced his wife, lest any man should charge him with adultery! This conduct, we find, displeased his God, who had previously commanded, that if any man committed adultery with another man's wife, he should surely be put to death along with the woman;[48] so he sent him a messenger to acquaint him thereof: which was the cause of much grief to David, who thought nothing of it during the nine months of her pregnancy, until the messenger came. But, lest he should be swallowed up with over-much sorrow,[49] his God sent him word, at the same time, that he should not die;[50] because the Lord is a God that changeth not,[51] and with whom there is no variableness nor shadow of turning:[52] for instead of enforcing the penalty of his law upon him and the woman, according to his former decree, he would now set it aside, and punish his other wives and children for his crime! Therefore, being a God of peace, he commanded that the sword should never depart from his house; and because he had formerly forbidden a man to lie with another man's wife, he now ordained that his neighbour should lie with his wives, in the sight of the sun;[53] which was accordingly done, shortly after, to the praise and glory of God, by Absalom, his own son, taking them all, ten in number,[54] to the top of the house, where God, whose eyes are too pure to behold iniquity,[55] could have a clear view of the nakedness and actions of all these women, and see fair play between them and Absolam![56] In short, this good man so followed the Lord in all his ways, and kept his commands,[57] that the Lord was pleased, in his tender mercy towards his chosen people, to move David for to number them, (although the holy men or ghosts, that wrote the book of Chronicles, say, that it was Satan, who provoked David to number the people,[58]) in order, I suppose, that he might know whether he had not chosen too many. For, we oftentimes read of

God employing his servants in numbering his people,[59] and doing other little jobs for him. Sometimes we read of a man measuring the length and breadth of a city;[60] at others, pourtraying a city upon a tile.[61] And once or twice he employed men as spies, to go and search the land for him.[62] However, it seems, by the census taken, that they were found to be too many by seventy thousand. So the Lord was obliged to send one of his flying soldiers, *because he delighteth in mercy,*[63] with a drawn sword in his hand, to slay these seventy thousand men.[64] *Query :* were the souls of these men sent to heaven or to hell, as they were not the transgressors, but only the innocent men that were numbered? I never could make out, exactly, the number of these men, in Israel and Judea, which you must acknowledge is necessary that I should know, or why was it written? We are told, in 2 Sam. xxiv. 9, that there were but 1,300,000 : while, in 1 Chron. xxi. 5, we find 1,570,000, I should rather suppose of the two, the latter to be most correct, because of the odd seventy thousand, that were slain. But the drawn sword frightened David so much,[65] that he knew not what he did, or he never would have given Ornan 600 shekels of Gold, by weight, for the same threshing floor,[66] which, we are told, he had bought of Araunah, for fifty shekels of Silver![67]

Moreover, this holy man after God's own heart, to convince the people that he was faithful even unto death, while upon his death bed, ordered his son Solomon to remember Joab, his faithful general, and not suffer his hoary head to go down to the grave in peace;[68] as a reward for his friendship and loyalty! Also, to convince Shemei of his forgiveness, which he had formerly sworn to him,[69] he commanded Solomon likewise to bring his hoary head down to the grave with blood.[70] Both commands, Solomon, like a dutiful and obedient son, strictly obeyed.[71] And, as a stimulus for his posterity, to imitate this good and pious man of God, (for all these things were written for our example, that we might be thoroughly furnished unto all good works,[72]) God ordained that he also should be the fore-father of his holy child, Jesus. Further, to prevent posterity censuring his conduct with the wife of Uriah, God made choice of her, from among all his wives, to be the fore-mother of this *holy* child, likewise: for Matthew expressly states that "David the King begat Solomon, of her that had been the wife of Urias." Luke seems to have been ashamed of her, as he neither mentions her name, nor that of her son Solomon, in his pedigree. Instead of which he says, that Jesus descended by Nathan the son of David.[73] Still we find it was by this woman, who was the mother of Nathan,[74] if Bath-shua, the daughter of Ammiel, and Bath-sheba, the daughter of Eliam,[75] be one and the same person!

Verse 7, "And Solomon begat Roboam."

This person, we find spoken of, in 1, Kings xi. 43, 1 Chron. iii, 10, and in 2 Chron. ix, 31, by the name of Rehoboam. And if Solomon had not been a very wise man, he certainly must have been greatly puzzled in providing distinct and proper names for all his children: for by having seven hundred wives and three hundred whores,[76] he must have had one thousand children at least; it being very natural for us to suppose, that to every woman, which he might fancy, the Lord would bestow *one* child at least! Though if we take into consideration the number of children that his sons had by their *small* number of wives, we have strong reason to suspect, that he must have had more, instead of less. For Rehoboam, his son, had eighty eight children, by only seventy eight women.[77] And Abijah, his grandson, although he would not allow himself more than fourteen wives, yet had thirty eight children.[78] If we had such men in our days, I know not what Mr. Malthus would say: for one man in those days, seemingly would get as many children as would stock a village! Witness Ahab, who had seventy sons, besides daughters, for his share.[69] But what surprizes me most is the wisdom of Solomon, who could govern one thousand women; when in the

present day, we can scarcely find a man able to manage one! Especially when we read, that there was not
one good for any thing, out of the whole thouasnd.[89]

We are likewise informed, that he spake three
thousand Proverbs, and his Songs were one thousand
and five.[81] Josephus, besides, says, that he composed
one thousand five hundred books of Odes and Can-
ticles : and thirty thousand books of Parables ! Is it
not strange, that those books, with all his sayings and
doings, during a reign of forty years, were not preserved by the holy men, or *Ghosts*, for the benefit of
future generations? What a vast deal of instruction,
might our Astronomers, Geographers, Geometricians,
Chemists, and all other professors of Arts and Sciences
have received, from these books, composed by the
wisest of all men,[82] if God had taken as much care of
them, as he does of the lilies and ravens![83] Indeed
there are many books refered to, in this holy book,
which might have proved as useful and instructive to
Christians, as those of Ruth and Esther, or even that
of Leviticus; seeing that the Priesthood being changed
there is made, of necessity, a change also of the law.[84]
Such as the book of the *wars* of the Lord :[85] the book
of Jasher :[86] the book of the *Acts* of Solomon :[87] the
book of Gad :[88] the books of Nathan, Ahijah, and
Iddo :[89] the books of Shemaiah :[90] the book of Jehu :[91]
the former epistles of Paul to the Corinthians,[93] and
Ephesians :[93] with the epistle to the Laodiceans :[94]
besides the prophecies of Enoch.[95] All of which are,
somehow or other, lost or mislaid : as they are not to
be found by either Jews or Christians. I would just
observe, before I leave Solomon, that out of his one
thousand women, God selected an Ammonitess,[96] who
was an Idolater, sprung from the connexion between
Lot and his youngest daughter, the night following
that in which his eldest daughter had played the same
game with him,[97] to be the fore-mother of this *holy*
child !

"And Roboam begat Abia." We find in 2 Chron.
xi. 30, that it is written Abijah; and in 1 Kings, xiv.

31, he is called Abijam ; but in Chron. iii, 10, we read
Abia. So that out of three evils, or names, Matthew
has wisely chosen the least. This man's acts, his ways,
and sayings, are likewise lost ; by being written, the
writer of the book of Chronicles says, in the story of the
prophet Iddo.[98] But I never could learn who wrote the
Chronicles ; or for what purpose they were written: they
being nothing more than a repetition of the two former
books of Kings. Whoever it was, it is evident that he
could not write them till after Iddo had written his story,
or he could not have referred to it therein. And this
Iddo, the prophet, we find, was grandfather to Zechariah,
that lived in the reign of Darius, King of Persia.[99]
Though Ezra says, that Zechariah instead of being grandson, was the son of Iddo.[100] Whence, it appears evident, that this story of Iddo could not have been written
until after their return from Captivity, in the reign of
Cyrus ; for Nehemiah informs us that Iddo was one of
the priests that returned with Zerubbabel,[101] consequently, the book of Chronicles could not have been
written until after this ; and the book of Kings must
have been still later, by its referring therein, to the book
of Chronicles.[102] How, then, should the authors of
these books know what were said and done by David,
Solomon, or Abijah, who all flourished five or six hundred years before they were in existence? We never
read that the Jews kept any records like other nations ;
even if they had, we may be assured that if Shishak,
Shalmaneser, or Pharoah-necho, did not take or destroy
them when they pillaged their land and temple, Nebuchadnezzar must when he set fire to the city and burnt
the house of God.[103] For we must remember, that in
those days, there were no books among the people, as
there is now-a-days ; printing being unknown both to the
holy and *unholy!* What books they had, were written
by priests, who, after reading them to the people, deposited them in the house of God, which was oftentimes
pillaged, and at last burnt. We read of no Bible or
Tract Societies in those days, nor of any books read by
the people. Those books which Daniel is said to have

tead, were written by Jeremiah, during his Captivity.[104]

Verse 8. " And Asa begat Josaphat : and Josaphat begat Joram ; and Joram begat Ozias."

This Joram or Jehoram, as he is sometimes called,[105] married the daughter of Ahab, whose house was such an abomination to the Lord ; always doing that which was evil in his sight ; who slew all his own brethren;[106] so that the Lord was obliged to smite him in his bowels, which in two years time tumbled out![107] This *holy* pair were also deemed worthy to adorn the noble list of ancestors of the *holy* child, Jesus ! But who Ozias was, I cannot yet discover : except it means Uzziah, mentioned in 2 Kings, xv. 13, 30.—2 Chron. xxvi. 1.— Isaiah vii. 1.—Amos i. 1. &c., called Azariah in 2 Kings xiv. 21.—xv, 1. and 1 Chron. iii. 12 : who, we find, was the father of Jotham that begat Ahaz,[108] called Achaz, by Matthew i. 9. Then how came Matthew to forget Ahaziah, the son of Joram;[109] (called Jehoahaz in 2 Chron. x. 17.) and Joash, the son of Ahaziah,[110] (called Jehoash, in Kings xi. 21, and xiv. 13.) also Amaziah, the son of Joash,[111] who we, find, was the father of this Ozias, alias Uzziah, alias Azariah ? So that if Mr. Holy Ghost moved Matthew to write this genealogy, either one or the other, must have forgotten those three persons, viz, Ahaziah, his son Joash, and his son Amaziah ; all three of different generations ! whereby it appears, that this Ozias, was the great-great-grandson of Joram, instead of son, as reported by Mr. Matthew.

Verse 9. " And Ozias begat Joatham ; and Joatham begat Achaz."

This Joatham means *Jotham*,[112] and Achaz, means *Ahaz* ;[113] the man for whom the Lord hired a razor, to shave his enemies [114] because he sacrificed to other gods and destroyed the house of the Lord![115] Another worthy ancestor of the blessed Jesus !

" And Achaz begat Ezekias;" called Hezekiah, by every other writer.

Verse 10. " And Ezekias begat Manasses ; and Manasses begat Josias." Called, by the prophets of old, Manasseh, and Josiah.

This Manasseh, we find to have been such a monster in filling Jerusalem with innocent blood, which he shed, that the Lord, upon his account, delivered his chosen people into the hands of Nebuchadnezzar.[116] Yet he was deserving a name in the holy list of ancestors! Josiah, it seems, was a good man, and did that which was right in the sight of the Lord;[117] for which the Lord suffered him to be slain by the hands of his enemies,[118] after having told him that he should be gathered to his grave in peace.[119] For we find that he was sore wounded in the wars, and he died through his wounds.[120] This, I suppose is " the peace of God," which I confess " passeth all understanding !"

Verse 11, "And Josias begat Jechonias, and his brethren."

In 1 Chron. iii. 15, we find that the sons of Josias, alias Josiah, were called Johanan, Jehoiakim, Zedekiah, and Shallum. In 2 Kings xxiii. 30, and 2 Chron. xxxiv. 1, we read that Jehoahaz was the son of Josiah; whom they made King in his father's stead : against whom, the King of Egypt came and took him prisoner : making his brother, Eliakim, King in his stead ;[121] but in 2 Kings xxiv. 8, we read that he was eighteen years old, when he began to reign! He, also, Nebuchadnezzar carried prisoner to Babylon ; where we are told, he remained in prison thirty-seven years ;[122] and made his brother Zedekiah King in his stead : though we read in 2 Kings. xxiv. 17, that Zedekiah, whose name was Mattaniah, before the king of Babylon changed it, was Jehoiachin's father's brother ! Perhaps you will say, that these are no mistakes, because they were all in. the family ! Thus, we find, that Jehoiakim, the son of Josiah, is omitted by Matthew : and that his son, Jechonias, who is called Jeconiah, and Coniah, in Jeremiah xxviii. 4, and xxvii. 1, was the grand-son of Josias, instead of his son, as reported by Matthew.   And in 1 Chron. iii. 16. we find that Jeconiah, was the son of Johoiakim, and brother to Zedekiah.

Verse 12, " Jechonias begat Salathiel, and Salathiel begat Zorobabel."

In 1 Chron. iii. 17, we find that Salathiel is the son of Jeconiah; but who is Zorobabel ? There is one Zerubbabel, mentioned in verse 19, but he was the son of Pedaiah, the brother of Salathiel, (17, 18) as is supposed. There is another Zerubbabel mentioned by Ezra, (iii. 8.) but he was the son of Shealtiel. So that the remainder of this genealogy remains evidently in obscurity. Indeed you must admit that it is quite clear the whole is a complete *mystery !* for, from David to Christ, Matthew has only given us twenty-seven generations; although according to the Bible chronology, there was an interval of one thousand and eighty years. Whence it appears, that on an average, one with the other, not one of those twenty-seven persons mentioned by Matthew, were born before their father attained the age of forty: which, if we review their respective ages, we shall find to have been impossible. For Amon was only twenty-four when he died.[123] Ahaz, thirty-six,[124] (and if it be true, that his son Hezekiah, was twenty-five years of age when his father died,[125] he must have been begotten before his father was eleven years old !) Josiah, thirty-nine.[126] Joram, forty;[127] but according to the book of Chronicles (xxii. 2.) his son Ahaziah, was born before his father! for it says that Ahaziah, the *youngest* son of Joram, (who died at the age of forty) was forty-two years old when he succeeded his father. Even if the book of Kings be correct, which says that he was only twenty-two years old when he succeeded his father,[128] yet, being the youngest son, his father Joram must have begun early to get children, if he died at forty ! This, it seems, neither Mr. Matthew, nor the Holy Ghost, could comprehend; so they left him out of their pedigree altogether.

Verse 16, " And Jacob begat Joseph."

Luke says, (iii. 23.) that Joseph was the son of Heli; of whom was born Jesus, called the Christ; being a word derived from the Greek word, *Christos,* that was commonly applied by the Greeks to some popular or celebrated character; which is a clear proof, that those who wrote those books, were not Jews; Christ, or

Christos, having no meaning in the Hebrew language; for in all the Jew books, the name of Christ, is never once mentioned. He whom the Jew Poets, or *Prophets* as they are called, wrote and spoke upon, was Cyrus, King of Persia, whom they called the Lord's anointed.[129] All Kings and Prophets were called the Lord's anointed.[130] Priests were anointed.[131] Even the Patriarchs, and followers of Jesus, were called the anointed;[132] it being a titular name of honour given by the Jews to certain individuals, as *Christos* was among the Greeks, whether they were anointed with oil or not.

In *Verse* 17, Matthew says, that all the generations, from Abraham to Christ, were three fourteens; which our vulgar arithmeticians say, are equal to forty-two. Though if you will take the trouble to enumerate them severally, you will find no more than forty: whilst Luke (iii. 23 24.) has made out fifty-five generations from Christ to Abraham.

I have now, Sir, concluded my enquiry into the characters of those persons who form the genealogy of Jesus, whom you call the Son of God! And I do assure you, that if it were mine, instead of his, I should certainly be ashamed of it: for such a list of whores and abominable monsters, I never heard of before. Therefore, if you, or the Holy Ghost, will convince me of my erroneous opinions, before the first of next month, you will, by that means, prevent me continuing the subject. If not, you may expect to hear from me again. Till then,

I remain, willing to receive instruction,

Your humble Servant,

JOHN CLARKE.

1 Mark xvi. 16.
2 Isaiah i. 18.
3   ,,   xli. 21.
4 Luke xx. 46—47.
5 Matthew xii. 37.
6 1 John iii. 15.
7 Genesis xxxiv. 25.
8 Proverbs vi. 16—19.
9 Genesis xxxix. 6.
10   ,,   xl. 19.
11   ,,   xli. 30.
12   ,,   viii. 22.
13   ,,   ix. 13—16.
14   ,,   xlii. 28—38.
15   ,,   xlvii. 20—24.
16 1 Timothy ii. 4.
17 1 Corinthians i. 25.
18 Genesis xi. 7.
19 Exodus xxxi. 2—6
20 Isaiah xxviii. 24—29
21 John v. 39.
22 2 Timothy iv. 13.
23 Judges xvi. 19.
24 Romans i. 20.
25 Acts xv. 18.
26 Ruth iv. 19.
27 Joshua ii. 1.
28 Matthew xi. 19.
29 Hebrews xi. 31.
    James ii. 25.
30 Ruth ii. 1.
31 1 Samuel xvi. 1
32 1 Kings xi. 3
33 Deutronomy vii. 3.
34 Ruth i. 1—4.
35 Genesis xix. 36—37.
36 Numbers xiii. 27.
37 2 Peter ii. 7—8.
38 Ruth iii. 12—14
39 Nehemiah xii. 36.
40 1 Samuel xiii. 14.
41   ,,   xviii. 25—27.
42 Isaiah lv. 3.
43 Job xii. 10.

85 Numbers xxi. 14.
86 2 Samuel i. 18.
87 1 Kings xi. 41.
88 1 Chronicles xxix. 29.   111
89 2 Chronicles ix. 29.
90   ,,   xii. 15.
91   ,,   xx. 31.
92 1 Chronicles v. 9.
93 Ephesians iii. 3.   vi̇
94 Colossians iv. 16.
95 Jude 14.
96 1 Kings xiv. 21.
97 Genesis xix. 38.   ,,
98 2 Chronicles xiii. 22.   ,,   xxiii. 29.
99 Zechariah i. 1.
100 Ezra v. 1.
101 Nehemiah xii. 4.
102 1 Kings xiv. 29.
          ,,   xv. 31.   ...
103 2 Chronicles xxxiv. 19.
104 Daniel ix. 2.   ,,
105 1 Kings xxii. 50.   ,,
     2 Kings viii. 16.   ,,
106 2 Chronicles xxi. 4—6.   ...
107   ,,   18—19.
108 2 Kings xv. 7—38.
— 2 Chronicles xxvi. 23
—   ,,   xxvii. 9.
109   ,,   xxii. 1.
     1 Chronicles iii. 11·
— 2 Kings viii. 25.

LETTER II.

TO DR. ADAM CLARKE.

THE GOSPEL ACCORDING TO ST. MATTHEW.

CHAP. 1.

Verse, 18. "Now the birth of Jesus Christ was on this wise; when, as his mother Mary was espoused to Joseph, before they came together, she was found with child of the Holy Ghost."

The meaning thereof, is, I suppose, that Mary was contracted, or promised in marriage to Joseph; but, before the national rites or ceremonies were performed, she was found to be with child! That such a circumstance as this should have occurred, no one will presume to question; we having so many instances, even in the present day, of young *maidens* being found with child before marriage. But the question is, who was this Holy Ghost that got her with child? We have just read the genealogy of Joseph, in Letter 1, supposing that he had been the father of Jesus: but now, when we have come to his birth, we are told in *Verse* 25, that he knew her not till she had brought forth her first born son! What utility then, can there be, in giving us the genealogy of Joseph, if Joseph were not his father? Matthew informs us, in *Verse* 1, that Jesus was the son of David, the son of Abraham: but if the Holy Ghost were the father of Jesus, Matthew should have given us the pedigree of this Holy Ghost, instead of that of Joseph, if a genealogy were considered so necessary, in order to prove that Jesus was descended from Abraham. However, for the credit of Jesus, I am glad to find some reasons for suspecting that he was not descended from such an

abominable wretch : for surely this Abraham is represented to have been such another monster as was David.
Read Gen. xxii. and you will there find that Abraham,
under the cloak of piety, persuaded his *only* Son, Isaac,
to go with him a three day's journey from home to a
solitary place, where he intended to stick a knife into
him, and roast him like an Ox ! You, Sir, are the father of
a large family, and probably could better spare one of
your children, than the man who has an *only* Son ; yet,
were you, in a dream, in a vision of the night, when
deep sleep falleth upon men ; in slumberings upon the
bed ;[1] to imagine that some phantom appeared, (for
you cannot suppose that God himself, could possibly appear to any man, when it is written, that *no man* shall
see him and live.[2]) and commanded you to take one of
your children to some by-place, and there slay and roast
him, could you so stifle all natural affection, all feelings
of humanity, as to comply with so absurd and diabolical a command ? Even were you so credulous as to
believe, that the message came from God, would you not
think him a tyrannical monster, for attempting to sport
with your feelings in that manner ?

I have heard some priests strain hard to persuade their
hearers that the offering up of Isaac was a type of
God's offering up of his son Jesus. Which, by the bye,
I think was no credit to this God ; for, surely, if he
were both an " all-wise" and an " all-powerful" being,
he might have found out some other method to satisfy
his *wrath* and *fury*,[3] than that of wreaking his vengeance
on his own innocent son ! But what similarity does the
one bear to the other ? Isaac did not suffer ; but Jesus
did. Abraham deceived Isaac, by pretending that he
was only going to *worship*, and then to return ;[4] but
surely, you will not pretend to say, that God deceived
Jesus ! Isaac, being a young man of twenty-five, was
not forced to yield to a feeble old man of one hundred
and twenty-five years of age ; but Jesus was, being
compelled by superior force. You, likewise say that
Jesus was the only begotten son of God ; whereas Isaac
was not the only begotten son of Abraham, (though

Paul says he was,[5]) because, he had, at that time, another son living, whose name was Ishmael;[6] and to whom, and to his mother, Abraham's barbarity is another instance of his unnatural feelings: for, after having first seduced the mother, with the help and consent of his own wife Sarai, and got her with child, he suffered his wife Sarai to treat her in so inhuman a manner, while in a pregnant state, that, rather than submit to such tryannical behaviour, the poor girl ran into the wilderness:[7] for, as Solomon says, it is better to dwell in the wilderness, than with a contentions and angry woman.[8] And, though she humbled herself and returned home, probably, for the sake of the child in her womb, yet, after she had brought him forth a son, which he so much desired, he had the barbarity to turn both her and the child out of doors; giving them only a bottle of water, and some bread, to go and perish in the wilderness:[9] although, at the same time, he had cattle, servants, and land in abundance![10] But Paul says, that those two sons of Abraham, were no more than an *allegory;*[11] by which it appears that Paul only considered it as a fictitious tale! Neither were the unnatural feelings of Abraham confined to his children only; for, even his own wife, on whom he doated, he would rather sacrifice to pagan lust, than endanger his own life for her, or even trust her to the mercy and protection of his God.[12]

But to return to the Holy Ghost; why have we not his genealogy, if a genealogy at all, be necessary? For without some account of his pedigree, we know nothing of him; having never heard or read of such a being before! We are only assured of his belonging to the masculine gender, by his capability of getting Mary with child; and that is all we know about him! Could I be assured, by any authenticated history, that such a person as this Jesus ever existed, I should imagine that it alluded to some Holy or High Priest, that got her with child: we have so many instances, even in our own days, of holy and high priests getting young maidens with child!

But this book is written in such an ambiguous and

unintelligible manner, especially the writings of Paul, in which Peter himself acknowledges, are some things hard to be understood,[13] that I cannot discover what is meant by this Holy Ghost? Some passages seem to favour the opinion of his being the High Priest, while others are altogether enigmatical. For instance; we find in Acts xiii. 2. that, when certain prophets and teachers came to Antioch, the Holy Ghost said, "separate me Barnabas and Saul for the work whereunto I have called them:" which evidently implies that some person in authority whom they well knew was speaking to them, seeing that they were not at all surprised at the voice. And when Peter tells us,[14] that "holy men of God spake as they were moved by the Holy Ghost," what else can he mean, but that those men who had sanctified themselves to the Lord, according to their law,[15] spake and wrote as the Holy or High Priest directed them? Even Jesus said, that "all manner of sin and blasphemy shall be forgiven unto men, but the blasphemy against the Holy Ghost shall not be forgiven";[16] because it was not lawful for any man to speak evil of or against the High Priest.[17] But when we find this Holy Ghost descending like a dove upon the head of a man at one time,[18] and like a parcel of fiery cloven tongues at another;[19] sometimes filling men and women;[20] at others converting their bodies into temples,[21] and many other curious freaks which this Holy Ghost is said to have done, we can have no idea what this Holy Ghost could be. Perhaps it was a nick-name given by the Greeks, in derision, to the Jewish High or Holy Priest, when they wrote this Quixotical story of Jesus; it being evident that it could not have been written by the Jews; for none of the rulers or prophets ever mentioned a word about such a being as a Holy Ghost: especially as we find that they never did, nor ever will believe a word about it; and surely they ought to know best. But whoever or whatever this Holy Ghost might have been that got her with child, why should he, as well as she, escape the punishment of the Jewish law?[22] Or how could Joseph be called a just man, who was not willing to expose this adulterous connection? Was he not amenable likewise to the law,[23] by his attempting to put her away privily? Though I cannot imagine how he could put her away privily, without privily putting her to death, if her appearance proved that she was with child; it being written that she was *found* with child, which could only be known by those who found her, but by her appearance; the nature of which, and the law of the Jews, on such an occasion, must have rendered it impossible for Joseph to put her away privily.

Matthew says, (*verse* 20) that "while he thought on these things, behold the angel of the Lord appeared to him in a dream, saying Joseph, thou son of David, fear not to take unto thee Mary thy wife, for that which is conceived in her is of the Holy Ghost."

That a man should have such a dream as this, I will not say is impossible: for, as Solomon said, a dream cometh through the multitude of business; and in the multitude of dreams and many words, there are also divers vanities.[24] But that the Jews could be expected to give any credit to such a dreamer, appears to me very improbable, especially as their law authorized, and even commanded them, to put all such dreamers to death, who should attempt to subvert their faith in their *one* God.[25] So that, like Luke, I must differ from Mr. Matthew, by rejecting all such absurdities as dreams; for he, conceiving that it would give the story a greater degree of plausibility, says[26] that the angel appeared (not in a dream, but) in a visible form, (not to Joseph, but) to Mary. No doubt but he found that Matthew's dreaming story would not be so readily received among the people, for the reasons already given; therefore he endeavoured to give it a more substantial colouring, by bringing the angel forward in reality; well knowing that the ignorant and weak-minded, were credulous enough to believe in the stories of witches, ghosts, angels, and such imaginary beings. Yet he ought to have informed us, how it was that Mary discovered that this angel came from God? seeing that Satan can transform *himself* into an angel of light,[27] and perform many *wonderful things*, as well as God himself!

But men in this age, who are so well acquainted with the schemes and contrivances which some women will make in order to avoid the stigma of harlotry, will not be imposed upon by either Luke or Matthew; of which both Mark and John seems to have been aware, by their avoiding to say any thing about the birth of this Jesus; although John had heard and seen all things from the beginning.[28] That such a woman as Mary, if she ever did exist, did play the harlot will not be disputed, it being a thing neither unnatural nor yet uncommon. But should a woman in the present age say that an angel, or even God himself, had come and told her that she should be with child, I doubt whether any sensible man would believe that it was produced without the help of man, supposing that she was afterwards, like Mary, *found* to be with child. I grant that there are many persons so credulous as to swallow any absurdity that is offered to them; such as the preternatural conception of Joanna Southcott; the tales of the "Arabian Nights;" "Haunted Tower," &c.: but because they are so weak-minded as to credit such idle and nonsensical tales of ghosts, witches, angels, and hobgoblins, should you, who are so well skilled in all the Arts and Sciences, submit your reasoning faculties to their credulity? No; surely your philosophy teaches you that immateriality cannot corporate with materiality. Besides, it is written that he that is joined to an harlot, is one body; for *two*, saith he, shall be one flesh.[29]

Then let us compare things and examine ourselves; proving all things, and supporting that which is just and true, not being like unto those who seem ever learning, and never able to come to the knowledge of the truth.[30] We are not ignorant of the craft and subtilty of priests, who, to extricate themselves from this dilemma, say that with God all things are possible. But this I deny; for it is impossible for God to *lie*;[31] and that which is crooked, cannot be made straight; and that which is wanted, cannot be numbered.[32] Still, admitting for the sake of argument, that this God could tell a lie if he chose, and alter the course and laws of nature, he must have some reason for so doing : and, by admitting this, we destroy his immutability ; as though he grew wiser, as he grew older : or why should he be obliged to change or destroy that which he had previously commanded or done ? Besides, admitting that this woman did bring forth a child without the help of man, for what purpose was the laws of nature thus changed, either in this or in any of those prodigious wonders said to have been done ? They did not convince the people ;[33] they only confounded them.[34] They did not, and have not, produced those effects which this God must have expected from them, or he never would have done them. Neither can I see where was the necessity of them: for if they were necessary in one age, they must be necessary in every age. And if God willeth that all men should believe them, all men should have the same grounds for believing. And should we admit the necessity of them, it would seem as if this God had made a cobbling piece of work of the system of things at first by his · being necessitated to mend them afterwards !

Now let us reason together a little further on this sub-ject. You say that God made all things good at first, but man spoilt them, because he would choose his own ways. (Isaiah lxvi. 3.) If I ask how ? you reply by his own free-will, whereby he became disobedient. Then why did this God give man this free-will ? Would it not have been far better for man, and more to the honour and glory of God, as he knew *all things* from the begin-ning, if he had with-held this free-will, as he did Abimelech from sinning ?[35] He need not then to have sacrificed his only-begotten son ; and would moreover, have prevented all the misery which you say is entailed upon all men in consequence thereof; and all those evils and abominations which have so grieved and distressed him ever since.[36] Though I cannot see how man can choose his own ways, if the Lord worketh in us to *will* and to *do* of his own good pleasure,[37] and *directs all our steps :*[38] especially, as it is written, that *all* our suffici-ency is of God,[39] and that it is he that hath wrought all our works in us.[40]

Again : you assert that God provided a remedy for the
evils which he knew would arise in consequence of man's
free-will.[41]   But does not this evince both folly and
cruelty ?   Should we consider that man *just* and *wise*,
who would give to his child a serpent with his bread,
whereby his life might become endangered ?'   Could he
extenuate such folly and inhumanity, by saying that he
had provided a remedy for the child ?   No ; surely you
will say that it is better to leave the head alone, than to
break it in order to apply a plaister ; for as Jesus intimates,[42] it is better to prevent an evil, than to permit,
and afterwards punish it. Besides, where is this remedy ?
All things appear to be now, as in the days of Solomon ;
who said, that the thing that hath been, is that which
shall be ; and that which is done, is that which shall be
done ; and there is no new thing under the sun.[43]   And
as PETER ANNETT justly observes, that if we read the
history of mankind, we shall find that " the common nature of man, as well as of the world, was ever the same :
and that no supernatural pretensions have mended it at
all.   Wisdom and Folly, Learning and Ignorance, Virtue and Vice, Slavery and Freedom, ever were, and still
remain ; and rule alternately in Persons, Places, and
Kingdoms. None were ever wholly good or wholly evil :
but the superiority of one over the other, by turns or in
certain cases prevailed. All seek their own good, according to their different conceptions of it, as their different
natures incline to, motives induce, and circumstances permit."   This is the fixed and invariable rule of human
conduct.   Then where was the utility of Jesus Christ
coming into the world ?   The works of evil are not destroyed, although one thousand eight hundred years have
elapsed, since you say he came for that purpose.[44]   He
did not convince the people when he did come ;[45] not
even his own family ![46]   How then can it be expected,
that we, who have neither heard nor seen him nor those
wonderful things, should believe ?   Besides we are told,
that he had the assistance of the Holy Ghost ; who, it
seems, had the power of converting three thousand souls
a day.[47]   *What made him leave off ?*   Or why did he

begin, if he did not wish to continue? If he had gone on at that rate, all men would long since have been converted. Is his arm shortened? Or did he, like God,[48] require refreshment? If so, he takes a long time to refresh himself; for we have never since heard of any such conversions, although you will allow that there never was a time when they were more needed! Now does not this doctrine exhibit a God that is a complete botch: first spoiling things; then mending them—and making them no better!

And if those things were done to produce faith, or if as you say, those things were done that we might believe, why are not the same things done now? Are we not as much entitled to a sight thereof, as those were for whom it is said they were done? And if it be *faith* that produceth wonders, why do not you, who profess to believe, shew us some? it being written, that all things are possible to him that *believeth.*[49] Yet although Jesus has given you such exceeding great and precious promises to enable you,[50] I very much doubt, if the salvation of the whole world rested on the performance of a single miracle, whether you, together with all those who profess to believe, could produce one to save it!

History informs us that there have been many juggling tricks of heathen and popish priests, and many impositions passed upon mankind, for the wonderful works of their Gods and their Saints. And if some men are so easily deceived without a wonder, surely a wonder-working man, a crafty juggler, or a dexterous knave, may be capable of deceiving many. Witness Mahomet, Prince Hohenlehoe, &c. But is it not owing to our ignorance of the secrets, artifices, and intrigues, made use of by those impostors, that the mind is thus filled with wonder and astonishment? Am I to ascribe those deceptive arts, which we often find exposed or discovered, to the interposition of a supernatural power, or an imaginary being? No; surely you would be the first to ridicule my folly and credulity. If I, then, dare not ascribe these wonders which are done in the present age, and in my presence, *to any power* supernatural, how much less should I ascribe those things, which are only said to have been done, thousands of years back, in the presence of men who, we are convinced, were far more ignorant, and far less informed, respecting the operations of nature, and the properties of matter, than men in this enlightened age; consequently more liable to be imposed upon, concerning things which reason cannot comprehend, nor you explain? such for instance as a woman being found with child by a Ghost, and still retaining her pucelage! But this book itself does not authorize you to draw such a conclusion. It no where states, nor even hints, that Mary, after her adulterous connection with this *Ghost*, was ever considered a Virgin; nor was her conception ever considered as miraculous, or it certainly would have been noticed by some of the holy men, if not often alluded to by Jesus himself. Even Paul would surely have eulogized the faith of Mary, in his catalogue of the faithful, as well as that of Rahab the harlot![51]

Luke says, that when the angel came to Mary, he told her that she should be with child;[52] and Mary replied, "how shall this be, seeing I know not a man?" which answer at that time was very proper, and the inquiry natural enough, she having not then known any man or Ghost, holy or unholy. Then "the angel answered, and said unto her, the Holy Ghost shall come upon thee." But the angel did not tell her, that after this Holy Ghost had come upon her, she should still retain her virginity; for this would have been degrading the powers of the Holy Ghost to an equality with old King David.[53] And what would you think of that being, who should insult the modesty of your daughter, in such a manner, by telling her that some man or ghost should come upon her, and get her with child? Surely, you would say, he deserved a good horse-whipping!

But you, being so well acquainted with the Hebrew Language, know full well that the passage in Isaiah (vii. 14.) to which Matthew alludes, in *Verse* 23, does not mean a vestal or pure virgin, in the original language, but *merely a young* unmarried woman; or what we term a spinster. Why then should you assert, that after this Ghost had been upon her, and got her with child, she was still a pure and undefiled virgin? You know that such would be as great an impossibility, as that of the daughters of Lot getting themselves with child by their own father, without his knowledge!

. Let us see, now, what authority Matthew had for referring to that particular passage, which was spoken by Isaiah, we are told, seven hundred years before the birth of Jesus; which Matthew says, was done that it might be fulfilled, which was spoken of the Lord by the Prophet, saying, "behold a virgin shall be with child, and shall bring forth a son, and they shall call his name EMMANUEL, which being interpreted, is God with us."

We have just seen, in *Verse* 21, that his name was to be called JESUS; how then can the name Jesus or Joshua apply to the word Emmanuel, admitting that it does mean God with us? Many persons were called Gods by the Jews, who were not named Jesus, as I have already shewn.[54] But when we look into Isaiah we find the name is Immanuel, and not Emmanuel, as Matthew states; and which alluded to some portion of land, of which Isaiah was speaking;[55] and no way applicable to God or Man. We will therefore inquire now into the circumstances, that induced Isaiah to speak of this virgin or young woman, and her child, and what was the thing signified thereby?

Isaiah says, that in the days of Ahaz, King of Judah, Rezin, King of Syria, and Pekah, King of Israel, made war against Ahaz, King of Judah, and Ahaz, who was of the house of David, was afraid, whereupon the Lord sent Isaiah to Ahaz, to bid him "take heed and be quiet; to fear not, nor be faint-hearted, for the fierce anger of those two Kings; who had said, let us go up against Judah, and vex it; and make a breach therein for us, and set the son of Tabeal King in the midst of it. Thus saith the Lord, it shall not come to pass." But, if we look into 2 Chron. xxviii. we shall find that instead of the Lord sending a messenger to comfort

and encourage Ahaz, in the time of his distress, he
delivered him into the hands of the kings of Israel and
Syria; (5) who smote him, and carried a great multitude of captives to Damascus; and two hundred
thousand captives and much spoil to Samaria; (8)
besides slaying one hundred and twenty thousand
valiant men in one day. (6)

Here we find are two different statements given of
the same transaction. Isaiah shows, that Ahaz was
protected by this Bible God, and promised success:
whilst in 2 Chron. xxviii. 10, we read that " the Lord
brought Judah low, because of Ahaz, King of Israel,
for he made Judah naked, and transgressed sore
against the Lord." How came the holy men of God,
who I suppose wrote this verse, to call Ahaz, King of
Israel, when we are told, that he was the King of
Judah, and defeated by the King of Israel, whose
name was Pekah?

Again, what credit can be given to any of these
Jewish tales, when we find it written in 2 Kings xvi.
5—20. that those two Kings, Rezin and Pekah, came
against Ahaz, and besieged him, but could not overcome
him; instead of which, Ahaz, with the aid of the King of
Assyria, overcame the King of Syria, and went to their
capital, Damascus. But in 2 Chron. xxviii, 20—27, we
read that the King of Assyria came and distressed him,
and strengthened him not. Moreover, that he sacrificed to the Gods of Damascus, which smote him;
besides shutting up the doors of the house of the Lord,
and making altars in every corner of Jerusalem, pro-
voking the Lord to anger by his abominations. Yet
the Priests would wish us to believe that this man was
so much the favourite of God, as to be indulged, in
preference to any other man, with a sign from the Lord
himself, concerning his only begotten son, seven hundred years before it came to pass! And if you can
condescend to men of low estate[5][6] you will oblige me
by explaining how Pekah, King of Israel, could come
against Ahaz, King of Judah, when we are told[5][7] that
Pekah *was slain in the twentieth* year of Jotham, the

father of Ahaz! Or how could Pekah be slain in the
twentieth year of Jotham, when we are informed[58] that
Jotham reigned only sixteen years, that Ahaz his son,
succeeded him in the seventeenth year of Pekah?[59]
And why, in all these accounts, we do not find the
name of Isaiah once mentioned, nor yet the virgin
story, which we will now take the trouble to examine?

Isaiah says, (vii. 10.) that the Lord himself spoke to
Ahaz, and bade him ask for a sign; as he seemed to
doubt of Isaiah's message. But Ahaz (good man)
would not tempt the Lord; (12) yet he would provoke
him to anger, by burning his children in the fire, and
sacrificing to other Gods![60] Then the Lord answered
and said, that he, the Lord, would give him a sign;
(14) for "behold," he says, "a virgin shall conceive,
and bear a son, and shall call his name IMMANUEL.
Butter and honey shall he eat, that he may know to
refuse the evil and choose the good; for before the
child shall know to refuse the evil and choose the good,
the land that thou abhorrest, shall be forsaken of both
her kings."

This then we find, to be the purport of the sign; viz,
that a child should be born, who was to be fed with
butter and honey; for by eating that only which was
good, such as butter and honey, he would have a greater
aversion to that which is bad, such as those stinking
clods of beef, &c. which are oftentimes given to us in
these times. And that before the child should have the
judgment to distinguish the one from the other, or as it
is said in Chap. viii, 4, "before the child shall have
knowledge to cry my father and my mother, the riches
of Damascus, (in Syria) and the spoil of Samaria, (in
Israel) shall be taken away, before the King of Assyria," and the land forsaken of both those kings,
namely, Rezin, the king of Syria; and Pekah king of
Israel. This was to be the sign. Ahaz was the person unto whom the sign was to be given; and Isaiah
was to be the instrument by which this sign was to be
accomplished. For he took witnessess to prove, that

he went in unto a prophetess, and got her with child: (viii, 2, 3,) which child, with some others that he had got, he declared should be for signs and wonders in Israel, from the Lord. (18.)

Now, prithee Doctor, please to inform me, how this woman, the prophetess, can be accounted a *virgin*, if it means a pure and undefiled woman, according to our acceptation of the word, when Isaiah himself confessed that he took witnesses in with him to see him getting her with child? Would not such a *virgin* be deemed an impudent *whore* in the present day, who would admit witnesses in to see a man getting her with child? For we do not read that she was the wife of Isaiah. You know that it was common in those days, for *holy* men of God, such as *priests* and *prophets*, to keep *whores* and *concubines;* witness the Levite, Hosea, David, Solomon, Samson, &c., &c.[6][1] Besides, what reference can this transaction have to the birth of Jesus? Did Jesus feast upon butter and honey? Are we not told that he was called a man, gluttonous, and a wine-bibber?[6][2] Was Ahaz living, unto whom the sign was to be given? or were those two kings invading the land of Judah, when the birth of Jesus took place? If you cannot answer these questions agreeable to reason, I must consider Mr. Matthew, if he wrote this account, to be no other than an ignorant impostor, and an abominable liar; it being evident that he had some base design in view, by his only quoting a part of the sign of Isaiah, and applying it to Jesus, instead of the whole: he well knowing that if he quoted the whole sentence, it would apply no more to Jesus, than it would to Pontius Pilate.

And why all this fuss about Jesus? What benefit have men received by his coming? Matthew said, (verse 21) that he should save his people from their sins. But do we not read throughout the book, that the people were as sinful after he came, as they were before? And have they not continued so even to the present day? Even the *bishops* and *priests* who have been filled with this Holy Ghost, by the laying on of hands, are not saved nor prevented from committing the most

abominable and atrocious sins. You yourself likewise
confess that you are a miserable sinner, or why pray
daily for forgivness ? Perhaps you will say, that it is
in consequence of the depravity of human nature, and
that by reason of the heart being so deceitful and desperately wicked,[63] we are not able to do those things
which we would wish to do.[64] If such be the case,
what good could Jesus do by preaching or even dying
for us ? He should have changed those deceitful hearts,
as *all power* was given unto him.[65] But instead of
doing that which had been promised by the prophets
ages back,[66] or saving them from their sins, he gave
power, to a set of ignorant and malicious wretches,[67]
to retain their sins, according to their own will and
caprice![68]

Should any God ask me to come and *reason* with
him,[69] I would ask him why he had made all their
hearts so desperately wicked ? it being written, that
it is he that fashioneth their hearts,[70] and *turneth* them
which ever way he willeth.[71] Surely it would have
been more to the praise and glory of God, if he had
made them with pure and holy hearts at first ; as the
potter, you say, has power over the clay to make the
vessel as he willeth.[72] He would then have prevented
those rivers of blood which have flowed through the
accursed[73] name of Jesus. Every man would then
have been able to enjoy the fruits of his own labour ;
which is now taken from him to support in idleness and
luxury, a swarm of useless animals, called Popes, Cardinals, Archbishops, Bishops, Priests, and many other
ambassadors,[74] of different degrees and denominations,
which this name of Jesus has sent among mankind :
also Churches, Chapels, Tabernacles, and Conventicles,
with all their gew-gaws, to please the fancies of those
pretended *ambassadors*. Neither should we, if every
man were impeccable, require Prisons, Bastiles, Record-
ers, Judges, Gaolers and Turnkeys, with all the host
of vermin that infest almost every street in every city,
parish, and village, and who are a reproach to every
civilized nation.

Trusting that you will answer the words of truth, to them that send unto thee,[7][5] I have addressed those two letters unto you, in order that thou mightest have perfect understanding of the first chapter " according to St. Matthew." And before the expiration of another month, I shall take into consideration, the second chapter, and lay it before you, in like manner, for your inspection.

Till then, I remain, as before,

Your humble Servant,

JOHN CLARKE.

NOTES TO THE FOREGOING LETTER.

1	Job xxxiii. 15.	40	
2	Exodus xxxiii. 20.	41	
3	Isaiah ix. 19.	42	
	Ezekiel vii 18.	43	
4	Genesis xxii. 5.		
5	Hebrews xi. 17.		
6	Genesis xxi. 21		..
7	,, xvi. 6—7.		..
8	Proverbs xxi. 19.		
9	Genesis xxi. 14.		
10	,, xiii. 6.		
11	Gallatians iv. 24.		
12	Genesis xii. 12.		
	,, xx. 2.		
13	2 Peter iii. 16.		..
14	,, i. 21.		...
15	Leviticus xi. 44.		..
16	Matthew xii. 31.		
17	Acts xxiii. 5.		,,
18	Luke iii. 22.		,,
19	Acts ii. 3.		... 3 23.
20	Luke i. 41, 67.		
21	1 Corinthians vi. 19.		
22	Deutronomy xxii. 23—24.	—	.
23	Leviticus v. 1.		...
24	Ecclesiastes v. 3, 7.		,,
25	Deutronomy xiii. 1—5.		
26	Luke i. 28.	62	
27	2 Corinthians xi. 14.	63	..
28	1 John i. 1.	64	
29	1 Corinthians vi. 16.	65	
30	2 Timothy iii. 7.	66	
31	Hebrews vi. 18.		
32	Ecclesiastes i. 15.	67	
33	John vii. 5.		
	., xii. 37.		
34	Acts ii. 12.		
35	Genesis xx. 6.		
36	,, vi. 6.		
	Amos ii 13.		
37	Phillipians ii. 13.		
38	Proverbs xvi. 9.		
39	2 Corinthians iii. 5.		

TO DR. ADAM CLARKE.

CHAP. II.

Verse 1, "Now when Jesus was born in Bethlehem of Judea, in the days of Herod the King, behold there came wise men from the East to Jerusalem, saying where is he that is born King of the Jews? for we have seen his star in the East and are come to worship him.

When we compare the account given of Jesus, according to Matthew, with that according to Luke, one would imagine that they were inspired by different Holy Ghosts: or that they were both endeavouring to excel each other, in giving the most romantic history of this individual. In the first place, what *wise* man would come to inquire of King George, saying where is he that is born King of England, for we have seen his star, and are come to worship him? The cases are similar. And if there were any truth in this account, why should we treat Judicial Astrology as being fallacious? But Luke says that they were shepherds in the country,[1] instead of wise men from the East, who saw a multitude of angels,[2] instead of a *star*, that spoke of peace on earth, and good-will towards men![3] Now Sir, as you profess to be a teacher sent by God, and whose fame is noised throughout all the country, be pleased to inform me which of these two accounts I am to believe? as it is written that he that believeth not shall be damned.[4] So that without some information I *am already damned*, not knowing which to believe : whether it was a *star* travelling before a company of men from one place to another, and resting over a manger as though it had been a fire balloon; or whether it were a multitude of angels speaking of peace on earth and good-will towards men : both accounts being so contrary to History, Science, and Reason.

If we examine history for the character of an angel, (which by-the-bye is only to be found in that history called *sacred*,) we shall find that all supernatural beings, instead of bringing good tidings of great joy,[5] have been the harbingers of misery and desolation to us poor mortals! And the description given of them in the *sacred* history, proves them to be a fornicating and most cruel race of monsters.

The first time which we read of one, we find him armed with a flaming sword;[6] standing sentinel over a tree against two poor naked and defenceless mortals, lest they should pluck its life-preserving fruit, and live for ever! *Query*: how many poor birds were slain in their attempts to pick from this tree? Or were there no birds, caterpillars, or insects in those days, which might have stolen a bit, and so have become immortal? Perhaps you will say that they were all *inspired* with good manners by the Holy Ghost, like the wild colt upon which Jesus rode! But I never could learn what became of this strange being with his flaming sword? Is he and the tree there still? If not, when and where did he go with it? as we hear no more of him nor his tree ever after. Surely God did not destroy them with every living substance, when he opened the windows of heaven,[7] and deluged the whole earth!

We next find them picking and choosing wives from among the daughters of men for themselves.[8] Though we have no account of the manner in which the marriage ceremony was performed: or whether they were obliged, like us, to pay a parish priest, for this liberty of rendering obedience to the first command of God? But the priests say, that they were not supernatural beings; they being only called sons of God, to denote good men; thereby distinguishing the children of *Seth*, from the children of *Cain*, who, they suppose, were all bad men, because their father unintentionally slew his brother. I say unintentionally, because it cannot be supposed that Cain could calculate upon the result of a blow given with a stick or a stone upon the body of his brother, (they having no sword nor pistols, nor yet bows and arrows, as we read of, in those days,) he never having before had any experience of such an effect. Yet the priests will not admit of this definition of the sons of God, when applied to Jesus: who was also called the son of God![9] But admitting this explanation to be correct, namely, that they were only good men, how could a good man, merely because he is good, cause a woman to bring forth giants, mighty men, or men of more renown,[10] than a bad man?

Again: whenever an angel was sent to any female, we find that his message was always impertinent and immodest; and delivered in such places and at such times, attended with such circumstances, as to give us strong reasons for suspecting his honour and chastity. As in the case of Hagar, Abraham's maid;[11] and his wife Sarai:[12] likewise Samson's mother,[13] and Mary, the betrothed wife of Joseph.[14]

But how happy we ought to consider ourselves in the present day, who are never troubled with such angelic visits; for whenever these creatures made their appearance to man, we always find that they had some murdering work in hand. Read the account of their visit to Lot,[15] and the destruction of Sodom, which immediately followed; when the Lord, to assist them, took the fire and brimstone out of heaven, and flung it down upon the people,[16] overthrowing all the cities, and destroying the inhabitants thereof, with the exception of all the righteous persons that could be found therein: which only consisted of drunken Lot,[17] (the man who so little regarded chastity as to offer up the bodies of his own two daughters to the lustful desires of a lawless mob![18]) his worldly-minded wife,[19] and his two incestous daughters! *But if Sodomites are so obnoxious in*

the sight of this Bible God, why does he not pour down
fire and brimstone upon them in the present day, instead of suffering them to escape punishment, as is the
case with the Right Reverend Father in God, Percy
Jocelyn, and many others in England, especially in
Turkey, where they are tolerated? Surely this ought
not to be winked at!

Behold another angel, standing between the earth
and heaven, with a drawn sword in his hand,[21] after
having slain seventy thousand men! At another time
we read of one who slew one hundred and eighty-five
thousand, all in one night![22] This one, I suppose, was
a captain in the army belonging to the God of battles;[23]
for Joshua speaks of one of these captains who came
to him with a drawn sword in his hand, with a most
important message, namely, to bid him *pull off his
shoe!*[24] I wonder who has the honour to be sword-
cutler to the armies in heaven? As to the one that
appeared to Gideon,[25] I cannot discover whether he
was only an angel, or the God himself, as both titles
are given to him. Yet let him be whoever or whatever
you please, I think he came on a very foolish errand,
else there is some mistake in the tale; for those Midianites, whom he ordered Gideon to slay,[26] were already
slain by Moses,[27] every man, woman, and child, excepting some young virgins, whom the chosen people
of God kept for their own private use, although it was
in consequence of an intercourse with them that the
slaughter was made,[28] and all their land given to the
tribe of Reuben.[29] How then could those Midianites
come up like grass-hoppers for multitude?[30] We also
read of another one who was prevented from murdering Balaam,[31] through a dumb she-ass speaking with
man's voice![32] Even the angel that came all the way
from Gilgal to Bochim, though he did no harm himself, yet he promised much.[33] Thus we find, that
whenever an angel makes his appearance, he never
speaks of peace on earth and good will towards men,
but always the contrary. And lest you should think
that these their actions were not sanctioned nor ap-

proved of by their master, as it is written his angels
he chargeth with *folly*,[34] I will now give you a description of HIS character, whom you call a God of love,
[35] and peace ;[36] who delighteth in *mercy*,[37] and doth
not afflict, willingly, nor grieve the children of men ;[38]
but styles himself a merciful, gracious, and long-suf-
fering God![39]

In the first place we find him creating every thing
out of nothing ; which *Christians* say is impossible :
for nothing cannot produce a something. We next
find him praising the work of his own hands, by saying
it was all good, yea *very good ;*[40] though Solomon said,
let another man praise thee, and not thine own mouth ;
a stranger, and not thine own lips.[41] Yet, in a few
days, he curses all these very good things which he has
just made, because a poor simple young woman happened to steal a little fruit belonging to him![42] And
this, it appears was placed there for the sole purpose
of tempting her to steal, or what could have induced
him to make it so good for food and pleasant to the
eye ? Surely here was a temptation sufficient to overcome any young woman, who might be placed in a
similar situation; for we may naturally suppose that
she was in a longing condition !

Yet notwithstanding the character which Nehemiah,
(ix, 32.) Daniel, (ix. 4.) and Nahum, (i. 2.) give of
this Bible God, we do not find him so black as the
clergy have painted him. They say that he was not
satisfied with mulipljing sorrows on the poor deluded
young woman, but that he actually doomed all her posterity, in consequence of her stealing his fruit, to suffer
an eternity of torments amidst fire and brimstone in
some other world ! A sentence more unjust and cruel,
could never have been given by the most tyrannical
monster that ever existed.

But from which passage in this book, the Bible, do
they obtain authority for so saying ? I cannot find one
that bears the least resemblance to such a condemnation
as that of eternal punishment for her disobedience. Jesus
never taught it : nor even as much as mentioned either

her or her husband's name, much less their fault: yet
they say that it was upon their account, and through
their transgression, *he* came! Neither did the prophets,
nor the apostles, as they are called, ever allude to such
a condemnation.   Doubtless if it had ever been decreed
by this God, he would have made it known to some of
the fathers, unto whom he spake by the prophets in
divers manners and at sundry times :[44] especially, as
"the Lord God will do nothing, but he revealeth,
(even) his secret unto his servants the prophets;"
(Amos iii. 7.) this being a subject of far more importance
to be made known, than the manner of robbing a bird's
nest, (Deut. xxii. 6.) or of manufacturing candlesticks
and snuffers![45]   But instead of any future punishment
in another world, as the priests say, the God of Moses
says expressly that their punishment shall be in this
world;[46] not a word about any other; and that he will
not extend the punishment upon the children, beyond
the fourth generation:[47] though Ezekiel's God says,
that the child shall not bear the iniquity of the father![48]

Solomon, who we find, was wiser than all men,[49]
consequently knew all those matters better than any of
our priests; yet neither he nor Moses, the chosen favourite of God, ever once mentioned the names of either
Mr. or Mrs. Adam, Devil, or Holy Ghost.   For we
must not suppose that the book of Genesis could have
been written by Moses, or he surely would not have
omitted saying so.   Besides there are several things
related therein, that could not have occurred till after
his death.   For instance; we read in Gen. xii. 6, and
xiii. 7, that when Abram was travelling through the
land of Canaan, "the Canaanite and Perrizite dwelled
then in the land;" which evidently implies that this
was written at a time when they were not in the land;
and which, we find, did not occur until the days of
Joshua; even then, and for several ages after, we read
that the Canaanites would dwell in the land; for they
having made themselves chariots of iron, crept into the
valleys, where neither the Jews, nor yet their God,
could drive them out!   (Judges i. 19, 27.) So that if

Moses wrote this account, it is as ridiculous as though any one in the present day, were to say, that when his Majesty, George IV, went over to Ireland, the Irishmen dwelt then in the land : but if in ages hereafter they should be driven out of the land, as was the case with the Canaanites after the days of Moses, then it might be said with propriety.

Again in Chap. xxxvi. 31. while speaking of the descendants of Esau, it says, "these are the kings that reigned in the land of Edom before there reigned any king over the children of Israel;" which you yourself admit could not have been written until after there had been some king reigning in Israel; which did not occur till many years after the death of Moses; Saul being made the first King in Israel. As a proof that this book of Genesis could not have been written until nine hundred years, at least, after the death of Moses, we find that the above verse, and the twelve that follow it, are an extract from 1 Chron. i 43—54; which could not have been written until after the Captivity, or how could the writer of the book of Chronicles, give the genealogy of Zedekiah and his descendants, in Chap. iii. 84 ?

Besides there are many passages, even in the other books that are ascribed to Moses, which prove that none of them were ever written by him; and as Moses himself never said that he wrote them, I cannot see what right the Priests have to say that he did. In the first place, it is evident that he could not write the last Chapter of Deuteronomy, which records his death. Neither can we suppose that he wrote the 12th Chapter of Numbers, wherein it is said "now the man Moses was very meek, above all the men which were upon the face of the earth," without considering him as an ostentatious braggart, which is the very reverse of meekness. In short, the style and manner in which these books are written, are sufficient proof, if further proof were necessary, that they were not written by Moses; for it is every where expressed that the Lord said unto Moses; and Moses *said unto the* Lord; or Moses said unto the people; and the people said unto Moses; and Moses began to declare; and Moses made an end of speaking; all evidently proving that some other person was writing the history of Moses : but in all that Moses is *reported* to have said himself, we find not a word about Adam, Eve, Ghost, Devil, or Hell, much less the immortality of a *soul!*

Paul, we find, speaks more about these things than any body else : yet he only says, that by one man sin entered into the world, and death by sin; so death passed upon all men, for that all have sinned :[50] which does not imply that death has passed upon all men for the transgression of Adam and Eve, but for their own sins, for ALL have sinned. Neither does it imply, that any of their posterity are to live in everlasting torments after death, in consequence of their sin; instead of which he says that as in Adam all die, even so in Christ shall all be made alive;[51] for as by the offence of one, judgment came upon *all* men unto condemnation, even so by the righteousness of one the free-gift came upon all men unto justification of life.[52] This, probably, is some of Paul's mystical jargon, to which Peter alludes when speaking of his writings; in all his Epistles, he says, there are some things hard to be understood. Surely, an all wise God would never have commanded Paul to deliver such an important message, if it alluded to the fall and recovery of man, in such an ambiguous manner, that those who are unlearned might wrest it unto their own destruction. But Paul says that God will destroy the wisdom of the wise, and bring to nothing the understanding of the prudent : because the world, by wisdom, knew not God. (1 Cor. i 19, 21.) How then is God to be known? If man's wisdom be too short, can folly reach him? And if those who are unlearned, wrest his messages to their own destruction, how is he to be known at all? or how are we to discover wherein the immortality of men is taught? Is it to be learnt from Paul's foolish and absurd allegory? when he says, in answer to an anticipated question which he expected some rational being would propose, viz. how are the dead raised up ? and with what body do they come?[54] he calls him a fool, in spite of the anathema of Jesus,[55] and says, that which thou sowest is not quickened, except it die ; so also is the resurrection of the dead ; it is sown a natural body, it is raised a spiritual body.[56] Herein we discover his ignorance of the laws of nature; and he ought to have his own epithet, *thou fool*, retorted upon himself, for almost every plough-boy knows, that if a grain die in the ground, it can neither quicken nor vegetate: whereas, if it do not die it may chance to bring forth thirty, sixty, or even an hundred-fold! Besides, we cannot imagine that an all-wise and merciful God would leave men ignorant of their dreadful state and condition till the days of Paul, whom we find to have been the chief of sinners,[57] even a *Blasphemer!*[58] Yet this is the man upon whom Christians build their Church ; notwithstanding the promise of Jesus, that it should be built upon Peter![59]

But this very book, the Bible, positively denies the immortality of man, by saying, that God placed a cherubim to guard the tree of life, lest man should eat thereof and live for ever.[60] And Solomon, who certainly knew the state and condition of man, as well as Mr. Paul, he being under the express tuition of his God,[61] tells us that man is but dust ; that all turn to dust again ; all go to one place ; as the one dieth so dieth the other ;[62] with this difference, that in consequence of the peculiar organization of man, his spirit or breath, goeth upward, whilst that of the beast, through his organic structure, goeth downward. Spirit and breath being often used as synonimous terms in these books.[63] Yet notwithstanding the declaration of the wisest of men, with the testimony of God himself, who assures us that he secured the tree of life, lest man should eat thereof and live for ever, the priests would make us to believe that man is immortal, in spite of God's anxious and providential care to the contrary! Besides without we had eaten some of the fruit of that tree we all know it to be a thing opposed to reason and experience, that this body, after having been made a part and parcel of numerous other bodies, should ever live again as the same identical individual. For as Shakspeare says, "a man may fish with a worm that hath eat of a king, and eat of the fish that hath fed of that worm." Therefore, agreeable to the sixth article of the Church of England, which was agreed upon by the Archbishops, Bishops, and the whole Clergy, in the convocation holden at London, in the year 1562, we are not bound to believe this story of *immortality* and eternal punishments; for it therein states, that " what soever is not read therein, (meaning the holy scriptures) nor may be *proved* thereby, is not to be required of any man, that it should be believed as an article of the faith." As to the dark parables and ambiguous sayings of Jesus, I shall endeavour to explain them hereafter.

And now though I have clearly shown that this Bible God is not so bad as the priests represent, yet I will prove him to be such a monster, that if I thought it possible for such a being to exist, his ears, if he had any, should be daily annoyed with my curses and execrations. First, read the account of the deluge, (though your philosophy teaches you that such a circumstance could never have occurred in the manner as described in this Bible;) here you find this monster drowning all the human race, with *every living* thing that he had made so very good, as though they had been all rats and mice![64] *Query;* were the fishes drowned also?

But what was his reason for this universal slaughter? You reply because he found that every imagination of the thoughts of men were only evil continually.[65] If such were the case, why did he not destroy them all, and make a fresh race of men, he being so expert at man-making, instead of preserving some of the old stock to engender the same corrupt nature, and those evil imaginations, throughout all subsequent generations? Do men gather grapes of thorns, or figs of thistles?[66] If a *corrupt* tree cannot bring forth *good* fruit,[67] how could it be expected that Noah, who was such a drunken beast and tyrannical parent,[68] should bring forth children different *from himself?* For what is bred in the bone, I have

heard say, will not depart out of the flesh! Then if, as
you say, mankind be this corrupt tree, why was it not
hewn down and cast into the fire?' instead of preserving
some of the most corrupted branches to bring forth fruit
after its kind; whereby, we are still by nature, born in
sin,[69] and thereby made the children of wrath.[70]

Besides, was it not this God that commissioned his
angelic gang to execute those bloody deeds of which I
have already spoken? Yet those monsters were not
sufficient to satisfy *divine* vengeance, fury, and wrath,[71]
but he must pick and choose certain individuals of the
most diabolical nature, such as Moses, Joshua, David,
&c., to assist in plundering, tormenting, and butchering
their fellow-creatures. And such pleasure did he derive
from the agony and dying groans of those poor mortals,
which he had made in his own image, that he would oft-
times take an active part himself in their destruction!
For instance; when Joshua was fighting and striving to
plunder the territories belonging to five kings of the
Amorites, so great was his rage that he took the stones
out of heaven and threw them down upon the people,
(pretty amusement for a God who delighteth in mercy!)
whereby more had their brains knocked out by those
great stones, then were slain by the swords of the people.[72]
And lest he should mistake and knock down the sun and
moon in his *fury*, he made them both to stand still, out of
his way, and wait until he had done pelting the people![73]
although he had formerly promised that while the earth
endured, neither day nor night should ever cease![74]

At another time, we read of his slaying fifty thousand and
seventy persons,[75] only because they had the curiosity to
peep into his travelling carriage; which by the bye was
no other than a little box of shittim wood![76] And once,
whilst shut up in this said box, which was drawn by oxen,
he slew Uzziah, one of the drivers, because he put forth
his hand to steady the box, when he thought, most probably, that the Lord was in danger of being upset![77]
Who would not come to the help of the Lord against the
mighty!

And have you not read how he treated his own chosen

people, when having enticed them away from a land
flowing with milk and honey,[78] wherein they had bread
and flesh to the full,[79] and did eat their fish and vege-
tables freely,[80] he led them into a barren wilderness,
wherein were neither bread nor water: and because they
complained of being starved and famished through hunger
and thirst, he sent among them a number of strange birds
from the sea; which as soon as they began to eat, yea,
while the flesh was yet between their teeth, ere it was
chewed, he smote them with a very great plague?[81] At
another time, for the same cause, he sent among them a
number of fiery serpents, which bit the people, and many
of them died.[82] Yet this Moses had the impudence to
tell the people that the Lord had kept them as the apple
of his eye,[83] and had only chastened them as a father
would his son.[84]

One time he destroyed twenty-four thousand persons
because one of them took a Midianitish woman and
brought her home publicly in the sight of all Israel:[85]
(not secretly, like some of our modern Christians:)
although Mr. Moses had, himself, taken a wife out of
the same nation, and which had moreover protected and
supported him when he fled out of Egypt, through fear
of Pharaoh, after he had barbarously murdered the
Egyptian.[86] Though Paul says that he forsook Egypt,
not fearing the wrath of the King;[87] and further declares that there were but twenty-three thousand slain
that day,[88] making a difference of one thousand men.
And as I often find whilst reading this *sacred* book, many
instances of a similar nature, I am constrained to declare,
though much against my will, that the *Holy Ghost*, if he
wrote this book, was not so temperate in his drink as he
ought to have been, whilst thus engaged: for surely, no
man in his sober senses, could possibly make such blunders as the following:—

First; we read in Genesis xv. 16, that God promised
Abraham that he would bring the people back again in
the *fourth* generation: but we find that they did not return until the time of Joshua; who distributed the
countries among them for an inheritance.[89] And this

Joshua we find was one of the *thirteenth* generation: for in 1 Chronicles vii. 22—27, we find that

1. Abraham begat Isaac,
2. Isaac begat Jacob,
3. Jacob begat Joseph,
4. Joseph begat Ephraim,[90]
5. Ephraim bagat Beriah,
6. Beriah begat Resheph,
7. Resheph begat Telah,
8. Telah begat Tahan,
9. Tahan begat Laadan,
10. Laadan begat Ammihud,
11. Ammihud begat Elishama[91]
12. Elishama begat Nun,
13 Nun begat Oshea, alias Jehoshua,[92] alias Joshua,[93] alias Jesus,[94]

who lived only one hundred and ten years;[95] whilst Abraham we find lived one hundred and seventy-five years,[96] although it is written in Genesis vi. 3, that God had promised that the days of man should be one hundred and twenty years !

But the Priests, who have such a knack of perverting the words of this God in order to render them unintelligible to the laity, that they might be induced to look to them only for an explanation of the words of this all-wise God, say that God did not by these words, signify that he would limit the days of man to one hundred and twenty years, but that he, in his *tender mercy*, gave them warning one hundred and twenty years before he destroyed them with a flood. Yet where can they find a passage throughout these books which will support such an assertion? Of course they had to wait, as Peter says,[97] while the ark was building; but we are not informed that they were ever acquainted with its purpose. Jesus says[98] that "they were eating and drinking, marrying and giving in marriage, until the day that *Noe* entered into the ark, and knew not until the flood came and took them all away." By this account it is evident that God meant what he said, (and not what the priests say,) which was, that the days of a man's life should be one hundred and twenty years; as men had been accustomed to live eight or nine hundred years and upwards. It was the knowledge of this which caused Moses, the man of God, to murmur, when he found that they were, in general, no more than threescore and ten.[99] And man still exists, although four thousand years have passed since those words were spoken *as we are informed;* which would not be the case if God had intended to destroy mankind in one hundred and twenty years. Besides, man was not destroyed; there being eight persons saved, whom I suppose you will admit belonged to that class of animals called Man!

I shall now select a few more passages out of those books which were written for our instruction, by men who spake as they were moved by the holy Ghost, in order to prove that if those holy men or Ghosts were not drunkards, they were not qualified to take charge of a ledger in any merchant's counting house in London.

Genesis xlvi 27 ......70 souls
Exodus xii 40 ......430 years   ,,
Numbers iii 39 ..Total 22,000

2 Samuel viii 4 ..700 horsemen   ...
  ,,   x 18 ..40,000 horsemen   ,,
  ,, xxiv 9 800,000 & 500,000   ,,
       13..7 years of famine
  ,,   24 ....50 shekels of silver
1 Kings iv 26 ....40,000 stalls   .
  ,, v 11 ..20 measures of oil   ii 10

  ,,   16........3,300 rulers   ,, ii 18
  ,, vi 2 ....House 30 cubits   ,, iii 4
  ,, vii 15 16 Pillars 23 cubits   ,, 15
  ,,   26 ....2000 baths   ,, iv 5
  ,, ix. 23 ....550 rulers   ,, viii 10
  ,,   28 ....420 talents   ,, 18
  ,, xxi 15 16 ..3 ℔ of gold   ix 16
  ,, xvi 15 16 ..In the 27th year of Asa, Omri began to reign

  ,,   23..In the 31st year of Asa, Omri began to reign, and he reigned 12 years, and he died; and Ahab his son reign-in his stead (28)   In the 38th year of Asa, began Ahab to reign. Kings xvi 29

2 Kings i 17..Jehoram, king of Israel began to reign in the 2nd year of Jehoram, king of Judah.

Jehoram, king of Judah, began to reign in the 5th year of Joram king of Israel. 2 Kings, viii 16

,, viii 25..In the 12th year

In the 11th year, ,, ix 29

,, 26...... 22 years old

42 years old 2 Chron. xxii 12

,, xvii 1..In the 12th year of Ahaz, (son of Jotham) Hoshea began to reign over Israel.

In the 20th year of Jotham, began Hoshea to reign. 2 Kings xv 30

,, xviii 1..In the 3rd year of Hoshea king of Israel, began Hezekiah, the son of Ahaz, to reign over Judah.

Pekah reigned 20 years in Israel. (2 Kings xv 27) Hoshea who succeeded him, reigned 9 years, (xvii 1) And in the 17th year of Pekah, began Ahaz to reign over Judah, who reigned 16 years, (xvi 1 2) leaving 4 years for Ahaz to reign after Hoshea.

,, 9..In the 4th year of Hezekiah the king of Assyria came up against Samaria, and besieged it.

At the end of three years they took it, in the 9th year of Hezekiah. 2 Kings xviii 10.

,, xxiv 8......18 years old

,, xxv 8 ....7th day

,, 19 ....5 men

,, 25

,, 27... .....27th day

,, 31

1 Chron. xi 11 ...300 men

Ezra ii 64 ..The Congregation were 42,360

,, 65 ....200 singers

245 singers, Nehemiah vii 67

,, 69 { 61,000 drams of gold / 5000 lbs of silver / 100 garments

41,000 drams of gold / 4,200 lbs of silver / 597 garments } Neh. vii 70—72

Neh. vii 66..The Congregation were 42,360

Total 31,089 Neh. vii 8—62

Psalm lxviii 17 The chariots of God are 20,000

Dan. i 1..In the 3rd year of Jehoiakim, came Nebuchadnezzar king of Babylon.

,, 21 .... 1st year of Cyrus

Dan. ii 1..In the 2nd year of Nebuchadnezzar, Daniel was made ruler over the whole province of Babylon.	Nebuchadnezzar sent Daniel to school, where he continued 3 years. Dan. i 5 18.
Matt. i 17 .... From Abram to Christ, 42 generations.	55 generations Luke iii 23—34
Matt. viii 28 ....2 men	1 man, Mark v 2.
,, xii 40 3 nights and 3 days	2 nights and 1 day, Mark xv 42 xvi 2.
,, xviii 1 . ...6 days	8 days, Luke ix 28
,, xx 29 30 .2 blind men	1 blind man, Mark x.46
Mark xvi 5 ......1 young man	2 men, Luke xxiv 3
Luke iv 25 3 years and 6 months	In the 3rd year, 1 Kings xviii 1
John xix 14 ..6th hour	3rd hour, Mark xv 25
1 Cor. xv 5..seen of the twelve	Of the eleven, Mark xv 14

Now Sir, what credit can be given to any thing that the Holy Ghost or his clerks have written? How can we be assured that Jonah was not three years in the whale's belly, instead of three days? Or that Isaiah was not thirty years instead of three, running naked about the town.[100] Besides it might have been forty years instead of forty days, that poor Moses fasted while God was writing out his commands for Moses to break, as God knew all things from the beginning! Even Samson might have slain ten thousand men instead of one, with the ass's jaw-bone! And instead of three hundred foxes which it is said that he caught,[101] it might have been three hundred tigers, the one being as easily caught as the other. But pray Doctor, what would you think that man deserved, whom you should see gathering together three hundred dogs or cats, and tying them tail to tail with a fire-brand in the midst, between two tails? would you not say that he ought to be severely punished for his cruelty and wantonness? It was well for Samson, that Mr. Martin, our Honourable Member for the county of Galway, did not live in those days! All these things being written for our instruction, are consequently of importance; else an all-wise God would not have taken the trouble of revealing them to us; it is therefore very requisite that we should be acquainted with the precise number of every particular. For could it be proved that there were thirty knives given to Sheshbazzar, the prince of Judah, by Mithredath, the treasurer to Cyrus king of Persia, instead of twenty nine as it is written,[102] what a sad mistake that would be!

Let us now return to the Midianites, the nation that protected Moses, after he had perpetrated the inhuman murder on the body of the Egyptian. We find that every man, woman, and child was ordered to be butchered by this God, to whom belong *mercies* and *forgivness*, though we have rebelled against him;[103] which order was faithfully executed by his servant Moses, the *meekest* man in the earth.[104] And for more proof of the *tender mercies* of God over all his works,[105] read Deutronomy 2nd and 3rd chapters, with the 8th and 10th of Joshua, and the two last chapter of Judges. The priests tell us that herein did God shew forth his *mercy*, in the butchering of those little innocent children; so we may be sure that they were safely lodged in heaven; by which means they were saved from the evil to come. If this be the best means of obtaining heaven, would it not be advisable for him to slay every child as soon as it is born? For man that is born of a woman, is but of few days, and those full of trouble![106]

But the slaughter of the Amalekites ought particularly to be observed, where every man, woman, child and suckling, were ordered to be slaughtered by this God, whose goodness endureth continually:[107] which also was done to the praise and glory of God, by Saul,[108] a man anointed of God for this purpose; but having unfortunately felt a spark of humanity towards an individual, a brother king, it so displeased this God of *love*, that he took his kingdom from him, and gave it to another;[109] one after his own heart, that would not stand upon such niceties. Though we must not forget that the man whose preservation offended God so much, was afterwards hewn in pieces before the Lord,[110] because he delighteth in *mercy!*

And how surprized are we to find that within ten years after this *slaughter, David is* obliged to slay them all over again![111] And although he was determined to do all things faithfully, by leaving neither man nor woman alive, lest they should bring tidings to Gath; yet as if the very devil were in those Amalekites, before the expiration of another year, they are alive again! and so numerous, as to invade David's territories, and burn Ziglag, his capital, with fire; carrying away captive all the women and children.[112] But mark, Doctor, the conduct of those Amalekites, whom you call Idolators; *they* did not hurt one woman or child, whom they had taken. Not so with the man after God's own heart; *he* butchered all that he could catch:[113] and not satisfied with the extermination of his enemies, he must first put them to the most exquisite torture, by burning them in brick-kilns, sawing them assunder,[114] and various other methods of shewing the sure *mercies* of David.[115] Well might Shemei cry out "thou bloody man;" for Saul only slew them by thousands, but David by ten thousands![116]

The destruction of those nations, you say, is a proof of God's displeasure at sin; they being Idolators, consequently were very wicked people, and were not fit to live upon the face of the earth. But the Bible positively asserts the contrary, by declaring that they were more humane, more generous, more honest, and more peaceable than the *chosen* people, that were raised up for the purpose of extirpating them. For proof, read the character of the people of Laish,[117] who were so peaceable and honest, that they needed no magistrates throughout the land. Yet the chosen people of God went secretly and smote them with the edge of the sword, and afterwards burnt their city with fire![118] But behold, we find written in the book of Joshua, (xix. 47.) three hundred years before this massacre is said to have been perpetrated, the very same transaction recorded, as having been already done in the days of Joshua. This I suppose, is the effect of inspiration!

Again, the conduct of the Amalekites, towards the captives is a proof of their humanity.[119] The noble and magnanimous spirit of Pharaoh,[120] and the two Abimelechs,[121] ought not to be overlooked, but compared with the mean, cruel, and blackguard conduct of this pure and holy God, whose eyes cannot behold iniquity; yet he had the indecent barbarity, to close up fast all the wombs of the poor women belonging to the house of Abimelech![122] In fact, the language of this God throughout the Bible, is most disgusting and filthy; he is always talking of whores and Sodomites,[123] and such like obscene and beastly things, which are not fit to be spoken of by any decent or modest person, either male or female;[124] besides indecently exposing his own back parts;[125] being ashamed, I suppose, to shew his face!

Is this conduct agreeable to the doctrine taught by Paul? who says, that it is a shame to speak of those things which are done in secret: that neither fornication, uncleanness, nor filthiness, should be once named among saints; that nothing should proceed out of the mouth, but that which is good and edifying; that it may minister grace to the hearers.[126] But what grace, or what instruction can we receive by being told that "she doated upon her paramours, whose flesh is as the flesh of asses; and whose issue is like the issue of horses;"[127] and many such like passages, which delicacy forbids me to expose?

As to his foolishness of which Paul speaks,[128] and his fickle-mindedness, instances are so numerous and so evident, that it would be wasting time to recount them all; therefore one shall suffice for the present. At *night* he ordered Balaam to go with the princes of Moab; and in the *morning* was angry with him, because he went.[129] As to his promises, his own servants could not depend upon his words, such a propensity had he for lying; or why should Jeremiah complain in such a lamentable manner,[130] when he cries out, "Ah! Lord God! surely thou hast greatly deceived this people and Jerusalem, saying, ye shall have peace, whereas the sword reaches unto the soul?" Again he says,[131] "Wilt thou be altogether unto me as a liar, and as waters that fail?" and in plain terms he tells him that he has been deceived by him.[132] Even his favourite David had reason to complain of his breach of promise.[133] Though there is no necessity for my referring to all those instances, which prove his unfaithfulness, for he acknowledges himself [134] that he gave them statutes that were not *good*, and judgments whereby they should not live; and that he had *deceived* the prophets. [135] In short, it became a proverb among the people, saying, "the days are prolonged, and every vision faileth." [136]

This is the God who would sometimes *sell* his people to those that would not buy them; [137] selling them for nought, as David says, (Ps. xliv. 12,) whereby his wealth was not increased by their price; which was the cause of his having so many creditors! [138] And this, I suppose, it was that induced him to send a messenger, to compromise matters, between him and his creatures, by speaking of *peace* and *good will* towards them. But what was the result of this embassy? Was it peace? If what Matthew says, be true, instead of peace, we find that all Jerusalem was troubled, and lamentation, weeping and mourning, were the consequences thereof. [139]

And why did this star appear to a foreign nation, in preference to his own chosen people? as we find that it was to them Jesus came; who was, moreover very cautious, lest his doctrine should be made known in any other place but Jerusalem. [140] Even there he did not wish his power to be made public. [141] Then why did not this star lead them direct to Bethlehem, where the child was, instead of going round to Jerusalem, thereby causing the death of so many little innocent children? Did not this star know the way to Bethlehem, without inquiring for it at Jerusalem? As Mr. Matthew seems to have had a strange propensity for gutting various passages in this book, and calling them prophecies, I suppose he was obliged to bring them round to Jerusalem, in order to accommodate this story to the passage, so as to form a prophecy. But as I know nothing of Mr. Matthew, or any of his acquaintance, I shall take the liberty of examining his prophecies; especially as I have already detected him in endeavouring to palm such passages upon us for prophecies, as cannot by any means be twisted into prophecy!

First let us inquire what became of this star after it

arrived at Bethlehem? What was its magnitude, and distance from the earth? And how and in what manner did these wise men discern when the star was over the house, or manger, wherein the young child lay?[142] as our *wise men* can never distinguish any particular city under any particular star which may be in the zenith; every one appearing perpendicular to the extent of more than one hundred miles. And the smallest of the stars which we now see, if within a thousand miles of our earth, would have covered and darkened the whole land of Judea, with all the surrounding nations. Though perhaps you will say that this star was made on purpose for Jesus, because it is expressly stated to be *his star;* if so, what did Jesus do with it? for Matthew takes no further notice of it; neither does Mark, Luke, John, Peter, James, nor even Paul, say anything about it; and surely some of them must have known or heard something of it, if it ever did appear. But admitting, that this star did appear, and did afterwards disappear like a ghost, how came it to pass that Herod and all his people in Jerusalem did not see it, as well as those foreigners? for it plainly appears that they knew nothing of it, by Herod sending to the wise men to enquire *diligently* when the star did appear. Yet, Matthew says, it came from the east to Jerusalem, and thence to Bethlehem! Peter talks of a star arising in the hearts of some people;[143] perhaps this was a star which arose in Matthew's brain, whilst reading Balaam's prophecy, who, in speaking of some bloody-minded king, which he expected would rise up from among such a blood-thirsty race of monsters as the Jews then were, says,[144] " there shall come a star out of Jacob, and a sceptre shall rise out of Israel, and shall smite the corners of Moab, and destroy all the children of Sheth;" such another fighting star I suppose, as that of which Deborah speaks![145]

Now, let it be whatever star you will, you must admit that it was an evil star, as it caused the death of so many little innocent children, which belonged to the kingdom of God;[146] upon which I shall descant in my next letter. For the present, I shall conclude, wishing that you may soon have honesty and courage sufficient, to acknowledge the truth.

Till then, I remain, as before,

Your humble Servant,

JOHN CLARKE.

NOTES TO THE FOREGOING LETTER.

1 Luke ii. 8.
2   ,,   13.
3   ,,   14.
4 Mark xvi. 16.
5 Luke ii. 10.
6 Genesis iii. 24.
7   ,,   vii. 11.
8   ,,   vi. 2.
9 Matthew xiv. 33
10 Genesis vi. 4.   46
11   ,,   xvi. 11.
12   ,,   xviii. 10
13 Judges xiii. 3
14 Luke i. 35.
15 Genesis xix. 13.
16   ,,   24.
17   ,,   35
18   ,,   8
19   ,,   26
20   ,,   36
21 1 Chronicles xxi. 16, 14.
22 2 Kings xix 35
23 2 Chronicles xx. 15.
24 Joshua v. 13, 15.
25 Judges vi. 11, 12.
26   ,,   16.
27 Numbers xxxi. 17, 18.
28   ,,   16.
29 Joshua xiii. 21.
30 Judges vi. 5.
31 Number xxii. 33.
32 2 Peter ii. 16.   64
33 Judges ii. 1, 3,   65
34 Job iv. 18.   66
35 1 John iv, 8.   67
36 1 Corinthians xiv. 33.   68
37 Micah vii. 18.   69

70	Ephesians ii. 3.		
71	Ezekiah xxv. 14. ●		
	Jeremiah xxi. 5.		
72	Joshua x. 11		
73	,, 13		
74	Genesis viii. 22.		
75	1 Samuel vi. 19.		
76	Exodus xxv. 10.		
77	2 Samuel vi. 6, 7,		,,
78	Numbers xvi 13.		,,
79	Exodus xvi 3.		
80	Numbers xi. 5.		
81	,, 83		
82	,, xxi 6.		
83	Deutronomy xxxii. 10.		
84	,, viii. 5.		
85	Numbers xxv. 9.		
86	Exodus ii. 21.		
87	Hebrews xi. 27.		
88	Corinthians x. 8.		
89	Joshua xvi. 1.		—
90	Genesis xii. 52.		
91	Numbers ii. 18.		
92	,, xiii 16.		
93	,, xiv. 6.		
94	Acts vii. 45.		
	Hebrews iv. 8.		
95	Joshua xxiv. 29		
96	Genesis xxv. 7.		,,
97	1 Peter iii. 20.		xx. 7.
98	Matthew xxiv. 38, 49.	133	
99	Psalm xc. 1, 10.	134	
100	Isaiah xx. 3.	135	,,
101	Judges xv. 4.	136	
102	Ezra i. 8, 9.	137	63.
103	Daniel ix. 9,	138	
104	Numbers xii. 3.	139	
105	Psalm cxlv 9.	140	,,
106	Job xiv. 1.	141	
107	Psalm lii. 1.		
108	1 Samuel, xv. 3, 8.		
109	,, 28.	142	
110	,, 33.	143	
111	,, xxvii. 11.	144	
112	,, xxx. 1.	145	
113	,, 17	146	

LETTER IV
TO DR. ADAM CLARKE

THE GOSPEL ACCORDING TO ST. MATTHEW.

CHAP. II.

Verse 3—6. " When Herod the King had heard these things, he was troubled, and all Jerusalem with him. And when he had gathered all the chief priests and scribes of the people together, he demanded of them where Christ should be born. And they said unto him, in Bethlehem of Judea; for thus it is written, by the prophet: and thou Bethlehem, *in* the land of Juda, art not the least among the princes of Judah: for out of thee shall come a governor, that shall rule my people Israel."

In my last letter I made a few observations on the troubles which all Jerusalem, with Herod, underwent, in consequence of those good tidings of great joy, which were to be to all people.[1] I now intend to examine the passage which is said to have been written by the prophet, whom we find to be Micah;[2] and which passage is quoted as foretelling the birth-place of this Jesus called the Christ.

But, before we examine the writings of Micah, it is requisite we should first know who he was, and in what age he lived: and consider also the difficulties attending the crediting of what are called prophecies. For Isaiah says, that there were prophets who taught *lies.*[3] And Jesus exhorts us to beware of false prophets,[4] for that many false prophets will arise, and shew great signs and wonders,[5] in order to deceive the people. Therefore, it behoves us to be careful in what men, who assume the name of prophets, we confide; by proving all things, and judging for ourselves.

First, we find him a contemporary of Isaiah and Hosea, as it is written that he lived in the days of Jotham, Ahaz, and Hezekiah, Kings of Judah;[6] in whose days we are told, Isaiah and Hosea were living.[7] Though I must confess that it appears very singular that they never notice each other in all their writings; seeing that they were all such conspicuous characters in the same nation; all denouncing the same judgments, namely, the desolation of Israel and Samaria. They all wrote in the same style, and in many places use the same expressions. In fact the writings of Micah, appear to be only an abridgement of those of Isaiah, similar to the epistle of Jude, which is a complete plagiarism of the second chapter of Peter's second epistle. They both begin in the same poetical strain, (Isaiah i. 2. and Micah i. 2.) and continue the subject in nearly the same words. (Isaiah ii. 2, 5. and Micah iv. 1, 4.) Their chief complaint, is, (like mine,) against the princes and the priests. For Isaiah says that the princes are rebellious, and companions of thieves;[8] that they beat the people to pieces, and grind the faces of the poor.[9] Also the priests and the prophets have erred, through strong drink; they are swallowed up of wine;[10] yea, they are greedy dogs, which can never have enough, and they are shepherds that cannot understand; they all look to their own way; every one for his gain, from his quarter.[11] Hosea says, that the King and the Princes are made *glad* with the wickedness and lies of the people; that they are all adulterers and sick with bottles of wine.[12] The prophet is a fool, and the spiritual man is mad;[13] that the priest also had forgotten the law of God; like people, like priest.[14] Micah says, that the princes hate the good and love the evil;[15] the rich men are full of violence,[16] and the prophets cause the people to err.[17] Then they all pretend to expect some deliverer, who would turn the people from their evil ways, and exalt them above the surrounding nations. Thus, Isaiah says, that Cyrus, the

Lord's anointed, shall perform the Lord's pleasure.[18] he shall not fail, nor be discouraged, till he have set judgment in the earth; and the Isles shall wait for his law, because the spirit of the Lord is upon him.[19] And all nations and tongues shall come and see the glory of God;[20] for the Lord will rejoice in Jerusalem and joy in his people.[21] Hosea says, that God himself shall deliver them, for there is no Saviour beside me saith the Lord; I will be thy King, and redeem them from death.[22] But Micah supposed that this deliverer would come out of Bethlehem Ephratah; who would stand and feed in the strength of the Lord, and deliver them from the Assyrian, who had laid siege against them. This man, also, was to be a ruler in Israel, who would waste the land of Assyria with the sword, likewise the land of Nimrod; by raising against the Assyrian, seven shepherds and eight principal men, as soon as he came into the land.[23] This is the passage referred to by Matthew, which you say, applies to Jesus. But what similarity is there between the character of this man, whom Micah said was to be the peace of the nation, and that given of Jesus? Instead of Jesus being the peace, we find that he was the common disturber of nations: even from his birth, the nation was troubled concerning him; and numbers of little innocent children lost their lives through him.[24] When arrived at the age of manhood, we find that there was always some uproar or other, caused by his parading the streets and entering peoples' houses, sometimes creating riots in the temple, and squabbles among the rulers,[25] till at length they were obliged to put him to death in order to restore peace and tranquillity to the nation. Moreover, Micah said that this man should be a ruler in Israel; but Jesus was no ruler, for we read that he would not be a King.[26] Neither did Jesus deliver them from the Assyrian, nor waste their land; for both Assyria and Judah were subject to the Roman Government in his days. And instead of all nations coming to Jerusalem to see the glory of God, Jesus said that it was shortly to be trodden under foot, and not one stone was to be left upon another.[27]   Even to this present day, though one thousand eight hundred years have elapsed since he came, as you say, yet the name of Jesus has obtained no authority in Israel, neither is it likely that it ever will.

Should it be asked who did Micah mean, I would reply that it is impossible for any man, in this age, to tell what a man meant two thousand years back, unless he had left us some clue, whereby we might discover the meaning.   For we find that there were two Kings of Assyria, Tiglathpileser and Sennacherib, who both threatened and distressed Israel and Judea :[28] but as he has not told us the Assyrian's name that was to lay siege against them,[29] nor who the seven shepherds and eight principal men were, we cannot tell rightly who it is that he meant.   Whoever it was, it cannot be of any importance for this generation to know ; we see plainly that it does not apply to Jesus, and that is all that is required at present.   Yet as we find those Jew poets making use of so many similes and figurative expressions, it is most probable that the shepherds and principal men, signify those princes and mighty men spoken of by Hezekiah, who helped him when Sennacherib invaded Judea.[30]   Besides, according to the Bible chronology, we find that this Mr Micah lived seven hundred years before Jesus was born.   Then if it be true what Solomon said, that no man knoweth what a day may bring forth,[31] how could Micah tell what seven hundred years might bring forth ?   Do you think that Judge Hale ever thought that he should be called *an old witch burner* in a public court (I cannot say of *justice*,) and his opinions concerning witches, &c., scouted as ridiculous and absurd by every sensible man in the nation ?   Yet, behold, such is the case in the present day.

If you suppose that those men were inspired by a something which you call a God, though I shall not yet attempt to argue with you concerning this imaginary Bible monster, I would ask why, if a God inspired those men to foretell those things, which must of necessity come to pass, because this God wills it, should man be punished for doing that which he is compelled to do? as this God must make man his machine to work with, in order to bring these things to pass. Whence, it is evident, that man cannot act otherwise than he does: else "the result of one free human action, might break every link of the chain to pieces," (for every creature is a link in the great chain of nature,) and so frustrate some particular part of the prediction. For instance: if Herod had not sent forth and slain all the children that were in Bethlehem, and in all the coasts thereof, the prophecy, said to have been spoken by Jeremy, would not have been fulfilled.[3 2]

Moreover, how is it possible for us to discover when those men of God spoke truth? seeing that they not only *deceived* the people, as Micah says, but oftentimes each other. Read the 13th chapter of the first book of Kings, where you will find that one of those men of God came out of Judah, unto Bethel, to inform Jeroboam that it was the pleasure of the Lord that human sacrifices should be offered upon his altar, and *men's bones* should be burned there! After he has given this information, as he had been commanded by this God who delighteth in *mercy*, and as he was returning home, he was overtaken by another man of God, belonging to Bethel, who entreated him, by urging the word of the Lord for his authority, to come back and take some refreshment with his brother prophet. But he refused to return, alleging as an excuse that the Lord had commanded him not to stop any where to eat or drink, because the Lord I suppose was impatiently waiting for his return; or why this hurry? However, it appears that this man of God did return in consequence of the man of God from Bethel telling him that an angel had commanded him to bring him back; but it is written, he *lied unto him.* Then if those prophets could tell lies, and deceive each other, how can we be expected to believe them? Besides, the sequel of this story shows us what danger there is in believing them; for we find that in consequence of his going back, to eat and drink with his brother prophet, he was met by a lion who slew him and stood by his carcase! Here is a strange perversion of justice; the lying prophet is left unpunished; whilst he who was deceived by his lies, is slain. That they were both *true* prophets cannot be disputed, for the one prophesied against the altar, and wrought a miracle upon Jeroboam, to confirm it: and the other foretold what should befal him before he got back. So that people ought to be upon their guard, and be careful how they receive this word of God, lest, like the prophet of Judah, they get punished for believing.

Again: to prove that a *true* prophet can tell lies, even Elisha sent Hazael to his master, the King of Syria, with a lie in his mouth, by bidding him say " thou mayest certainly recover," although, at the same time, he knew that he should *surely die.*[33]

Sometimes we find them quarrelling and fighting with each other;[34] one charging their God with putting a lying spirit into the mouth of the other; yet both lay claim to the spirit of God! For when the one struck the other on the cheek he asked him, " which way went the spirit of the Lord from me to speak unto thee?" Even in their writings, they abused and denounced judgments against each other. Hosea says, (ix. 8) that the prophet is a snare of a fowler in all his ways. Micah says, (iii. 11.) that they only *divine for money,* and deceive the people. (5) Jeremiah in his lamentations, says, (ii. 14.) that they had told the people vain and foolish things, in order to turn away their captivity. Isaiah says, (ix. 15.) that they teach lies, and are swallowed up of wine. (xxviii. 7.) Zechariah says (xiii. 2—4.) that the Lord will root them all out of the land, and make them ashamed of themselves. That they must mean each other, who have wrote these books, is evident by what Jeremiah says, (xxiii. 34.) that the prophet who shall say, " the burden of the Lord," him will the Lord punish, both him and his house; and because they say thse words, " the burden of the Lord," the Lord will forsake them, and cast them out of his presence (38, 39.): which words, we find, were oftentimes made use of by Isaiah, Nahum, Habakkuk, Zechariah, and Malachi, when uttering their denunciations against any city or country, such as Egypt, Tyre, Babylon, &c.

Besides, God himself not only deceived the prophets[35] and made the people to err, but he actually instructed them in the art and mystery of lying. Do we not read that when the Lord commanded Samuel to go and anoint David King of Israel, in the stead of Saul, Samuel was fearful, and said, *how can I go? if Saul hear it, he will kill me?*[36] But the Lord, whose judgments are unsearchable, and his ways past finding out![37] could soon find out a way to remove these fears, by bidding him take an heifer, and say, "I am come to sacrifice to the Lord." Oh! what a blessed thing is religion! it covereth a multitude of sins!

And how is it that there are no prophets in the present day? Is the art and mystery of prophesying lost? Or is mankind arrived at that degree of perfection, that they stand in no need of it? We find that there are many persons who lay claim to the *spirit of God*, and are even admitted into his privy council; yet, I suppose, you will allow that they know no more of futurity, nor even the truth of things which are past, than I do. And if what we read of prophets be true, I think we have not much cause to regret their non-existence. For we find that they being men subject to like passions as we are,[38] were capable of doing a great deal more mischief with their *divine* powers, than we poor creatures are! For instance; we are told that Elijah destroyed one hundred and two men for obeying the orders of their King; although they delivered their message in the most respectful and submissive manner,[39] yet did this man of God destroy them with his divine power. At another time we read of his slaying eight hundred and fifty men, because they differed from him in opinion.[40] In like manner would the "gangs" do in the present day, if they had but the power: for we see them (like Elijah,) instead of endeavouring to

convince those who differ from them, that their opinions
are erroneous, inclosing them within *stone walls*, bound
with iron; where they leave them to linger out their
useful days, unregarded and unconverted! If you say
that Elijah was only an instrument in the hand of God
to punish evil doers, read where he prayed earnestly
that it might not rain, and it rained not on the earth for
the space of three years and six months;[41] whence it is
evident that the just must suffer with the unjust, if it
rained not upon all the earth during that time; for
even in Israel, Jesus said, there were many widows
beside the one at *Sarepta*, unto whom Elias was sent.[42]
But what mighty evil could there be in a company of
little children, who upon seeing a queer-looking bald-
pated old man go past them, cried out, there goes bald-
head, that should cause this bald-pated blessed man of
God to curse them? which curse caused two she-bears
to come out of the woods, (close by the city) and tear
forty and two children of them![43] It is well for little
children, that there are no Elishas in the present day;
though we do not find little children assembling together in such multitudes, nor she bears lurking so near
a city in this age.

We moreover find that many of those prophecies, by
their own confession, were never fulfilled. For instance;
God bade Jacob go down into Egypt, promising him
at the same time, that he would surely bring him up
again;[44] yet we never read that he returned again
alive; unless you call bringing his dead bones back[45]
fulfilling the promise; which I think, would be but a poor
consolation to a living man, when ordered to go to a
foreign nation, to be told that his *bones* shall be brought
back again! Another time, God promised, if this book
is to be believed, that Josiah should die in peace;[46]
but we are told, he died sore wounded in the war![47]
And when God sent word to Hezekiah, saying "set thine
house in order, for thou shalt die, and not live: we find
that through Hezekiah boasting of his own righteousness, by telling the Lord how good he had been, and
shedding a few tears, the Lord changed his mind, and

added fifteen years to his days.[48]   If this be the case, how can future events be foretold ? or what confidence can be placed in prophecies, if this God repent, or changes his mind in this manner ?

We read, also, that this God said that he would bring a sword upon Egypt, and give the land to Nebuchadnezzar; and that he would cut off man and beast, so that the land of Egypt should be laid waste and desolate, from the tower of Syene, unto the border of Ethiopia, for the space of forty years; during which time neither man nor beast should pass through it.[49] Yet when did this happen ?   History does not inform us that Nebuchadnezzar ever conquered Egypt within its own rivers; although Isaiah said, that their waters should fail from the sea, and the river shall be wasted and dried up—the fishers also shall mourn—and they that spread nets upon the waters shall languish.[50]   If God meant what he said, when did all this happen ? If he did not, what did he mean ? and if we cannot tell his meaning, of what use is the prophecy to us ?[*]

In another part we find him speaking more explicitly to Jeremiah;[51] for after having bade him take great stones, and hide them in a certain place, near the King of Egypt's Palace, he says that Nebuchadnezzar shall set his throne upon these very stones which were hid in the sight of the men of Judah.   When did Nebuchadnezzar ever fulfil this prediction ? And if he never did, it is evident that he never will, seeing that he has long since gone to that place,

" From whose bourn no traveller returns."

Again, how can we in the present day, be assured that the prophet and the historian were not one and the same person ?   If so, it was very easy to prophecy and fulfil, as he could then accommodate facts to prophecies, and prophecies to facts!   We discover that the 18th, 19th, and 20th chapters of the second book of Kings, are nearly word for word the same as the 36th, 37th, and 39th chapters of Isaiah.   Therefore, we cannot

* Peter Annett.

tell that those prophecies which might have been fulfilled, were not written, until after those facts, said to
have occurred, had taken place. For instance; the
dispersion of the Jews among all nations, was foretold, it
is said, by Moses:[52] yet it is possible, that this prediction was not written until after they were so scattered: for we read that in the days of Ahasuerus,
they were scattered abroad, and dispersed among the
people, who inhabited one hundred and twenty-seven
provinces, from India, even unto Ethiopia. (Esther
i. 1, and iii. 8.) Even Nehemiah, (i. 8.) seems to confess that they were then scattered abroad among the
nations. And long before then, ten tribes out of the
twelve, were dispersed by Shalmaneser, King of Assyria, and placed in different countries. (2 Kings xvii.
6.) But when they were subject to the Romans, we
find that they were living in every nation under heaven.[53] Though I never heard that Julius Cæsar ever
found any Jews among the ancient Britons when he
came over; neither could I ever learn that the Spani-
ards found any among the Americans, when they discovered that land; though that was not until fifteen
hundred years after they were said to be living in every
nation under heaven!

As to any person foreseeing or judging that a numerous sect or description of persons should be scattered throughout all nations, it needed not the aid of
divine inspiration. Experience shews that every sect
soon finds its way to distant nations; witness the
Methodists!

But there are men possessing such great political
foresight—who anticipate events on the mere principle
of cause and effect—by which they often predict the
general consequences of certain measures, long before
they happen. And many singular coincidences have
occurred which might be adduced as the result of a
prophetic spirit. Such as the writings of Seneca,
wherein he states that " in late years, ages shall arive,
when the ocean shall relax the bounds of the universe,
and a mighty land shall be laid open, and Typhys shall

unveil new worlds, and Thulè shall no longer be the utmost extremity of the earth."* This was written upwards of fourteen hundred years before America was discovered by Columbus. Yet Seneca did not lay claim to *divine* inspiration ; he was an heathen poet. See how accurately his prediction was fulfilled! Here is the discovery of some mighty land, or a new continent, announced fourteen hundred years before it happened! a thing which must have been thought incredible in his days, as it was received only as an idle chimera of the brain, when Columbus first proposed the attempt. But Seneca, calculating on the progress which had been made by nautical inventions, considered that it would still advance to that degree of excellence, when men would boldly launch forth into the wide and hitherto impenetrable ocean, where it was probable there might be lands, which, to them, were then veiled and undiscovered.

Though this may be considered only as a single, solitary, and isolated prediction ; whereas the prediction of Moses was an highly complicated prophecy, comprehending a very considerable number of distinct particulars : then I say that each of those particulars must be shewn to have been accurately fulfilled ; otherwise the prophecy is rendered untenable, and stript of its *divine* authority. To prove which, let us examine the prophecy as it is written in the 28th chapter of Deuteronomy.

First : it is said in *Verse* 49, that "the Lord shall bring a nation against thee from far, from the end of the earth ; a nation whose tongue thou shalt not understand." Did Shalmaneser, the Assyrian, who took the ten tribes captive, come from far ? or Nebuchadnezzar from the end of the earth ? Were they not both neighbours, comparatively speaking ? And was the Syrian tongue unknown to them, when they besought Rabshekah to speak to them in that language, because they understood it, they said ? (2 Kings xviii. 26.) Or the Chaldeans from whom they were descended ? (Genesis

* Senec. Med. ver. 375. 380.

xi. 28, 31.) Even the Romans, although the Jews were dispersed abroad, as has already been shewn, long before they were subdued by them; yet even they did not come from far unto them.

Verse 50. "A nation of fierce countenance, which shall not regard the person of the old, nor shew favour unto the young." Did not Nebuchadnezzar shew favour to the young, when he brought up Daniel and his fellows in his own establishment, and made them rulers over his kingdom? (Dan. 1 and 11.) And many of the people that were dispersed abroad seem to have been in a flourishing condition, or they would all have gladly embraced the offer of King Cyrus to return to their own land. Instead of which, many staid till Ezra came, some till Nehemiah, and many went not at all; as we find that after those days they were still scattered abroad from India to Ethiopia. And those that did return, do not seem to have been hardly done by, when we find them capable of giving such an abundance of gold and silver towards defraying the expences of building a house for their God. (Neh. vii. 71, 72.) And in the days of Ahasuerus, we find that they were not only protected, but suffered to amuse themselves at their old favourite games, namely, the butchering of their neighbours! (Esther ix.) And if the Romans shewed them no mercy, it was what they might have expected, seeing that they themselves never shewed any; being strictly forbidden by their God, who charged them to shew them no mercy; neither should their eye have pity upon them, but consume all the people whom he should deliver into their hands. (Deut. vii. 2. 16.)

Verse 52, 53. "And he shall besiege thee in all thy gates, until thy high and fenced walls come down, wherein thou trustedst—and thou shalt eat the fruit of thine own body." In the days of Moses, they had neither walls nor gates; yet admitting that this was spoken by Moses, he knowing that in consequence of their tyranny, injustice, and cruelty to others, they would be held in such abhorence by all nations, (Ezra

iv. 15.) that such must consequently be the result of a siege, before they could be brought to surrender; for not having shewed mercy to others, they could not expect any themselves. But as this was done . three hundred years before the Babylonian Captivity, when Benhadad, King of Syria, was besieging Samaria, (2 Kings vi. 28.) we cannot be assured that this was written *before* that event took place. Besides, in Jeremiah (xix. 9.) we find the same words made use of as a prophecy against Jerusalem; although he acknowledges himself, that he knew that these things were done! (Lam. iv. 10.) Then what dependance can be placed on these pretended prophecies, when the prophet becomes his own historian?

Verss 60, 61. "Moreover, he shall bring upon thee all the diseases of Egypt which thou wast afraid of, and they shall cleave unto thee. Also every sickness, and every plague, until thou be destroyed." When has this been fulfilled? Are they more subject to disease than other people, excepting that which they bring upon themselves, through dirt and filth? Or are they yet destroyed? although they disobeyed the commands of Moses upwards of three thousand years back, within a century of his decease! (Judges iii. 6.) And is it not strange that while they kept the ordinances of their law these things came upon them; and when they did not keep them, these things scarcely ever happened? In the wilderness they were often visited by a plague, the sword, fiery serpents, or some other thing, which were continually destroying them, although under the authority of Moses himself.

While the Judges ruled in Israel the famine was so great, as to cause numbers of them to leave the promised land, and go to sojourn in other countries. (Ruth i. 1.) And although they were so intimately acquainted with their God, as to ask counsel, and receive answers from him, yet did he permit them to slay each other, until one whole tribe was nearly destroyed: having slain among themselves no less than sixty-five thousand one hundred and thirty persons! (Judges xx.) While the men of Bethshemesh were rejoicing that the ark of the Lord was come amongst them again, he slew fifty thousand and seventy men. (1 Sam. vi. 13, 19.) Even while that *holy* man of God, David, reigned over them they were visited with a three years famine; (2 Sam. xxi. 1.) and shortly after seventy thousand men died through a pestilence. And although from David to Zedekiah, there reigned many Kings in Judah, who provoked the Lord to anger by doing that which was evil in his sight, yet no conqueror, nor plague, visited them, until Josiah began to break down the houses of the Sodomites and adhere unto the laws of Moses! (2 Kings xxiii. 7, 25.)

Verse 68. " And the Lord shall bring you again into Egypt with ships—and there ye shall be sold for bondmen and bondwomen, and no man shall buy you." Did Shalmaneser or Nebuchadnezzar carry them over land, into Chaldea and Assyria with ships? That they have been oppressed and persecuted I will admit. So have the Catholics, the Protestants, and every sect, even the *Infidels!* when under the dominion of those that were more powerful. But to fulfil the prophecy, we ought to see them bondmen and bondwomen in every nation. Instead of which, they are not only living at their ease, free from plagues and bondage, but are actually the brokers of the nation : aye, and of the whole world too!

Verse 37. "And thou shalt become an astonishment, a proverb, and a bye-word among all nations." Their hard-heartedness, their avarice, their cruelties, and national ferocity, were tokens quite sufficient to convince Moses, that they would soon become proverbial among all nations, whether in subjection or not. But these same expressions were likewise used by Jeremiah, (xlii. 18. and xliv. 12) nine hundred years after the time of Moses. And the only bye-word, or proverb, of which I know, concerning a Jew, is, the common saying, that such an one is as *rich as a Jew!* I cannot think that this can be any great curse upon them.

In Leviticus xxvi. 43, we read that the land also

shall be left of them, and shall enjoy her sabbath while she lieth desolate without them. Which clearly proves that these predictions did not extend beyond the Babylonian Captivity, as it evidently alluded to the land enjoying her sabbaths during the seventy years captivity, spoken of by Jeremiah. (See 2 Chron. xxxvi. 21.) Then how can this prophecy be said to be fulfilled in every particular, when we cannot find its accomplishment in one? Do they now, or have they ever since their captivity, acknowledged any other God besides the God of Moses? And yet this was to be, it is expressly stated, the consequence of their captivity: even Gods of wood and stone.[54] No sect, not even Christians, have suffered more through persecution, for adhering to their religion, than the Jews have; neither are there any that are more tenacious of the laws and institutions of Moses, than they are even in the present day. And instead of their being few in number, as was predicted, through wild beasts, plagues, &c. (Lev. xxvi. 22.) they are now more numerous than ever: especially, when these words were spoken they did not then exceed seven hundred thousand persons, (Numb. xxvi.) while now, they are supposed to exceed nine millions, scattered throughout the world.

As to their being a separate people from all others, it is not possible for them to be otherwise, without their breaking the law of their legislator; who has forbidden them to marry with any other sect; and to which, we find they have in general strictly adhered: considering themselves the chosen people of God, and ever looking for a deliverer, who shall rise up from among them. These, with laws amd customs peculiar to themselves, like the gypsies, have preserved them separate in all ages amidst the various revolutions which have happened in their day. All which, being considered, I can see nothing wonderful in them excepting their pertinacity. This is the prophecy upon which Christians would rest the genuineness and authenticity of the Bible; and which I have now found to be a sandy foundation.

Again: is it not reasonable for us to expect, that whenever a prophecy is delivered, it would be so plain and explicit, as to show at once the intended purpose? For why should that be dark and mysterious, which is most necessary to be clearly understood? What admonition, or what instruction can we receive from inexplicable prophecies, which may be construed and applied to many very different cases? Do you think that an all-wise and benevolent God would take delight in puzzling and distracting the brains of his creatures, if he wished that all should arrive at a knowledge of the truth? Then why should the words of this God be more incomprehensible than the words of men? One man can make himself understood by another; but no man can say that he understands what God means; else why should there be such diversities of opinion concerning these writings? And if the trumpet give an uncertain sound, who can prepare himself for the battle?[55]

Peter says that no prophecy of the Scripture is of any private interpretation.[56] Then why are they not clearly and universally understood? Jesus himself was obliged to expound the Scriptures to them[57] who we might have expected were most acquainted with them. But no: we find the Scribes and Pharisees, whose business it was to expound these Scriptures, did not know them.[58] And if they did not understand their own prophets, how should we, who are both strangers and foreigners? Though we have strong reason to suspect that Jesus himself did not understand them, or why did he imagine that his days were to be the last? For verily, he says, "this generation shall not pass till all these things be fulfilled."[59] And what were those things? Why, that after the destruction of Jerusalem, the sun should be darkened, and the moon should not give her light; the stars also should fall from heaven, and the sign of the son of man should appear in heaven; whence he would with all his angels; who would by the sound of a great trumpet, gather together all his elect from the four winds![60] I suppose by this account, that they have musical instrument makers in heaven, as well as sword cutlers! And although he could not tell them the exact day nor hour when these things would happen,[61] yet it would be before they had gone over the cities of Israel;[62] for the gospel must be preached to every creature;[63] therefore, says he, "take heed to yourselves, and keep sober, lest that day come upon you unawares."[64]

The Apostles also seem to have held the same opinion; for Paul says the ends of the earth are come upon us,[65] we who are alive, and remain unto the coming of the Lord;[66] who will come in a little while, and will not tarry:[67] for the gospel has been preached, he says, to every creature under heaven;[68] yea the sound thereof, had gone forth through all the earth, and the words unto the ends of the world: it being made manifest and known unto all nations.[69] If Paul spoke truth, what need is there of sending missionaries to and fro through all the earth, if every nation has had this gospel preached to them eighteen hundred years back? Even Peter says the end of all things is at hand; be sober, looking for and hastening unto the coming of the day of God.[70] But John puts the matter beyond all dispute, by saying, " Little children, it is the last time; as ye have heard that antichrist shall come, even now are there many antichrists; whereby we know that it is the last time."[71]

Perhaps you may shrug up your shoulders, and say these are things which cannot be comprehended by carnal minds; because the natural man receiveth not the things of the spirit of God.[72] Then how is the natural man to come to the knowledge of the truth? You may reply that it was for this purpose the priesthood was instituted, in order that they might explain the words of this God to the ignorant and carnal-minded man. But can they explain them? Do they not all cry out, great is the mystery of godliness?[73] And have they not always been fighting, quarrelling, and persecuting each other, ever since they have been written? Even Paul and Peter could not agree in opinion concerning them![74] Besides, is there a priest in Christendom that will accept the challenge which I gave in a public court, to prove before our most gracious Sovereign, George IV. King of Great Britain, and defender of the Faith, that these books were only invented and composed by ignorant and designing men ? A pretty sort of a God he must be, who cannot make himself understood without employing a parcel of interpreters, supposing that they could explain them ! But I tell you that there is no God that employs them ; they are employed by fools and knaves ; and although they give thousands, yea millions, year after year, to have these words explained, still there are none that can understand them ; no, not one ! Why is it ? Because there never was, nor ever will be such a monster as this bible thing, called a GOD ; a proof of this I shall give you shortly. Consequently, these words are the words of base designing men, contrived to enslave the minds and bodies of their simple fellow creatures, while they themselves are living in ease and voluptuousness, in direct opposition to the commands of that God whom they preach ; who has commanded, they tell us, that man should eat his bread in the sweat of his face until he returns to dust.[75] Even Paul says,[76] " that if any would not work, neither should he eat." Therefore, if they call preaching work, they violate that day themselves, of which they say it is written, "in it thou shalt do no manner of work, thou, nor thy man-servant, nor thy maid-servant, nor thy cattle." For how often do we see these Reverend, and Right Reverend Fathers in God, (I might add others, but I do not wish to be too personal,) after they have been preaching and enforcing the above command, step into their carriage, with which their man-servants and cattle have been waiting at the door, ready to carry them to participate in some extravagant and un-necessary luxuries which have been prepared by their maid servants at home ? These are the men, whom, we are told, this God has appointed to explain his word ! which word, as Peter Annett justly observed, might pass for heavenly light if there were no human reason in the world, but that the latter puts the former out, and discovers its palpable darkness. I shall therefore conclude my observations for the present, on the nature of prophecies ; and with Jeremiah say, [77] that every man is mad, who maketh himself a prophet. And every man who attempts to pervert the writings of another, as Mr. Matthew has done, is both an imposter and a liar.

Verse 11. '' And when they were come into the house, they saw the young child with Mary his mother, and fell down and worshipped him : and when they had opened their treasure they presented unto him *gifts*, gold, frankincense, and myrrh.''

We read in Exodus, (xxiii. 8.) that this God commanded the Jews to take no gift ; for the gift blindeth the wise and perverteth the words of the righteous. Yet we find the holy mother of this holy child, receiving gifts from strangers; which is a clear proof to me, that when interest is in the case, the commands of this God are laid aside. Witness Solomon, who received gifts year by year; [78] although he knew that a gift destroyed the heart; [79] and that when a King receiveth gifts, the land is overthrown![80]

Verse, 13. "And when they were departed, behold, the angel of the Lord appeareth to Joseph in a dream, saying, arise and take the young child and his mother, and flee into Egypt, and be thou there until I bring thee word ; for Herod will seek the young child to destroy him.''

This verse implies a foreknowledge of certain events ; but did not this foreknowledge, or prescience, also know that a vast number of innocent children would lose their lives in consequence of this flight? Where then is the wisdom and power of this God, if he could not preserve the life of his only son, without occasioning the death of others? Though, as I shall probably show, at the conclusion of this work, by the similarity which exists between the life of Jesus and the life of Moses, that the one is only a modification of the other, I will only here just observe a slight variation, which is, that instead of flying out of Egypt, as Moses is said to have done, through fear of Pharaoh, Jesus is said to have fled into Egypt, through fear of Herod. However they are both commanded to return, and that too for the very same reasons. Compare Exod. iv. 19. with Matt. ii. 20

Verse. 14, 15. "When he arose and took the young child and his mother by night and departed into Egypt; and was there until the death of Herod, that it might be fulfilled which was spoken of the Lord by the prophet, saying, out of Egypt have I called my son."

Although Mr. Luke had promised Theophilus to write every thing in order,[81] relating to Jesus, yet we find that he makes no mention of his going into Egypt: but on the contrary he assures him, that after Jesus had been circumcised, (circumcise the son of God!) and the days of his mother's purification were accomplished, (which were forty and one, after the birth according to the Jewish law,[82]) he was brought to Jerusalem; and when they had performed all things according to the law of the Lord, they returned into Galilee to their own city Nazareth; whence they came to Jerusalem every year,[83] until he was twelve years of age, (without fearing any person,) after which time, we hear no more of him until he is baptized, at the age of thirty. But Matthew says, that he departed into Egypt, and that this was done to fulfil that which was spoken by the prophet, saying, "out of Egypt have I called my son."

By searching the prophets I find these words in Hosea; who, when reminding the Jews of their primitive state, said that Jacob fled into the country of Syria, and Israel served for a wife, and for a wife he kept sheep; and by a prophet the Lord brought Israel out of Egypt, and by a prophet was he preserved.[84] And in another place he says, when Israel was a child, then I loved him, and called my son out of Egypt.[85] I wonder what Matthew will call a prophecy next? it being evident that Hosea was speaking of the events that had occurred, which was the calling of Israel out of Egypt by Moses, who is here called a prophet; and the children of Israel whom the Lord calls his son, [86] even his first-born,[87] were at the same time reminded, that when they were so called, they sacrificed unto Baal, and burned incense to graven images.[88] Surely this needs no further comment, the imposition being so clear and obvious to every one.

Verse 16. "Then Herod when he saw that he was

mocked of the wise men, was exceeding wroth, and sent forth and slew all the children that were in Bethlehem, and in all the coasts thereof, from two years old and under, according to the time which he had diligently inquired of the wise men."

That such an order as this should have been given by Herod, who only held his office under the Roman Government, is highly improbable; especially as we find, that it was not the manner of the Romans to deliver any man to die, before he who was accused, had the accusers face to face, and had license to answer for himself, concerning the crime laid against him; as was the crime with Paul.[89]   How then could Herod send forth such a decree against little children, who could not answer for themselves?   Besides, could not the parents of these children appeal unto Cesar with as much propriety as Paul, who we find was allowed that privilege?[90] And how came John the Baptist to escape?   Luke speaks of his jumping in his mother's *womb*,[91] but says nothing of his jumping from this slaughter!   Neither do we find that Jesus or any of his historians, (besides Matthew,) ever alluded to such an inhuman massacre; which gives me reason to conclude that the whole is nothing but a fable.

Verse 17, 18. " Then was fulfilled that which was spoken by Jeremy the prophet, saying, in Rama was there a voice heard, lamentation and weeping, and great mourning. Rachel weeping for her children and would not be comforted because they are not."

On referring to Jeremiah, I find that he, like the rest of his profession, promised glorious days to the Jews : for behold, he said " the days come, saith the Lord, that the city shall be built from the tower of Hananeel, unto the gate of the corner.[92] I will build thee, and thou shalt be built, O virgin of Israel.[93] For I will bring them from the north country, and gather them from the coasts of the earth : and they shall come with weeping and with supplications will I lead them. For he that scattereth Israel, will gather him ; and I will turn their mourning into joy." " Thus saith the Lord, a voice was heard in Ramah, lamentation, and bitter weeping : Rachel weeping for her children, refused to be comforted for her children, because they were not. Thus saith the Lord, refrain thy voice from weeping and thine eyes from tears; for thy work shall be rewarded saith the Lord; and they shall come again from the land of the enemy. And there is hope in thine end, saith the Lord, that thy children shall come again to their own border.[94]" These are the words of Jeremiah, which Matthew has selected to make of them a prophecy, for Herod's slaughter ! But this prophecy, like the last, needs only comparing with the transaction, to discover the imposition. How could those children, whom Herod is said to have slain, come back again to their own border, from the land of the enemy? It is evident that Jeremiah thought nothing of Herod, or Jesus either, having enough to do to think of his own captivity. He therefore endeavoured to comfort the people by assuring them that the Lord would redeem them from captivity, and bring them again into their own land. Surely this prophecy would have applied much better to England in the last war, than to any massacre in Judea; when many Rachels were weeping for their children, who were then taken prisoners, but have since returned to their own border, from the land of the enemy.

Verse 22. " But when he heard that Archelaus did reign in Judea, in the room of his father Herod, he was afraid to go thither; notwithstanding being warned of God in a dream, he turned aside into the parts of Galilee."

By this verse, it appears that Joseph had some doubts of the providential care of his nocturnal visitor ; else he had not sufficient faith in his own dreams. Yet the christian religion is entirely founded upon this dreamer of dreams !

Verse 23. " And he came and dwelt in a city called Nazareth ; that it might be fulfilled which was spoken by the prophets, he shall be called a Nazarene."

Was there ever such a bare-faced imposition as this? Matthew would persuade us now, that the announcement of Samson by the bible-angel, applied to Jesus; there being no other passage which bears the least resemblance throughout the writings of all the prophets, but this one in the book of Judges, (xiii. 5,) wherein the angel is said to have appeared to the wife of Manoah; who, after giving her instructions, as to the manner in which the child should be brought up; says for "the child shall be a Nazarite unto God, from the womb." Oh! Doctor, come out from among them; shake off the dust from your feet at them, and enter the land of liberty. Do strive to enter the straight gate of *wisdom* and *truth*, for few there be that find it! Now if thou put the brethren in mind of these things, and study to shew thyself a workman, by rightly dividing the words of truth, thou need not be ashamed.[95] For some there be, who profess that they know God, but in works they deny him; by giving heed to Jewish fables, and commandments of men, that turn from the truth.[96] But verily I say unto you, they have their *reward;* like the prophets of old, they make a pretty penny by it. As Micah says, (iii. 11.) the priests teach for hire, and the prophets divine for money; which was exemplified by Elisha receiving, as one present only, forty camels' burden of every good thing in Damascus![97] it being customary for Kings and princes to hire these prophets to lead the people captive at their will.[98] Even a poor man who had lost his way, dare not ask a man of God, (Samuel) to set him right, without giving him a present.[99] But be you not like unto them, and I shall remain, as usual,

Your humble Servant,
JOHN CLARKE.

NOTES TO THE FOREGOING LETTER.

1 Luke ii. 10
2 Micah v. 2
3 Isaiah ix. 15
4 Matthew vii. 15
5 Matthew xxiv. 24.
6 Micah i. 1
7 Hosea i. 1
  Isaiah i. 1

8 Isaiah i. 23
9   „   iii. 15
10 „   xxviii. 7
11 „   lvi. 11
12 Hosea vii. 3, 5
13   „   ix. 7
14   „   iv. 6, 9
15 Micah iii. 2
16   „   vi. 12
17   „   iii. 5
18 Isaiah xliv. 28
—   „   xlv. 1
19   „   xlii. 1, 4
20   „   lxvi. 18
21   „   lxv. 19
22 Hosea xiii. 4, 14
23 Micah v. 1, 8
24 Matthew ii. 3, 16
25   „   iv. 25
    „   xxi. 12, 23
    Mark ii. 2, 4
26 John vi. 15
27 Luke xxi. 6, 24
28 2 Chronicles xxviii. 20
— 2 Kings xviii. 13
29 Micah v. 1, 5
30 2 Chronicles xxxii. 3
31 Proverbs xxvii. 1
32 Matthew ii. 16, 18
33 2 Kings viii. 10.
34 1 Kings xxii. 23, 24
35 Ezekiel xiv. 9
36 1 Samuel xvi. 2
37 Romans xi. 33
38 James v. 17
39 2 Kings i. 9, 13
40 1 Kings xviii. 19, 40
41 James v. 17.
42 Luke iv. 25—26.
43 2 Kings ii. 23—24.
44 Genesis xlvi. 4.
45   „   l. 13.
46 2 Kings xxii. 20.
47 2 Chron. xxxv. 23   24.
48 Isaiah xxxviii. 1—5
49 Ezekiel xxix. 8—12.
50 Isaiah xix. 5—10.
51 Jeremiah xliii. 8—10
52 Deuteronomy xxviii. 10.

LETTER V

TO DR. ADAM CLARKE.

CHAP. III.

Verse 1. " In those days came John the Baptist, preaching in the wilderness of Judea."

I cannot proceed further, without observing that this appears to me to be a strange sort of a place for a man to preach in; where we are told there were wild beasts, and nothing to feed upon but locusts and wild honey.[1] Few of our modern preachers, I believe, would submit to such fare!

Verse 2. "And saying, repent ye, for the kingdom of heaven is at hand."

This we are informed was foretold one thousand eight hundred years back ; yet we have since heard nothing of its accomplishment. If, as you say, this kingdom of heaven signifies the kingdom of God, which Paul described as righteousness, peace, and joy, in the Holy Ghost,[2] you destroy its existence, as a substance, by reducing it to a figure as Jesus did, who compared it to a grain of mustard seed, a merchantman, a net, and various other things ;[3] which gives me reason to suspect, that he himself did not believe in the bible account of heaven-making : especially as he never once alluded to that job!

From the Bible we learn that this Heaven is not a figure, but a " part and parcel" of the universe ; as it is stated therein, that after the Bible God had divided the

light from the darkness, three days before either sun,
moon, or stars, were made, he commanded a firmament
to appear in the midst of the waters, and it was so!
This firmament that was between the waters, he called
Heaven ;[4] and the waters which were under, or below
the heaven, so called, he named *Seas.*[5] The great
Atlantic and Pacific Oceans being, I suppose, unknown
to the Bible-God and his secretary; which is not to be
wondered at, they being located in so small a portion
of ground, at the extremity of the Meditteranian Sea;
which, together with the Red Sea, were the only two
principal seas that were known to them. But the
waters which were above the firmament, or heaven,
they have some how or other forgotten to name. However, we can learn from various passages in this book,
that those unnamed waters above the firmament or
heaven, were what were afterwards called *clouds.* For
God tells Jeremiah, (xxiii. 24.) that he fills both heaven and earth; which Jeremiah laments by saying,
thou hast covered thyself with a cloud ;[6] and this appears to have been his uniform livery; for when
acting as outrider or guide to the Israelites, a cloud
was his only covering.[7] And further, to convince us
that this heaven is placed beneath the clouds, we read
that when God opened the windows of heaven,[8] the
waters, of which clouds are formed, came through,
and covered the high hills that were under the whole
heaven. Fifteen cubits upwards did the waters prevail,
and the mountains were covered.[9] That is, the mountains in their neighbourhood; it being evident that
fifteen cubits of water could never cover such mountains
as the Andes, in South America, and many others,
which are in some places above ten thousand cubits in
height. Neither would fifteen cubits of water cover
the walls of Newgate: but I suppose that they had no
Newgates in those days, else all flesh need not to have
died!

So it appears that John was correct, when he said
that this kingdom of heaven was at hand; for if this
book is to be believed, the heaven spoken of, alluded to

the atmosphere with which we are surrounded, and which is between the waters above, and the waters or seas below. For proof: did not God, while in a great passion, threaten Zephaniah, (i. 3.) that he would consume man and beasts, with the fowls of the heaven, and the fishes of the sea: which you must acknowledge, could mean no other than the fowls of the air. However, it is a good thing for our worthy Aldermen, that this God is not a man of his word, else they would have fewer dishes for their civic feasts! Besides whenever this God calls to any of his creatures out of heaven, they can always hear him very plainly;[10] which proves it to be at hand, and not afar off. Jacob has moreover assured us, that he has seen the gate of heaven, through which the angels go up and out, by means of a ladder, situated between H____ and Beersheba![11]

As we find on earth, that every kingdom is divided into principalities, provinces, counties, &c., so we find that this heaven is divided also into principalities, thrones, dominions, &c. there being many different ranks and stations in it; else how could every man be rewarded according to his work?[12] Some are called great, and some least:[13] differing in glory, as one star differeth from another.[14] Though I cannot see much difference in the stars, save that which is caused by their distance; owing to my not being possessed of the *eye of faith*, I suppose.

Paul informs us that he was caught up into the *third* heaven, that is no doubt the third floor; where he heard the lodgers or inhabitants thereof, speak things which it appears he was ashamed to repeat; they being not lawful for a man to utter.[15] If they had been good and edifying, ministering grace unto the hearers, we may be assured that Paul would have communicated them to us. And by what more we learn from him, neither is it lawful for a man to imitate their actions; for no sooner was he arrived there, than they began to buffet him in a most shameful manner. I suppose it was for not giving the messenger of Satan a satisfactory answer, when sent to him; perhaps to know what he wanted there? as we read that there are principalities, powers, and spiritual wickedness in high places.[16] It is then most probable that this third heaven was Satan's territories, or how should Satan's messenger find him there? or by what authority could he buffet an ambassador of Christ, if he had not been found trespassing on forbidden ground? However, as we find that Paul was a queer odd fellow, being born out of due time;[17] not knowing whether he was in the body, or out of the body, yet possessing two bodies, a natural body, and a spiritual body;[18] forming two men, the outward man, and the inward man, or the old man, and the new man;[19] being a dead man, and a live man,[20] compounded together, it is therefore most probable that such a being got kicked out of Satan's territories, for being a fool; which he acknowledged himself to be, when he wrote to the Corinthians;[21] besides being rude in speech, and contemptible,[22] as no dependance could be placed on him, through his craftiness;[23] sometimes he was one thing and sometimes another,[24] serving either party to obtain that which suited best his own interest.

Elijah, we are told, went to heaven in a whirlwind;[25] which probably was the first heaven; it being unreasonable to suppose that the King of heaven would grant him permission to ascend higher, attended with such a storm. That there must be different heavens cannot be disputed, by David saying that the waves of the sea sometimes mount up to the heaven;[26] which certainly could not mean the same heaven that the men of Babel were determined to reach;[27] else God would have betrayed the same fear at the waves, as he did at the tower of Babel; which probably, if he had not come down and prevented its completion, might have reached his heaven of heavens![28]

Should further proof be required to demonstrate that this heaven which the bible God made, is at hand, and not afar off, being the space between the seas below, and the clouds or waters above, it is the short interval of time which elapsed between the conversation of Jesus with his disciples, and his entry into heaven.[29] This proves the ignorance of our forefathers, who taught that this heaven was situated somewhere beyond the sun ; nay some even thought that it was placed far beyond the fixed stars! But were this the case, how could Jesus have got into heaven so soon, when you tell us, that a cannon ball would not reach the nearest of these fixed stars, within 2,000,000 of years ? Therefore, admitting that Jesus flew one thousand times swifter than a cannon ball would fly from the mouth of a cannon, he cannot have reached this heaven yet, according to their account of it. But, if we admit the Bible account to be correct, namely, that the atmosphere which surrounds the earth, is the heaven that the bible-God made, then the sudden entry of Jesus into it, will seem more plausible; concerning which, I shall speak more hereafter.

Verse 3. " For this is he that was spoken of by the prophet Esaias, saying, the voice of one crying in the wilderness, prepare ye the way of the Lord, make his paths straight."

If we look into the "Gospel according to St. Mark," we shall perceive that he has found out more prophets that spoke of John ; for he says, that it is written, " behold, I send my messenger before thy face, which shall prepare thy way before thee ;"[30] which words I find, in part, written in the book of Malachi, (iii. 1.) and which Mr Mark has thought proper to connect with the words spoken by Isaiah. (xl. 3.) But if we notice, Isaiah says, make straight in the desert a highway for our God. Instead of which, Matthew, Mark, and Luke, have all written, make his paths straight. A clear proof that they copied each other, without regarding the words or meaning of Isaiah ; whereas, John differs from them all![31]

As Jesus has enjoined all those who read, to understand what they do read,[32] let us inquire what did Isaiah and Malachi mean, when they spake these words unto the people ? and what reference can they have to the preaching of John the Baptist ?

First, we find that Malachi, like the rest of the prophets, poured forth maledictions on the priests, (so true it is, that two of a trade can never agree, by saying, that the Lord had *cursed* them,[33] because they had not kept his ways, as the messengers of the Lord of hosts ought to have done, but had corrupted the covenant of Levi.[34] Therefore, he tells them, that he will send a *messenger*, (nothing here about *faces*) that shall prepare the way before him; that is, before Malachi, for it is Malachi who is speaking, and he expressly says *before me.* "Then will the Lord visit his temple; and the messenger of the covenant he also shall come, him whom ye delight in, saith the Lord of hosts."[35] Now what relation has this passage to the preaching or person of John the Baptist? How could the people delight in a man of whom they had never heard? For, if John the Baptist was the messenger of the covenant that was promised, he did not come till nearly 500 years after those persons were all dead and buried, according to the Bible chronology. And, instead of the people *delighting* in him, when he did come, he was only known to them a short time, having been brought up in a desert:[36] and as soon as he made his appearance among them, he was put in prison for using seditious language, and shortly afterwards beheaded.[37]

This messenger of the covenant, it is evident, means a teacher of the law, or an interpreter, as Job (xxxiii. 23.) calls them; who says, "that there were one among a thousand, to shew unto man his uprightness;" to whom Isaiah (xlii. 19.) also alluded, when he said, that the Lord sent Messengers to the people in his days; *teachers* to instruct them in the right way, whenever they should turn to the right hand or to the left.[38]

Besides, the character of John did not answer the description given by Malachi of the messenger; for he asks, who may abide the day of his coming? and who shall stand when he appeareth? for he is like a refiner's fire—he shall sit as a refiner, and purify the sons of Levi.[39] Whereas, John had nothing to do with the sons of Levi, more than the sons of other people. And instead of sitting as a refiner and purifier of silver, he is described as being more like unto an old washer-woman by the river side!

But who was this Malachi? In what age did he live? as we find him placed after all the other prophets: Though, this does not prove that he was the last, as none of the others are placed in a regular order, according to their succession; for Amos, and Micah, who lived in the days of Uzziah and his son Jotham, are both placed after Jeremiah, who lived in the days of Zedekiah, 160 years after the days of Jotham. Also Nahum, Joel, and Jonah, the last of whom prophecied, it is said, long before the reign of Jeroboam, the son of Joash, King of Israel;[40] yet they are placed after Daniel and Ezekiel, who lived during the captivity! Neither is it a proof that Malachi lived after the captivity, in consequence of his name not being mentioned in either the book of Chronicles or Kings; as none of the others are mentioned, excepting Jeremiah, Isaiah, and Jonah. But there are some grounds for supposing that he must have lived long before the captivity, (if such a man did ever exist) seeing that he makes no allusion to the captivity, like the others who lived after it. And his language convinces us, that he must have lived at a time when they had their priests and temples, by his saying, that the people had *robbed* God in tithes and offerings. Therefore, he commands them to bring meat into the house of the Lord, and the tithes into the store-house.[41]

As I have already shewed you, in my first letter, that this book contains many typographical errors, is it not possible, that this Malachi was the same prophet who lived in the days of Ahab and Jehosophat, kings of Israel and Judah, called Micaiah,[42] who heard the Lord send forth a *lying spirit* into the mouths of 400 prophets? There is not so much difference between Micaiah and Malachi, as between Ozias and Azariah; who are both spoken of as being the same person, viz. the father of Jotham;[43] for if Malachi were trans-posed, and the letter *l* changed for an *i*, it would form the word Micaiah: especially as he promised to send the prophet Elijah to them,[44] who, we are told, was living in the days of Micaiah, and who better answers the description given of him by Malachi, as a dangerous and terrible character, and of whom Ahab was greatly afraid.[45] Besides, here were some reasons for comparing him to a refiner's fire, when we learn that he could procure fire to consume whole companies of men at a time.[46] But we are informed, that he was taken into heaven: it is therefore unreasonable for us to suppose, that God would send him out of it again, to take upon him the form of John the Baptist, and get his head cut off by an Infidel! -

If further proof be wanting to demonstrate that John the Baptist could not be Elijah, it is his own testimony; when he told them plainly, that he *was not :*[47] and surely you will admit, that he ought to know best himself who he was, notwithstanding what Mr. Jesus has said to the contrary.[48]

Besides, Luke tells us, that his father was a priest, named Zacharias, and his mother's name was Elizabeth, the cousin of Mary the mother of Jesus.[49] He also relates a frolicksome adventure of the Holy Ghost and his parents; who, after he had overshadowed Mary, the mother of Jesus, went and *filled* Elizabeth, the mother of John.[50] And when Zacharias was struck dumb by one of those angelic monsters, called Gabriel, as soon as he opened his mouth, this Holy Ghost jumped in and filled him likewise![51] And, although those very strange pranks were noised about the hill country of Judea, neither Matthew, Mark, nor yet John, take the least notice of them, but lugs the "baptist" into the wilderness at once, where we find him preaching and *baptizing ;* an ordinance nowhere commanded, foretold, nor related, as having been practised before. But what does Isaiah mean by saying, "the voice of him that crieth in the wilderness, prepare ye the way of the Lord?"

By his writings we are informed, that he foretold the destruction of Jerusalem and the captivity of the Jews.[52] Though, if we consider the strength and numbers of their neighbours, who were, at this time, thirsting for dominion and wealth, we need not be surprised at any man, possessed of a warm imagination, predicting the

captivity of a wealthy and undisciplined handful of men,
as the Jews then were, compared with the Egyptians
and Babylonians; especially, as they, by their former
conquests and cruelties, had rendered themselves objects
of envy and hatred to the surrounding nations, who
kept records of their perfidious and evil practices.[53]
But we have proofs from various passages that the book
of Isaiah, like that of Jeremiah, was written long after
the captivity. If so, as I said in my last, it was very
easy to prophecy and to fulfil. Sometimes we find him
lamenting the desolation of the cities, by saying, (not
in the spirit of prophecy, but of affliction,) "Be not
wroth, very sore, O Lord, neither remember iniquity
for ever: behold, see, we beseech thee, we are all thy
people. Thy holy cities are a wilderness, Zion is a
wilderness, Jerusalem is a wilderness, our holy and our
beautiful house, where our fathers praised thee, is burnt
with fire; and all our pleasant things are laid waste.[45]"
At other times, he says, "the spirit of the Lord is upon
me; because the Lord hath annointed me to preach
good tidings unto the meek,—to proclaim liberty to the
captives—and they shall build the old wastes, they shall
raise up the former desolations, and they shall repair
the waste cities."[55] And, in the passage quoted by
Matthew he says, that "every mountain and valley shall
be made level, and the rough and crooked places plain
and straight; and they shall make straight in the desert a highway for our God;—for the glory of the Lord
shall be revealed, and all flesh shall see it together."[56]
Therefore, he tells them to "sing a new song unto the
Lord, and let the wilderness and the cities thereof lift
up their voice."[57] Now, prithee, tell me, Doctor, what
has all this to do with John the Baptist, or his preaching? Did John build up waste cities, and level mountains and valleys in the wilderness while he was there?
Or did he reveal the glory of this God to all flesh? It
is written that he shewed some few individuals him
whom he thought was the Christ, and whom he de-
signated as the lamb of God;[58] but was that revealing
the glory of God unto all flesh? when we find,
that there were but a few weak-minded illiterate per-

sons that placed any confidence at all in this Jesus, as none of the rulers believed in him ;[59] and their confidence was all destroyed when they saw him expire on the cross; else they would not have treated the account of his resurrection as an idle tale.[60]

Verse 5. 6. " Then went out to him Jerusalem and all Judea, and all the region round about Jordan, and were baptized of him in Jordan, confessing their sins."

This is not to be wondered at, for, if in the present day a man were found, say, for instance, in Hyde-park, clothed with camel's hair, and only a leathern girdle about his loins, doubtless he would attract the gaze of most of the inhabitants in London and its vicinity: and, among them, enow of fools, who would, rather than be deprived of the sight of such a prodigy, suffer themselves to be splashed, or even ducked, in the serpentine river, if there were no other way of obtaining an interview. Though, I should trust, that the modesty and decency of Englishwomen would prevent them from exposing their delicate limbs in such an indecent manner. For, if they did not entirely strip themselves, they must have rendered themselves objects of ridicule amongst the men ; as it appears, that they were all baptized indiscriminately together in those days![61]

But what authority had John for baptizing? I cannot find that he ever received any commands from this God to that effect. Neither did any of the prophets predict or practise such an absurd and ridiculous action. And pray, who baptized John? Yet, admitting that, if the people suffered him, he had a right to dip them, what authority can that be for baptizing us? Jesus baptized none ;[62] and Paul declares, that Jesus sent him not to baptize, but to preach ;[63] although, we do find, that he baptized Crispus and several others.[64]

That which you say God has commanded, namely, circumcision, we leave undone ; whilst that which God never thought about, that do we. Oh! wretched creatures that we are! who shall deliver us from the body of this craft? I thank those, who through the medium of the press, have brought to light the hidden things of darkness.

This baptism, or immersion, appears to have been only a penance, imposed upon the people by this wild man, as a remuneration for his exhibition ; for we cannot find that God ever ordained such an ordinance. He moreover tells them, that he should *decrease*, that is, his work and value, (like all other exhibitions when public curiosity is satisfied,) while that of Jesus should increase ;[65] because he was a novelty ; and, no doubt, had told him, that he was about to establish a new religion of his own ; not consisting of ordinances, meats and drinks, beggarly elements, days, months, times, and years ; nor yet of holy days, nor sabbaths.[66] Why then, as Paul says, should we be subject to ordinances?[67] Great stress is laid on those supposed commands of Jesus, when he bade them go and teach all nations ; baptizing them in the name of the Father, the Son, and the Holy Ghost ;[68] for he that believeth and is baptized shall be saved.[69] But what does this baptism mean ? Are we to suppose that all the nations were to be dipped in a river ? No, certainly, baptism is a *doctrine;*[70] and although it was in some instances made use of as an ordinance, by endeavouring to wash an Ethiopian eunuch white, and keeping the people at Jerusalem clean, yet it was only used as a figure for the time then present, like unto the ordinances of the first covenant;[71] which consisted in meats and drinks, and divers washings.[72] For if it were not possible for the blood of bulls and of goats to take away sins, how can water make the comers thereunto perfect?[73] By comparing Acts ii. 38. with iii. 19. we find, that to be baptized signifies being converted ; that is, a change or conversion, which should take place in the life and conduct of any person, agreeable to the propositions of the bible God ; who had formerly told Ezekiel, (xviii. 11.) that if the wicked man would turn from all his sins that he had committed, and keep all his statues, and do that which is lawful and right, he shall surely live, he shall not die. Here is nothing about ducking or splashing of faces ! For it matters not to God whether you eat bread with unwashed hands or not.[74] It is not, as St. Peter says, the putting away the filth of the flesh, but the answer of a good conscience;[75] having our hearts sprinkled, (or cleansed) from an evil conscience, and our bodies (or conduct) washed (or regulated) with pure water;[76] that is, with the word of their God, which is said to be pure, converting the soul.[77] Paul says, when writing to the Ephesians, (v. 26.) that Christ gave himself for the Church, that he might sanctify and cleanse it with the washing of water by the word, which view of the subject accords with the prayer of Jesus, when he said, sanctify (or cleanse) them through thy truth, thy word is truth.[78]

That the apostles and brethren considered water batism of little or no consequence, is evident, by the injunctions laid down by them, after the dissension and disputation concerning circumcision. For it seemed good to the Holy Ghost, (or holy priest,) to lay upon the people no greater burden than these necessary things; which were, to abstain from meats offered to Idols, and from blood, and from things strangled, and from fornication; from which, they said, if ye keep yourselves, ye shall do well.[79] Here is neither circumcision, nor yet baptism, enforced as being necessary to salvation! If you imagine that Jesus would not have submitted to it, had it not been found necessary to fulfil all righteousness, then you must admit that circumcision is likewise necessary, for Jesus also submitted to that.[80]

Again, where do the priests obtain authority for baptizing young children? They say that it is agreeable to the institution of Christ; but I cannot find that Christ instituted water baptism at all. Jesus himself baptized not;[81] neither did he ever enforce it upon any one, as being necessary to salvation; for surely if he had thought so, he would have urged it upon the rich man in the gospel,[82] and many others whom we have no right to suppose were ever baptized, they being Jews, who regarded no other rites and ceremonies than those contained in the Mosaic law. It is then plain that this baptism was only a penance or imposition imposed upon the people by John, which caused Jesus to comply with it, when he suffered himself to be baptized ; thereby rendering unto John his due, which was the fulfilling of all righteousness.

But the baptizing of children, in particular, is no where suggested, there being not a single passage to authorise it, or an instance recorded as a precedent : every sentence convincing us that a man must believe before that he can be baptized. Philip would not baptize the Eunuch until he had acknowledged Jesus to be the son of God.[83] Peter would not baptize Cornelius and his friends until he found that they had believed.[84] Paul was not baptized until he was convinced.[85] And those who were baptized by John were baptized confessing their sins.[86] How can little children believe or confess sins ? Besides, did not Jesus command them first to teach all nations ? for he that believeth first and is baptized (or converted) shall be saved.

Moreover, what presumption it is for any man or woman to assume the title of God-father and God-mother (newly invented names.) How can they insure that a child, a stranger to them, shall perform those things which they promise in his name ? Solomon says (Prov. xi. 15) that " he that is surety for a stranger, shall smart for it ;" which things you acknowledge yourself, are never done, such as the keeping God's holy will and commandments, and walking therein all the days of his life. Surely, if there be any meaning in the word blasphemy, it must be this! I have been baptized and confirmed, have often received, what you call, the sacrament of the Lord's supper. Yet, what better am I for all those things ? Then if those things do not regulate the conduct and consciences of men, of what good are they ? Surely, it would have been far better if myself and parents had applied our money towards purchasing things that were useful and necessary for our bodies, instead of giving it away upon such fooleries. But John exacted no money for baptism, the gratification which he derived from ducking the people was quite sufficient for him. Neither did any of the apostles demand or receive money for any thing which they did. No : when money was even offered to them, they spurned at it, by saying, thy money perish with thee, because thou hast thought that the gift of God may be purchased with money.[87]   They kept no equipage ; for gold and silver they had none,[88] but laboured, working with their own hands for their support, that they might not become chargeable to the people ;[89] oftentimes, naked and hungry : and instead of pompous palaces, with liveried servants, they had no certain dwelling place belonging to them.   Neither did John, nor any other baptist among them, require any splendid and costly baptistaries to be built for them.   They could baptize in any place, let it be a pond, a river, or a prison.[90]   Whereas, now if a man has not money to pay a priest for baptising his child, it may go to hell and be damned ; as they say that none can enter the kingdom of God, except he be regenerate, and born anew of water and of the Holy Ghost ; because, he is born in original sin, and in the wrath of God.   Yet, notwithstanding their certainty of all this, very few will trouble themselves about it, when there is no money to be got.

Verse 7. "But when he saw many of the Sadducees and Pharisees come to his baptism."

This proves what I have already stated, that this ducking in the river, was only a penance, imposed by John, for his exhibition ; or why should the Sadducees, who believed in no resurrection, angel nor spirit,[91] come to his baptism ? which, moreover, shows the insufficiency of those tales, related by Abraham, Moses, Samuel, and others, concerning Witches, Ghosts, and Angels ; seeing that a few Jews, chosen expressly by this God, for the purpose of convincing the whole world, could not agree among themselves, concerning those things ; of which, some of them must have had ocular demonstration, if what Matthew writes be true ; for he says, that the graves opened, and many dead bodies arose, and appeared to many in the city, after the resurrection ; which, we are told, was not until the third day after the graves were opened, at his crucifixion ; consequently, they must have been all that time going to and fro in the city.   Yet Paul says, that these

Sadducees would not believe. Then if they, whose fathers were the prophets, would not believe, why should we, who are both foreigners and strangers?

Verse 13. "Then cometh Jesus from Galilee to Jordan, unto John, to be baptized of him."

The last account given by Matthew of Jesus is, that when a child, he dwelt with his parents in a city called Nazareth.[92] From which time we hear no more from him, until we find him coming to be baptized; which, according to Luke, was not until he was thirty years of age. Though Luke relates an anecdote of him, stating that when he was only twelve years of age, he was found disputing with the doctors in the temple, who were astonished at his understanding and answers.[93] A proof that the Jewish doctors were more liberal in tolerating FREE DISCUSSION than the Christian doctors; who will not suffer any man to speak beside themselves in their temples; wherein they crow like a cock upon its own dunghill. After this he is represented as increasing in wisdom and in stature,[94] which we might naturally suppose, without the aid of a ghost to tell us, it being very natural for lads of his age to grow wiser as they grow older, likewise to increase in stature. But, from various passages, we have good reason to suspect that he was, during this interval, working with his reputed father as a carpenter;[95] (The son of God a carpenter!) though none of his historians give any account of his proficiency in that business, whether he made any improvements in it by his ingenuity, industry, or divinity. Indeed, I wonder that the Church of Rome, among all its holy relics, have not preserved some notable thing or other, which he, of course, must have made, during that time, as a specimen of his workmanship. But, no, as Woolaston said, they have not kept so much as a three-legged stool, or even a pair of nut-crackers! Neither have his historians informed us whether he attended any public place of worship, and disputed again with the doctors, after he had increased in wisdom and in stature: or whether he grew slothful and negligent, suffering the people all that time to live and die ignorant of his mission. For if he came to destroy the works of the devil, surely the sooner he began about it the better. This conduct of Jesus seems unaccountable; it could not be for the want of talent, seeing that at twelve years old he astonished the doctors with his understanding and answers; besides, we know that it does not require such extraordinary talents to preach or make a sermon. A Methodist, although a poor mechanic, styling himself a miserable sinner, need not tarry until he is thirty years of age, before he is qualified by the Holy Ghost for preaching. Why then should Jesus, who was full of the Holy Ghost from his infancy, lose so much time? We do not read that he ever converted any of his shopmates during his obscurity, not even his reputed father, nor any of his brethren![96] Indeed, I somehow think, that he must have spent this part of his life, like the generality of carpenters, in Bacchanalian revels, or some such idle and pernicious pastimes, until either his brain became distempered, or he had acquired a degree of cunning and ingenuity sufficient to qualify him for deluding and imposing upon the credulity of his ignorant countrymen; of which I shall treat in my next, when I examine his first miracle said to have been done in Cana.

But in whose name was he baptized and all Judea with him? as it is the name of the Father, Son, and Holy Ghost, which now constitutes baptism; without which, you say, the sprinkling or ducking would avail nothing. You, moreover add, that baptism is an outward sign of an inward and spiritual grace or death unto sin; that repentance is required of all them who come to be baptized. If so—what need had Jesus of baptism, when we are informed that in him was no sin,[97] consequently he could not repent? Besides, it is written, that his parents had performed all things according to the law;[98] he had been circumcised agreeable to the Jewish law, what righteousness then was there left for him to fulfil, that it should be deemed necessary to baptize him? Moreover, according to our present baptismal ceremony, we are commanded to renounce the devil and all his works. But, we read, that as soon as Jesus was baptized, he became very intimate with the Devil, they visiting several places together during the space of forty days! of which I shall treat in my next letter.

Verse 16. "And Jesus, when he was baptized, went up straightway out of the water; and, lo, the heavens were opened unto him, and he saw the spirit of God descending like a dove, and lighting upon him."

Herein Mr. Matthew has omitted the most important information that could be given to us; which is, whether it was the gate, the doors, or the windows of heaven that were opened; or whether it was on this side of the sun, or on the other side of it: by this omission, he has left our priests and wise men still to puzzle and distract their brains about its situation. However, it is evident that it must be somewhere "at hand," as John said, by his hearing the voice so plain. Neither has he informed us what became of the dove afterwards, whether it was caught and preserved in a cage, as a heavenly curiosity: or whether they saw it return into heaven. If they did, surely the gate, doors, or window, must have remained open long enough for them to have seen, or discovered, something of its internal structure, as we do not read that there were any porters in heaven before Peter arrived there. But, perhaps, it was only the ghost of a dove! Trusting, Sir, that you may throw some light upon this dark subject, I subscribe myself,

Your humble Servant,

JOHN CLARKE.

NOTES TO THE FOREGOING LETTER.

1 Mark i. 6—13
2 Romans xiv. 7
3 Luke xiii. 7.
4 Genesis i. 8.
5 „ „ 10.
6 Lamentations iii. 44.
7 Exodus xiii. 21.

LETTER VI.

TO DR. ADAM CLARKE,

CHAP. IV.

Verse 1. " Then was Jesus led up of the spirit into the wilderness, to be tempted of the devil : and when he had fasted forty days and forty nights, he was afterwards an hungered."

Both Matthew and Luke make this excursion into the wilderness, the next occurrence in their history of Jesus after his baptism.

Mark says expressly that it was immediately :[1] whilst John, who knew all things from the beginning,[2] takes no notice of it ; but says, that the next day, after his baptism,. he invited two disciples to spend the day with him ; and the day following he walked forth into Galilee, where he found Philip and Nathaniel.[3] The third day he went with his mother to a marriage feast at Cana.[4] After which, he went home and staid some time at Capernaum, until the passover, when he went up to Jerusalem,[5] making no mention of either the devil or wilderness. How the priests will get over this blunder I. cannot tell ; for, according to John, (and we have as much right to believe him as any of the others,) instead of fasting in a wilderness along with a devil, for forty days, he was feasting with his friends at Cana !

And what manner of Spirit was that which could lead Jesus into such a dreary place, in order that he might be tempted of the devil ? It surely could not be a good spirit, for James says (i. 13,) that God tempteth no man ; but that every man is tempted when he is

drawn away of his own lust and enticed. Though
Mark says that the spirit drove him into the wilderness: if this were the case, Jesus cannot be blamed for
going there, as we all know that there is a great
difference between leading and driving. Yet I cannot
tell how it was possible for a bad spirit, or, as James
calls it, his own lust, to lead or drive the Son of God
about, when we are told that he was filled with the
Holy Ghost,[6] except this Holy Ghost signifies the
Spirit of the Lord, which Jesus seems to insinuate as
being upon him.[7] If so, it is then easily accounted for;
as we all know that the Spirit of the Lord was a cruel
and malignant spirit, or it never would have caused
Jephtha to make that rash vow, through which his
daughter lost her life.[8] Neither would it have led
Samson to gamble, and afterwards to rob and murder
thirty men, in order to make good his loss.[9] But what
employment were the Devil and Jesus engaged in
among the wild beasts, that should require a space of
forty days to perform? as we find that the three temptations did not commence until those forty days had
expired, when the Devil first asked Jesus to make
bread out of stones; a thing less difficult, I should
think, for him to do, than making bread and fish out of
nothing; especially as he found himself an hungered.
And the other two temptations were evidently not
made in the wilderness; the one being on a pinnacle
in the city, and the other on an exceedingly high mountain, whence Jesus could see all the Kingdoms of the
round world! which mountain, we are well assured,
could not have been in the wilderness, or it would be
there still; having no account handed down to us of
any natural mountain being brought low by John the
Baptist. Moreover, what had become of all the locusts
and wild honey? Surely, if that food could support
John for so many years in the wilderness, it might very
well have supported Jesus for forty days!

This being the first passage throughout the book
wherein we read of such an animal as a Devil, it is
necessary to inquire into his nature, as he seems to have
been a very powerful being, by his carrying Jesus

whithersoever he thought proper. The Jews, we find, charged Jesus with being a friend to the Prince of Devils;[10] which accusation does not appear to be entirely groundless, as we always find that he was remarkably civil to those Devils whenever he met with any of them, always granting them any favour which they requested;[11] which complaisance, probably, might have been one of the conditions made between Jesus and the Devil while they were together in the wilderness, (for we find by Isaiah xxviii. 15, that an agreement may be made with hell) for the instructions which Jesus might have received in the art and mystery of magic. I cannot imagine what else could employ their time together in a wilderness, during a space of forty days. Though, if what the priests say be true concerning this Devil, I am sure it would have done him more credit, and been much more to his honour and glory, if he had, like St. Dunstan, taken the Devil by his nose, or even by his collar, if he had one, and cast him into some of the lowermost dungeons in hell, or some other such dismal place; he would then have preserved his own life, by preventing him from getting into Judas Iscariot, besides the many evils and troubles which he has since brought upon mankind. But I suppose that if he had done so, the priests would have grumbled, for without a Devil they could not so easily frighten the people out of their money.

Besides, is it not curious that no one ever saw or heard of a Devil before they saw Jesus? And that as soon as he left them, away went the Devils! for no Devil has ever been seen since. Though John said that they were only to be for a short time:[12] and as he is the only one among them all that has attempted to describe a Devil, let us read what he says about them in his Revelations; for in his Gospel he takes no more notice of them than if there never were such animals.

In the 12th chapter of Revelations, he informs us that it was a great red Dragon, (by which it appears that the Devil is not so black as he is painted!) having seven heads and ten horns. If God made the Devil, why did he make him with seven heads, when he himself has but one, if man be made in the image of God? Besides he had a very long tail, and a mouth large enough to contain a flood of water! He was considered as being one of the wonders in heaven, a woman being the other! (1) But this red Dragon, or Devil, or Satan, or Old Serpent, as he is called, having a quarrel with one Mr. Michael, they and their angels or soldiers fought together, when Mr. Devil got the worst of the battle, and was cast out of heaven into the earth, whereto he fell like lightning, as Jesus says,[13] with all his army. In consequence of which, he became very wroth with the inhabitants of the earth, and went about to and fro seeking whom he might devour.[14] I think, Doctor, that if Mr. Michael had cast him into some other world, the inhabitants of this would have been under greater obligations to him: for we find that he soon got into Peter,[15] upon whom the Church of Christ is built,[16] and has kept his station ever since!

If this Dragon, or Devil, be the Satan which is spoken of in the book of Job, we find, that in Job's days he and the bible God were very friendly and sociable with each other; inasmuch, that God refused Satan nothing which he requested; although it might distress and torment his own *upright* and *faithful* servants; yea, even to the death of some of those creatures, which he had been at the trouble of making and rearing up to the age of maturity.[17] By which, I somehow suspect, that this Satan was the most potent of the two; at least, that he "held divided empire with heaven's high King." Or why should a God of love, who doth not afflict willingly, nor grieve the children of man,[18] suffer such an adversary to walk up and down to and fro throughout the earth, distressing and destroying those creatures which he had made for his glory,[19] without either opposing him or making any resistance?

Moreover, if we examine every transaction of those two conspicuous characters, namely, God and the Devil, as related in this book, we shall find, that the Devil succeeds in almost every thing, except in the battle with Captain Michael and his army, whilst poor God and his plans are continually frustrated by this Devil; some of his faithful servants are cast into prison by him;[20] others are obliged, even a poor old woman, to carry him on her back, for a certain number of years;[21] and Joshua himself, although a High Priest, could not get measured for a new suit of clothes, without this Satan standing before him to resist him;[22] and any one of God's subjects may, it appears, be taken captive by him at his will;[23] it being utterly impossible for any mortal man to guard against him, in consequence of his invisibility; therefore, as St. Paul says, he must be the God of this world.[24] Though, it is very strange that he who is said to be the Lord of hosts, and God of battles,[25] after having defeated the Devil, by the valour of Captain Michael, should suffer and permit him to annoy us, with impunity. It does not look as though he had much regard for the creatures which he has made in his own image!

Besides, it appears so inconsistent, that this Bible God should say, thou shalt not kill—thou shalt not steal—thou shalt not commit adultery; and yet permit this Devil, whom no man can guard against, or attack, in consequence of his superior faculties of invisibility and immortality, to lead men into the commission of those very things, which this God has said, and commanded, shall not be done. When a man commits murder, they say, directly, that he was instigated to do it by the Devil. If a man have, what are called, wicked thoughts, it is the Devil, they say, that suggests them, or if his passions overcome his reason, it is the Devil's fault; and if he exercise his reason, should it be concerning certain creeds and doctrines, he is then told, that it is still the working of the enemy! This is like the government of a certain country, first enacting laws against sedition and treason, and then sending persons with superior powers, (money) to lead them into the commission of those said crimes. There is no distinguishing mark upon this Devil, as there was upon Cain,[26] whereby he might be known : for he can, if he chuses, transform himself into an angel of light, at any time.[27] So that man ought not to be blamed for any thing that he doeth, he being only a machine for the

Devil to work with. As Paul says, it is not I that do it, but sin, which they say, is of the Devil,[28] that dwelleth in me.[29] Therefore, I think, that it would be an act of policy and wisdom, if the Magistrates and rulers of every country were to enter into an holy alliance, muster all their forces, and attack this Devil; or if they cannot find him in consequence of his invisibility, let them send an ambassador, with a petition to the court of heaven, praying that this God, would send Captain Michael again, with his angels, to utterly destroy or extirpate from this earth, all the devilites that he cast among us at first. Then would mankind be at peace, having no instigator or prompter to rob and murder one another.

But, what have I written? I believe the Devil is at my " elbow," prompting me to blot it out again; for if this should ever happen, what would the priests do? the Devil being the only weapon that they can handle. If you go to a Catholic priest, and tell him that his dogmas are not true, he will tell you that the Devil will be sure to have you, and that when you get into his clutches, he will boil, roast, or fry you at his pleasure. If you go to a Protestant priest and tell him that his creed is disputable, he will also tell you that you will be damned to all eternity, and that this Devil will have the tormenting of you. In short, go to what priest you will, whether he be a Calvinist, a Lutheran, a Whitfieldite, a Wesleyan, or any other "an" or " ite," he will tell you, that, if you won't believe them, and them only, the Devil will be sure to have you, and will burn your soul in hell with fire and brimstone!

Some say that the Devil is now in hell, preparing the place, and devising tortures for us, against we get there. Though, by the bye, I am almost ashamed to acknowledge my ignorance of that place; but, really, I have never yet been able to learn whereabout hell is situated, or when the foundations thereof were laid; as I can only find, by this book, that God made heaven and earth; but not a word about making hell. Some think that the sun is hell! others, there are, who suppose that the comets are so many hells, appointed in their orbits, alternately to carry the damned into the confines of the sun, there to be scorched by its violent heat; and then to return with them beyond the orb of Saturn, there to starve them in those cold and dismal regions. The Mahomedans, say that hell has seven gates, the first for Mussulmen; the second for Christians; the third for Jews; the next for Sabians; then the Magians; next Pagans; and seventh, or last, for the hypocrites of all religions. But as I intend to search the scriptures again, lest peradventure I may have overlooked it, I shall postpone this subject to a future letter. In the meantime, I must confess that it appears somewhat parodoxical, for the Devil to be in hell, while the Bible positively asserts, that he is going to and fro in the earth, seeking whom he may devour; dwelling at a place called Pergamos.[3 0]

And what is more strange, the priests say that this very Devil or Satan, was the Serpent who spoke to Eve! Is not this, like many other tales which they tell us, false? there being not a single passage throughout the Bible which authorizes them to ground even a supposition, that such was the case. This book states, that that Serpent, which had the impudence to open his mouth and tattle to Old Mother Eve, was doomed by the Bible God to go upon his belly, eating dust all the days of his life.[3 1] For my part, I never could, for the life of me, imagine how that Serpent went before; whether he jumped along the ground upon the point of his tail, or upon his head? Some there are who suppose that he went upon his back; if so, I should think that it was a blessing instead of a curse, for surely it is more convenient and less difficult to go upon the belly, than upon the back! Though, according to Isaiah, this prediction was not to be fulfilled, until the Wolf and the Lamb fed together; then shall dust, he says, be the Serpent's meat.[3 2]

And how those persons discover their ignorance of the laws of nature, when they suspect that the serpent must have walked erect, prior to his conversation with Eve; besides being endued with the gift of speech, as well as reason, through Eve manifesting no kind of surprise when he accosted her. How could any animal speak without being possessed of the organs of speech? for surely, they will not presume to suppose that God opened the mouth of the serpent for this vile purpose, as he did the mouth of Balaam's ass.[33] Or how could an animal walk, without having legs to walk with? For if he had legs and organs of speech, he could not have been a serpent; whereas Paul tells us positively, that it was a serpent that beguiled Eve.[34] If this argument held good for the one, it certainly must for the other; then we might as reasonably conclude that the ass of Balaam spoke and reasoned before; seeing that Balaam testified no more surprise at the voice of his ass, than Eve did at the voice of the serpent.

I likewise think that you certainly must have forgotten yourself, when you considered that this serpent belonged to the ape or ouran outang kind; as you are well aware, that neither apes nor ouran outangs go upon their bellies, any more than dogs or cats; neither do they eat *dust* all the days of their lives; some of them being very dainty: surely this is making a *monkey* Bible of it altogether!

Perhaps some will say that this Devil, or Satan, got into the serpent, as he got into Judas Iscariot, or into the swine by the same means as the holy Ghost got into Elizabeth, Mary, and many others. If this were the case, why should a just and upright Judge punish the poor serpent who could not help the Devil getting into him any more than Judas could? Why not punish the Devil, he being the aggressor? instead of which, he is suffered to escape, and permitted to continue the same evil course with impunity. It is not the custom for human judges to convict the weapon which has taken away the life of any man, and acquit the criminal. It was well for the Devil that Newman Knowlys was not his judge, or he would not have heeded the serpent any more than he did my little book, but would have cast the Devil at least for *three years* into some dungeon or other. Though, it is written, that, " God's way's are not as our ways."[35] The one being *human* justice, and the other *divine;* be it as it may, I am sure that neither is *moral* justice.

Again, I have heard some people say, that this Devil was one of the fallen angels who kept not their first estate.[36] How could this be, when we are told that they were chained under darkness unto the judgment of the great day; which proves, that an angel has only got a limited power, by this restraint that is laid upon them; whereas, Satan has not only unbounded liberty, but reigns as God of this world, and Prince of the power of the air.[37]

Besides, according to the calculation of the priests, this Devil has 999 immortal souls out of every thousand, which this bible God makes. Jesus himself acknowledged that not every one who saith Lord, Lord, shall enter the kingdom of heaven;[38] the gateway being so very narrow, there are but very few persons that will be able to find it:[39] for many are called, but few chosen.[40] And as Paul has declared, that he gets into the hearts of some people,[41] it is evident, that he must have an unlimited existence; consequently, must see and know all things as well as the bible God, by his omnipresence. Though, how they can both be omnipresent, I am at a loss to discover; as God says that he himself fills heaven and earth.[42] And how this Devil and the Holy Ghost can get into the heads and hearts of men, without some one seeing them go in or out, is still more wonderful; for we find that as soon as one goes out the other pops in, as they cannot agree at all together in one place.[43] In consequence of which, the holy men of God, who spoke as they were moved, seem to have been greatly puzzled to know which was which. For instance, the writer of the first book of Chronicles (xxi. 1) says, that it was Satan who provoked David to number the people; whilst the writer of the second book of Samuel (xxiv. 1) says, that it was God that moved him. This, also, is another example of divine justice, punishing the innocent people that were numbered, and suffering the principal aggressor (David) to remain unpunished. Though, for my part, I cannot see any fault in a King numbering his subjects; for, as Jesus says—What King, going to make war against another King, sitteth not down first, and consulteth whether he is able to meet him or not? which can only be done by numbering his forces. [44]

Besides, this God himself often commanded his servants to number the people, both before and after this transaction. [45] But as I intend in my next letter to confine myself in particular to an inquiry into the existence of this God, I shall make no further observation at present upon his conduct, but merely point out, before I conclude this devilish subject, the discordance which prevails among these divine historians, relating to the three temptations of this devil with Jesus. First, Matthew says that Satan took Jesus into the city, and sat him upon a pinnacle of the temple, before he took him to the mountain. Luke says that he took him first to the mountain, and afterwards to the pinnacle. Whilst Mark mentions neither: and John denies it altogether.

"Who shall decide when doctors disagree?"

Verse 12. "Now when Jesus heard that John was cast into prison, he departed into Galilee."

According to Matthew, Mark, and Luke, we find that as soon as Jesus was baptized, before he could return into Galilee, or call Peter and the others, John the Baptist was cast into prison; whilst John positively denies it, by saying, that he was not. Jesus having been to Galilee, and called several; then to Cana; then to Capernaum; staid there some time; thence to Jerusalem; and thence into the land of Judea, where John was baptizing, at a place called Enon, near to Dalem; for, he says, John was not yet cast into prison. [46] That one of them, if not both, must speak false, I trust you will acknowledge.

Verse 13. "And leaving Nazareth, he came and dwelt in Capernaum, which is upon the sea coast, in the borders of Zabulon and Nepthalim: that it might be fulfilled, which was spoken by Esaias the prophet, saying, the land of Zabulon, and the land of Nepthalim, by the way of the Sea, beyond Jordan, Galilee of the Gentiles; the people which sat in darkness saw great light; and to them which sat in the region and shadow of death, light is sprung up."

As I have detected Mr. Matthew already lugging in unconnected sentences, and palming them upon us as prophecies; I shall be very cautious in receiving any more without due examination. Therefore, let us see whether Isaiah did say so; and if he did, what did he mean?

We find, as I before stated in my second letter, that Isaiah told Ahaz, King of Judah, that the Lord had hired a razor, (the King of Assyria,) to shave his enemies;[47] when, after he had done, he should "pass through the land of Immanuel, (Judea) and break the people to pieces,"[48] because they did not seek after God, but after those who had familiar spirits. Then they should look upward, and curse both God and their King, through vexation. "And when they looked unto the earth, they should behold trouble and darkness, dimness of anguish; for they should be driven into darkness, because there was no light in them."[49] Nevertheless, Isaiah says, "the dimness shall not be such as was in her vexation, when at the first he lightly afflicted [the land of Zebulon and the land of Naphtali] and afterwards did more grievously afflict her [by the way of the sea beyond Jordan in Galilee] of the nations. The people that walked in darkness have seen a great light; they that dwell in the land of the shadow of death upon them hath the light shined. For unto us a child is born, unto us a son is given," Isaiah's son, which he got of the prophetess,[50] and which, with some others that he had got, were to be for signs and wonders in Israel;[51] "and the government shall be upon his shoulder; and his name shall be called Wonderful, Councellor, the Mighty God;" it being common among the Jews to call Kings and Princes, and even Prophets, Gods, down to the time of Herod;[52] "the everlasting Father, the Prince of Peace, of the increase of his government and peace there shall be no end, upon the throne of David, and upon his kingdom, to order it, and to establish it with judgment and with justice, from henceforth even for ever."[53]

These are the words of Isaiah; but what reference can they have to Jesus travelling from Nazareth to

Capernaum, seven hundred years after they were spoken? Isaiah speaks of a circumstance that had already taken place, and should continue henceforth, that is, from his days. It seems, that the son, whom he had just got by the prophetess, he expected (like many fond and foolish parents) would become a great and wise man; who should have charge of the government of the country, and govern the people with judgment and justice; shining among them as a great light in the midst of darkness. Then their dimness would not be as it was when they sought familiar spirits and wizards, fretting themselves and cursing both God and their King: for which God only at first lightly afflicted them; but did afterwards more greviously afflict them, particularly about those parts in Galilee, beyond Jordan. And this kingdom, so established, should remain for ever; that is, as long as his son lived, or perhaps longer. For we are not to suppose that when we read of ever, or everlasting, that it signifies a continuation without end; it being evident, by referring to many passages, that it could not mean longer than a certain period or duration of time. For instance, when we read of a man having his ear bored through with an awl, it was to be a sign that he should serve his master for ever.[54] This, certainly, did not imply beyond his life, neither could it extend beyond the Jubilee, when all were released from servitude and bondage, without any exception.[55] Neither was Jonah compassed about with the bars of the earth for ever, when he was at the bottom of the mountains in the belly of the fish; seeing that the fish, after three days, vomited him out again upon dry land.[56] Paul also says, that Christ has perfected for ever, them that are sanctified;[57] yet Mr. Wesley says, in his "Plain account of Christian Perfection," that we are surrounded with instances of those "who lately experienced all that is meant by perfection. They had both the fruit of the spirit, and the witness. But they have now lost both; there is no such height or strength of holiness as it is impossible to fall from." And Paul says, "let him that thinketh he standeth, take heed lest he fall,"[58] for if he do

Peter says, " that his latter end is worse than the beginning."⁵⁹ How then can they be perfected for ever, if it be possible for them to turn again like the dog to his vomit, or the sow that was washed to her wallowing in the mire ?

We read also, of an everlasting priesthood ;⁶⁰ yet, when Christ came the priesthood was changed,⁶¹ because they had corrupted the covenant, and the Lord had cursed them.⁶² Indeed, the anointing ceased with their kingdom, as we never read that any were anointed after the Babylonian captivity. Again, when speaking of everlasting possession,⁶³ we find that that possession has long since been given up ; the Turks having possession of that which was promised to Abram, and his seed, for an everlasting possession : likewise the everlasting statutes, they being not good ;⁶⁴ and the everlasting covenants, they being faulty, were done away by a new covenant.⁶⁵

That this is the true meaning of Isaiah's words is evident ; and Matthew could be no other than an impostor for endeavouring to pervert the true sense of them, in the manner in which he has done. If you take notice of the division that I have made while writing the first verse of the ninth chapter you will find that he has only taken the names of the towns and places therein mentioned, (which I have enclosed within brackets) without ever noticing the subject, leaving the matter altogether senseless.

Verse 18. " And Jesus walking by the sea of Galilee, saw two brethren, Simon, called Peter, and Andrew, his brother, casting a net into the sea ; for they were fishers. And he saith unto them, follow me, and I will make you fishers of men : and they straightway left their nets, and followed him. And going thence, he saw other two brethren, James, the son of Zebedee, and John, his brother, in a ship with Zebedee, their father, mending their nets ; and he called them, and they immediately left the ship and their father, and followed him."

Luke says, (v. 3.) that he entered one of the ships, where he sat down and taught the people ; and that, through his power, they obtained a miraculous draught of fishes; but neither Matthew, Mark, nor yet John, have said a word about it. John expressly states, that the *beginning* of his *miracles* was at a marriage feast in Cana. And instead of his walking by the sea side, from one ship to the other, as Mark says, (i. 19.) or entering into any ship, as Luke says, he was passing by a place, where John the Baptist was standing, talking with two of his disciples; who, as soon as they heard the Baptist say, behold the Lamb of God, went directly and followed Jesus home, and staid with him all that day; making mention of neither ships, nets, nor fishes.[6 6]

Verse 23. "And Jesus went about all Galilee, teaching in their Synagogues, and preaching the gospel of the kingdom, and healing all manner of sickness among the people."

Before Jesus began to preach, John relates a miracle, which, he says, was performed by Jesus in Cana of Galilee. And as neither Matthew, Mark, nor Luke, have thought proper to notice it, I think it is necessary that we should; therefore, before we proceed further, let us examine it, this being the first miracle that he performed, according to John.

John says, that, there was a marriage in Cana of Galilee, and the mother of Jesus was there; and both Jesus was called and his disciples to the marriage. And when they wanted wine, the mother of Jesus saith unto him, they have no wine; Jesus saith unto her, woman, what have I to do with thee? mine hour is not yet come. His mother saith unto the servants, whatsoever he saith unto you, do it. And there were set there six water-pots of stone, after the manner of the purifying of the Jews, containing two or three firkins a piece. Jesus saith unto them, fill the water-pots with water, and they filled them up to the brim. And he saith unto them draw out now, and bear to the governor of the feast; and they bare it. When the ruler of the feast had tasted the water, that was made wine, and knew not whence it was, (but the servants that drew the water knew,) the governor of the feast called the bridegroom, and saith unto him, every man at the beginning doth set forth good wine; and when men have well drunk, then that which is worse: but thou hast kept the good wine until now.[67]

I believe it is customary with the Jews, as with all other nations, upon such occasions as these, to have some kind of pastime and diversion, such as music, dancing, singing, sometimes cards, &c. in order to produce mirth and hilarity; wherein levity and excess are oftentimes indulged: for which reason, few grave or seriously disposed persons are ever invited. If they be, few will accept the invitation; excepting, with a pious intention of delivering a seasonable exhortation, suitable for the occasion; by admonishing the parties to beware of Satan, that he tempt them not to incontinency;[68] or to discourse on the conjugal duties and blessings of matrimony; generally concluding with prayer, &c. But, as I do not find that Jesus or his mother ever taught, preached, or prayed, upon this occasion, I much doubt whether they were such pious characters as the priests would fain make us to believe. And if they did not themselves indulge in any excess, they surely must have been idle spectators of it in others, as it seems that they had well drunk; and you know, that it is written, come out from among them, and be ye separate; touch not, taste not, handle not, which all are to perish with the using;[69] not even with him, though he be called a brother, Paul says, if he be a drunkard; with such an one not to keep company.[70]

But, the sequel of the story proves to me, that they not only participated in the excess, but were the principal cause of promoting the intemperance. And by the snappish and senseless reply, which Jesus made to his mother, I am inclined to think, somehow, that he was more than "half seas over," especially, as he had the character of being a *Wine-bibber* and a *Glutton.*[71] At any rate, you must acknowledge that it was very unbecoming in a dutiful son to answer his mother in that surly manner, especially, when she was advising him for his good. For what other reason could she have in telling him, that there was no more wine, but that she thought it was high time for him to go home? She could have no knowledge of his working a miracle, never having seen, him do one before; it being written that this was his beginning of miracles. But we find that Jesus, like a man whose senses had flown out as the wine flowed in, forgetting his relationship to his mother, as well as the fifth commandment of his God, answered and said, *Woman what have I to do with thee? mine hour is not yet come :* signifying that she being a woman, might go home if she pleased, as all women ought to do, when they find the company almost drunk; but as for him who was a man, it was time enough yet; his regular hour, I suppose, was not yet come. He, therefore, like a "jolly good fellow," in order to prevent a deficiency of wine from being any excuse, was determined to raise the wind somehow or other, so had recourse to a stratagem, which ignorant persons call a miracle, by going and manufacturing a large quantity of water with certain ingredients, with which, no doubt he was well acquainted, and probably had furnished himself with, ready for the occasion ; whence the water became coloured, like wine. This being at a time when the company were well drunk, escaped detection, and so obtained the character of a miracle.

If this transmutation were the effect of any supernatural operation agreeable to the will of God, it certainly would have proved itself consistent with utility and wisdom ; whereby man might be induced or constrained to honour and obey him with *fear and trembling,* not in *rioting and drunkenness,*[72] as is always the case when men have well drunk.

But why were the pots first filled with water ? Could not he, by whom the worlds were made from nothing,[73] have made this wine from nothing ? Surely, a miracle cannot be too great ; but by being too little, it brings it down to a mere juggling trick. How often do we find men capable, not only of deceiving the palate, but the sight also, with the mere charm of " hocus, pocus, fly, and begone ?" And, why should he have made such a prodigious quantity ? Would not a few bottles, or at most, *a dozen of wine,* have been sufficient for a

score of godly people, after they had *well drunk?*
Instead of which, we are told that he made upwards of
one hundred gallons!—enough, probably, to intoxicate
the whole of the inhabitants of such a small town as
Cana. As to its being better wine than that which
they had at first, I doubt whether we ought to consider
them as competent judges; for after men have *well
drunk*, they seldom can distinguish good from bad;
which, I believe, most vinters and keepers of taverns
well know by experience!

Again, if this man were sent from God, as some say,
to work this miracle, it must have been productive of
some good. But, what good effects did this produce?
Were any converted from their evil ways in consequence
thereof? Or, did it produce a conviction of his divine
authority? No! we do not read that there was one
among them that believed in him, except his disciples,
who, it seems, were a few weak-minded, illiterate, and
credulous men, whom he had selected out, as fit objects
for him to work upon, through their ignorance and
imbecility; no, not even his own brethren![74] Surely
you will admit, that his own family were as well
acquainted with his abilities as those ignorant strangers
called his disciples. His own father, with whom he
had been working so many years, never bears testimony
to any one miracle which he is said to have wrought.
Neither did his mother, even on this occasion, consider
it as a miracle; it being more than probable that it was
by her assistance the trick was effected. She, finding him
unwilling to come home, takes the hint; being acquainted, no doubt, with his ingenuity, orders the servants to
procure him whatever he should stand in need of. He,
therefore, in order to take the advantage of their absence,
caused them to fill those six stone water-pots, containing
from sixteen to twenty four gallons each, which he knew
would occupy them a considerable time, during which
if he had not all things ready necessary for the trick,
he or his mother would have time suffiient to procure
them. And as we find that there are men, even in the
present day, who can change wine into blood; why should
we be surprised at Jesus changing water into wine?

But, as it is probable that some of your friends have never read the *Discourses of Woolston, upon the Miracles*, I will, for their edification and amusement, give you his opinion upon this wine-and-water story. Indeed, he has confessed, that his veneration for the holy Jesus, would not permit him to treat this story in his own name, so has recourse to the stratagem of personating a Jewish Rabbi, like the writers of " Religious Tracts," who oftentimes introduce a Jew in their fictitious tales, to help them out in the argument. He, therefore supposes that a Rabbi would give his opinion upon this story, in the following manner :—

" You Christians pay adoration to Jesus, whom you believe to be a divine author of religion, sent of God, for the instruction, reformation, and salvation of mankind ; and what induces you to this belief of him, is (besides some obscure prophecies, which you cannot agree upon, and which neither yourselves, nor any body else understand the application of) the history of his miracles. But I wonder that you should have a good opinion of him for his miracles, which if he wrought no better than what are recorded of him, by our Evangelists, are, if duly considered, enough to alienate your hearts from him. I cannot spare time now to examine into all of them, but according to the cursory observation I have made on them, there is not one so well circumstanced as to merit a considerate man's belief, that it was the work of an omnipotent, all-wise, just, and good agent. Some of them are absurd tales, others foolish facts, others unjust actions, others ludicrous pranks, others juggling tricks, others magical enchantments : and if many of them had been better and greater operations than they are, and of a more useful and stupendous nature than they seem to be : yet the first miracle that he wrought, viz, that of his turning water into wine, at an extravagant and voluptuous wedding at Cana of Galilee, is enough to turn our stomachs against all the rest. It is in itself enough to beget in us an ill opinion of Jesus, and to prepossess us with an aversion to his religion, without further examination into it. It is enough to make us suspect his other miracles, of what name soever, to be of a base, magical, and diabolical extraction ; or he had never set up for a divine worker of miracles, with so ill a grace.

" Would any sober, grave, serious, and divine person, as you Christians suppose Jesus to have been, have vouchsafed his presence at a wedding, where such levities, diversions, and excesses (in our nation of the Jews, as well as in all others) were indulged on such occasions, as were not fit to be seen, much less countenanced by the *saint*, you would make of him ? If your Jesus, his mother, and his disciples had not been merry folks in themselves, they would have declined the invitation of the bridegroom ; nay, if they had been at all graver and more serious people than ordinary, no invitation had been given to such *spoil-sports :* but boon companions they were, and of comical conversation, or there had been at a wedding no room for them.

You Christians may fancy what you please of Jesus and his mother's saintship ; but the very text of the story implies, that they were lovers of good fellowship, and excess too, upon occasion ; or he had never, upon her intimation, turned so large a quantity of water into wine, after all or most of the company were far gone with it. You may suppose, if you please, that all were sober, and none intoxicated, and that the want of wine proceeded from the abundance of company rather than excess in drinking ; but why then did John the Evangelist use the word ΜΕΘΥΔΩΣΙ, which implies, that they were more than half seas over ? And if Jesus and his mother had not both a mind to *top* them up, the one would not have requested, nor the other have granted, a miracle to that purpose.

" Whether Jesus and his mother themselves were at all *cut*, as were others of the company, is not so certain. She might have been an abstemious dame for ought we know ; though, if old stories are true of her familiarity with a *soldier*, of whom came her *chara deûm soboles*, in all probability she would take a dram and a bottle too. But it looks as if Jesus himself was a little in for it, or he had never spoke so waspishly and snappishly to his mother, saying, *Woman, what have I to do with thee ?*

mine hour is not yet come; which was very unbecoming
of a dutiful son, who, excepting when he ran away
from his parents, and put them to sorrow and trouble
to look him up, (Luke ii. 48) was, and is still in heaven,
say the Roman Catholics, a most obedient child. You
modern Christians may put what construction you can
upon the words above of Jesus to his mother, to salve
his credit ; but the fathers of your church* confess
them to be a sharp and surly reply to her, which, if it
did not proceed from the natural badness of his temper,
derived, *ex traduce,* from his supposed father, yet, was
certainly the effect of drinking; and that's the more
likely, because it is a broken and witless sentence, such
as fuddlecaps utter by halves, when the wine's in and
the wit's out. Your modern commentators are sadly
puzzled to make good sense of this broken and abrupt
sentence of Jesus, and a pertinent reply of it, to what
his mother said to him, *they have no wine.* If you will
bear with me, I'll help you out at this dead lift, and
give you the true meaning of it; thus :—Jesus's mother
being apprised of a deficiency of wine, and willing, as
well as the bridegroom, that the company should be
thoroughly merry before they parted, intimates to her
son, (whom she knew to be initiated in the mysteries
of Bacchus) that they had no wine; but before she
could finish her request to him, he, mistaking her
meaning, imagines that she was cautioning him against
drinking more wine, and exhorting him to go home;
whereupon he takes her up short and quick, saying,—
Woman, what have you to do with me ? (for that too is
the English of the Greek) I'll not be interrupted in
my cups, nor break company, for *mine hour is not yet
come* to depart. But after he rightly apprehended her,
he goes to work, and rather than the company should
want their fill, by trick of art, like a punch-maker,
meliorates water into what they called wine. That
this is the obvious interpretation and natural paraphrase
of the words before us, shall be tried by the absurd

---

* Christus asperius respondit, quid tibi & mihi, Mulier ?—*St.
Chrysost. in Loc. Johan.* Vide & *Theophylact. in Loc.*

comments now-a-days put upon them, that are enough to make a considerate man laugh, if not hiss at them.

"Some ancient heretics very gravely inferred from this expression—*woman, what have I to do with thee*—that Mary was neither a virgin, nor Jesus her son, or he had never accosted her with such blunt language, that implies they could not be so akin to each other. This was a perplexity to St. Augustin, and gave him some trouble to explain the expression, consistently with her virginity (for all she cohabited with the old carpenter) and his filiation. But this being a quibble, that has been long since dropped, I shall not revive, nor insist on it. But that the expression above does suppose a little inebriation in Jesus, I may aver; neither is there a better solution to be made of it.

"The *fathers* of your church, being sensible of the absurdity, abruptness, impertinence, pertness, and senselessness of the passage before us, according to the letter, had recourse to a mystical and allegorical interpretation, as the only way to make it consistent with the wisdom, sobriety, and duty of the holy Jesus. But you *moderns*, abandoning allegories and mysteries on miracles, have endeavoured, I say, to put other constructions upon it, as may comport with the letter, and with the credit of Jesus : but, how insipid and senseless they are, I appeal to any reasonable man, who will give himself the trouble to consult them upon the place, and save me the pains of a tedious and nauseous work to recount them for him.

"But to humour the Christian priesthood at this day, I will suppose Jesus, and his Mother, and disciples, though fishermen, to have been all sober, grave, and serious at this wedding, suitably to the opinion that his followers now would have us to entertain of them. But then, it is hard to conceive them less than spectators, and even encouragers of excess and intemperance in others ; or Jesus, after their more than sufficient drinking for the satisfaction of nature, had never turned water into wine ; nor would his mother have requested him to do it, if I say, they had not a mind, and took pleasure in it too, to see the company quite *stitched up*.

"A sober, prudent, and wise philosopher or magician, in the place of Jesus, if he had an art or power to turn water into wine, would never have exercised it upon such an occasion ; no, not to please his best friends, nor in obedience to the most indulgent parent. What would he have said in such a case ? Why, that the company had drank sufficiently already, and that there was no need of more wine. That the bridegroom had kindly and plentifully entertained his guests, and he would not for the honour of God, who had endowed him with a divine power, be at the expense of a miracle, to promote the least intemperance. Whether such a speech and resolution in Jesus, upon this occasion, would not have been more commendable than what he did, let any one judge.

"If I were a Christian, I would, for the honour of Jesus, renounce this miracle, and not magnify and extol it as a divine and good act, as many now-a-days do. I would give into, and contend for the truth of that gloss, which the Gentiles of old, by way of objection put upon it, viz. That the company having exhausted the bridegroom's stock of wine, and being in expectation of more, Jesus, rather than the bridegroom should be put to the blush for deficiency, palmed a false miracle, by the help of the governor of the feast, upon a drunken crew ; that is, having some spirituous liquors at hand, mingled them with a quantity of water, which the governor of the feast vouched to be incomparable good wine, miraculously made by Jesus ; and the company being, through a vitiated palate, incapable of distinguishing better from worse, and of discovering the fraud, admired the wine and the miracle ; and applauded Jesus for it, and perhaps became his disciples upon it. If I, I say, were a disciple of Jesus, I would give this story such an old turn for his credit. And I appeal to indifferent Judges, whether such a daubing of the miracle, to remove the offence of Infidels at this day, would not be politically and wisely done of me. Whether modern Christians may be brought into such a notion of this supposed miracle, I know not ; but really there is room enough to suspect such a fraud in it.

"But supposing Jesus's change of water into wine to have been a real miracle; none commissioned of God, for the reformation and instruction of Mankind would ever have done it here. Miracles, must be such things, as are consistent with the perfections of God to interest himself in. And again, they must argue not only the power of God, but his love to mankind, and his inclination to do them good; which this of Jesus is so far from, that it has an evil aspect and tendency, as is above represented; consequently it is to be rejected and no longer esteemed a divine miracle. Neither is Jesus to be received as a revealer of God's will for it.

" No doubt, but your Christian Priests would have us Jews and Infidels to believe the whole company at this wedding, for all what is intimated by St. John to the contrary, to consist of sober and demure saints; I will suppose so : but then, what occasion had they at all for wine ? What reason could there be for God's power to interpose and make it, especially in so large a quantity, for them ? I conceive none. If any of the company had been taken with fainting fits ; and Jesus, for want of a cordial bottle, had created a cheering dram or two, I could not have found any fault with it ; though, even here, if he had restored the patient with a word of his mouth, it had been a better miracle, than making of wine for him. But, that he should make for a company of *sots*, a large quantity of wine, of no less than twelve or eighteen firkins of English measure, enough to intoxicate the whole town of Cana, is what can never be accounted for by a Christian, who should, one would think, wish this story, for the reputation of Jesus, expunged out of the New Testament.

" Besides, if Jesus had really and miraculously made wine, which no power or art of man could do, he should, to prevent all suspicion of deceit in the miracle, have done it without the use of water. You Christians say, that he is the original cause of all things out of nothing : why then did he not create this wine out of nothing ? Why did he not order the pots to be emptied of their water, if there were any in them, and then, with a word of his mouth, command the filling them with wine instead of it? Here had been an unexceptionable miracle, which no Infidel could have cavilled at, for any thing, but the needlessness of it. But this subject matter of water spoils the credit of the miracle. The waterpots, it seems, are to be filled, before Jesus could do the notable feat. Is not this enough to make us think that Jesus was an artificial *punch maker?* Could not he create wine without water for a transmutation? Yes, you'll say, he could; what was the reason then, that he did not? This is a reasonable question to a learned priesthood; and a rational answer should be given to it. A question too it is that as heretofore been under debate. Some said that the water might be made use of, to abate the immensity of the miracle, which otherwise for its greatness might have surpassed all belief. But this reason will not do. A miracle cannot be too great in itself, if well attested, to transcend credit; but it may easily be too little to conciliate the faith of a freethinker.

" The fathers of your church fetched a reason for the use of water here from the mystery. But since mysteries on miracles are set aside by the priesthood of this age, they are to assign another and good reason of their own ; or this miracle is to be rejected, as a piece of art and craft in the operator, if for no other reason than this, that Jesus used water to make wine.

" All that I have to say more to this miracle, is, that it is to be wished, if Jesus could turn water into wine, that he had imparted the secret and power to his disciples of the priesthood of all ages since; which would have been the greatest advantage to them in this world. He has empowered them, they say, to remit sins which few old sinners think themselves the less in danger for. And he has enabled them, some say, to transubstantiate bread into flesh, and wine into blood; which none but foolish and superstitious folks believe they ever did. And he promised to invest them with a power to do greater miracles than himself; even to remove mountains, and to curse trees; but I thank God they never were of so strong a faith, as to put it in practise, or we might have heard of the natural state, as well as we do

M

now of the civil state of some countries ruined, and overturned by them. But this power to transmute water into wine, without labour and expence, would have been of better worth to them, than all their other priestly offices. Not that our conduits would thereupon run with wine, instead of water; or that wine would be cheaper and more plentiful than it is now, excepting among themselves, if they could withal curse vineyards. They would make the best penny they could of their divine power. And as surely as they can now sell the water drops of their fingers at a christening, at a good rate, they would set a better price on their miraculously made wine: and give a notable reason for its dearness, namely, that miracles should not be *cheap*, which would bring them into contempt, and lessen the wonder and admiration of them."

Thus ends the invective of a supposed Jewish Rabbi against this miracle. And as Mr. Woolston has favoured us with several such like observations, on the miracles of Jesus, I shall take the liberty of laying them before you in order that you may take them into consideration, and decide accordingly, when I come to treat on them. As Elihu told Job, "Let us choose to us judgment; Let us know among ourselves what is good," (Job xxxiv. 4.) rightly dividing the word of truth,[75] and carefully avoiding giving heed to Jewish fables, and commandments of men that turn from the truth.[76] Men who will compass sea and land to make one proselyte; and when he is made, they make him two-fold more the child of hell than themselves.[77]

Matthew further says, "that he went travelling about, followed by great multitudes of people from all parts, healing all manner of sicknesses, and preaching the Gospel of the Kingdom."

In so doing Jesus might be justified, as neither he nor any of the holy men of God knew anything of printing, it being a thing unknown in those days; consequently, they had no other means of publishing or making known this new Kingdom, but by preaching or proclaiming it about the streets to the people. But I cannot see what occasion there is for preaching in these days, when printing is so much in fashion. Even if the preachers had a new thing to acquaint us with, they could easily make it known through the medium of the press ; by which means we should have a better opportunity of proving all things, and judging for ourselves, that which was right, as Jesus and Paul have both advised.[78] Instead of which, that which they preach now is an old thing, having been preached throughout the earth, if what Paul says be true,[79] 1800 years back ; and must be by this time, nearly worn out !

Besides, by what I can learn, Jesus preached gratis ! whereas, in the present day, people are *obliged* to pay the preachers a most enormous sum, for preaching that which but few, compared with the multitude, ever go to hear. And those that do go, might stay at home and learn, by reading the same books, the same things which they learn by hearing the preachers read ; besides saving their money and time, and being less prejudical to their health ; for, surely, nothing can be more injurious to the constitution of the human frame, than being penn'd up together in a cold, damp, and pestiferous place, like so many wethers and ewes at a fair.

If we employ men for teaching us, that which we may easily know of ourselves ; we might as well employ preachers to tell us that George the Fourth, is King of England ! For if Jesus were the Son of God, and did those things which they say he did ; we shall learn the truth equally as well, if not better, by reading and *judging for ourselves*. Jesus commanded that we should search the Scriptures ;[80] he nowhere commands that we should employ Popes, Archbishops, Cardinals, Bishops, and all those ridiculous titles, which some men have given to themselves, to search them for us.

Neither did he think any thing at all about us, as I have already shewn you in a former letter ; it being evident, that he thought *his* days were the last. And if God did employ any one to explain his words for him ; surely, he would never employ such ugly old men, and beardless boys, as we now see starting up everywhere, as servants of the Lord. I think that it would have been more to his credit, if he had written them in a plain and intelligible manner at first, so that all might have easily understood them, without having recourse to the assistance of others, who are evidently as ignorant, and know no more of God and his words than those who employ them; he would then have saved us all this trouble and expence, besides, prevented that effusion of blood, which has been shed in consequence thereof. However, as I intend, in my next letter, to make an inquiry into the evidences, that prove the existence of this being, called a God, about whom there is so much talk; I shall conclude for the present, and remain,

Your humble Servant,
JOHN CLARKE.

NOTES TO THE FOREGOING LETTER.

1 Mark i. 12.
2 1 John i. 1
3 John i. 35—43
4 „ ii. 1
5 „ ii. 12—13
6 Luke iv. 1
7 „ „ 14—21
8 Judges xi. 29—40
9 „ xiv. 6—19
10 Matthew xii, 24
11 „ viii. 31
12 Revelation xii. 12.
13 Luke x. 18
14 1 Peter v. 8
15 Matthew xvi. 23.
16 „ „ 18.
17 Job i. 15—19
18 Lamentations iii. 33
19 Isaiah xliii. 7
20 Revelations ii. 10
21 Luke xiii. 11—16
22 Zachariah iii. 1—5
23 2 Timothy ii. 26
24 2 Corinthians iv. 4
25 1 Samuel xvii. 47
— 2 Chronicles xx. 15
26 Genesis iv. 15

LETTER VII.

TO DR. ADAM CLARKE,

THE GOSPEL ACCORDING TO ST. MATTHEW.

CHAP. V.

Verse 1. "And seeing the multitudes, he went *up* into a *mountain*, and when he was *set*, his disciples came unto him; and he opened his mouth, and taught them, saying, Blessed are the pure in heart, for they shall see God."

In Luke vi. 12, we read, that "Jesus *went out into a mountain to pray, and continued all night in prayer to God.* (Why should Jesus spend so much time in prayer to God, if he himself were "very God of very God?" especially, as he condemned the practice of making long prayers.[1]) And when he had chosen his Apostles "he came *down* with them, and *stood* in the *plain;*" and there he taught the people.

Mark says, (iii. 19.) that, as soon as he came down from the mount, they *went into an house,* where they began to *eat bread;* instead of preaching on the mount or in the plain! while John takes notice of neither *mount, plain, or sermon!*

It is not my intention at present to unfold the doctrine contained in this sermon, but merely to consider the promise that is held forth to those who are *pure in heart,* namely, a sight of God: it being in consequence of this *idea* that I am excluded from society, torn from the bosom of friends and relatives; and doomed to linger out, in an uncomfortable and dreary mansion, three of those years, in which,

> Man, guided by a virtuous mind,
> Might every day some pleasure find,
> If free to act, and *unconfin'd*.

It therefore, behoves me in a special manner, to make some inquiry into the nature of this GOD. What is it? or whether such a thing either does, or ever did exist? finding, that many "Cloud capp'd towers," and "gorgeous palaces," which have been, are now no more; it might have happened that this God, through length of days, like all other things, has long since ceased to exist.

First, let us inquire what is meant by the word GOD? In the course of my travels, especially in Africa, I have been shewn several things which the natives called *Gods;* some made out of wood, some out of stone, others out of ivory, &c. And in one place, I saw *men* and *women* worshipping that, which they called a *God,* while the Christians, who were with me, called it a *Crocodile!*

The "powers that be," in England, tell us that the word *God,* implies a sovereign, intelligent Creator, and Governor of all things; who is a Spirit, or no *thing;* yet capable of moving matter, or every *thing;* an invisible being, whose power is equal to his will; incomprehensible, yet punishes with the greatest severity, those who *know him not;* which makes our inquiry concerning it the more necessary, in consequence of its importance. But, alas! how very few there are who trouble themselves about it. The greater portion of mankind being daily employed in labouring to procure, not only that which is necessary for themselves and families, but in addition thereto, superfluities for others, have no time for making inquiry after this *one thing* so *needful;* but leave it to those who may, possibly, be deceived themselves, or have an interest in deceiving others.

Some, there are, who are exempted from this labour; yet, their time is so occupied in the pursuit of pleasure, that they neither have time nor inclination to think on this subject, which is so opposite to their natural propensities; others there are who have much leisure time, but in consequence of some defect, or imperfection in their reasoning faculties, are rendered incapable of *judging for themselves.* And among those who are capable, few, yea, very few, have honesty and courage sufficient to induce them to impart the result of their inquiries to their fellow creatures; being prevented either by fear or interest. For if any have the fortitude to avow it, they not only expose themselves to the censure of the ignorant, but to the malevolence of the interested "powers that be;" whence, it becomes indispensibly necessary, that this *God* should be manifested in a plain, evident, and notorious manner. And surely, if he were desirous that all men should know him, and acknowledge him for their Lord and Creator, he would not avoid exhibiting himself in the most conspicuous manner, both unequivocal and unquestionable. As we find that he has not, by the diversity of opinions concerning him, it is a convincing proof that he does not wish to be made known; consequently, men are to blame for troubling themselves about him. For, if it were even true, as we are told, that it is in consequence of our understanding being so darkened, that we are not able to comprehend him, he would either, in the first place, if he had any hand in the making of us, have prevented that darkness, or would, afterwards, have enlightened it. They further tell us, that this God has made himself known by revelation, and this revelation informs us that he is made known by his works.[2] But if known by his works, what need is there of revelation? And if known by either, why should so many men of exalted minds, still doubt of his existence; or need so many thousands of volumes to prove it?

We find that this God, whom revelation makes known, is an inconsistent being, full of strange whims and contradictions. One, upon whom there can be no dependence, as he himself confesses, that he deceived the prophets.[3]

He boasts that he is almighty ; yet curses the people because they came not to his help against the mighty.

Genesis xvii. 1
Judges v. 23

When he made heaven and earth, he said that all things contained therein, was *very good;* yet the stars are not pure, nor the Heavens clean in his sight ; besides a number of birds, beasts, and creeping things, which are an abomination to him ; even man, whom he made in his own image, had a portion of matter, which he considered superfluous ; or why command Abram to cut it off ?

Genesis i. 31
Job xxv. 4
Job xv. 15
Leviticus xi. 15
Genesis xvii. 11

He rested from all his works, and was refreshed ; yet he is continually working in us to will and to do of his good pleasure.

Ex. xxxi. 17
Phill. ii. 13

He commanded that the seventh day should be kept holy ; but the priests say, that he has since changed his mind, transferring the holiness from the seventh to the first day of the week ; notwithstanding it is written, that, with him there is no variableness, *neither shadow of turning.*

Exodus xx. 10
James i. 17

He is slow to anger : yet, he slew 50,070 persons in an instant for looking into his travelling box.

Psalms cxlv. 8
1 Sam. vi. 19

His anger endureth but a *moment;* yet, when it is kindled, he makes his people to wander in a wilderness during the space of forty years.

Psalms xxx. 5
Numbers xxxii. 13

He kept them as the apple of his eye, by hanging their heads up against the sun to dry !

Deut. xxxii. 10
Numb. xxv. 4

He chasteneth his people as a father would his son ; first seeing them famishing with hunger, before he would give them meat ; and then, when given, smiting them with a very great plague, while the meat *was between their teeth, ere it was chewed.*

Deuter. viii. 5
Numbers xi. 33

As he delighteth in *mercy,* he commands his people to shew no mercy nor pity upon their captives.

Micah vii. 18
Deut. vii. 2, 16

He is very pitiful, and of tender mercy ; therefore promises that their infants shall be *dashed to pieces !* and their women with child *ripped up ! !*

James v. 11
Hosea xiii. 16

He doth not afflict, nor grieve the children of men willingly ; yet smites them with emerods in their secret parts ; pelts them with great stones ; sends fiery serpents, plagues, pestilence and grievous famines, among them.

Lam. iii, 33
1 Samuel v, 9
Joshua x. 11
Numbers xxi. 6

His mercy endureth for ever, by raining fire and brimstone upon them at one time, and drowning them all, like a parcel of rats at another.

1 Chro. xvi, 4
Gen. xix. 24
—— vii. 21

.He has no desire to see the nakedness of a man, but has a strong propensity to discover the secret parts of a woman ; he being very expert in the opening and closing of wombs.

Exod. xx. 28
Isaiah iii. 17
—— xlvii. 31
Gen. xxix. 31
—— xx. 18

He says that he hath no pleasure in the death of the wicked ; yet hardens the hearts of the nations, that they may be destroyed.

Ezek. xviii. 3
Josh. xi. 20

He willeth that all men should come to the knowledge of the truth and be saved ; so sends them a strong delusion, that they might believe a lie and be *damned*.

1 Tim. ii. 4
2 Thess. ii. 11

He justifieth the ungodly, but will not justify the wicked.

Rom. iv. 5
Exod. xxiii. 7

He forgiveth their iniquities and remembereth their sin no more ; yet will by no means clear the guilty.

Jer. xxxi. 34
Ex. xxxiv. 7

He punishes the just for the unjust ; and makes the wicked ransom the righteous.

1 Peter iii. 18
Prov. xxi. 18

He cuts off the righteous and the wicked, because he delights to exercise loving kindness, judgment, and righteousness in the earth.

Ezek. xxi. 3
Jer. ix. 24

He appoints some kings to utter destruction, and chooses the poor of this world, to inherit his kingdom ; yet, of a truth, he is no respecter of persons.

1 Kings xx. 4
James ii. 5
Acts x. 34

He loved Jacob, and hated Esau, because his ways are equal.

Mal. i. 2, 3
Ezek. xviii. 2

He will not allow his priests to take to wife a woman who is a whore ; but commands them to take a wife of whoredoms, one who is an adulteress.

Lev. xxi 7
Hosea i. 2
iii. 1

He says thou shalt not commit adultery ; yet promises them, that their wives shall be ravished, while their children are being dashed to pieces.

Exod. xx. 14
Isaiah xiii. 16

He makes foolish the wisdom of this world, by destroying the wisdom of the wise ; although he knows that when made fools they say in their heart, that there is no God.

1 Cor. i. 19, 2
Ps. liii. 1

He gave them statutes that were not good, and judgments whereby they should not live ; because his ways are just and true. — Ezek. xx. 25, Rev. xv. 3

His eyes are too pure to behold evil ; yet while the people were waiting for good, evil came from the Lord. — Hab. i. 13, Micah i. 12

He is the creator of evil ; yet the earth is full of his goodness. — Isaiah xiv. 7, Ps. xxxiii. 5

None can stay his hand, or say, what doeth thou? yet Moses could prevail upon him, to repent of the evil, which he thought to do unto the people. — Dan. iv. 35, Exod. xxxii. 14

He is not a man to repent ; yet weary with repenting. — 1 Sam. xv. 29, Jer. xv. 6

His eyes are in *every place ;* yet he had a difficult matter to find Adam, when he hid himself from the presence of the Lord. — Prov. xvi. 3, Gen, iii. 9

His eyes are running to and fro throughout the earth ; yet he must come down to see whether things be so or not. — 2 Chr. xvi. 9, Gen. xviii. 21

He is near to them that call upon him ; yet those who do, complain of his being *afar* off. — Ps. xxxiv. 18, —— x. 1

He dwelleth in *thick darkness;* yet no man can approach him, by reason of the great light. — 1 Kgs. viii. 12, Ps. xcvii. 2, 1 Tim. iv. 16

He wishes that all men would seek him ; though his most upright and faithful Servant, knew not where to *find him.* — Jer. xxix. 13, Job xxiii. 3

He filleth heaven and earth ; yet may be crammed into a little box of shittim wood. — Jer. xxiii. 24, Ex. xxv. 8, 10

He is willing to be made known, yet ashamed to shew his face. — Hosea ii. 20, Ex. xxxiii. 23

No man can see his face and live, yet Moses, and likewise Jacob, saw God face to face, as a man speaking with his friend. — Ex. xxxiii. 20, —— 11, Gen. xxxii 30

No man hath seen him at any time ; though seventy nobles not only *saw* but did *eat and drink* with him. — 1 John iv. 12, Ex. xxiv. 10, 11

His voice was never heard at any time ; yet all the people of Israel acknowledged to have heard it. — John v. 37, Deut. v. 24

It is impossible for him to lie : yet he promises not to perform that which he had previously sworn to perform. — Heb. vi. 11 / Num. xiv. 30

He teaches some to lie, and sends a lying spirit into the mouth of others, yet lying lips are an abomination in his sight.

He says, that whoso sheddeth man's blood, by man shall his blood be shed : yet, his favourites may shed blood with impunity.

He is good, and doeth good ; so sends an evil spirit among the people, that they may deal treacherously with each other, and get slain.

He promised to visit the sins of the fathers, upon the children, and children's children ; yet, he says, the son shall not bear the iniquity of the father. — Exod. xxxiv. 7 / Ezek. xviii. 20

He says that the children shall not be put to death for their fathers ; yet he had seven of Saul's sons hung up before him, for their father's fault. — Deu.. xxiv. 16 / 2 Samuel / xxi. 9, 14

To him belong mercies and forgiveness, though we have rebelled against him ; yet he commanded Saul to go and smite Amalek, for their forefathers' transgression ; to *spare them not*, but utterly destroy every man, woman, child, and *suckling*. — Dan. ix. 9 / 1 Samuel / xv. 2, 3

A thousand years being only in his sight, but as yesterday, he set a bow in the clouds, to remind him of his promise. — Psalms xc. 4 / Gen. ix. 16

He knoweth the secret of the heart ; yet must be acquainted with the wants of his creatures, before he can, or will assist them. — Psalm xliv. 21 / Phill. iv. 6.

One time he bids them not defraud, nor deal falsely with their neighbours, nor yet to covet any thing belonging to them : at another time, he commands them to borrow all they can, and spoil their neighbours, the Egyptians. — Lev. xix. 13 / Exod. xx. 17 / —— iii. 22

He suffered Cain to take away the life of his brother ; although the soul of every living thing, and the breath of all mankind were in his hand. — Gen. iv. 9 / Job xii. 10

His enemies he cast down into hell, and delivered them *into chains of darkness*, reserving them to the judgment of the great day ; yet, they are going to and fro throughout the earth, and sometimes mounting up into heaven. — Jude 6 / Job i. 6, 7

He forbids them to make any graven image, the likeness of any thing that is in heaven or in earth ; yet, shortly after, commands them to make two cherubims.	Exod. xx. 4 —— xxv. 18
He forbids them committing adultery ; yet, if what the Priests say, be true, he himself committed adultery, with a poor carpenter's wife ; but instead of fixing the *horns* in the poor carpenter's head, he, himself, carries them in his hand.	Exod. xx. 14 Hab. iii. 4
He is angry in the morning at the performance of that which he had commanded, the preceeding evening, should be done ; yet he says, *I change not!*	Numbers xxii. 20, 22 Mal. iii. 6
One minute he will not go, the next, he will go with the people ; although, it is written, that he is of one mind.	Exodus xxxiii. 3, 14 Job xxiii. 13
In short, we find him an illiberal, and an uncharitable God ; one who will not suffer any other God to exist beside himself ; starving all the other Gods of the earth, that men may serve him alone.	Exodus xx. 3 Zeph. ii. 11
Sometimes a God of peace ; sometimes a man of war.	Heb. xiii. 20 Exod. xv. 3
Sometime a God of love ; at others, a God of Fury.	1 John iv. 8 Jer. xxi. 5
Sometimes like a Shepherd ; at others, like a Bear.	Isaiah xl. 11 Lam. iii. 10
Sometimes like a mighty man ; at others, like a drunken man.	Isaiah xlii. 13 Ps. lxxxviii. 65
Sometimes like a moth,—at others, like a leopard.	Hosea v. 12 —— xiii. 7
Sometimes like the Satyr in Æsop's fable, blowing both hot and cold.	2 Sam. xxii. 9 Job xxxvii. 10
Sometimes like a Devil, going about like a *roaring Lion*, devouring all he can catch.	Peter v. 8 Hosea xi. 10 —— xiii. 8
One that cannot be trusted, because he revealeth secrets.	Dan. ii. 28
One who tolerates Bigamy, Slavery, and Emasculation.	Deut. xxi. 15 Joshua ix. 27 Isaiah lvi. 4, 5

N

One who has cattle on a thousand hills: yet is   Psalms i. 10
always borrowing from his needy creatures.   Prov. xix. 17

One who is a Spirit,[4] that hath neither flesh nor
bones;[5] yet he is described as having a head,[6] with
hair,[7] face,[8] eyes,[9] nose,[10] mouth,[11] lips,[12] ears,[13]
tongue:[14] besides feet,[15] hands,[16] arms,[17] fingers,[18]
loins,[19] heart,[20] bowels,[21] blood,[22] organs of generation,[23] and back parts;[24] possessing a soul,[25] with all
the passions, sensual desires, appetites, powers and
faculties, which are found in the human body!

Although never bound 'prentice to any trade or calling, yet he professes to be a gardener,[26] a tailor,[27]
a *God*-midwife,[28] a house builder,[29] a draughtsman,[30]
a butcher,[31] a grave-digger,[32] a schoolmaster,[33] a stone
mason and graver,[34] a potter,[35] a doctor,[36] a threshing instrument maker,[37] a barber,[38] a cook,[39] and
slave-dealer.[40]   Besides an instructor of ploughmen,
threshers,[41] and candlestickmakers.[42]

He is not only a murderer,[43] a tyrant,[44] a liar,[45]
a fool,[46] a deceiver,[47] and a blackguard,[48] but he is a
consuming fire.[49]   Therefore, as Paul has informed us
that it is a fearful thing to fall into his hands,[50] the
sooner, I think, that we get rid of him the better.   For
what indulgence or mercy can we expect to receive
from one, who would not spare his only begotten son!

It appears, from this description of the God of the
Jews, that they have made their God exactly in their
own image.   And no doubt, had those Jews found
themselves in the shape of an elephant, they would have
given to him a proboscis or trunk, with a tail, and all
things pertaining to an elephant.   It being unnatural
for any species who entertain any idea of a Creator, to
imagine that he can possibly be different from themselves; whether they be men, beasts, birds, fishes, reptiles, or insects.   They, therefore, must necessarily
ascribe to him a greater extension of parts, with properties and qualities superior to themselves, in order to
qualify him for a Creator.   This then, I find, has been
the case with the Jews, and all other human animals
who have described their supposed Creator or God, as
being like unto a very old man, or ancient of days,

living in great splendour and magnificence; they not doubting, but, that he, who has made all these very fine things, such as gold, silver, and precious stones, must have a large stock of them himself, for his own state and convenience.* Therefore, as I can have no idea, how a spirit, that hath neither flesh nor bones, can participate in any pain or pleasure, natural only to flesh and bones, I cannot receive this Jewish revelation, as being at all necessary, or disclosing anything more than their own ignorance of themselves and the objects which surrounded them.

But what kind of a God do those works make known? Men calling themselves DEISTS say that he is made known by his works, in the creation. Moreover, that it is only by a careful and attentive study of those works, that men can arrive at any knowledge of his existence. For if we want to know his power, the immensity of the universe declares it. And the unchangeable order, by which the whole is governed, sheweth forth his wisdom. His liberality and goodness are seen by the abundance with which he supplies all his creatures, both the just and the unjust.

Yet, with all due respect to those who maintain these opinions, the more I study and consider those things, the less do I perceive of *order*, *wisdom*, or *liberality*. And, as great men are not always wise, neither do the aged understand judgment, you will, perhaps, hearken unto me, whilst I also will show mine opinion.[51]

First, respecting *immensity*. I cannot conceive any possible limits or boundaries to space, which could render it otherwise; for if there were any limitation, still, there must be a something beyond. And instead of an *unchangeable* order pervading the universe, we find, that every thing is continually changing; even the minds and bodies of men. Do we not find, that

---

* I admit that the Christians are an exception to this statement; for if Christ be "the express image" of God, (Heb. i. 3.) he is always represented as being a young man. Why Christians should paint the "express image" of God at all, in almost every parish church, when he has strictly forbidden them to make any likeness whatever of him, can only be answered by those who have made him.

where an island once stood now flows a body of water; where a river once ran, now stands a solid rock; stars that have formerly been recognised, are now no longer seen; and where they have never been before observed, there we see them clearly? Comets, earthquakes, inundations, volcanoes, &c. convince us that nothing is unchangeable; but that all things being in motion, must necessarily change their position; consequently, their figure, shape, and external appearance. Whence, it follows, that that which was *order* in one age, may be considered *disorder* in another; even that which is *order* in one country, may, at the same time, be *confusion* in another; and sometimes, in the same nation, certain things may be considered, by some persons, as being in *perfect order*, while others may deem them quite *irregular;* from the government of a country to the headdress of a female! Order and disorder are only expressions, by which persons denote the views that they have of particular objects, as they relate to, or affect themselves, in their different stations of life, according to their several judgments. For, if the surrounding objects which we find arranged in the present manner, had been found in any other position, we should still have concluded that they were all right, and in perfect order, by our co-ordering ourselves to them. Thus, if man had found himself possessed of four legs instead of two, with which he might have outrun the hound; or with wings like the eagles, wherewith he could soar above the kite; and if women had the tail of a peacock, all would have been considered in order; as men would have accustomed themselves to use those appendages, and women would have exulted at their embellishment.

As for liberality, I can see none; we scarcely get any thing without much toil and labour. What would the earth bring forth of itself, if let alone? As Byron says,

"The earth yields nothing to us without sweat."

Our principal food, in this country, I believe, would consist of briars, thorns, weeds, grass, and such like, if man did not tear up and force the earth, with much care and labour, to bring forth those fruits which we

deem so necessary for our existence.   Even then, there
is no certainty that we shall enjoy them after they are
thus produced ; for sometimes we perceive the elements
as if they were conspiring to blast both our hopes and
precious fruits together.   Besides birds, beasts, and
devouring insects, are continually eating, destroying,
and trampling down those fruits, which have been thus
brought forth, with so much toil and anxiety.

And where is justice equitably ministered ?   Do we
not see some who appear to be highly favoured and
protected, enjoying every good and pleasant thing
which the earth, by the help of man, bringeth forth ;
whilst others seem totally neglected and forsaken, not
having sufficient to satisfy the cravings of their natural
appetites ?   Yet they who enjoy all the comforts and
good things of this world, are, in general, the most
licentious and unthankful.

" Is this just dealing, Nature ?"

And where is goodness or wisdom displayed in filling
the earth with so many miserable and needy creatures,
without an independent or unfailing provision ?   We
see that dogs, cats, and every species of animal, but
man, are provided with sufficient clothing during life,
both useful and ornamental.   And scarcely do we ever
find one of them, if unrestrained, perishing through
lack of food, as is often the case with intelligent man !
Besides, man, styled the lord of the creation, is not
only dependent upon beasts and worms for their assistance and support, but he is actually a slave to them.
How many smiths, farriers, farmers grooms, ostlers, &c.
are there employed in washing, currying, shoeing, feeding, and waiting upon them day and night ?

Then the world is framed so badly, every thing so
ill-contrived, which proves the want of an intelligent
mind in its formation.   First, we find that two parts
out of three are barren and desolate, through excessive
heat and extreme cold ; producing only sandy deserts,
hills of snow, and plains of ice.   Then, see the treacherous quick-sands, deceitful morasses, rocky mountains,
hideous caverns, horrid chasms, frightful precipices,

ruinous valleys, and burning mountains, casting forth clouds of smoke, sulphurous flames, and calcined rocks, while streams of melted minerals cover the adjacent plains with boiling fiery lava.

Again, the violent tremulations and sudden quakings of both the earth and the sea, which sometimes bury whole nations of people, without either performing or waiting for the *sacred* rites and ceremonies, so *necessary* for their interment. Even the elements are so badly constructed, that they cannot perform their respective functions, without sending forth destructive fires in flashes of lightning, and torrents of rain, which often cause inundations, floods, &c., whereby large tracts of cultivated land are laid waste; and oftentimes flocks, houses, even men, women, and children, are destroyed by their irresistible progress. Moreover, while the earth in one place appears to dissolve like water, in another it is like iron, (compare Deut. xxviii. 23, with Lev. xxvi. 19.) yielding neither fruitful rains, nor cooling dews. Then, the roaring tempest and boisterous hurricane, caused by the agitated air, before whose power "stout ships and lofty buildings seem as chaff;" all prove the want of an all-wise and benevolent being, in the construction of this globe of matter.

Say; would not an all-wise and benevolent being, whose power was equal to his will, have framed a world more suitable, and less destructive to its inhabitants? He would have cleared it of burning sands and icy plains, both useless and destructive. He would not have made such waste of stuff, in building those lofty mountains, which are impassable; and barren wildernesses, which are uninhabitable; with such large tracts of superfluous ocean. He would, moreover, have embellished it with pleasant mounts, instead of cragged rocks; the seasons would have been regular; the climates convenient; and the lamps would have distributed an equal and sufficient portion of light to all the inhabitants. Neither would he have made any animal but such as would be useful and agreeable with each other. No serpents, hyenas, crocodiles, hawks, sharks, rats, monkeys, and many other species of beasts, birds, fishes, reptiles, and insects, which are not only useless, but of a destructive nature. Trees, plants, and fruits, would all have been free from their pernicious juice; and metals, with minerals, from their dangerous metallic effluvia.

Besides, if he had intended to exalt one animal above the rest, as lord and master of the whole, he would have endowed him with power and qualifications suitable to his dignity and office. Especially, if he wished to exhibit him as a masterpiece of workmanship, he would, doubtless, have manufactured him in a superior manner to the rest. He would have given to him that nature, by which fire should not consume, nor waters overwhelm him. His parts would have been so constructed, and in such order, that rocks nor pits should harm him. Neither would he have suffered so many of his years to be wasted in old age, infancy, and sickbeds; above all, perishing before he is born, through an untimely birth.

But what is man, who is said to be in the image of this Bible-God? Is his mechanism more wonderful than the insignificant flea? Is he not a puny, ignorant, filthy, and the most helpless animal in existence? When he makes his appearance, he causes more trouble and pain than any other animal. Birds, beasts, or fishes, need no surgeons, gossips, nor foolish toys. The little animal, which sucks the filthy swine, will follow its dam as soon as dropped. But man, proud man! is sometimes many months before he can waddle, or even bear the weight of his own body. And how filthy! how loathsome is the helpless infant! Would it not perish in its own filth, if not carefully attended to? surely, it is worse than a *beast*. Besides, how ignorant? give it food, or poison; a knife or a coral; it will put either to its mouth; whereas, the fowls and fishes will, with surprising sagacity, pick and single out their proper nourishment from among a thousand useless and obnoxious weeds, &c. And many persons, though arrived at the age of *discretion*, know not the proper quantity and quality of the food most suitable for their constitution. (This description of the human animal

is not confined to the "swinish multitude," but wil
with equal justice, apply to Kings, Lords, and Com
moners.) Birds can, without any experience, build thei.
nests. Bees, without serving any apprenticeship, can
make their cells. Spiders can weave their webs un-
taught; the ants can build their store-house; the
beaver his hut, without any pattern. But man, intelligent man! must serve a tedious apprenticeship before
he can learn any useful employment; and oftentimes,
after all, turns out but an indifferent workman. Besides, what a frightful monster would he appear, if the
operations of his nature were not continually checked?
his hair would grow like eagles' feathers, and his nails
like birds' claws.[52] (By the bye, how did Mr. and Mrs.
Adam, with all their family, cut their hair and nails,
before Tubalcain made them knives or scissors? Were
this paradisiacal family like unto the wild Indians? or
did their God stand Barber to them as well as Tailor?)

And why should man, more than any other animal,
be subject to pain, disease, and deformity, which seem
to be so indifferently distributed, without any regard to
moral character? If this God be the author of all
things, he certainly must be the author of those tormenting pains attending the gnawing gout, and racking
gravel; the burning heat of a fever, and the cold
shivering of an ague. Can wisdom and goodness be
the cause of evil? Surely, you will not say that the
man who hath been tormented for years by the stone,
or gradually devoured by a cancer, or he that is
wasting inch by inch, under the baleful influence of
some other disease, is a monument of divine mercy!
Even our natural enjoyments are often succeeded by
the most excessive pain. Not a day passes, but we are
liable, in some way or other, to suffer the keenest
sorrow, bitterest anguish, and most poignant griefs,
through the various casualties arising from the complicated nature of the surrounding objects. The loss of a
relative, treachery from friends, disappointment in
business, tyrannical acts of rulers, domestic broils,
besides a number of heart-rending and distressing
cases, produced by fire, water, cattle, thieves, &c.,

which occur daily to some one or other, are convincing proofs of the anarchy which prevails throughout the whole system; which would never be permitted if under the controul and power of a good and beneficent being, whose power was equal to his will. Would it not then be more to the credit of this God, if his *God-ites* would confess, that he was deficient in power, or he would readily remove those evils which so grievously afflict his creatures? We might then be inclined to pity his weakness, and recommend him to the consideration of some *Virtuoso*, as an harmless outlandish animal or *nondescript!* But, by admitting him to be omnipotent, while these evils exist, he becomes an object of fear and hatred, instead of love and admiration.

Again, if the Creator of men and tigers, dogs and cats, rats and mice: were an intelligent and merciful being, he would have fashioned all their hearts alike, so that the wolf might dwell with the lamb, the cow and the bear lie down and feed together, and the sucking child play on the hole of the asp. Instead of which, we find that each class of animals live only by the destruction of another; as the decomposition of the one is necessary to the recomposition of the other. Hence, the earth is ever the same, neither increasing nor decreasing; for if it loose some parts by giving birth, it increases as others cease; being both *tomb* and *womb*. Is this consistent with infinite benevolence, to ordain that the *destruction* of one animal should be so essential to the *preservation* of another? Observe the spider; see what pains, what labour, he takes in preparing his net for the heedless fly! Then behold the entangled prisoner struggling to regain his liberty; "while the fell tyrant rushes on his prey, murders the defenceless victim, and revels in his blood!" Did this merciful being create spiders? Yes, you say, for spiders cannot make themselves. Look at the eagle pouncing upon the poor defenceless lamb; the hawk with the sparrow; the cat with the mouse. Yet, what are these compared to the actions of the erect monster, man? who trepans, oppresses, or destroys, not only every other animal in existence, which come within his power, but even his fellow bipeds! He is not satisfied with slaughter of those animals, which he considers necessa for his preservation, but must even butcher his o' species. And he who can slay the most, receives t highest honour and greatest reward. Witness th "bloody automaton," Wellington, with all his inferna deluded machines, that have hired themselves out t butcher the human race; to cut any man's throat whet ordered; to slaughter their brethren either wholesale or retail. We seem struck with horror at the thought of a tomahawk and scalping-knife of the uncivilized Indian; but the boarding pike, the bayonet, the cutlass, are considered as merciful instruments of the enlightened and civilized Christians!

I know that fools, and interested priests, ascribe this ferocious and carnivorous appetite, to the depravity of human nature, in consequence of what they call "the fall of man;" but they say that it is not the will of God that it should be so. Then, if his power be equal to his will, why doth he not correct or amend this depravity? He had a good opportunity, when he once destroyed them all but eight persons, whom he considered as being *righteous* and *perfect*, or why did he preserve them? And if he found their nature perfect, how can we, whom they say are descended from those eight perfect persons, be polluted by any thing antecedent to them? Surely, he would have displayed more wisdom and goodness, if he had corrected their nature, and fashioned their hearts alike, so that they might dwell together in peace and friendship. Instead of which, we find that no community, not even a small body of men, can dwell together any length of time, without strife, contention, sometimes rapine, and murder; in consequence of their disposition and temperament not being in union with each other, resulting from their peculiar organization. Whence men see the necessity of making laws, and appointing arbitrators, to secure themselves from the vicious propensities of those unfortunate organized beings. And if those laws are not sufficient to restrain vice from injuring society, we have ocular demonstration that the dread of future punishment, however horribly represented by fire and brimstone, weeping and gnashing of teeth, &c., will never prevent iniquity from abounding in every town, street, and family: although there be no scarcity of hired men, to remind them of those pre-ordained terible things. And though many others, belonging to certain societies and institutions, are continually creeping about, disseminating this terrible doctrine; yet, as Jesus said, "*it must needs be that offences come!*" (Matt. xviii. 7.)

In consequence of these evils, and many other deficiencies which might be named, it appears that man has no just reason to conclude, that this world was ever formed by an intelligent Architect; therefore, there can be no such a being as a Creator and governor of all things, commonly called a GOD. And the reason why men say that there is, is because they are either ignorant of the properties and qualities of matter, or they have an interest in deceiving the people.

Many arguments have been advanced, and ingenious comparisons made to illustrate those arguments, or evidences of of the existence and attributes of this God; such as the prospective contrivances that are exhibited in the human body; implying a contemplation of the future, which they say could only belong to intelligence. For instance, the teeth, though formed, are lodged within the gums, and there detained for some months, until they are wanted; as their further advance would not only be useless, but extremely in the way of a new-born infant, while in the act of sucking. But would not the infant, if possessed of those teeth, act like the worm of the beetle? the teeth of which being already formed, begins to gnaw as soon as it escapes from the shell. But by being deficient of these pointed bones, called teeth, the infant is naturally inclined to extract its nourishment from whatever might be put into its mouth, by a mechanical compression of its lips. And why should the infant be deprived of that, which will cause it so many restless nights and days of anguish to obtain? Did this said intelligence, *contemplate* the future misery which this infant would experience in what is commonly called cutting those teeth? which, after having cut, seldom last but a few years, before another group appear, which drive out the others to make way for themselves. This chopping and changing is likewise attended with much pain and misery by the owners; such as no benevolent being, who *contemplated futurity*, would ever have designed, if possessed of power equal to his will. The whole of Mr. Paley's arguments may be answered in the like manner; let this suffice at present.

Another argument is advanced, to prove the possibility of the existence of an invisible being, superior to man, which is, that notwithstanding a blind man cannot see such a thing as colour, yet colour doth exist. Although I grant that it is no proof that there can be no such thing as colour, because a man born blind cannot see it; for, if he cannot see it because he is blind, others can who are not blind: but where is the man who can say that he has seen this God at any time? And if he is not to be seen or known, he can be of no more use to us than colours would, if all men were blind.

The only reason which they give for his invisibility is, that he is a spirit which cannot be seen. But, what is a spirit? or how can it be known, if it cannot be seen? Is it not the essence, or the effluvia, extracted or produced from some body of matter; which body must have weight, figure, extent, and boundaries, thereby occupying, necessarily, some portion of space? If so, this destroys all ideas of omnipresence; consequently, omniscience and omnipotence. Then, if he be a spirit, where is the body whence this spirit emanates? as you are well assured that there can be no spirit without some material substance to produce it.

Again, it is demanded, why should an universal idea of some being, possessing intelligence, pervade the minds of all men? But this is not true; there is no universal idea of it? Instead of which, there are scarcely any two men that can agree in opinion upon the subject. As all our ideas are acquired by the sensation produced through some external object, agitating or operating upon our animal spirits, so those ideas of omnipotence, &c., are produced by a cursory view of those surrounding objects; and not being able to comprehend the true cause, they have been attributed to that which their several imaginations dictated; which is evident, by the different ideas or notions that different nations have of this unknown cause; whereby, it is always represented under different forms, and in a different manner, with different laws, customs, &c.; which prove it to be only a chimera of the brain, founded in ignorance : or it would be as universally and apparently understood, as the ideas of pain, pleasure, hunger, thirst, copulation, &c. in all of which, mankind readily concur; because they are known and felt by all men; they being demonstrated to the mental faculties of the inhabitants of *New Zealand*, as well as to those in *Old England.*

And now I presume, you are ready to ask, whence came matter? Could unthinking matter fashion itself into such various forms and figures, as those objects which surround us? Those questions I am not bound to answer; not being ashamed to confess my ignorance of subjects that cannot be demonstrated by either you or me, in the present day; my object being to expose the fallacy of the present doctrines, without presuming to set up others. Let us first clear away the rubbish, in order that we may have clear and good ground to build upon. Neither can I think it of any importance to this generation, what was done, probably, millions of ages back. I shall therefore assert nothing but what may be demonstrated to the meanest capacity. The arts and sciences are rapidly advancing towards attaining a knowledge of that, which at present, seems to be but obscurely or *dimly seen.* It suffices me to know, that matter does exist, and our principal inquiry should be, how to make the best use of it, for our own comfort and preservation. Therefore, the answer that I would make to the inquiry, " whence came matter?" would be such as you would make, if questioned, whence came God? viz. that matter *is*, always *was*, and always *will be*, matter *without end*. Amen.

Thus have I endeavoured to prove, that there cannot exist such a being as that which is called a GOD; and, although some persons may take up the language of David, and say that I am a *fool* for so thinking,[53] they cannot say that I am a murderer, a tyrant, a rebel, a robber, an adulterer, an hypocrite, or a liar, like him; a character, which I trust you will acknowledge to be more dangerous and baneful to society, than a *fool* like me, who only says that THERE IS NO GOD.

Then, why am I excluded from society? If there be a God, possessing those attributes you ascribe to him, is he not big enough, and old enough, to take his own part, without having recourse to the aid of such insignificant worms,[54] as men are represented to be in his sight? Surely, he is the same to day as he was yesterday. If he could, on former occasions, prove himself a God, why does he not now? Is he on a journey, or is he sleeping? Cry aloud, ye priests, who make no small gain of this your craft;[55] your God is in danger, and must be *awaked*,[56] else his kingdom will be *rent* from him,[57] and given to another, even to his enemy, the PRINTING-PRESS; whose voice not only *shakes the earth*, but even the *heaven* itself;[58] filling the earth with the knowledge of its glory, as *the waters cover the sea!*[59]

I have now concluded my observations on the promise held out by Jesus' to those who are pure in heart, viz., a sight of GOD, and find it deceitful. If a man be pure in heart, or more properly speaking, an honest and upright man, he will need no visionary promises; he will possess that solid and substantial blessing, which neither man, devil, nor God, can either give or take from him. The ear hath not heard, nor the eye seen, neither has it entered into the heart of an *hypocrite*, to conceive the blessings which that man enjoys, who fears neither God, devil, nor man. Wishing you speedily the enjoyment of that blessing, I subscribe myself,

Your humble servant,

JOHN CLARKE.

NOTES TO THE FOREGOING LETTER.

1 Matthew vi. 7.
2 Romans i. 20.
   Psalm xix. 1.
3 Ezekiel xiv. 1.
4 John iv. 24.
5 Luke xxiv. 39.
6 Isaiah lix. 17.
7 Daniel vii. 9.
8 Jeremiah xvi 17.
9 Proverbs xv. 3.
10 Isaiah lxv. 5.
11   „ lv. 11.
12   „ xxx. 27.
13 Psalm xxxiv. 15.
14 Isaiah xxx. 27.
15 Ezekiel xliii. 7.
16 Numbers xxi. 17.
17 Jeremiah xxi. 5.
18 Psalm viii. 3.
19 Ezekiel i. 27.
20 Genesis vi. 6.
21 Jeremiah iv. 19.
22 Acts xx. 28.
23 John iii. 16.
24 Exodus xxxiii. 23.
25 Isaiah i. 14.
26 Genesis ii. 8.
   Isaiah xli. 19.
27 Genesis iii. 21.
28   „ xxix. 31.
—   „ xxx. 22.

29 Exodus i. 21.
   „   xxv. 9.

Deuteronomy xxxiv. 6.
Isaiah liv. 13.

Isaiah lxiv. 8.
Jeremiah xxx. 17.

42 Exodus xxxi. 6—8.

49 Hebrews xii. 29.
50   „ x. 31.
51 Job xxxii. 9—10.
52 Daniel iv. 33.

1 Kings xviii. 27.
1 Samuel xv.

LETTER VIII.

TO DR. ADAM CLARKE.

SIR,

In consequence of the irregular and contradictory statements given by Matthew, Mark, Luke, and John, of almost every circumstance relating to, or connected with, the life of Jesus, I find that it is not possible to trace, with any degree of precision, every particular in a regular and successive 'manner; therefore, must abandon the idea of following him throughout the various incidents of his life, in a progressional course; and, instead thereof, take a general review of the whole, descanting upon each particular, as they may happen to occur. For, according to John's account, he wrought miracles before he began to preach,[1] whilst Mark and Luke say, that he began to preach before he wrought miracles![2] And those miracles, as well as the parables, which they say he spoke, are related by each of them, as having been done and spoken at different places, and upon different occasions. Even the precepts and injunctions, which are contained in his sermon, that were, according to Matthew, delivered upon a mount, on *one* occasion, Luke says, were delivered by him, at various places, at different times, and under different circumstances; part of which, are only to be found scattered throughout his writings; and those in an imperfect and confused manner. I shall, therefore, as I find that he spent a great part of his time in curing bodily diseases, and casting out devils, first examine the subject of exorcising devils.

According to Matthew, Mark, and Luke, we learn,

that Jesus was an exorcist, by their saying that Jesus went about casting out devils. But, surely, we ought not to consider that his casting out devils, was of that extraordinary nature as to constitute a miracle! A miracle, according to the general received opinion, signifies something done contrary to the laws or general course of nature, which cannot be done by human powers. But this exorcising devils, was as common in those days, as the exorcising of worms, by Dr. Gardiner's pills, is in ours. Do we not find that there were different parties, who travelled about like itinerant quack doctors, casting out those devils, who greatly offended the partisans of Jesus, because they would not join them?[3] Besides, Jesus himself says, "if I by Beelzebub cast out devils, by whom do *your sons* cast them out?"[4] He also acknowledged, that many shall cast out devils, besides him and his disciples.[5] Which clearly prove, that whatever those devils were, the casting of them out was never considered as being any thing wonderful or miraculous by the Jews. Indeed, by the multitudes that were continually brought to Jesus, they appear to have been so numerous, in those days, that one is apt to think that hell had broken loose as soon as Jesus made his appearance; for we never read before that there were any such animals existing. However, it is some consolation to this generation, that he took them all away with him; as none are to be found of such a description in the present day, although there is so much talk about them.

Nevertheless, admitting that no other person besides Jesus could have been found sufficiently qualified or capable of casting out those devils, I cannot think that we are justified in calling it a miracle, or the effect of any supernatural power. We find that in the present day there are many persons who can do with their own natural powers that which, perhaps, no other person is capable of performing; yet, we do not consider them as supernatural agents, or speak of their work as miraculous; for let their display of art be ever so great, we only consider the men as being ingenious artists, and admire their works accordingly.

It was formerly dangerous for a man to display his art or ingenuity, or even to endeavour to improve his intellectual faculties; but those days of state-enforced-credulity are passed; in which, there were laws for punishing of that, which no person ever did or could do. And, although many persons has suffered death, in all its aggravated circumstances, through the accusation, we now find that they suffered innocently; being judged and condemned, by weak-minded and ignorant men, among whom, was Matthew Hale, for doing of that which could not have been done. And, notwithstanding our legislature has repealed those laws, as being absurd and erroneous, yet our sapient judges are compelled still to be governed by the sentiments and opinions of those ignorant judges; having only discarded those nonsensical notions, which they consider as being useless and unprofitable, but have retained others, equally as absurd, because they find them necessary for their own immediate interest. However, since the law for the punishment of wizards, witches, &c. is annulled, and men are in no danger of being *burnt* for their ingenuity, we find them starting up every where, displaying greater *miraculous* powers, and which tend more to promote the comforts and happiness of mankind, than any which are said to have been done by Moses, Elijah, or Jesus. For, I verily believe that, if they had put all their heads and hands together, they never would have been able to analyze the atmosphere, by separating the oxygen from the nitrogen and azotic gases, or even have turned out a spinning-jenny! It is true, that it is written, they could cover the people with lice :[6] consume men with preternatural fire;[7] and destroy fig trees with their curses;[8] yet none of those miracles were productive of so much good to society, as the publishing of our police reports, or even the ignition of the gases, by which our shops and streets are illuminated. All of which, with many other useful and beneficial contrivances and inventions, they were entirely ignorant.

And, is it not strange, that although there were such multitudes continually brought to Jesus and his disciples, that were possessed with those devils, yet John never takes the least notice of them, or even so much as mentions one circumstance relative to Jesus casting out devils? Indeed, if we had only his gospel to go by, we should never have learned that there were such animals in existence! He seems not even to have known that his master was ever acquainted with the devil; although the other three historians say that he was forty days with him in the wilderness; or he was ashamed of the story, as he never takes the least notice of it. It is true, he says, that the Jews charged Jesus with having a devil,[9] and Jesus charged Judas with being a devil;[10] so this accounts for the Jewish accusation. But, we are also told, that Satan entered into Judas;[11] whence it seems that satan and the devil were two distinct beings. Though, if satan be the devil, and Judas *was* the devil, how the devil could the devil get into the devil? Yet, this same devil, *alias* Judas, is appointed to sit upon a throne, and judge one of the twelve tribes of Israel.[12] Oh, poor Israel! the tribe, whose lot it will be to have a devil for their judge, will be in as sad a condition as they who now have a *Recorder*. Let you and I pray, if we get to heaven, that we fall not under the jurisdiction of *Newman Knowlys;* else we had better go to hell at once out of his way! As it appears by this account, that judges will be deemed necessary in heaven, so it is most likely that he will have a berth there, if any be worth having. It seems, also, that those devils were subject to many infirmities, as well as us poor mortals! for we find that there were deaf devils, and dumb devils.[13] But as there is not much to be learnt from those who are deaf or dumb, we will pass them, and examine those that are more intelligent; which class, I think, may be denominated the pig-driving devils.

According to Mark and Luke, there was a *man* in the country of the Gadarenes, whose abode was among the tombs;[14] but Matthew says, that there were *two men* who were so exceeding fierce, that no man could pass by the way where they were.[15] Luke, further says, that this *man* was oftentimes driven by the devil

into the wilderness; whence, it appears that this was
the place wherein the devil kept his pandemonium or
council chamber; as we find, that it was in the wilderness where Jesus first met with him; and, although
they *kept* this man bound with chains, yet would he
break the bands, and run into the wilderness. This
clearly proves what indifferent mechanics there were
among the Jews in those days; as I am well convinced
that were his excellency, the Prince of Devils, but
once committed to Newgate, our keepers would soon
find chains and *bands* strong enough to keep him safe.
But, if they were such dangerous characters, and it
was impossible either to tame or confine them, would
it not have been better to have depatched them, as they
did every other dangerous animal? The Jews, we find,
were not very dilatory in slaying their neighbours, even
brethren, when circumstances did not justify them in
so doing,[16] as this would have done, had they took up
stones and cast at him, until they had despatched him.
We, sometimes, ourselves, under certain circumstances,
find it necessary to destroy, by suffocation, or otherwise,
a fellow creature; and the action is not only approved
of, as being lawful, but, is moreover prescribed. Would
not this have been an act of humanity towards the poor
sufferers, as well as policy in the rulers, for the safety of
others?

Again, we are told, that as soon as he saw Jesus, he
came and worshipped him. Surely, this could not have
been a devil, especially, as he acknowledged Jesus to
be the *son of God*. For, if what John says be true,[17]
every spirit that confesseth that Jesus Christ is come in
the flesh is of God; and hereby, he says, ye know the
spirit of God. Then Jesus asked him what was his
name; whence it appears, that Jesus did not know all
things; and he answered, and said, my name is Legion,
for we are many. Now a Roman Legion, some say,
consisted of 666 soldiers, and according to others, 6666;
but, I think, that either of these numbers were too
many to stow themselves within the body of one man!
Mark says, that they besought Jesus not to send them
out of the country; and Luke says, that they besought

him not to send them into the deep, but to suffer them to enter a herd of swine, that were feeding upon an adjacent mountain; when Jesus, according to their request, without any hesitation, gave them leave to go. Then went the devils out of the man, and entered into the swine; and the herd ran violently down a steep place, and were choaked. But Mark and Matthew are more explicit; they say, that they run into the sea, (being about two thousand) and were choaked in the sea. Yet Luke has just informed us, that they besought Jesus not to send them into the deep; which, I suppose, you will admit, signifies the sea, or some such watery place.

If we admit, that those swine were suffered to be kept by those Gadarenes, which, I think, is very improbable, that the Jews, who held swine in such an abomination, should have suffered them to be kept in or near their land, yet, this action will not accord with the description which Peter gives of Jesus.[18] He says, that Jesus went about doing good. But, it does not appear to me, that there was much goodness or justice in destroying those poor little pigs, as neither they nor their masters ever insulted or molested Jesus or any of his followers, as we are informed; even if they had, Jesus should, according to his own doctrine, have returned good for evil.[19]

Perhaps, you will say, that Jesus destroyed those pigs to convince the Gadarenes how abominable swine were in his sight, also to punish them for keeping that which had been so strictly forbidden and prohibited by the Lord. Then why did God make them? for if he did not actually fashion and frame them with his own hands, he must have been privy to their formation, as the *soul* of every living thing is in his hand;[20] neither can a sparrow fall to the ground without his knowledge.[21] But, we are told, that he made all things at first; consequently must have made pigs, for pigs, they say, cannot make themselves; likewise a number of other animals, such as the camel, the hare, the coney, the eagle, the vulture, the kite, the raven, the cuckoo, the swan, the owl, the mouse, the snail, and many others,

both in the water and out of the water, which are said
to be such an abomination in his sight, that whosoever
or whatsoever is touched by their dead bodies shall
likewise be an abomination in the sight of God, they
being all unclean;[22] excepting black *beetles* and *grass-
hoppers*, which may be eaten freely, without giving any
offence, for they are *clean!*[23] Therefore, if God knew
all things *from the beginning*, he must have known that
those animals, including the pigs, would be such an
abomination in his sight; and if so, why did he make
them? Would he not have displayed more wisdom
and benevolence, if he had, while the clay was in his
hand, moulded and fashioned them in some other shape
or figure, and so have prevented their *abominable*
existence? It may be said, that probably he did not
know their *abominable* nature, till after he had made
them and seen their ways. Then, why did he not
destroy them, as he did the human animals, when they
became so obnoxious to him? Why did he take such
precautions to have them so carefully preserved? Are
we not told that he gave strict orders to Noah, to take
with him into the ark, a *male* and *female* of every kind
of *unclean* beast, in order that their kind might be
preserved and propagated?[24]

Therefore, all things considered, by taking a fair and
impartial review of the whole, I think that Jesus was
not justified in destroying this property belonging to
the swine-herds; and as I cannot find that he ever
made them any remuneration for their loss, which must
have been considerable, I must candidly confess, that
he acted in a most barbarous, wanton, and malicious
manner. For if he were so poor himself, that he could
not afford a place wherein he might lay his head,[25] yet
he might have easily called up by his power, one of his
fishy agents, that would have soon brought him whatever he might have deemed sufficient to satisfy the pro-
prietors for their loss.[26] And as he did not, I do not
wonder at their eagerness to get rid of him by sending
him out of their coasts.[27] Indeed, I wonder most that
they did not sue him for damages! as I am well assured, that if any man in the present day, were to be

guilty of the like scandalous action, he would soon have a tipstaff, or a police officer at his heels. Moreover, had he lived in the days of that *enlightened*, that *pious* and *eminent* man, Judge Hale, he would surely have got burned for witchcraft!

Besides, this Devil's action will not agree with his doctrine, wherein he tells them, that when a spirit is gone out of a man, he walketh through *dry places* seeking rest;[28] whereas, we find that those devilish spirits sought just the contrary, by running into the sea!

Again, what became of those Devils, were they choaked too? If not, according to this same doctrine, they must have gone home and brought with them *seven* other legions worse than themselves, and have taken possession of the man again, after they had found him empty, swept, and garnished; making his state seven times worse than it was at first. So that the swine-herds were not only deprived of their property, in a wanton and shameful manner, but the man himself was greatly injured thereby.

We also read that he cast out many other Devils from various persons of both sexes; one woman in particular, out of whom there went seven Devils.[29] Now, as you are better acquainted with Devils than I am, can you inform me what became of those Devils, or where they went to after they got turned out? For, if they were suffered to go at large, without either confining or destroying them, he might as well have let them staid where they were; as we might suppose that they would very naturally, when turned out of one, thrust themselves into another; admitting that they did not choose to return to the same premises again as soon as his back was turned.

Matthew says, moreover, that these things were done, that it might be fulfilled which was spoken by the prophet, saying, *himself took our infirmities and bare our sicknesses.*[30] But how was this fulfilled in the person of Jesus? We never read that he was sick, or even possessed with one of those Devils. Instead of which we, in general, find him enjoying perfect health, if a good appetite be a sign thereof, by his eating and drinking with every one who invited him. Let him be saint or sinner, it was all alike to Jesus, so that he could get his belly filled! Very different from the doctrine of Paul, who says, with such a one, *no not for to eat.*[3][1]

By examining those words of the prophet, to whom Matthew alludes, I find that they have quite a different meaning to that for which Matthew has quoted them. But, as not only this passage, but the whole of the chapter in which it is contained, has been so ably and fully explained by that celebrated philanthropist, THOMAS PAINE, I will take the liberty of extracting his observations thereon, as they cannot be read too often by an inquirer after TRUTH.

He begins by stating that "this affair of people being possessed by Devils, and of casting them out, was the fable of the day, when the books of the New Testament were written. It had not existance at any other time. The books of the Old Testament mentions no such thing. It starts upon us all at once in the book of Matthew, and is altogether an invention of the New Testament-makers, and the Christian Church. The book of Matthew is the first book where the word devil is mentioned. (The word devil, being a personification of the word evil.) We read in some of the books of the Old Testament, of things called familiar spirits, the supposed companions of people called witches and wizards. It was no other than the trick of pretended conjurors, to obtain money from credulous and ignorant people, or the fabricated charge of superstitious malignancy, against unfortunate and decrepid old age.

"But the idea of a familiar spirit, if we can affix any idea to the term, is exceedingly different to that of being possessed by a devil. In the one case, the supposed familiar spirit is a dexterous agent, that comes and goes, and does as he is bidden; in the other he is a turbulent, roaring monster, that tears and tortures the body into convulsions. Reader, whoever thou art, put thy trust in thy Creator, make use of the reason he endowed thee with, and cast from thee all such fables.

"The passage alluded to by Matthew, (for as a quotation it is false,) is in Isaiah, chap. liii. verse 4, which is as follows :—' Surely he (the person of whom Isaiah is speaking) hath borne our griefs, and carried our sorrows.' It is in the preter tense.

" Here is nothing about casting out Devils, nor curing of diseases. The passage, therefore, so far from being a prophecy of Christ, is not even applicable as a circumstance.

" Isaiah, or at least the writer of the book that bears his name, employs the whole of this chapter (the 53rd) in lamenting the sufferings of some deceased person, of whom he speaks very pathetically. It is a monody on the death of a friend; but he mentions not the name of the person, nor gives any circumstance of him, by which he can be personally known ; and it is this silence, which is evidence of nothing, that Matthew has laid hold of, and put the name of Christ to it; as if the chiefs of the Jews, whose sorrows were then great and the times they lived in big with danger, were never thinking about their own affairs, nor the fate of their friends, but were continually running a wild goose chase into futurity.

To make a monody into a prophecy is an absurdity. The characters and circumstances of men, even in different ages of the world, are so much alike, that what is said of one may, with propriety, be said of many: but this fitness does not make the passage into a prophecy ; and none but an impostor or a bigot would call it so.

" Isaiah, in deploring the hard fate and loss of his friend, mentions nothing of him, but what the human lot of man is subject to. All the cases he states of him, his persecutions, his imprisonment, his patience in sufferings, and his perseverance in principle, are within the line of nature ; they belong exclusively to none, and may with justness be said of many. But if Jesus Christ were the person the church represents him to be, that which would exclusively apply to him must be something that could not apply to any other person; something beyond the line of nature ; something beyond the lot of mortal man ; and there are no such expres-

P

sions in this chapter, nor in any other chapter in the Old Testament.

"It is no exclusive description to say of a person, as is said of the person Isaiah is lamenting in this chapter, 'he was oppressed, and he was afflicted, yet he opened not his mouth; he is brought as a lamb to the slaughter, and as a sheep before his shearers is dumb, so he openeth not his mouth.' This may be said of thousands of persons who have suffered oppressions and an unjust death with patience, silence, and perfect resignation.

"Grotius, whom the bishop esteems a most learned man, and who certainly was so, supposes that the person of whom Isaiah is speaking, is Jeremiah. Grotius is led into this opinion, from the agreement there is between the description given by Isaiah, and the case of Jeremiah, as stated in the book that bears his name. If Jeremiah were an innocent man, and not a traitor in the interest of Nebuchadnezzar, when Jerusalem was besieged, his case was hard; he was accused by his countrymen, was persecuted, oppressed, and imprisoned, and he says of himself, (see Jer. xi. 19) 'but, as for me, I was like a lamb, or an ox, that is brought to the slaughter.'

"I should be inclined to the same opinion with Grotius, had Isaiah lived at the time when Jeremiah underwent the cruelties of which he speaks; but Isaiah died about fifty years before; and it is of a person of his own time whose case Isaiah is lamenting in the chapter in question; which imposition and bigotry, more than seven hundred years afterwards, perverted into a prophecy of a person they called Jesus Christ."

Should further proof be required to show that this passage can have no relation to the person of Jesus, we have only to read the ninth verse of the same chapter, wherein it states that this person, of whom Isaiah is speaking, *had done no violence.* Which no man, surely, will presume to say of Jesus, when we are told, that he acted in a most violent and outrageous manner, by making a scourge of small cords, with which he drove out the people from the temple.[3][2] And this will now lead me to an examination of that transaction, which also is called a miracle!

If ever any man could have accomplished such an undertaking, it certainly must have been a prodigous miracle; as he must not only have spoken differently from other men, but he must have appeared, by something terrible and majestic in his countenance, more than mortal, to have effected it: which alone would have been sufficient to have convinced the people of his authority, without their coming directly after to ask him for a sign;[33] especially as this castigation was executed on such a multitude of people, who were none of his disciples, nor of those who paid any regard to his sayings and doings. But this action will not agree with the description which Matthew says Isaiah gives of him; which was, that he shall not cry, nor lift up, nor cause his voice to be heard in the streets.[34] As I have already shewn that these words, said to have been spoken by Isaiah, alluded to Cyrus, king of Persia, I need not say any thing more upon that subject; it being evident that they can not apply to Jesus, who was continually parading the streets with multitudes at his heels from all parts; whence it appears, that he must have employed his lungs in a stentorian manner, or how could such multitudes hear him preach? Even the houses into which he went were always beset by the mob:[35] and we all know what tumults there are occasioned by a disorderly and lawless mob of people gathering round the house of any individual. Indeed, I do not wonder at the eagerness of the Jews to get rid of him, expressed by their crying out, *away with him and crucify him;* it being evident that he must have been a pest to society in those days. And no man, placed in such circumstances as was Pontius Pilate at that time, could do otherwise than as he did, if he had any regard for his Sovereign, when the whole nation charged him with being a mover of sedition, by stirring up the people, and perverting the nation, through his strange and nonsensical doctrines;[36] especially, in those turbulent times: for we find that an insurrection had just broken out, which had been attended with the most aggravated crimes, namely, robbery and murder;[37] which might, for what we know, have originated through Jesus himself, as it said that at one time they wanted to make him a king. And, although he would not then accept of the honou yet this might have been policy in him at that time considering that his partisans were not strong enough t support him; neither could he place any confidence ii them; for although it is written, that at one time they were for making him a king, yet at others they were foi stoning him;[39] through which he was oftentimes obliged to play at hide and seek with them. If he had no traitorous design, why did he not, when they wanted to make him king, preach a sermon to them, wherein he might not only reprimand them for their disloyalty, but enforce their allegiance to their lawful Sovereign? for surely this must have been the highest pitch of rebellion! But no, he would not even satisfy them by a direct and explicit answer, whether it was lawful to give tribute unto Cæsar or not; evading the question by merely saying, "*Render unto Cæsar the things which belong to Cæsar;*"[40] which was a mere shuffling and equivocating answer, to avoid one more explict, which he was unwilling to give.

And if they had entertained no suspicions of his traitorous intentions, why should they have put that question to him? Whence, it is evident, that he was strongly suspected of being a revolutionist, one who wished to subvert the order of the government; and the injunctions to his followers proved it, when he told them that they should not act towards each other as did the kings of the Gentiles,[41] who exercised lordship over the people, and were called *benefactors* for so doing. It cannot be supposed that he ever intended to equalize his followers, or why should our bishops and archbishops have such splendid mansions and sumptuous fare, while so many pious and devout Christians have scarcely food to eat, or a place wherein to lay their heads? He certainly spoke these words with a view to expose the folly and degradation of those who tamely submitted to the authority of their lordly oppressors, whom he called foxes,[42] serpents, vipers, blind-guides, and hypocrites; comparing them to painted

sepulchres, full of dead men's bones and uncleanness.[43]
But, whatever his intentions or designs were, I am fully
persuaded that were any man in the present day to act
in the same disorderly and outrageous manner as he is
said to have done, he would either be confined in
Bedlam as a lunatic, or else popped into some cage, in
order that he might be brought to justice, to answer for
such a breach of the peace.

John says that when Jesus went into the temple he
found some who sold oxen, and sheep, and doves, and
the changers of money, sitting there. This account
appears to me very strange, that men, who were so
remarkably strict in the observances of their rites and
ceremonies, as not to eat bread with unwashed hands,
and who had such a veneration for their temple, should
suffer it to be polluted with filthy cattle and money-
changers; especially such a stupendous and magnificent
building as that must have been, which had occupied
forty and six years in building,[44] to be now converted
into a market-place for cattle! Can we suppose, that
the citizens of London, who pay less attention to their
cathedral, than the Jews did to their temple, would
suffer such a noble edifice as St. Paul's to be filled with
oxen, sheep, doves, stock-jobbers, &c.? No, surely;
nor yet around its walls, much less within them.

Admitting that the Jews were permitted to sell oxen,
sheep, doves, &c., in some of the porticos or avenues
which led to the temple, how could those things pollute
it, when we are told that they had formerly been carried
or driven into it for presents and sacrifice? Did not
the mother of Jesus take into the temple, for *sacrifice*,
those very things which her son is now driving out?[45]
Truly, if those things were for the use of the temple,
there could have been no more harm in selling them
there, than the sale of Missionary Notices, &c., in
Hinde Street Chapel, which are there now sold for the
use of the Methodist temples.

There are some persons, who, not considering in what
manner this flogging and driving was performed, cry
out, was not this a miracle, and proof of his Godship?
Yet, those who are supposed to have been witnesses of

the action did not consider it as any miracle, or as being any.thing wonderful ; or, why should they come directly after, and demand a sign of him, whereby they might be convinced that he had authority to act in that outrageous and unlawful manner? But, did Jesus give them any sign ? No, he said-that no sign should be given to them, because, as he before told them, they were a *wicked and an adulterous generation.*[46] Which, I should have thought, was the very reason why a sign should have been given to them ! If signs were necessary to any nation, they, certainly, needed one more than a righteous nation; for they that be whole need not a physician, only those who are sick. Moreover, Jesus told them, himself, that he came not to call the righteous,. but the sinners.[47] Then why did he not give the sinners a sign ? Peter has informed us that he gave them both signs and wonders ;[48] which, if he ever did, they surely would have been given to those who so earnestly requested them. But as we find that he gave neither the one nor the other to those who stood so much in need of them, we have strong reasons to suspect that he could not ; consequently Mr. Peter must have been greatly mistaken, when he said that he gave them both.

If we consider all the circumstances attending this driving the buyers and sellers out of the temple, we shall find that it was not done by his own individual powers, natural or supernatural, but by multitudes that followed him. Matthew, Mark, and Luke, all agree in saying that it was done as soon as he came to Jerusalem in triumph, when whole multitudes were at his heels : which opportunity, it is very natural for us to suppose, Jesus embraced, in order to try the dispositions of the people towards him, whether or not they were willing to support him in his newly-acquired regal dignity; for it appears that they had just hailed him, *the King of Israel.*[49] So he began, first, by upsetting one of the money tables, which, no doubt, pleased his followers, as they, by the scramble, became great gainers ; and which, as a natural consequence, must have produced a great bustle among them. It is therefore most likely that many others were capsized; when the noise and confusion, arising therefrom, must have been quite sufficient, not only to frighten away the cattle, but their keepers likewise, without his driving them. I have oftentimes thought, while passing through Exeter Change, that if a mob, consisting of two or three thousand persons were to rush through it, how easily all the boxes with the trinkets, &c. might be knocked down and plundered, as the poor merchants' money boxes were by Jesus and his followers.

As to the time when the robbery took place, for surely it cannot be called any thing else, the historians of Jesus are not all agreed. Indeed, there are but very few things upon which they are agreed! John makes it appear as being the first thing that he did after the wine and water story; and that he did not ride into Jerusalem until some time after this fray; whilst the rest inform us, that it was done immediately after he rode into Jerusalem That both accounts cannot be true, is evident: that both may be false, is possible.

John, moreover, seems to ascribe this action of Jesus to his zeal for the house of God. But why should he have been so remarkably zealous for that house, when he knew that it would be shortly thrown down and polluted, in the most shameful manner? For he tells them that they shall see the abomination of desolation, spoken of by Daniel the prophet, standing in the holy place, (whoso readeth, he says, let him understand.[50]) Why then did he not prevent that abomination from standing in the holy place, if he were so zealously attached to that house, instead of permitting and pre-ordaining its defilement, as all power was given unto him?[51] Though, if it were foretold by holy men of God, that such should be the case, it is evident that God himself had not much regard for the house; therefore, Jesus had no need to have put himself into such a passion about it.

According to Luke, it appears that Jesus, when he spoke these words, alluded to the destruction of the city and temple by Titus, which happened forty years after his supposed death; by his saying, "when ye shall see Jerusalem compassed with armies, then know that the desolation thereof is nigh."[52] Therefore, as he has advised those who read to understand what they do read, let us examine those writings of Daniel, wherein he is said to have foretold these things, six hundred years before they happened.

By his writings, or those which are ascribed to him, we find that he was continually dreaming about wild beasts, kings, and such like animals. That, when in one of those visionary flights, he foresaw that two kings, whose hearts were bent upon mischief, would sit together at one table, and speak lies to each other.[53] Surely there needed not the aid of divine inspiration to make this known; it being very natural for us to expect that such would be the case when two kings got together : a circumstance which has often occurred since those words were spoken, even in our own days ! He tells us, moreover, that one of these two kings, should come and pollute the sanctuary of strength, and take away the daily sacrifice, placing the abomination that maketh desolate instead thereof;[54] which, we are in-informed, in another passage, should continue for two thousand and three hundred days.[55]

Now all these things had been done two hundred years before these words were alluded to by Jesus, when Antiochus Epiphanes, King of Syria, took Judea, and entered into Jerusalem ; where he forbad the burnt-offerings, drink-offerings, and sacrifices in the temple ; which prohibition continued about two thousand three hundred days, or upwards of six years, until the temple was purified and cleansed by Judas Maccabeus. He also placed the image of Jupiter Olympus in the temple, which was such an abomination to the Jews ; having previously polluted the temple, by sacrificing an hog therein. And history further informs us, that prior to this event, Antioch did sit and eat at the same table with Ptolemy Philomater, king of Egypt. Whence, it is evident, that this book must have been written after the cleansing of the sanctuary, by Judas Maccabeus, in or about the year 165, B. C. For it cannot be supposed that God would take the trouble of moving Daniel to write such useless nonsense about kings eating together, four hundred years before they were in existence; especially as they were such an abomination in his sight; or why should he give orders to Ezekiel, to remove their carcases from him,[56] and at other times, consign their flesh for food to the fowls of heaven?[57] He assures us himself that they were only things which he gave in his anger, and takes away in his wrath.[58]

But there is another passage in the writings of this Daniel, which speaks of abominations and desolations in his own days; whence it appears that these words were a general phrase amongst the Jews, and applied to all such events. He says, "That the people of the prince that shall come shall destroy the city and the sanctuary, and the end thereof shall be with a flood; and unto the end of the war, desolations are determined. And he shall confirm the covenant with many for one week: and in the midst of the week, he shall cause the sacrifice and the oblation to cease; and for the overspreading of abominations, he shall make it desolate, even until the consummation, and that determined, shall be poured upon the desolate."[59]

Although this is nothing better than a confused jumble of words put together without either order or sense, still we can discover in them enough to convince us that they could not, nor were not intended to apply to those times to which Jesus alluded; namely, the destruction of Jerusalem, by Titus, the son of Vespasian, the Roman Emperor: for how could Titus cause that to cease which did not exist? We have no account that there were any daily sacrifices offered in the temple during the life-time of Jesus, or in the days of his disciples. Instead of which we have just read, that this temple was converted into a market-place for beasts, money-changers, and such like beings. Neither does history inform us that Titus ever overspread it with abominations, as Antioch did before, and Adrian after him; or that he ever made any covenant with them for one week. Instead of which, according to Josephus, the Jews would not covenant with him, they being forbidden so to do by their Mosaic law. Whence it is plain, that Daniel was alluding to his own times; which, I think, we shall find by a careful and attentive examination of the chapter.

In the beginning of this chapter, (the ninth,) he says that, "In the first year of Darius, the son of Ahasuerus, of the seed of the Medes, which was made king over the realm of the Chaldeans, instead of Belshazzar, the son of Nebuchadnezzar;[61] in the first year of his reign, I Daniel understood by books, the number of years, whereof the word of the Lord came to Jeremiah the prophet, that he would accomplish seventy years in the desolations of Jerusalem." This being in the reign of Cyrus, king of Persia, must have been very near the expiration of those seventy years; or why should the Lord stir up the spirit of Cyrus to make proclamation throughout all his kingdom, for the return of the Jews,[62] if the time predicted, was not quite or nearly accomplished? When Daniel discovered this, he began to make his supplications to the Lord, praying him to defer not, but to open his eyes, and behold the desolations of the city; to forgive them their sins, and cause his face to shine upon the sanctuary that is desolate, for his own sake, (17—19) which had been consumed with fire, by Nebuchadnezzar, King of Babylon.[63] Surely, nothing can be more plain, to convince us, that Daniel was speaking of his own times, and of the fulfilling the predictions of Jeremiah; which I think was quite enough for him to think about, without troubling himself with what should befal it 600 years after it was again built up.

While he was thus engaged in prayer, a *man*, whose name was *Gabriel*, came and told him, that as soon as he began to make his supplications the commandment came forth; (23) which clearly proves that this *Darius the Mede* was make king over the Chaldeans in the first year of Cyrus, king of Persia, the year in which the *commandment came forth*, for the return of the captive Jews. You will probably say that this account will not agree with the history of Persia, by other historians, because they, who ascribe a reign of twenty years to Cyrus, fix the siege of Babylon in the eleventh year of his reign; while those, who suppose him to have reigned thirty years, fix it in the 21st year of his reign. But the book of Daniel, being *sacred* history, is certainly entitled to more credit than *profane* history; therefore we must abide by this, which was written by *divine inspiration*, as being the most correct.

This proclamation, or commandment given by Cyrus, for the return of the captive Jews, was communicated to Daniel, who was at that time chief president of Babylon,[64] by Mr. Gabriel; who had, as soon as he heard of it, set off immediately from Persia, being *caused to fly swiftly*, for the express purpose of informing Daniel thereof, at Babylon; adding further, that there were still seventy weeks determined upon his people and upon the holy city, to finish the transgression, and to make an end of sins, and to make reconciliation for iniquity, and to bring in everlasting righteousness, and to seal up the vision and prophecy, and to anoint the most holy. (24) That is, that there were yet seventy weeks to come before the prophecy of Jeremiah would be accomplished; when the punishment for their transgressions would be finished, and an end made to their sins. For the Lord had likewise promised, by the mouth of Jeremiah, to give them, when they returned from their captivity, one heart and one way, by putting his fear into their hearts; so that they should not depart any more from him.[65] Then would a reconciliation be made for the iniquity of Manasseth, upon whose account the Lord had brought this captivity upon Judah, for the innocent blood that he had shed,[66] which the Lord said that he would not pardon. Then would be brought in that everlasting righteousness, foretold by all the prophets, and the prophecy accomplished and sealed: when the *holy* men should be anointed again, as formerly, to serve in the house of the Lord; which he had now *stirred up the spirit of Cyrus* to build for him.

This is the prophecy which has puzzled the brains of so many learned men, and thrown those chronologers into inextricable difficulties who have felt an interest in endeavouring to extend those *seventy weeks* to the days of Jesus and the destruction of the temple at Jerusalem by Titus, the Roman General. And the only method which they could take to accomplish this was by presuming that when Daniel said weeks, he meant weeks of years, or seven years for one week. What blasphemy, to pervert the words of holy men of God, who spake as they were moved by the Holy Ghost! For if they wrote one thing while they meant another, how should a *way-faring man* understand any thing that they have written? He could not be assured, but that a day signified a year, or a day of years, if a week signifies seven years, or a week of years. And then he might as reasonably suppose, by this way of reckoning, that instead of forty days which poor Moses fasted on the mount, while God was writing with his *finger* the commandments upon two tables of stone, [67] it signified forty years! Though, I verily believe, that I could find many a man in London, who could write them all out in *forty hours*, and upon such stones as would not so easily break, if thrown down upon a mount, [68] by the most violent, much less by the *meekest man on the earth!*

But to convince those unbelievers that Daniel meant what he said, we have only to look at a few verses following these, wherein he tells us that he was mourning three full weeks; during which time he ate no pleasant bread, neither came flesh nor wine into his mouth; neither did he anoint himself at all, till three whole weeks were fulfilled. [69] Surely, no person can suppose that the chief ruler of Babylon would so demean himself, as to eat no flesh nor drink wine during the space of twenty-one years, (if one week means seven years,); or even to neglect washing and anointing himself during all that time. But for three weeks it were possible that he might have so done, when the *King's business* [70] did not require his presence, if he thought it necessary?

Yet, admitting that these *seventy weeks* meant seventy weeks of years, or four hundred and ninety years, still they could not extend to the destruction of

Jerusalem, by Titus. As the Bible chronology informs us, that from the first year of Cyrus, the year in which the commandment came forth, to the death of Jesus, there was an interval of five hundred and seventy years; and the destruction of Jerusalem did not take place, until nearly forty years after *his* supposed death.

I have already shewn, in a former letter, how easy it was for a man to prophecy after he had seen the facts take place; so we find it exemplified in Daniel. For, as he lived, it is written, until the *third* year of Cyrus,[71] (which, we have a right to conclude, was after the seventy weeks had expired that commenced in his first year,) he could state the time that it took them to build the city, and the walls thereof, with any other particular circumstance attending it. As a proof, see how accurately he has divided those seventy weeks, as they were employed.

First, he says, that there were seven weeks from the going forth of the commandment to restore and to build Jerusalem; which, we find, was given in the first year of Cyrus unto the Prince or Messiah, signifying a Saviour, or one sent to redeem them from captivity; as the Lord had promised them by Isaiah, that Cyrus should build his City, and let go all his captives.[72] Which, if it were not written that he should be cut off in sixty two weeks after, one would suppose that it meant the time that it took Cyrus, the Lord's anointed, to come to Babylon, in order to give Sheshbazzar, the prince of Judah, those vessels belonging to the house of the Lord, which Nebuchadnezzar had formerly taken to Babylon, and deposited in the house of his Gods,[73] and which were so impiously made use of by Belshazzar, his Son.[74] But history informs us that Cyrus reigned twenty or thirty years; by which, it is evident, that it could not apply to him, if the commandment came forth in the first year of his reign. It might, probably, have alluded to Sheshbazzar himself, being a prince of Judah, who was sent by Cyrus with the captives; and the time which it occupied him in going from Babylon to Jerusalem with his cargo, in order to restore and re-

Q

build it.[75] Though, I should rather suppose that it meant Michael, one of the chief princes, who stood up so for the people;[76] as he says, at that time, (when he standeth up for them) *the people shall be delivered*; and who, moreover, is represented as being the only prince who did assist them.[77] For whenever an angel or messenger was sent to Daniel at any time, no one, but this Michael came to help them, when they were prevented or hindered by the Prince of the kingdom of Persia.[78] But, whoever it meant, it cannot be of any importance to this generation. It is evident that this cannot apply to Jesus; as he did not come within seven weeks, nor yet in seven weeks of years, after the commandment came forth from Cyrus, at the beginning of Daniel's supplications. Besides, he says, that this Prince or Messiah should continue threescore and two weeks, and should then be cut off; which evidently will not apply to Jesus. For if those weeks mean weeks of years, Jesus must have lived 434 years (being the number of threescore and two weeks of years) before he was cut off; which, I trust, you will acknowledge was not the case with him.

If we wish to understand what we do read, agreeable to the advice given by Jesus, we must not construe words according to our own wishes and fancy, but read them as they are written. Daniel says, that in threescore and two weeks the street and the wall should be built, even in troublesome times. Which, by referring to Ezra, we find to be about the time that it took them to rebuild ·their habitations, that formed the street. He says, that in the second month of the second year, after their return, they began to set forward the work of the house of the Lord.[79] By this time, we may presume that they had nearly built their street; and the second month of the second year nearly fulfils the threescore and two weeks, the time spoken of by Daniel. The inspired writers seldom mind an odd week or two to make up their figurative number seven, which is always used in some shape or other upon almost every event. And here you see the old proverb verified; when they had got their own houses built up, they did not care whether God had a house to lay his head in or not ; for, some years after, we find that Haggai, the prophet, reproves them for dwelling in their ceiled houses, while the house of their God was lying waste.[80]

Ezra informs us also that the times were very troublesome, as the Samaritans, who were the secret adversaries of Judah and Benjamin, troubled them exceedingly in the building.[81]

Then, it is further written, that, after these seven weeks, and threescore and two weeks, the Messiah (meaning him who was sent to deliver them from their captivity) should be cut off ; and the people of the prince that shall come shall destroy the city and the sanctuary, which they had built during the threescore and two weeks. These words, we may reasonably suppose, were added thereto after the death of Daniel ; which you will admit to be very probable ; the same trick having been played with the last chapters of Deuteronomy and Joshua ; likewise the last seven chapters of the first book, with the whole of the second book of Samuel: none of which could possibly have been written by their reputed authors, who were deceased at the time that they were written. Besides, there is strong reasons for doubting whether Daniel ever wrote any part of this book at all ; for, in the beginning of the book, it is written, that Daniel continued even unto the first year of King Cyrus ;[82] which surely could not have been written by Daniel himself. However, it is evident, that he must have been very far advanced in years, supposing that he was but seven years old when taken captive by Nebuchadnezzar, in the third year of Jehoiakim, King of Judah ;[83] though, by the bye, Jeremiah says that Nebuchadnezzar did not begin his reign till the fourth year of Jehoiakim ;[84] but this, I suppose, is the effect of inspiration ! Then Jehoiakim reigned eight years in Judea after Daniel's captivity. After him, Zedekiah reigned eleven years, before the seventy years captivity commenced. If Daniel lived all those years to the third year of Cyrus, he must have been nearly one hundred years of age ; consequently, could not have been living when Artaxerxes sent messengers, and made them cease building by force and power.[86] Even they who had seen the house of the Lord in the days of Zedekiah, were described as being ancient men.[87]

Again, it is written that he, (meaning the prince) whose people were to destroy the city and the sanctuary, shall confirm the covenant with many for one week. This cannot mean the same prince who was called the Messiah; because, at the expiration of the sixty-nine weeks, he was to be cut off. And the only prince that we can find who made a covenant with God, was Ezra; who, after these things, in the seventh year of Artaxerxes,[88] came from Babylon to Jerusalem; when he advised the people to put away all their strange wives, which they had taken from the people of the land,[89] and to make a covenant with God to that effect. This proposal was agreed upon, and proclamation throughout Judah and Jerusalem was made, in order that the people might come and confirm the covenant with Ezra; which probably occupied them a whole week; as it is written, that they were three days assembling together. And, in consequence of the great rain which fell at that time, it is not to be wondered at, if they were three days more in getting their consent, they being obliged to sit in the street during the time.[90] Especially, as Nehemiah informs us, that the princes, the Levites, and the priests, had to seal this covenant, besides all the people entering into a curse and oath, that they would abide by it.[91] So that this must have been the covenant confirmed with many for one week, which is alluded to in Daniel: though it is evident that there is some defect or omission in the passage, which you acknowledge to be the case with many passages in those books. As, for instance, when the Lord sent an angel to Joshua, all that we can learn of this important embassy was to bid Joshua take off his shoe, (Joshua v., 15) and Joshua did so! And, what then? Surely the Lord would not send an angel out of heaven to bid a man take off his shoe, unless something more important was to follow, which is omitted in this chapter,

But the historical parts of the book of Ezra and

Nehemiah are written in such a manner, so discordant and desultory, that it has been found impossible for the most *learned*, much more for a *fool*, to connect them together in any regular order. First, we read that Sheshbazzar came to Jerusalem with Zerubbabel and others, in the first year of Cyrus; when they built their habitations and laid the foundation of the house of their God, and stirred up the spirit of Cyrus, charging him to build him an house at Jerusalem.[92] Why then was it not built, and the Jews firmly established, to fulfil the prophecy of Isaiah, who said that Cyrus, the Lord's anointed, should build the city, and perform the pleasure of the Lord?[93] Was it his pleasure to permit the adversaries of Judah to trouble and prevent their building his holy house, leaving it unfinished, not only during the reign of Cyrus, but of Ahasuerus and Artaxerxes, until the second year of the reign of Darius?[94] History informs us that Jerusalem was destroyed by Nebuchadnezzer in the year 587, B.C. That Cyrus began in 560, B.C. That the conquest of Babylon did not take place until the year 539, B.C. which was in the 22nd year of his reign. Admitting that the first year of Cyrus, spoken of in Ezra, alluded to the first year of his reign in Babylon, still, how were the seventy years' captivity completed, from 538 to 587, the year in which they returned from captivity, being the first year of Cyrus, King of Babylon?

Bishop Newton, in order to get over this difficulty, supposes that the captivity is dated from the third year of Jehoiakim, when Nebuchadnezzer first came against Jerusalem. But the Bible positively asserts that the captivity did not commence until the final destruction of Jerusalem, in the eleventh year of Zedekiah. How else could the land enjoy her sabbaths, while Jehoiakim (who reigned eight years after his defeat in his third year,) and Zedekiah were reigning and fighting in it? The word of the Lord, it is written by Jeremiah, was, that, until the land had enjoyed her sabbaths; for as long as she lay desolate, she kept sabbath, to fulfil three-score and ten years.[95]

Again, history informs us that the successors of

Cyrus, were Cambyses, his son, and Smerdis, the
magician, previous to Darius. Who then were the
Ahasuerus and Artaxerxes mentioned by Ezra, as reigning prior to Darius? Artaxerxes Longimanus did not
begin his reign until upwards of twenty years after the
death of Darius! in the seventh year of whose reign,[96]
we find that Ezra came to Jerusalem to teach the people
and confirm the covenant. The temple having now
been finished about sixty years, as Darius reigned thirty-
six, and his Son Xerxes twenty-one, before Artaxerxes
began to reign; we now leave them, seemingly, established in their city, with the house of the Lord, and
their former privileges of worship. But when we come
to read Nehemiah, he says that, in the twentieth year
of Artaxerxes, he came to Jerusalem, and behold! it
is all laid waste; the gate being burnt with fire, the
walls broken down, and the people in great affliction.[97]
Who were they that had done this, after the Lord had
stirred up the spirit of Cyrus to build him an house,
in order that he might rejoice in Jerusalem, and joy in
his people?[98] We do not read that they again incurred
his displeasure, by serving other Gods. Then why did
he permit them to be so ill treated and afflicted; especially as he had promised to watch over them for
good?[99]

Then we find that Nehemiah was obliged to build it
up again; the people working with one hand, while
they held a sword or weapon of defence in the other.[100]
Surely these were the troublesome times spoken
of by Daniel! And who was this Nehemiah? It
appears that he was cup-bearer to the king; who, together with the queen, had given him authority to
come and build the city, supplying him with an escort,
and letters of authority to the several governors of the
neighbouring towns, to assist him in the building.[101]
Then, how could those petty governors withstand the
mandate of such a mighty king as Artaxerxes, by causing them to build their city in such a state of alarm and
danger? We also find this Nehemiah to have been
one of those savage monsters that disgrace the Jewish
history; for he acknowledges himself, that he cursed

and smote the people; plucking off their hair, and making them swear by God to do that which he had no right to enforce.[102] For, if God be no respecter of persons, what difference can it make to him, whom a man takes to wife? If there were women not fit for a man, why did he make them? Are they not of all nations made of one blood?[103] Yet, this Nehemiah many times reminded God to remember him for good, for what he had done,[104] as though he had been a profitable servant unto the Lord!

Moreover, the book of Daniel is written in such a discordant and romantic strain, that one is almost inclined to believe it fabulous! First, it says that Daniel was taken captive by Nebuchadnezzar; that being a child, he was sent, with several others, to the King's establishment, where he was fed and taught the Chaldean tongue, at the charge of the King. In the second chapter we find that in the second year of the reign of Nebuchadnezzar Daniel was made ruler over the whole province of Babylon. How was this possible, when we have just read that in the first year of Nebuchadnezzar he was but a child, sent to school, where he staid three years, according to the King's commandment? (Daniel i. 15, 18.) Some bishops and priests, in order to reconcile this difference, say that this Nebuchadnezzar was the son of the former; but this either proves their villainy, or their ignorance. History does not inform them that there were two Nebuchadnezzars; neither does the Bible. Instead of which, it expressly states that the son and successor of Nebuchadnezzar, who conquered Judea, was named Belshazzar. Indeed, it seems that the writer of the book of Daniel expected that some bishop or priest would pervert the true meaning of his words; therefore, to guard against it, he has repeated no less then three times in one verse, that it was the father of Belshazzar who brought the children from Judea; by saying, the King, Nebuchadnezzar, thy father, the King, I say, thy father.[105] And Belshazzar himself asked Daniel whether he was of the captivity of Judah, whom the King, his father, brought out of Jewry? Jeremiah speaks of a King of Babylon, that succeeded Nebuchadnezzar, but his name was Evil-merodach;[106] who, according to history, did not reign above two or three years, and was called Ilouarodam.

Again, we read that this Nebuchadnezzar made an image of gold, whose height was threescore cubits, or nearly one hundred feet, and the breadth thereof six cubits, or ten feet. This image, being nearly half the height of our monument, made of gold, was set up to be worshipped by people of all nations and languages;[107] yet, in the preceding chapter we read that this same Nebuchadnezzar acknowledged the God of Daniel to be the only true God of Gods and Lord of kings.[108] This appears inconsistent; but when we read that he would cast into a fiery furnace those whom he had just made rulers over his kingdom[109] for their wisdom and understanding, because they refused to worship any other God besides the *true* God, acknowledged to be such by him to Daniel, this seems incredible. Besides, where was Daniel? He certainly was included among the princes, rulers, governors, and people, who were commanded to fall down and worship this image; yet, there was no accusation brought against him, it was only against the three men, Shadrach, Meshach, and Abednego. Did Daniel fall down and worship it, or did he sanction it in others? Where was his wisdom and understanding at this time, that he could not convince the king of his folly and injustice? To credit the story of the three men coming out of the furnace *unhurt* would be ridiculous; being a circumstance contrary to the course of nature, which, we may be well assured, God would never alter, even if he could, without having some grand object in view, such as the conversion of a whole nation at least: but here we do not find that there was any good at all done by it; seeing that the people and the lords of the nation were as impious as ever after this notorious and wonderful miracle.[110]

Daniel says further, that Nebuchadnezzar saw *four men* walking in the midst of the fire, and the form of the fourth was like the Son of God. What God did he mean; as there are gods many and lords many?[111] We do not read any where that the Bible god had any family; and if he had, how could Nebuchadnezzar, who was an idolator, know any of them? Besides, he must have had sharper-sighted organs than ordinary to enable him to distinguish a man in a blazing fire, as that is represented to have been; especially as we may naturally suppose he must have been a distant spectator; the fire consuming all those who approached any ways near to it.

Again, this Nebuchadnezzar, Daniel says, was turned out to grass like an ox! Is it not strange that the butchers did not get hold of him? for we do not find that there was any distinguishing mark set upon the *royal* beast! This metamorphosing was not uncommon among the ancients; for we read in other Bibles or books that Actæon, a famous hunter, was turned into a stag; and Lycaon, a king of Arcadia, was metamorphosed into a wolf. Even Jupiter himself, when he wanted to kiss a pretty girl, would transform himself into a bull!

Besides, I never could learn how Daniel came to be so disgraced; for in the days of Nebuchadnezzar he was made chief ruler over the whole kingdom; but in the days of Belshazzar, the son of Nebuchadnezzar, he was unknown to the king; and the highest honour which he could possibly confer upon Daniel was to make him third ruler in the kingdom.[12] There is still another story concerning Daniel, which appears to me *almost* incredible, viz., that being, as I have already shewn, nearly one hundred years of age, he should be made ruler over an hundred and twenty princes; and when at this advanced age, invested with such power and authority, he should be thrown into a den of lions by a believing king for praying to his God, who had shown them all such signs and wonders. Believe this who can; I cannot.

Bishop Newton has made a *great* fuss about Daniel's *little* horn, his ram, and his goat; but, as he has just filled *two hundred* octavo pages, abounding with quotations from apocryphal books, to support his assertions, (which books he pronounces fabulous) in endeavouring to explain two pages of the word of this God, it will require, by the same rule of proportion, just 20,000 volumes to explain what *he* means. This, however, I must defer until another opportunity. If it will please our sapient rulers to continue their loving-kindness towards me, as they have hitherto done, by furnishing and providing me with food, such as it is, and lodging free from rent and taxes, I shall endeavour to answer the dissertations of the Bishop; flattering myself with being as competent as himself to explain the words of an unknown God.

I find that his principal object is to prove that this God of the Bible was more concerned about those four kingdoms, viz., the Assyrian or Babylonian, the Persian, the Macedonian, and the Roman, than he was about other empires. Why should not Great Britain deserve a prophecy as well as they? Are not our legislators and clergy equally as eminent for *piety* and *wisdom* as theirs were? In fact, has not this God got more supporters in the British empire than he had among the Assyrians, Persians, &c.? They had no Bible nor Tract Societies as we have. Even the empires of the Tartars, the Saracens, and the Turks claim equal privileges, through the extent of their dominions and the period of their existence. Besides, did not this Bible God know that our most *gracious* and *religious* Sovereign, George the Fourth, would defend the faith for him? Then why did he not make a wild beast of him also; as Sir Isaac Newton as well as Bishop Newton, confesses that those four kingdoms are represented by the four wild beasts of which Daniel speaks; particularly the Medes and Persians, who for their cuelty they say are represented by the bear; though Daniel himself informs us that they are represented by the ram;[113] between which and the bear there is a vast deal of difference. But perhaps the Bishop is more acquainted than Daniel was with those four-footed animals.

However, if the Medes and Persians for their cruelties were represented by the bear, by what beast must the Christians be represented? Surely, the cruelties of Cambyses, Ochus, or any other Persian tyrant, were not equal to those that have since been practised by Christians. Read the account of the bloody massacre at Paris, on the blessed St. Bartholomew's day, in 1572;

also the massacre in Ireland in 1641 ; with the continual burnings in Smithfield, and other places, both of
Protestants and Papists ; not forgetting South America,
and the East Indies, even in the enlightened eighteenth
century ! besides all the unknown horrid tortures, practised at the *holy* tribunal of the inquisition ; which,
within 250 years from its establishment in 1480, burnt
or roasted no less than 34,00 persons, and all for the
glory of God (!) besides inflicting various capital punishments on near 300,000 more. I have no need to
remind you of the truly enlightened nineteenth century;
the imprisonments, fines, &c. inflicted on certain individuals by the Christians being " as notorious as the sun
at noon-day."

To conclude, we find that all prophecies being of
such an equivocal, ambiguous, and delusive nature, no
particular explanation can be given to them ; they
being applicable to so many events. Whence they will
admit of various accomplishments and completions ;
having this privilege belonging to them in consequence,
namely ; that if they fail in one thing, they may
seem good in another. Jesus might therefore have
laid hold of this passage, or those who wrote for him,
as we do not find that Jesus could write himself fit to
be seen. The only time when he attempted to write,
being with his finger on the ground; when, being
ashamed of it, as I suppose, rubbed it out again directly,
as no one has ever presumed to inform us what he
wrote on the occasion.[114] But, whoever it was, whether
Jesus, Matthew, or Luke, he thought, no doubt, that
the desolation would apply to the destruction of the
city, by Titus, the same as when destroyed by Antiochus.
Though it will apply with equal justice to Aurelius
Adrian, when he built a temple to Jupiter Capitolinus
in the same place where the temple of this God once
stood, seventy years after Titus had destroyed it ; and
even to the Mahomedans in after ages, when they converted it into a mosque.

As to his driving and flogging the people out of the
temple, admitting that he did it only because they did
not hold the same sacred opinion of this temple as him-

self, is a proof of his intolerant spirit; which spirit he breathed into his followers,[115] who have communicated or transmitted this same inbred intolerant spirit down to the present generation. For ever since they became possessed of power, they have been flogging and driving out of the world, with the same blind and fanatical zeal, as he did these out of the temple, all those who presumed to differ from them about things of which they were all ignorant. And rather than stand all the day idle, when they could get no one else to persecute and drive about, they would quarrel and strive to drive each other out. That you may be enabled to drive this spirit out of them, is the sincere wish of

Your humble Servant,

JOHN CLARKE.

NOTES TO THE FOREGOING LETTER.

1 John ii. 1.
2 Mark i. 21·
   Luke iv. 16.
3 ,, ix. 49.
4 ,, xi. 19.
5 Matthew vii. 22.
6 Exodus viii. 17.
7 2 Kings i. 10—12.
8 Mark xi. 21.
9 John viii. 48.
10 ,, vi. 70.
11 ,, xiii. 27.
12 Luke xxii. 30.
13 ,, xi. 14.
   Mark ix. 17.
14 ,, v. 2.
   Luke viii. 27.
15 Matthew viii. 28.
16 Exodus xxxii. 27—28.
   Judges xx. 48.
17 1 John iv. 2.
18 Acts x. 38.
19 Matthew v. 44.
20 Job xii. 10.

38 ,,
39 ,,

43	Matthew xxiii. 27—33.	Ezra iv. 1—4.
44	John ii. 20.	Daniel i. 21.
45	Luke ii. 24.	„ i. 1.
46	Mark viii. 12.	Jeremiah xxv. 1.
—	Matthew xvi. 4.	„
47	„ ix. 13.	
48	Acts ii. 22.	„
49	John xii. 13.	„
50	Matthew xxiv. 15.	„
51	„ xxviii. 18.	
52	Luke xxi. 20.	
53	Daniel xi. 27.	
54	„ 31.	
55	„ viii. 14.	
56	Ezekiel xliii. 9.	
57	Revelations xix. 17—18.	
58	Hosea xiii. 11.	
59	Daniel ix. 26—27.	
60	Deuteronomy vii. 2—3.	
61	Daniel v. 30—31.	
62	Ezra i. 1—3.	
63	2 Chronicles xxxvi. 19.	
64	Daniel vi. 2.	
65	Jeremiah xxxii. 39—40.	
66	2 Kings xxiv. 4.	
67	Deuteronomy ix. 10.	
68	Exodus xxxii. 19.	
69	Daniel x. 2—3.	
70	„ viii. 27.	
71	„ x. 1.	
72	Isaiah xlv. 13.	„
73	Ezra i. 7.	„
74	Daniel v. 2.	
75	Ezra i. 11.	
76	Daniel xii. 1.	
77	„ x. 21.	„
78	„ 13.	
79	Ezra iii. 6.	
80	Haggai i. 4.	

LETTER IX.

TO DR. ADAM CLARKE.

Sir,

Notwithstanding the many appeals that I have made to your Christian charity, entreating you to point out, in the spirit of meekness, any error which I might have unfortunately made, in this my inquiry into the life of Jesus, you have never once condescended to favour me with your opinion. I therefore, not being willing to ascribe or impute your silence to a contempt of *men of low estate*, nor yet to your incapacity of appreciating my conclusions, have reasonably concluded it to be a mark of your approbation; not doubting, but that if there were any error or misrepresentation contained in my letters to you, beside those which may be ungrammatical or typographical, (as wheat seldom grows without tares,) you would, before this, have readily and cheerfully embraced the opportunity of correcting me. This persuasion encourages and stimulates me to proceed in the further investigation of the life of this Jesus, called the Christ. And though some persons may imagine that I am scheming to obtain a bishopric, or some other ecclesiastical benefice, I assure you Sir, that nothing is further from my views : my only object, unlike the generality of theologians, being the *salvation* of mankind and their *eternal* happiness. I therefore earnestly entreat your serious attention to the following observations.

Previous to the driving the buyers and sellers out of the temple, Matthew, Mark, and Luke say, that Jesus rode into Jerusalem upon an ass ; which circumstance should have been noticed before, had not John placed this triumphant ride a long time after the temple story.[1] And as there is something marvellous in the tale, it will not, I trust, be taken amiss, if we inquire into the particulars.

Matthew says, that when they drew nigh unto Jerusalem, Jesus sent two of his disciples into a village, where he told them they should find an *ass* tied, and a *colt* with her; loose them, he says, and bring them unto me.[2] But Mark and Luke, considering that the *ass* and *colt* were not both required for one man to ride upon, leave out the story of the *ass*, by saying that it was only the *colt* that was brought to him.[3] While John, who wrote his narrative some time after the rest, having discovered that the tendency of this robbery would invalidate the credit of Jesus, shrewdly omits it, by saying that it was a young *ass* which Jesus *found!*[4]

In the first place, whose ass was this? Mark says that it was tied by the door; and Luke says that the owners of the ass inquired of the two disciples why they loosed him? which clearly proves that the ass or colt did not belong to Jesus or any of his disciples, but to some one or more persons unconnected with them. Then what legal claim had Jesus to this ass? It is evident that he did not ask permission, by his telling them, that should any man ask why they loosed him, to say that the Lord had need of him. So if they could have got the ass clear off, without any one perceiving them, they were to bring him; if not, they were to excuse themselves by this answer. But would this answer justify any person in the present day, if detected loosing an ass or colt, which the owner thereof had tied to his door? Our legislature punishes horse-stealing with death, but ass-stealing is only considered a minor offence, punishable with seven years transportation : though I cannot see any difference in the disposition of the man who steals an ass, and him who steals an horse. James says,[5] that whosoever offends in one point of the whole law, is guilty of all. Therefore, if Jesus only broke the tenth commandment, by coveting his neighbour's ass, he was, according to James, equally guilty with the man who breaks them all ; for

"by one sin is the law broken, as sure as one crack
will break a pitcher, that can never be made whole
again."

This story of running away with an ass or a colt, or
a colt with the ass, for there is no method of knowing
which account to believe, cannot, I think, add much to
the honour and glory of Jesus; as we do not read that
the ass was ever restored again to the owners; besides,
it being a precedent for ass-stealing with impunity; as
Shakspeare says,

> "Thieves for their robbery, have authority,   ·
> When Judges steal themselves."

I would therefore advise our priests to expunge this
story altogether; or say of it as John did, when he
said, that Jesus *found* the ass. Even then, according
to the Mosaic law,[6] he would not be justified in detaining it, much less employing it to his own use, until he
had made diligent inquiry after the owner. Instead of
doing which, we find that he employed it in the most
ostentatious manner possible, by riding upon it in triumph to Jerusalem; it being formerly as great an
honour for a Jew to ride upon an ass, as it is in the
present day to ride in a coach and six. Do we not
read, and it is particularly remarked, that the thirty
sons of Jair, who was one of the Judges in Israel, rode
on thirty ass-colts,[7] as an instance of their high rank
and authority, they having thirty cities belonging to
them? Another Judge in Israel, who had forty sons,
and thirty nephews, are all likewise described as having
ass-colts to ride upon.[8] Moreover, the 250 princes of
Israel, who were famous in the congregation, and men of
renown, had asses to ride upon; for what other purpose
could they employ asses in a wilderness?[9] Even Balaam
the prophet rode upon an ass along with the princes of
Moab. (Numbers xxii. 22.)

Matthew says, that all this was done, that it might·
be fulfilled, which was spoken by the prophet, saying,
tell ye the daughter of Sion, behold, thy king cometh
unto thee, meek, and sitting upon an ass, and a colt the
foal of an ass.[10] But, as neither Mark nor Luke has
taken any notice of this prophecy, it is most probable

that this, like the rest of Mr. Matthew's prophecies, is one of his own making. I shall therefore search the prophets, and see what they have said upon the subject.

The passage to which Matthew alludes, I find to be written by Zechariah, (ix. 9.) who lived in the reign of Darius, king of Persia; who, together with Haggai, prophecied or taught the people, while they were building the house of the Lord.[11]

This Zechariah, to encourage and stimulate the people in their work, relates many wonderful and curious things, which he told them he had seen in dreams and visions; with a view of comforting and cheering their dejected spirits; always endeavouring, by some whimsical or fanciful image, to prefigure their future happiness and dominion over the Gentile nations; such as horns without heads, women with wings, mountains of brass, flying rolls, red horses, and a strange variety of such like symbols and figures;[12] by which he obtained a good report among the people as a prophet. While in those pleasant moods, he tells them that although the Lord had separated himself from them these many years, [13] (alluding to the captivity,) yet now he was returned unto Zion, where he would dwell in the midst of Jerusalem; they should be his people, and he would be their God.[14] He further tells them that the Lord had commanded him to take silver and gold, and make crowns, and set them upon the head of Joshua, the son of Josedech, the high priest, and say, thus saith the Lord, behold the man, whose name is the BRANCH, because he shall grow out of his place, and shall build the temple; he shall bear his glory, and sit and rule upon his throne; for he shall be a priest upon his throne.[15] Therefore, he says in the passage to which Matthew alludes, "Rejoice greatly, O daughter of Zion, shout, O daughter of Jerusalem: behold, thy king cometh unto thee; he is just, and having salvation; lowly, and riding upon an ass, and upon a colt, the foal of an ass."

The only thing in this passage, that has the least affinity to the case in question, is the ass. Joshua, the son of Josedech, rode upon an ass, and Jesus, the son of Mary (for there is no knowing who was his father) rode also upon an ass. Have not many men and women rode upon asses besides Jesus, who never considered themselves as the subjects of prophecy? Then how can this prophecy apply exclusively to Jesus? Supposing that Jesus procured this ass, in order to apply this passage to himself, and so construe it into a prophecy, it being not so difficult to fulfil; and if, instead of stealing, he had borrowed, or even purchased it for the occasion; yet there is not so much similarity between the two asses, as to deserve the name of a prophecy. One ass carried the king of Jerusalem; the other carried Jesus the Carpenter, who was king of no place in this world, as he himself acknowledged to Pilate.[16] It is evident that Zechariah never intended his king's ass to apply to the ass of Jesus, by his saying to the people who were then dwelling at Jerusalem, "behold! thy king cometh unto thee." Jesus, instead of being king, was not even respected among them; or why should they be always moved, whenever they saw and heard him, to cast stones at him? Besides, Zechariah bids them to rejoice when his king cometh; but if all men are in danger of being damned through not believing in this Jesus, there is not much cause for rejoicing at his coming. But Zechariah does not inform us that the ass upon which his king rode was stolen; then how can the ass itself apply to the stolen ass of Jesus? If the ass of Jesus had spoken, like the ass of Balaam, and assured the people that he was the identical personage of whom Zechariah had spoken, it might have been worthy of recording; but as it did not please God to open his mouth, in order that he might convince the people of it, I cannot see any necessity for holy men of God to trouble themselves about such a contemptible animal as an ass, especially as the story is of so little credit to the life of Jesus, admitting that it was foretold.

Moreover, Zechariah said, that his king was just and lowly; but, surely, no one will presume to say thus much of Jesus, after having read so many of his violent and unjust actions. The sequel of the story itself proves that, instead of being lowly, he was quite the reverse; or he would never have permitted the people to degrade themselves in the manner described, by spreading their garments and strewing palm-branches in the way before him, besides making as much noise, and paying him the same honour, as if he were Alexander the Great! If Jesus had been a meek and lowly person, he certainly would have rebuked them for this disorderly conduct; especially when requested so to do by those who did not agree with such tumultous behaviour.[17] Instead of which, he publicly encouraged it, by saying, that if they should hold their peace, the stones would immediately cry out. Surely, this was what some people call a thumper! But, I suppose, as Shakspeare says,

"Great men may jest with saints; 'tis wit in them;
But in the less, foul profanation.
(For) that in the Captain's but a choleric word,
Which in the Soldier is flat blasphemy."

I wonder that Mr. Matthew did not allude to Jacob's benediction,[18] wherein he says that " the sceptre shall not depart from Judah, nor a lawgiver from between his feet, until Shiloh come; and unto him shall the gathering of the people be: binding his foal unto the vine, and his ass's colt unto the choice vine." Perhaps he thought that the description there given of *Shiloh* would not reflect much honour to the person and conduct of Jesus; because it is further written, that his eyes shall be red with wine, and his teeth white with milk, that he would wash his garments in wine, and his clothes in the blood of grapes; which is no other than a figurative description of a bloated drunkard!

However, setting aside the absurdity of·God inspiring men to prophecy about jack-asses or jenny-asses, if humility be praiseworthy, the ass, I think, was entitled to the greatest share; seeing that he never once attempted to open his mouth and chatter like the ass of Balaam; neither did he act like the rest of his species, who, without a great deal of trouble in breaking them in, are very unruly and difficult to manage when ridden upon. But this one, though never ridden upon before by any man, had, nevertheless, the humility and good manners to carry his burthen quietly, without any grumbling, or even kicking, or throwing off his rider; else we might be sure that some one among them would have said something of it.

Besides, this story will not agree with the account given of Jesus by John in other places, when he says that prior to this Jesus walked no more openly among the Jews.[19]   Perhaps it may be said that riding upon an ass is not walking; but we are told that he walked publicly afterwards through the temple;[20] and Luke says that he taught daily in the temple.[21]   How could this be, when John says that a commandment had been given by the chief priests and pharisees,[22] that if any man knew where he was, he should shew it, in order that they might take him?   Can you think that any man proscribed by law would be suffered to make such a public and pompous entry into London, without being arrested; especially, if he received those honours which are alone due to the Sovereign; for John says that they hailed him as King of Israel?[23]   If this would not be permitted in a free country, how can we believe that it was ever suffered to be done in a conquered nation like Judea?

After Jesus had thus entered into Jerusalem, and driven the buyers and sellers out of the temple, Matthew says (xxi. 18.) that he went to lodge in Bethany; and in the morning, as he returned into the city, he hungered; when, seeing a tree afar off, he went to it, if haply he might find any thing thereon: but when he came to it, he found nothing but leaves, for the time of figs was not yet. (Mark xi. 13.) Then Jesus said unto it, let no fruit grow on thee henceforward for ever; and presently the fig tree withered away.

The first thing which attracts our notice on this subject is the singular appetite of Jesus, who could not walk a distance of fifteen furlongs,[24] (about two miles) without feeling himself an hungered; when we are informed that at other times he could fast for forty days together!   But where was Judas with the bag? Surely

they would not all set out together without providing
something for their breakfast, supposing that Mr. Lazarus or Mrs. Mary and Martha neglected to get it ready
for them in time ; as it appeared by John's account that
Jesus lodged with them.   It could not have been in consequence of the low state of their finances, seeing that
it was but the preceding day when they upset the money-
changers' tables ; when, we may reasonably suppose,
they replenished their stock in the scramble. Moreover,
one would have thought that Jesus would have been the
last among them to complain of hunger ; instead of
which, we find him to have been the only one.   This
certainly proves the truth of the Jewish accusation,
when they said that he was a wine-bibber and a glutton.[25] Besides, we are told that such was his voracious
appetite, that he could not rest quietly in his grave
after he was dead and buried, but must needs get up
again to eat broiled fish and honey-comb.[26]

The next thing with which we are surprised is his
astonishing ignorance of the nature of things, exemplified in his expectation of finding figs upon a tree at a
time when the leaves were only put forth ; this being,
according to John, but a few days before the passover
took place, which was held on the fourteenth day of the
first month ;[27] consequently, must have been about the
latter end of March. Some persons suppose that it
was not uncommon for figs to become ripe in that
country at that season of the year ; but if that were
the case, why should Jesus, after he had thus learned by
experience, say that the fig tree did not shoot forth
till summer was nigh at hand?[28] Besides, Mark says
expressly that the time of figs was not yet. Whence
it appears plainly that Jesus did not know all things,
but had need of much instruction ; or he had never gone
to a tree afar off, to look for fruit before the leaves were
hardly put forth.

And why should Jesus, who is held forth to us as an
example of patience in suffering, show so much im-
patience and ill-nature, when he found himself disap-
pointed of his usual meal? for it is written, that he
cursed the tree.[29] Paul taught his followers to bless

and curse not.[30] But Jesus blessed little children and cursed trees! These things, James says, ought not so to be, for blessing and cursing should not proceed out of the same mouth.[31] Woolston says that this action of Jesus was as foolishly and passionately done, as if a man were to throw the chairs and stools about the house, because his dinner was not ready for him at a certain time, or before it could be got ready for him ; and no more to his credit than if a yeoman of Kent were to go and look for apples at Easter, (the supposed time that Jesus sought for those figs,) and because he could find none, cut down all his trees! Surely, if such folly were wrought in England, Theodore Hook, or Dr. Stoddart, would make a pretty jest of it. Indeed, I oftentimes wonder how some men can stand up in the midst of an assembly and read such a tale without laughing at it!

But, supposing that Jesus had found any figs upon this tree, would he have been justified in taking them? We do not read that he had any land or trees of his own ; therefore this tree must have been the property of some other person. We cannot suppose that figs grew wild, like our nuts and berries, or how can that prediction ever be fulfilled, which said,[32] that every man shall sit under his own fig tree? And although, in this instance, Jesus did not commit theft, because there were none to steal, yet he must have committed it already in his heart, by longing for those figs, as much as the man, who looketh upon a woman, to lust after her, commits adultery in his heart.[33]

One of our *Reverend* Priests, the other day, almost crippled a poor boy for robbing his orchard of a few apples. How would he have served Jesus if he had found him in it ; especially if he had destroyed his apple tree as he did this fig tree? Surely they had no need of false witnesses[34] to lay an accusation against him. If the proprietor of this tree, together with the swine herds, the money changers, and the owners of the colt, had come forward, when Pilate demanded of the people what evil he had done, he never would, after hearing of these charges, have said that he could find

no fault in him.[35]   At any rate, I am convinced that
if Jesus lived in the present day, and committed such a
malicious and flagrant act of folly and injustice, he
would stand but a poor chance of escaping the tread-
mill !

Some persons, rather than doubt the veracity of his
historians, suppose that Jesus took a secret opportunity
of applying his carpenter's axe, before hand, to the root
of this tree ; by which means the leaves withered away ;
which, they say, would be the consequence, within
twenty-four hours, if acted upon in this manner.   For,
according to Mark, it was not until the morning after,
when they passed by the same way, that the tree was
discovered dried up from the roots.[36]   Though, in what
ever manner it was done, you must acknowledge that it
was a spiteful and malicious action, somewhat resembling the fable of the dog in the manger, who, because
he could not eat the hay himself, was determined that
no one else should.   I have often heard stories of
witches, fairies, and such like imaginary beings, who
would, for some private grudge, envy, or dislike, smite
their neighbour's cattle, sometimes their persons, with
some languishing distemper or disease, until they, like
the tree, withered away, or were otherwise destroyed.

St. Augustine, one of the fathers of the church, said
in his 89th sermon, that if Jesus had, instead of cursing
the fig tree, caused it immediately to bring forth the
desired fruit, by the word of his mouth, there could not
have been so many objections against it.   Which, I
think myself, would have given an hungry man more
satisfaction than the sight of a barren tree ; besides
exhibiting a greater display of divine power.   But the
spoiling of the tree, as Woolston said, is in its nature
of such a malevolent aspect, that it is enough to make
us suspect the beneficence of Jesus in his other works ;
and to question whether there might not have been some
latent poison and diabolical design, under the colour of
his fairer pretentions to Almighty power.   If this
action were recorded of Mahomet, instead of Jesus, our
divines would, long since, have discovered the devil's
foot in it, and have concluded, that Satan provoked

Mahomet to curse the tree, with the design of exposing him for a wizard, and his Mussulmen, in all ages, as fools for believing it. But, it is written, that the foolishness of God is wiser than the wisdom of men!

This action of Jesus, seems to have been such a blot upon his character, that neither Luke nor yet John would notice it. Instead of which, Luke endeavours to turn it off by way of parable; giving it a more favourable turn, in laying the blame to the barrenness of the tree; which, unless it produced fruit in the course of three years, was to be cut down.[37] But if this cursing the fig tree be only a parable, why may not all the rest of his miracles be so likewise? Indeed, the whole of his life may be nothing more than a fictitious tale or parable, there being no proof whatever that such a personage ever did exist.

The accounts which we have transmitted to us, by those persons who could not have written them until a long time after his supposed death, are no more authenticated than the preternatural conception of Johanna Southcote, the miracles of Prince Hohenlohe, or the adventures of Robinson Crusoe, will be to those who may live 500 years hence. In fact, if any party of men were to find themselves interested in espousing those tales, which we, in the present day, know to be false, they might grow into authority, and be received as sacred truths, in after ages, by those who may feel more inclined to take things upon trust, than take the trouble of examining into them.

Surely you will acknowledge that the writings of Daniel De Foe are deserving of more credit than the writings of those men whose names are recorded in this book, called the New Testament; there not being so many contradictions nor improbable events related in his " Adventures of Robinson Crusoe," as in the life of Jesus; nothing contained therein that is contrary to the well known laws of nature; consequently, less subject to controversy and dispute, to which the New Testament has been subjected, in all ages, even from its origin. Neither was the life of Robinson Crusoe written in an age when men were most liable to be

imposed upon, as this book was; the latter being
written before printing was invented, when men had
not such opportunities of refuting it, by circulating
their opinions concerning it, as in the present day.
Few persons, excepting children, are so credulous as to
place any confidence in the history of Robinson Crusoe,
although there is nothing contained therein but what is
both possible and probable.

Many persons, among whom was the Rev. Mr.
Fletcher, of Maddely, considered it as unreasonable for
any man to suppose that twelve or thirteen poor simple
men, like Jesus and his apostles, could impose on a
whole nation of people, by working sham miracles, if
the people had not had indisputable evidence that those
men were empowered by God. For, he says, those
things were not done in a corner; they were known to
a distant King, (Agrippa,) as well as to many honourable persons of Cæsar's household. How absurd, he
says, would it be, if thousands of wise Englishmen and
sensible Frenchmen, in the present day, were to suffer
themselves to be deluded by a tale, told by twelve or
thirteen Hottentots, who should cause them to worship,
and put their whole dependence of future happiness on
a certain Hottentot, whom the Hottentot nation had
hanged for an imposter. How then, he asks, can we
suppose, that thousands of wise Greeks and learned
Romans, should have taken for themselves, as their
Saviour, the very man of whom his own countrymen,
the Jews, had been ashamed, and put to death for an
impostor; and which country, both Greeks and Romans
despised? Besides, he says, what could induce those
men to carry on such a deception, if it were a deception? Instead of riches and honour, gold and silver
they had none. They were considered as the filth and
off-scouring of the earth; and endured unparalleled
hardships. (How much unlike, is this description, to
that which is given of those in the present day, who
pretend to follow them in all things!) Neither were
they under any delusion respecting their treatment:
having been assured thereof, by their master, what they
were to expect, and what as truly followed, even suffer-

ing the most cruel deaths to support the truth of Jesus. Can we think, he asks, that they were men different from ourselves, who loved pain better than ease, and poverty more than riches ? How absurd would it be, he says, to suppose that twelve of the greatest Epicureans in England would agree among themselves to preach abstinence day and night, for a number of years, and fasting throughout the three kingdoms, merely to have the pleasure of starving themselves to death! Surely then, he says, it is as ridiculous to suppose that a few poor fishermen, by means of a lie, told without wit, wrote without elegance, having only stripes and imprisonment for their pains, could thus foil a multitude of Jewish and Pagan priests, who had learning, oratory, prejudice, custom, wealth, profession, laws, governors, and emperors on their side, as to suppose that David killed Goliah with a grain of sand, and afterwards cut off his head with a blade of grass ; or that sailors sunk men of war with a puff of their breath ; and soldiers battered down ramparts with snow-balls !

He further asks, why should Saul of Tarsus, a man of sense and learning, and surprising intrepidity, be seduced by nobody knows who, to preach a parcel of lies for nearly thirty years, undergoing such matchless hardships, with such astonishing zeal, even to death, to support that of which he had been so exceedingly mad against all those who did believe ? Besides the constant appeal to the Jews themselves ; for surely, he says such a miracle as that recorded by all the Evangelists of Jesus feeding so many thousands of persons with a few loaves and fishes, if it were an imposition, must have been detected by some one among them who were eye-witnesses of it.

These arguments, I acknowledge, might have some weight in the scale against infidelity, if Mr. Fletcher had first proved that those poor fishermen ever existed, and did those things which are recorded of them. Or that Saul of Tarsus, lived and acted in the manner he has described. It is recorded of Don Quixote, that he did many wonderful things, yet few persons will be found so credulous, as to believe in them. As to those men being under no delusion, as Mr. Fletcher has thought, respecting their treatment because they were before-hand apprised of it, I must beg leave to differ from him. Admitting, that they did exist, and suffered those things which he has described, were there not many splendid promises held forth to encourage them to proceed? Were they not to have for every house that they left for his sake, an hundred? Let it be whatever it might, whether houses, lands, brothers, sisters, fathers, mothers, wives, or children, they were to receive an hundred fold, now in this time, and in the world to come, eternal life,[38] where they should sit upon thrones and judge the twelve tribes of Israel.[39] Surely, here were strong and powerful temptations, sufficient to induce many a credulous man to forsake his house and family, even in the present day! But these promises would not entice the rich man to forsake his all, at the request of Jesus;[40] they only prevailed on those, who had nothing to lose; and which being never fulfilled, as we read of, prove them to have been deceitful. Some imagine that those promises were fulfilled in some other world; but Jesus expressly stated that they should be fulfilled now, in this time. Surely we are not to suppose that a man who forsakes his wife and child in this world will have an hundred wives and children in another, when Jesus declared, that in that world they neither marry nor are given in marriage.[41] Besides, either in this world or in any other, how can a man have an hundred fathers and mothers? The Mahomedans promise plenty of wives in their new world; but do not make themselves so ridiculous as to promise more fathers and mothers than are absolutely necessary.

To enquire into the truth or falsehood of any book is commendable in every man who wishes not to be deceived; and if they find one part not consistent with truth, they have an indisputable right to question the whole; especially when no proof can be advanced, to warrant the authenticity and genuineness of the rest.

Most persons who have examined the history of the church, admit that the books of the New Testament did not *publicly* exist till at least one hundred years after

the supposed life of Christ: and if they had no public
existence, how can we be assured that they had ever
any private one before? It is written in this book that
Paul wrote some of his Epistles at Rome when brought
the second time before Nero;[42] and that Jesus lived in
in the reign of Tiberius Cæsar, when Pontius Pilate
was governor of Judea.[43] But, unless we had proofs,
or some reference to proofs, that such were the case, we
are not authorised to give it credit upon the bare assertion of this book itself. One witness is not sufficient
to rise up against any man for any iniquity;[44] neither
can one witness be sufficient to establish another man's
honesty, much less his own; as you have justly observed,
that one man may be mistaken, or so violently prejudiced, as to impose even on his own judgment, or so
wicked as to endeavour, through malice or interest, to
deceive or even compass the life of his neighbour.
Therefore, it is absolutely necessary that every thing of
importance, which may concern the interest of society,
should be established by the mouth of two or three
witnesses at least;[45] it being less probable that two
or more would conspire together to deceive or destroyed
their neighbour; and even were they so inclined, their
seperate examination might lead to a discovery of their
conspiracy.

Although it is written in this book that Paul lived
in the reign of Nero, and Jesus in the reign of Tiberius
Cæsar, yet we have no proof that it was so, independent
of the book itself. There were many eminent historians and poets, who lived in those reigns, such as Livy,
Ovid, Celsus, Patercules, Persius, Quintus Curtius, Lu-
can, and others, all Romans, consequently, as well
acquainted with the affairs of the nation, its conspicuous
characters, and every remarkable circumstance which
occurred therein, as those of Cæsar's household, or distant Kings. And as neither King Agrippa nor any of
Cæsar's household, not even Cæsar himself, has written
any thing upon the subject, I cannot think that the
allusion made to them in this book is proof positive
that they were ever acquainted with the persons whose
names are contained therein.

The testimonies of Tacitus, Pliny the younger, Ignatius, Irenæus, Quadratus, Suetonius, or Justin Martyr, can be no more convincing to us that such a person as Jesus ever existed, than those who might now make allusion in their writings to the adventures of Robinson Crusoe will be to those who may live 1600 years hence. As they all lived and wrote 1600 years back, within one and two hundred years after the supposed existence of Jesus; consequently, what they wrote must have been from hearsay or tradition, (printing being unknown,) upon which, as Jesus himself acknowledged, no dependence can be placed. (Matt. xv. 2, 3.)

As for Clemens, Origen, Jerome, Lactantius, Athenagoras, Annatolius, Aristides, Arnobius, Eusebius, and others, whose writings are brought forward as certain proofs of the validity of the gospels and epistles, they all living in the third and fourth century after those things which they say had ocurred, could not vouch for the truth of them, more than we can now for the existence of witches, &c., said to have existed two hundred years back. They could only receive their information from the writings of those before them; not one of which that they allude to were written before the days of Pliny, the Proconsul; who, as I have already shewn from their own confession, lived in the second century. In fact, we have better and more substantial ground to build our faith upon, concerning things done two hundred years back, than they had; because we have it transmitted to us in a number of printed copies circulated among all classes of people; which, if not consistent with truth, would be, by the same means, contradicted or refuted; as numerous other printed copies would be circulated, contradicting the statements, if false; of which criterion to judge between truth and falsehood they were deficient; printing being to them unknown. They were consequently obliged to write all their copies; which, we may reasonably conclude, must have been but very few, especially as writing was so little practised in those days; it being a universal maxim among the fathers of the church to teach their adherents that " Ignorance is the mother of devotion."

For, Paul told the Corinthians that God would bring
to nothing the understanding of the prudent, and
destroy the wisdom of the wise ;[46] so cautions his followers to beware of philosophy,[47] and to be careful for
nothing,[48] but the making of prayers and supplications;
which commands we find that the fathers of the church
strictly obeyed ; not like the disobedient and the apos-
tates of the present day, who are so anxious about
establishing national schools, universities, societies,
institutions, and various other seminaries for promoting
knowledge, and obtaining wisdom and understanding in
all things.

Those copies then being written by those men, whom
we now call Catholics, how can we be assured that they
were correctly copied from the original; as none of the
original manuscripts, which were written by the persons whose name they bear, were ever preserved ? We
know not the men that were employed to copy them;
whether they were sufficiently qualified and honest, or
whether they might not have been illiterate, prejudiced,
or interested persons ? The oldest manuscript, of which
we know any thing, is that in the British Museum,
called the Alexandrine, which was written entirely in
capitals, by an Egyptian woman, we are told, named
Thecla, in the fourth century, and presented to Charles
the first, in the seventeenth century, by the patriarch
of Constantinople.* This manuscript has many different readings to that called the Vatican, which was
written, they say, about a century after the former.
Now, who was this Egyptian woman, or any of those
persons who had a hand in copying the originals, which,
they tell us, were written by the men whose names they
bear ? Paul, when writing to Timothy, admonished
him to continue in the things which he had learned and
been assured of, knowing of whom he had learned
them.[49] If Timothy could depend upon the honesty
and veracity of those persons whom he knew, and from
whom he had received instructions, he might have been
justified in believing those things. But, as we know
nothing of the writers of these copies, how can we be

---

* Prideaux.

assured of their integrity and honesty? And as Jesus found no fault with Thomas, for not believing without ocular demonstration,[50] notwithstanding the many wonderful things of which he had been an eye witness, he, surely, cannot find fault with us, for not believing, who have never seen either him or any of his wonderful works. Man, you know, is not at liberty to think for himself; he must think as his own ideas, notions, or sensations compel him; else all men would think alike of the same thing, if their ideas and sensations were alike; which we find is not the case, there being very few persons who do think alike of the same thing. Then if men are not free to think, how can they be free to act? If thought is the cause, how can the effect be free, which arises from that which is confined? Shall we be damned then for this cause, over which we can have no controul?

The advocates for this book of books, have advanced, as a proof of their genuineness and authenticity, that the writings of its opponents have been overpowered by the arguments and evidence adduced in its favour. But of this I am not assured; whether they have ever been fairly answered or not? or whether there has not been some foul play in this pretended conquest? In the present day we have undeniable proof that this book will not stand the test of examination, by an impartial and unprejudiced inquirer. Neither is there one who dares to espouse its cause, with fair argument, against its opponents, without having recourse to the "strong arm of power." But we read that there were men who publicly opposed it as being fallacious, as soon as ever its contents were made known; by the same means with which it was propagated, namely, by written copies; among whom were Celsus, Porphyry, Peregrinus, Crescens, Lucian the Roman philologist, and a number of others, whose writings have been all destroyed, or artfully withheld from public inspection: these being the means employed by those who felt interested in supporting those books, to suppress every thing that had a tendency to overthrow them. In the reign of its first royal advocate, Constantine, we are informed that many persons who differed in opinion concerning those books, were banished, and all their books burned, or otherwise destroyed. In all ages this has been their practice, from Paul at Ephesus, where they burned books to the value of 50,000 pieces of silver,[51] to the reign of Henry the Fourth, King of England; when they dug up the bones of Wickliffe, the Reformer, and burnt them, together with his books.

According to Origen, who wrote in the third century, we find, by some quotations in his writings, that Celsus had written a book, a century before, entitled, "The True Word," in opposition to the doctrine of Justin Martyr, his contemporary. Which book, Origen, it is said, ably and clearly refuted; but unless we had the "True Word" of Celsus, to examine, how can we be certain that such was the case? Porphyry, who lived near the end of the third century, wrote, it is recorded, no less then fifteen, some say, thirty books, against these Christian books, Why were not those writings of its opponents, as carefully preserved as those of its advocates? Does not this look very suspicious?

There are passages in three different books that are brought forward as invincible arguments in proving the existence of Jesus, and the sect of persons, called Christians, at the time ascribed to them; namely, in the first century, before the destruction of Jerusalem, by Titus, the son of Vespasian. The first is from the writings ascribed to Tacitus, who could not have written them within forty years after Jerusalem was destroyed; consequently, what *he wrote* must have been from some other copy or tradition handed down to him, neither of which does he acknowledge.

He says, that Rome was nearly consumed by fire, during the reign of Nero, prior to the destruction of Jerusalem by Titus. That this calamity was generally imputed to the wickedness of Nero; but who, "in order to divert suspicion from himself, substituted fictitious criminals; and with this view, he inflicted the most exquisite tortures on those men, who, under the vulgar appellation of Christians, were already branded with infamy—they died in torments, and those were imbittered by insult and derision. Some were nailed on crosses; others sewed up in skins of wild beasts, and exposed to the fury of dogs; others again smeared over with combustible materials, were used as torches to illumine the darkness of night. The gardens of Nero were destined for this melancholy spectacle, which was accompanied with a horse race, and honoured by the presence of the Emperor." (Tacit. Annal. xv., 38—44.

This story altogether seems incredible, that a monarch, who had been brought up and instructed by that eminent philosopher, Seneca, should set fire to his own city, in order to form a pretext for tormenting and destroying his own subjects, by imputing the act to them. That a man, when possessed of absolute and arbitrary power, will become despotic, no one will attempt to dispute; we having had so many instances of its possibility. But, that he should torture and destroy his own subjects, merely to make sport with their sufferings, can never meet with credit from an unprejudiced mind; especially, when we learn from the same authority, that after his death, many young females, in the dead of night, " used to strew flowers over his tomb." Surely no female, however interested in his fate, while living, could have felt such sympathy and respect for him, if he was the monster described. David, the monster, sawed his enemies asunder, and burnt them in brick-kilns, but never tortured his own subjects, merely to sport with their sufferings.[52]

Besides, admitting that this is no interpolation, of which we cannot be assured, how can we tell but Tacitus wrote with a prejudiced mind, through envy, hatred, or uncharitableness towards the family of Nero? as some historians, you know, will do. Nero being long since dead, Tacitus could write what he pleased, there being no one living, at that time, to contradict him. Even if there were, his account might be to them unknown; as his writings could not be circulated to a great extent, during his life, in consequence of the difficulty arising in copying them. We discover something like prejudice in him, when he seems to insinuate that it was reported that Nero amused himself, during the conflagration, by "singing to his lyre the destruction of ancient Troy." And, although he only mentions it as having been a rumour among the people, yet how readily we find Suetonious and Dion Cassius, transcribing it as a matter of fact! Tacitus acknowledged, as a fact, that Nero manifested much prudence and humanity on the occasion, by throwing open the imperial gardens to the distressed multitude, and erecting temporary buildings for their accommodation; besides supplying them with corn and provisions at a very low price. Why then should we throw aside the subject matter of fact, and embrace those prejudiced reports? Moreover, all who have read the writings of Tacitus acknowledge him to have been a very credulous man, upon whom no dependance can be placed.

But there are no other historians who lived between the days of Nero and the time when Tacitus wrote, not even Philo nor Josephus, who give any account of this persecution of Christians, by Nero. Those who have since alluded to it in their writings, such as Suetonius and Dion Cassius, received their information thereof from Tacitus, which is nothing more than hearsay evidence to us, consequently tantamount to none at all.

Josephus mentions a sect of Jews, called Galileans, by way of derision, "who were branded with infamy," but says nothing of persecuting Christians, or Nero's pastimes! And if such a sect of persons did exist in his days, and did those things which are related of them, he certainly would not have omitted noticing of them; he, holding an official situation amongst them at the same time. Livy relates (xxxix. 13—17) that a number of persons, called Bacchanals, were discovered (about the supposed time of Christ) and punished for their licentiousness and depravity. Surely this cannot allude to the disciples of Jesus! But, according to the testimony of this book, the New Testament, this sect of persons, called Christians, must have been well known, not only in Judea, but in Pontus, Gallatia, Capadocia, Asia, and Bithynia.[53] Yet neither Josephus nor any other historian or poet, seems to know anything of them or their gospel, although it is said to have been preached to every creature under Heaven.[54]

There were many other things, such as the slaughter of the children by Herod; the opening of the heavens at the baptism of Jesus; the beheading of John the Baptist, after he had baptized all Judea and Jerusalem; the purchase of the field of blood, which this book says was known to all the dwellers at Jerusalem;[55] the total darkness at the crucifixion of Jesus; the strange appearance of the dead bodies to their friends in the city; the wonderful pool of Bethesda in Jerusalem, wherein 'an angel came to heal the diseased;[56] the persecution of the Christians by Herod, when James the brother of John was killed by the sword;[57] the stoning of Stephen; besides the disturbances occasioned at various times by Paul and Peter; if these, and many other notable occurrences, which are related in this book, ever did transpire, is it likely, that Josephus, who was so remarkably particular, in relating the most trivial events, would have omitted them? Besides, the two greatest philosophers and historians of the age, Seneca and Pliny, the natural historians, would surely never have suffered such a surprising phenomenon, as that of the total darkness, to escape their observation.

As to the passage which christians formerly used to bring forward as an argument, from Josephus, relative to the person of Jesus; I need not waste time in making any observations thereon; as the most strenuous advocates of christianity admit it to be an interpolation; consequently no *sensible* man will ever presume to advance it again as an argument in its favour; which, by being proved and acknowledged to be an interpolation, shews what mean artifices and miserable shifts Christians have been obliged to make use of, in order to support their tottering fabric.

The other passage is from Pliny the Proconsul, commonly called the younger, to distinguish him from his uncle, Pliny the Elder. He was contemporary with Tacitus, and wrote, in the reign of Trajan, a letter, stating therein the conduct of a certain class of men, calling themselves Christians, and inquiring of the

Emperor his pleasure concerning them : to which Trajan replied, that "if they are brought before you and convicted, let them be capitally punished." But this was no persecution as is represented. Yet this is the principal foundation that Christians have for considering Trajan a Persecutor! Neither is it a proof that they had been long in existence : but on the contrary. For if they had been scattered abroad throughout Rome and Asia, as this book testifies, before the destruction of Jerusalem, Pliny need not to have sent from Bithynia to Rome, an account of their existence and conduct, as a matter of surprise and novelty ; for they would have been well known to Trajan at Rome, who would there, if so inclined, have issued forth his mandate concerning them, without waiting for Pliny's information and inquiry. We are told that Paul dwelt *two whole years* at Rome,[58] preaching and teaching those things contained in what is called the gospel, no man forbidding him. Surely here was a fine opportunity for the word to run and be glorified, having such a free course. Yet during an interval of fifty years, between Paul and Trajan, it does not seem to have been known at Rome.

But what was Pliny's accusation against those Christians, that should induce Trajan to direct him to punish them, if convicted? It appears that in those days, there were many associations formed, and private meetings held in various parts of the country, which excited the suspicions of the magistrates: insomuch that Pliny deemed it expedient to issue forth a general edict against them ; consequently the meetings, which were probably the "love feasts" of the Christians, fell under the meaning of the prohibition. But as their religion taught them not to fear those who could only kill the body,[59] they gave no heed to the edict, but obstinately persisted in attending their sequestered places. And although those meetings might have been harmless and innocent in themselves, yet their secrecy and mysterious conduct, gave rise to many conjectures. Some, perhaps, instigated by malice or envy, pretended to confess and relate the secret mysteries and ceremonies of the societies ; which, whether true or false, was quite sufficient to justify Pliny's inquiry and Trajan's answer. It being asserted, that, in their dark recesses, "a new-born infant, entirely covered with flour, was presented, like some mystic symbol of initiation, to the knife of the proselyte, who, unknowingly, inflicted many a secret and mortal wound on the innocent victim of his error; that, as soon as the cruel deed was perpetrated, the sectaries drank up the blood, greedily tore asunder the quivering members, and pledged themselves to eternal secrecy, by a mutual consciousness of guilt. It was as confidently affirmed that this inhuman sacrifice was succeeded by a suitable entertainment, in which intemperance served as a provocative to brutal lust; till at the appointed moment, the lights were suddenly extinguished, shame was banished, nature was forgotten; and as accident might direct, the darkness of the night was polluted by the incestuous commerce of sisters and brothers, of sons and mothers." (See Gibbon's inquiry into the progress of the Christian Religion, chap. xvi. for his authorities.)

Surely Trajan was justified in saying, that if they were *convicted*, upon such charges as these, let them be *capitally punished*. We have ourselves daily experience to what heights of folly and madness superstitious frenzy and fanaticism will lead some persons who are affected therewith. Not long since, a young woman, infected with the plague of methodism, hanged her little brother in order to send him spotless into heaven! In fact, we seldom can see a weekly newspaper, either in town or country, without reading some ridiculous transaction or violent assault upon the life of individuals, by those infected with this spirit of fanaticism. The extravagant and ridiculous actions of the Ranters, the Jumpers, and the Revivalists, would almost persuade us, that the above charge against the Primitive Christians, was not altogether groundless, at least, not improbable.

Some Christian writers have considered it as an incontestible evidence of the genuineness and authenticity of the New Testament, in consequence of their being no contemporary of the evangelical writers, not even

Josephus, who have left anything on record to invalidate the truth of them. But this can be no evidence; for if there never were such a man as Jesus, or writings concerning him, in their days, how was it possible that they should write against them? When they, in after ages, did write, as I have already shewn, their writings were, as soon as known, destroyed, or otherwise withheld from public inspection; which the Christian fathers admit to have been the case with the writings of Celsus, Porphyry, and others.

Again, in whose hands were those copies that were written, prior to the invention of printing? We find that when the first edition of the Bible was printed, in the sixteenth century, the scriptures were almost unknown to the laity; and so little learning had the Clergy themselves among them, that Bishops were obliged to testify their synodical acts by proxy; which were done, generally, in the following curious manner: "As I cannot read myself, A. B. hath subscribed for me." Or, "As my lord bishop cannot write himself, at his request, I have subscribed." Whence, it is evident, that the M. S. copies must have been like a sealed book, secreted among a few individuals, who kept them in in their own private possession; and who might, for what we know to the contrary, have altered, corrected, and revised them, to suit their own purpose, according to their own pleasure. Hence arose so many different readings, amounting to upwards of 30,000, which were found among these copies when they came to be collected together for the purpose of being printed; the number of which, we are told, did not exceed 287, that could be found throughout the whole world! Then how can we tell which was correct, or whether any one of them was like unto the original that was written by the author, whose name it bears? Even since then, in 1603, there has been another edition printed, the title-page of which confesses that the former has been *altered*, *corrected*, and *revised*, agreeable to the command of King James I., who had been told by Dr. Reynolds that the first edition, then extant, did not correspond with the original. And, although he had upwards of fifty learned men employed in altering and correcting this first edition, to answer the original Greek manuscripts, who were, no doubt, inspired by the *Holy Ghost,* yet you acknowledge that it is still in an imperfect and disordered state, and needs another alteration, correction and revision. Is this, then, the *sacred* book upon which we are to rest our " eternal state ?" Away with such an idea. The word of a God would be as clearly understood among all people, nations, and languages, as the word of Nebuchadnezzar. [60] It would serve them as a lamp to their feet, and a light to the paths of all his creatures.[61] Instead of which, this is only a *stumbling block to the Jews, and foolishness to the Greeks.*[62]

These things being so well known, what confidence can be placed in such books ? or what security have we, to assure us that the copies were not altered by the monks and friars, in whose possession they were before thay were printed ? The advocates of Protestantism advance, as a proof that they were not altered during those dark ages of superstition, the fact that their internal evidence was brought forward by the Reformers, as an argument against the Romish Church ; which had been acting all that time, they said, contrary to its precepts. But, this is still disputed : and if a majority of persons are admitted to decide a question, this will be in favour of the Catholics; who greatly exceed in number those of the Protestants ; and will not admit of the explanation and construction of those precepts and passages, singled out by the Reformers or Protestants : many of them having, moreover, testified, and sealed their testimonies with their blood, that there is no contrariety whatever between the precepts of this book and the doctrines of the Romish Church. Should we admit that they were not *wilfully* altered by those who were possessed of them, yet, you must acknowledge that they have undergone many variations, through translating them from one language to another; which is proved by the diversity of readings, not only between the Samaritan, the Chaldaic, the Septuagint, the Ethiopic, the Greek, the Syriac, the Coptic, the Arabic, the Persian, the Vulgate or Latin, the Slavonic, the Gothic, the Anglo-Saxon, the Sahadic, the Armenian, and many others, but in the English translation also; as the first Bible, called the Bishop's Bible, has many different readings from that printed afterwards in 1603.

If we examine the history of the Church we shall find, that in the reign of Constantine, the first Christian emperor, there were found a number of Gospels and Epistles, that were written by various persons, whose names are now mostly buried in oblivion, amounting to nearly one hundred; among which there were forty gospels, that were respected and believed to have been written by divine inspiration, as well as those of Matthew, Mark, Luke, and John; some of them are yet extant. Constantine having rendered himself odious in the eyes of his subjects, by his atrocious acts of cruelty and injustice, discovered that in those gospels and epistles, there were promises of pardon held forth for all manner of sin and blasphemy, [63] to those who would believe, or say they believed, in those books. He thereupon readily embraces the offer, by complying with its conditions, its rites, and ceremonies. Having made himself an object of hatred and detestation to his subjects, first, by his cruelty towards Maximin, his father-in-law, whom he destroyed with all his family; then, as soon as invested with power, he found means to put his colleague, Licinius to death, in a most treacherous and infamous manner; whereby he became possessed of the supreme command of the empire: he then thought that by establishing and promulgating these *glad tidings*, which certainly were such to all people of his character, that all old things would be done away, by the blood of Jesus, which, it is written, cleanses from all sin ; [64] by which means he, being made a new man, might obtain through this book what he never could by his conduct, namely, a good report.

Therefore, as this book stated that Jesus had promised to all those who should believe on him, full pardon for all manner of sin, no matter what, whether robbery, murder, sodomy, or any other species of crime, excepting speaking evil of the Holy Ghost, a personage by-the-by, whom Constantine knew no more about than you or I do, it became a matter of policy in him to countenance and support this book; to accomplish which, a Synod was appointed, in order that they might take into consideration the best and most effectual means of establishing it; when 318 persons, who are now called the Fathers of the church, attended: And having collected together as many of the gospels, epistles, and sybelline oracles, as could be found, from those who had them in possession, decided by *vote*, that those four gospels, namely, Matthew, Mark, Luke, and John, with the epistles annexed to them, should be received and maintained as the *true word* of God, given by *divine* inspiration. While the others, such as the gospel of the Virgin Mary, the gospel of the Infancy, the gospels of James, Peter, Barjonas, and upwards of thirty others, with the epistles of Barnabas, Clemens, Ignatius Hermes, &c., were thrown under the table as being spurious; although they had been previously received and believed to have been as much the work of *divine* inspiration as the others! This reminds me of a number of criminals, being tried at the Old Bailey, whether they were guilty, or not guilty? Those that were found guilty of fraud, were condemned: and those that were supposed to be innocent were acquitted and suffered to go at large. Hence came Mr. Matthew and his gang!

Now, we know that it is not impossible, but that a majority of Jurymen may condemn an innocent person, under suspicious circumstances; and acquit a guilty person upon favourable evidence. Therefore, those "fathers of the Church," being but men, might have been misled by their judgment, through false evidences or appearances, the natural consequence of their fallibility. Though I must confess, that it appears strange, yea "passing strange," to me, that the words of a GOD should be left to the judgment of those men whom we find to have been the most ignorant and superstitious of all mortals: the Creed of St. Athanasius, who was one of those judges of the word of God, being a proof. This Creed passes sentence of "God's wrath, and everlasting damnation" on all those whom *we* "deem God's

foes." Well might Archbishop Tilletson wish *we* were
" rid of it !"

And what good effect had this religion upon the
habits and morals of Constantine ? Did it influence his
actions and change his evil disposition ? No ; certainly
not. Why should it ? The promise of pardon, with all
the blessings attending, were only given to the most
guilty and depraved. The honest, just, upright, and
charitable man was rejected ;[65] even were there ninety-
nine righteous persons out of every hundred, they were
not thought worthy of notice equal to the guilty wretch.
So that Constantine, after he was baptized, and professed to believe in this book, had a greater stimulus to
pursue his evil and vicious propensities, than before ; in
order that he might be found worthy of the notice of
heaven, and entitled to share its favours. Therefore,
being at that time jealous of his own son, Crispus, in
consequence of the good report which he had obtained,
by his amiable qualities, so opposite to those of his
father, among the people, over whom he was appointed
governor, he had him secretly murdered ; because he
found, no doubt, that the shedding of blood was the
first step to an acquaintance with this God. Witness
Abel, who obtained the preference to his brother, by
shedding the blood of the firstlings of his flock ;[66]
whereas Cain offered nothing but dry roots wherein
was no blood; consequently, could produce no sweet
smelling savour for this God of blood.[67] Abraham,
also, whose good will, to shed the blood of his only son,
was accepted for the deed. Then Moses, before this
God would speak to him, must first shed the blood of
an Egyptian. Phinehas, the son of Eleazer, won the
favour of this God, only, by shedding the blood of a
man and woman,[68] while they were fulfilling the first
command, given by this God, to his creatures. (Gen.
i. 28.) In short, every man who was favoured and
protected by this God, were all " men of blood !" such
as Joshua, Ehud, Samson, David, Samuel, Solomon, &c.
and, whenever a woman could dispense with those
tender and delicate feelings, so natural to their sex, and
adopt the ferocity of a monster, like Jael, who could

drive a nail through the temples of a man, and after-wards cut off his head, she was sure to be "blessed above all women."[69] At last, his only son, finding that nothing would satisfy his father but BLOOD! BLOOD! BLOOD! volunteered to keep a "fountain" continually open for him; wherein he might revel at his pleasure.

Constantine having now become a candidate for heaven, by the murder of his own son, in imitation of his God; and having his government also strengthened, by the aid of a religion, which taught the people to submit themselves to the "powers that be," they being ordained by God,[70] became more intolerant and despotic than ever. We find that the people were continually oppressed by enormous taxes, raised merely for the sole purpose of enabling him to build those splendid and pompous palaces, for himself and his favourite clergy; unto whom his prodigality became excessive. Dr. Lardner, in endeavouring to extenuate his faults, says, that "we should be willing to make allowances in favour of princes, and especially of long reigns." What allowances need be made for princes, if the "powers that be," are ordained by God? Is not the heart of a king, in the hand of God, who turneth it whithersoever he will?[71] Surely, then, whatever Constantine did, must have been agreeable to the will of God, who worketh in us, to do of his good will and pleasure,[72] and consequently needs no excuse. But, if allowances are to be made in favour of princes, who, during a reign of thirty years, are amply provided with every thing necessary to render their own lives happy, and oppor-tunities of alleviating the sufferings of their fellow-creatures, yet, instead thereof, oppress, afflict, and aggravate their sufferings, what allowances should be made in favour of that poor distressed mortal who, destitute of the common necessaries of life, endeavours to support his starving family by some dishonest action? A temptation from which princes are wholly exempted.

A state religion, once established, we may reasonably conclude, would soon influence many to accord there-with. So it occurred here. Those who had been the most strenuous opponents, now became its most zealous defenders; and nothing could equal the intolerant spirit manifested by those state-protected Christians, when they destroyed their former idols; razed their temples and persecuted their Pagan priests; which conduct the priests of the present day commend, as being agreeable to the will of their God. But when Julian, the nephew of Constantine, came to the throne, he acted in a more liberal and charitable manner, by giving free toleration to all religions; which conduct has drawn upon him, by those same priests, the appellation of an "Apostate, and the enemy of all that was good." Yet they acknowledge that he was "chaste, temperate, learned, and vigilant, wearing the appearance of piety and devotion." But, as it was not under a Christian form, they have denounced him as being "witty, wicked, and hypocritical." How can a man be an hypocrite, if he openly and publicly denies what he does not believe? They only are hypocrites who profess to believe what they do not. He was called an apostate, because he would not employ nor sanction the same intolerant spirit, like his uncle, but countenanced all religions—whether Jewish, Pagan, or Christian, and persecuted none. He only prohibited those seminaries of vice, called Christian Schools; which, under the cloak of piety, had been instituted in the reign of Constantine; and which were, and are still, in the present day, the nurseries for every kind of vice and immorality. For proof, search the brothels, the taverns, and gaming-houses, of Oxford and Cambridge.

He was also called witty and profane, because he wrote, they say, many puns and sarcasms on the Christian religion; which, if he had not had good ground to build his puns upon, he could never have ridiculed it in the manner they have described. Indeed, all the persecutions which the Christians had suffered, prior to his day, must have arisen through the views which their persecutors had of the evil tendency of their doctrines, which taught men to make themselves eunuchs, for the kingdom of heaven's sake,[73] it being not good for a man to touch a woman,[74] if he could possibly avoid it. They were, likewise, forbidden to swear;[75] consequently, no dependence could be placed upon their allegiance, by which they could be of no more use to the state than the Quakers are to ours, because their weapons of warfare were not carnal, but spiritual;[76] which could be no more serviceable in knocking down ramparts, or sinking men of war, than Mr. Fletcher's *snow-balls* and *sailor's puffs!*

Tacitus informs us, that when this " mischievous sect" was accused of setting fire to the city of Rome, " the confessions of those who were seized discovered a great multitude of their accomplices, and they were all convicted; not so much for the crime of setting fire to the city, as for their hatred of human kind."* This was one of the precepts given by Jesus, when he told them, that if any man who came to him did not hate his father, and mother, and children, and brethren, and sisters, he could not be his disciple.[77] These doctrines, together with their endeavours to overthrow the national and ancient religion of the land, which religion was harmless and inoffensive of itself, as it exacted no tithes from those who did not choose to follow it, were surely quite sufficient to excite the vengeance of both rich and poor towards them.

But how did Christians act themselves when they became possessed of power? Did they adhere to the same precepts which they had endeavoured to inculcate into the minds of their persecutors, such as returning good for evil, and instructing with the spirit of meekness those who had fallen into the snare of the devil? Or were they more patient and gentle to all men[78] than their persecutors had been to them? No; we find them congregating together from all parts, to subdue, with the sword, like Mahomet, all those who would not acquiesce in their creeds. Hence the bloody Crusades, in which upwards of *two millions of precious souls* were inhumanly butchered; and all to no purpose! Surely, if this had been the word of a God, and he a *prayer-answering* God, here was a fine opportunity of giving this word free course; whereby it might have run and

---

* Tacit. Annal. xv, 44.

been glorified. But, no: Mahometanism prevailed, and still prevails, in spite of sword, gunpowder, prayers, or intrigues; covering a greater extent of ground than that which was, long since, to have covered the earth as the waters cover the sea;[79] although founded six hundred years after the supposed time of the invention of the Christian religion!

As an additional proof that these books could not have been written at the time they profess, they speak of things which could not have occurred until after their supposed dates. Paul wrote to different *churches;* which are generally supposed to singify large assemblies of people, in those different towns and cities. Even Jesus himself speaks of a church in his days, that had authority to decide controversies.[80] But, if such churches or assemblies existed among the Jews prior to the destruction of Jerusalem by Titus, would not Josephus, who is very particular in noticing every sect among the Jews, or some other poet or historian, especially Philo or Pliny, have alluded to them, in some way or other, in their writings? For those things could not have been done in a corner, as Mr. Fletcher says; they must have been notorious to the whole empire, by their having consecrated bishops. There is no proof, I grant, that Theophilus, to whom Luke wrote his gospel, was a bishop; but if you suppose that he was, there was no bishop of that name until the middle of the second century. Whoever he was, it is evident that the gospel by Luke could not have been written until after many others had been not only written, but circulated among the people, by the manner in which he addresses Theophilus. He begins by saying, " Forasmuch as *many* have taken in hand to set forth in order a declaration of those things which are most surely believed among us, even as they delivered them unto us; which from the beginning were eye-witnesses and ministers of the word: It seemeth good to me also, having had perfect understanding of all things from the very first, to write unto thee in order, most excellent Theophilus." This evidently implies, that many persons had formerly written and preached those things before he took it in hand; which writings he certainly must have considered as being imperfect, or why should he presume, much more take all that trouble, to write them over again especially with so many variations? He not only contradicts many of their statements, but he actually differs from Matthew respecting the person of this Jesus. By his account, Jesus was the grandson of Heli, descended from Nathan the son of David, and brought up in Gallilee; whereas, Matthew says that Jesus was the grandson of Jacob, who descended from Solomon, the son of David, and brought up in Egypt. Moreover, by his address to Theophilus, it appears plainly that Luke himself was not an eye-witness or minister of the word, as were the many to whom he alludes.

Matthew, also, when relating the story of the Watch,[80] says, that "this saying is commonly reported among the Jews until this day." Yet Philo, nor Josephus, who were both Jews, knew nothing of this saying, any more than they did of the field of blood, which Matthew says, was called unto this day,[81] or surely they would have noticed it, if it had been known, as it is written, unto all the dwellers at Jerusalem.[82] Besides, how could Jesus have been cotemporary with John, called the Baptist, when Jesus says, that "from the days of John the Baptist, until now, the kingdom of heaven suffereth violence?"[83]

It may be said by some persons, indifferent to truth or falsehood—Well, what matters it when these books were written? they are written: that is evident; and if not written in the first, let them be dated from the second century. To this I reply, that it matters a great deal; for if those books were not written prior to the destruction of Jerusalem, in the year 70, A. D., it proves their imposition in relating things, as predictions, which were not written until after their accomplishment; for instance, the destruction of the temple and the city, foretold, it is written, by Jesus. This discovered, destroys likewise the credibility of those things said to have been done and written in the reigns of Tiberius and Nero. What dependence could be placed in the writings

of any man who should attempt to write an account of
the life and transactions of some obscure individual,
who might have lived one hundred years back, unless
we were assured that he had his narrative transmitted
to him down from the individual himself, or from some
eminent historian of the age in which he lived? And
if this individual were such a conspicuous character as
Jesus is represented to have been, who, it is written,
was to be a light to lighten the Gentiles, and the glory
of Israel, [84] is it likely that all the historians of the age
and country in which he lived would neglect to notice
him? Yet, this is the case with all those who lived in
the first century, the supposed age in which Jesus lived.
Moreover, if those books are proved to have been
written in that age, called the second century, and the
authors detected in antedating them to an age, in which
it is found to be impossible that the persons alluded to
therein could have lived and acted in the manner
described, without being noticed by some historian of
the age, these things not being done in a corner, it
proves the whole history to be a fictitious tale.

You may, probably, inquire—Whence came those
Christians who were found by Pliny in the second
century? They must have had their origin in some
country, and in some age, prior to his discovery. This
I will admit; but this will not prove that they had
those gospels and epistles written in his days; but, on
the contrary. For we may be well assured, that these
would have been the first and most important of all
things for him to have seized, if he wished to put down
the sect; instead of which, he does not so much as
notice a single book belonging to them.

If we refer to this book itself for their origin we shall
find that they were originally Jews; who, being disgusted with the Jewish religion, in consequence of its
absurdities and painful rites and ceremonies, which they
said were a yoke too heavy for them to bear, [85] embraced
the doctrines of Plato, an eminent Philosopher, who
flourished about 350 years before the Christian era is
dated; in the same manner as the Protestants sprang
from the Catholics, and the various sects again from

the Protestants. For the Jews were no more unani-
mous in their religion than any other nation. All
have a variety of sects; because religion itself is
only a phantom of the mind; consequently, no settled
nor universal opinion of it can be had. It is unlike the
generality of things which are substantial, and may
be demonstrated to the mind of man; such as fire,
water, &c., concerning the nature of which no man
differs from another. All agree that fire produces
heat, and water will form its own level; and particular
modes of religion, which is a nonentity or ideal thing,
cannot be universally received, unless all men are organized alike, and possessed of the same mental faculties.

The Jews, we find, had many sects among them at
the time when those books were professedly written,
notwithstanding the many promises which they say had
been given to them 700 years before that they should
all have one heart and one way.[86]   There were the
Pharisees, the Sadducees, the Herodians, the Galileans,
the Libertines,[87] the Nazarenes, and many others,
mentioned by Josephus, but not recorded in the Jew
Bible.   Those persons, called Christians, to whom
Pliny alluded, evidently sprang from that sect which
had formerly been called Nazarenes,[88] but had adopted
the name of Christians at Antioch, in Greece.[89] I
have already shewn you, in my first letter, that the
word Christ is derived from the Greek word, Christos,
a titular name of honour bestowed by the Greeks on
some or any particular celebrated character; consequently, Jesus could never have been called the Christ
in Judea, prior to the change of Nazarenes to Christians at Antioch, Christ not being a Jewish name.

These Nazarenes, no doubt, took their name from
either the name of their place of residence, where some
popular preacher of their sect resided; like the Wesley-
ans, who derive their name from Wesley, their preacher;
or the Moravians, from Moravia, where they first originated; or like many others, in a similar manner. Jesus
we are told, was born in Bethlehem; but he was called
Jesus of Nazareth,[90] a place distant 60 miles from
Bethlehem.   Whence it appears from this book, that

the Nazarenes derived their name from this Jesus of Nazareth, who, no doubt, was some popular preacher among those of his own persuasion, and who also might have been the first public preacher of this new doctrine, like Johanna Southcote was among those of her followers.

Although we admit thus far, that such a man as this, named Jesus, might have lived and preached in Nazareth a different doctrine from the other sects, having certain rites and ceremonies, perhaps peculiar to himself and followers, yet there is no evidence that he said and did those incredible and extraordinary things which are ascribed to him. If some person in the present day, or in after ages, were to write the life of Johanna Southcote, saying therein that she had fed 5,000 men, besides women and children, in Hyde Park, with only 5 loaves and two little fishes, besides going through every city, town, and village in England, raising dead persons to life, and curing all manner of sicknesses, would this said book, itself, be sufficient authority for persons in after ages to believe that those things were actually done, unless they were corroborated by the writings of other historians? Even should they discover in the History of England, or in any other book, that such a person as Johanna Southcote did exist, unless it spoke of those strange and wonderful things, which the narrator of her own history might relate as having been done by her, would they be justified in placing implicit confidence in it themselves? No surely; much less to enforce a belief in others. It being natural for men to expect that when a national historian, in particular, is writing of the times in which he is living, he will give an account of every remarkable occurrence that concerns the nation; especially of such unnatural and extraordinary things, as those supposed to have been done by Jesus.

In process of time these Nazarenes, called Christians. increased in number like every other sect: for what sect, however absurd and ridiculous, but will soon gain some proselytes? Witness the Swedenborgians, Ranters, &c. While they were thus scattered about in this state, they were noticed by Pliny in consequence of their private meetings, contrary to his edict, which I have already noticed. But no Gospel or Epistle was ever written before the days of Pliny; which is fully manifested by his silence. The question now is, when were they written? This cannot be precisely answered as we have no precise date; but of this we may be assured, that they were not written before the days of Pliny, in the reign of Trajan, 110, A. D.

As there is scarcely any one sect but what has had some clever or ingenious advocate among them, possessing greater abilities than his fellows, why should we not give the same honour to the sect of Christians? After the days of Pliny we find that there were several men, such as Ignatius, Clemens, Barnabas, and many others, who all wrote gospels and epistles, some of which are now extant in the present day: and which also were believed by the ignorant and superstitious to have been written, under the immediate superintendence of God, by those men; and were received as the pure word of God until the Synod, assembled in the reign of Constantine, rejected them as being superfluous and containing rather too many absurdities. There is not the least doubt but that those men took the ground work of their plot from the Jewish history of Moses, by new-modelling his life to shape one for Jesus of a less violent and offensive nature, which I shall probably endeavour to prove hereafter. They also, at the same time, endeavoured to regulate his life and actions in such order, that they might have some appearance of application to the actions and writings of the Jew poets, whom we have since called prophets;* by which means they were easily construed into prophecies, by illiterate and weak-minded persons; but a careful examination of them will soon convince any sensible man of the imposition. These men, writing of an individual, who had lived and died perhaps one hundred years before any of that age were in existence, could write whatever their fancy dictated concerning the individual;

---

* Paul called himself an heathen poet, a prophet. (Titus, i. 12)

there being no one living to refute them. And among such a multitude of ignorant persons, without books or learning, it was surely very easy to obtain some credit, and gain proselytes; even should a man have said that he had found an old book or manuscript, in some old ruinous house, in which he might have been rummaging, as Hilkiah did; when he said, that he had *found* the book of the law of the lord, while he was clearing of the house! [9] [1] Whenever I read this passage, I cannot help thinking, what a careless God this was of the Jews, to suffer his law to lie mouldering away in an obscure corner for so many years, when it had been so often wanted. Why did he not give Isaiah, Hezekiah, or some other of those holy men, information thereof? or did he not himself know where it had been put? And is it not, moreover, strange, that those sacrilegious Kings, who so often pillaged the house of the Lord, never met with it in their researches? especially, as we are told, that this law was written on two tables of stone, and deposited in the ark, by Solomon, which could not have been put in an obscure corner. [9] [2]

Thus, we have traced the origin of the Christians, who, according to these books, were originally called Nazarenes, a Jewish sect; so called from their founder, a man named Jesus, residing in the city of Nazareth, admitting the account given of him in these books to be so far correct, of which there is not the least shadow of proof. This Jesus probably possessed more abilities than his ignorant neighbours; having read, most likely, some of the writings of Plato, the Grecian philosopher, and imbibed his notions, and then taught them to his countrymen, some of whom, upon his recommendation, believed in this Platonic doctrine; till at length they formed companies among themselves to discuss the subject, and adopt ways and means of rendering themselves notorious, in order to obtain more proselytes. This was done by substituting baptism for circumcision; which was more agreeable and less painful to the nature of man than that of circumcision. In this manner they lived, no doubt, as a despised sect by the rest of the Jews, from whom they had seceded, till Pliny brought them into notice by his convicting some of them of malpractices, as soon as they began to increase in number. Some of them, such as Ignatius, Clemens, Barnabas, and others who assumed the name of Matthew, Mark, Luke, John, Paul, Peter, &c., conceiving that a plausible reason should be given for the hope that was in them,[93] undertook to write a marvellous history of the man who, they supposed, first founded their sect; having his name and residence perhaps handed down to them by tradition. After one was written another copied it, making what alterations he considered necessary. This accounts for the various readings in Matthew, Mark, Luke, and John; which names, whether real or fictitious, can be of no consequence to us. It is evident that they did not exist, nor write those books, in the age to which they allude. It being clear and obvious to every man acquainted with history that they lived after the reign of Trajan, and wrote of things which they said were done in the reign of Tiberius. A true statement of those things they likewise considered was not altogether absolutely necessary; for if the truth of God abounded more through a lie than otherwise, they considered that they would not be judged as sinners.[94] They, therefore, forbade any man, even the angels of heaven, to preach or teach anything else but what they themselves had written,[95] anticipating that the time was but short when those who wrote would be as those who wrote not;[96] consequently, no time was to be lost in disputing about foolish and unlearned questions, which only engendered strife and shipwrecked faith;[97] well knowing that sensible men would scoff and laugh at those sayings and doings of whom they bade them beware.[98] Thus they prevented their adherents from examining into the truth or falsehood of their writings, till at length they became firmly established under the protection of Constantine. Whether such a "made up story" deserves more credit than the story of Robinson Crusoe, I will now leave to your consideration and judgment.

Before I conclude this letter, I will make a few

observations on the tale of feeding 5000 men, by Jesus, with a few loaves and fishes, as Mr. Fletcher has advanced this as an undoubted proof of his divine power and mission : it being so notorious, he says, that it was impossible for it to have escaped detection by one or other of this great multitude, if it were an imposition or trick of art.

This miracle is related by Matthew, as having been repeated by Jesus. The first time, he says, Jesus fed 5000 men, besides women and children,[99] which, we may naturally conclude, made up a total number of 10,000 persons. The next time, he says, there were but 4000 men, beside women and children,[100] which may likewise be reckoned as being equal to 8000 persons : this latter circumstance Mark acknowledges, with this difference, that instead of 4000, beside women and children, there were but 4000 in all.[101] In another passage, he refers to the feeding of 5000, but does not record the transaction nor mention the women and children.[102] Luke and John, both differ from Matthew and Mark, as they speak of the 5000 men only, with the exception of the women and children,[103] but say nothing of the 4000. What strange and unaccountable contradictions in a notorious and public action, of which they all profess to have been eye-witnesses !

In the first place, let us inquire what could have induced so many thousands of men, women, and children to ramble after Jesus in a place wherein, if we had not already been informed, we might very naturally suppose, dwelt wild beasts, or some noxious and offensive reptiles which inhabit every desert place in those countries. Again, how far was this desert place from their habitations, that should cause the 4000, besides women and children, of whom both Matthew and Mark speak, to continue with him for three days together? Or with what could they be employed, day and night, during those three days in a wilderness, fasting and fainting? It could not have been to hear him preach, for John says that whenever he attempted to speak or preach to them they became so exasperated

that nothing less than stoning him would satisfy them.
Besides, as he was continually going about in their
streets and cities, preaching and healing all manner of
sicknesses, what need had they to leave their houses
and employment to follow him into a desert place,
much less to carry out their sick, exposed to the
elements, up into a mountain to him? Neither can I
imagine where such continued numbers of sick, lame,
blind, and diseased persons could come from, if he made
perfect cures of all he took in hand. It certainly
implies that the Jews were either a very imperfect race
of beings for God's chosen people, or that Jesus was
not a proficient in his business. For, wherever he
went, although he had been oftentimes before in the
same place, and cured such prodigious numbers, even
all that were sick, still there were multitudes always
brought to him again. And notwithstanding his fame
was noised about in every city, yet Peter and John,
shortly after his decease, could find more multitudes of
sick persons round about Jerusalem that required
healing;[104] one of them, we are told in particular,
that had been lame from his mother's womb.[105] Why
was not this man brought to Jesus during all this time?
Or how could Jesus teach daily in the temple,[106]
without seeing this man who was laid daily at the gate
of the temple? All which convinces me that Jesus
was no better than a Quack, or surely some of the
professional gentlemen among the Jews would have
entered a protest against him if they had found
their interest anywise affected by his practice.

However, it appears, that those 4000 men, besides
women and children, staid with him three days, during
which time they had nothing to eat. Could not some
of the men have gone to the neighbouring towns and
cities, and have purchased some necessaries for themselves and families instead of keeping them fainting and
famishing in that desert place during the space of three
days? Though one would think that there would
have been some chapman, vintner, apple, or ginger-
bread woman, that would have jumped at the opportunity of supplying such a multitude of men, women, and

children, with their commodities. Besides, how did they all sleep together during those three days? Surely it would be unnatural for us to suppose, that such a multitude of men, women, and children, should continue such a length of time, without taking their natural rest, especially during the nights. Did they all huddle together, higgledy-piggledy? or were they likewise portioned out to sleep together in companies of fifties, as when they were sorted out for feeding?

Matthew says, that Jesus had compassion on the multitude, because they had been with him three days, and had had nothing to eat. Would he not have shewn more compassion, if he had fed them, in that extraordinary manner, on the first day, instead of keeping them three days without food? Or even if he had sent them to the neighbouring towns and cities, to lodge and refresh themselves, during the night season, supposing that he did not choose to quit the desert place himself, I think it would have evinced more compassion in him, and been much more to his credit. Therefore, instead of ascribing this action of Jesus to any benevolent feelings, I consider it as the effect of a hard-hearted and cruel disposition, or he never would have kept them from food and rest all that time; especially the poor children, when he could have supplied them with bread and fish so cheap and expeditious. But if you take notice, the sequel of the story shews, that his own party were not without food during those three days; for they had left among them, on the third day, no less than seven loaves, besides a few little fishes!

Mark mentions only *one* person that was brought to him for healing, while in this desert place, who was both deaf and dumb,[107] instead of all this *multitude* of which Matthew speaks; whom, after he had cured, he charged strictly, that he should tell no man thereof. Why should he wish this to be kept a secret, if he did those things that the people might believe? If he, unlike those who publish abroad their abilities for interest, were not interested in it, still, his compassion for the afflicted might have induced him to charge the man to proclaim it on the house-tops, that those who were in the same predicament might have come to him and been healed in the like manner. But by telling him to keep it a secret from the rest of the world, he displayed an ill-natured and selfish disposition, contrary to his own injunction to his followers, when he bid them let their light so shine before men, that they might see their good works, and glorify their God.[108] Yet, behold! how inconsistent is this command with what follows. In the sight of this great multitude, he immediately after performs a much more wonderful and stupendous miracle! Surely, if he were so mistrustful and fearful of one man making known his power, he never would have committed himself to so many thousands. Jesus promised that if men had but faith as a grain of mustard-seed, they might do greater miracles than ever he did.[109] What a pity it is that our *Archbishops* and priests have not so much as half a grain among them all; if they had, surely they would not suffer so many poor creatures, who, they say, have all immortal souls, to languish, pine away, and expire, through lack of a little bread and fish, at the gates of their splendid and pompous palaces and mansions, as is now often the case, through lack of this faith and food!

John says, that when Jesus fed the 5000, they got the loaves and fishes from a lad that was present. Whence, it appears, that those persons could not have been fainting, like the others, through lack of food, or they would never have suffered a lad to retain five barley loaves and two fishes among them unsold, supposing them all so honest as to keep from plunder. We are not told whether those fishes were ready dressed or not; but still we are led to inquire, what could have drawn this boy into a desert place with those loaves and fishes? If he did not attend there for the express purpose of selling them, we have a right to conclude that he was neglecting his master's business; consequently, Jesus was to blame in detaining him there. If he did go there as a chapman, it is strange that he should have been the only one to supply such a multitude.

John, moreover, says, that after they had all eaten and were filled, they wanted to make Jesus a King,[110] when Jesus, in order to avoid this indignity, retired into a mountain himself alone, while his disciples were rowing in a boat at sea. Luke, although he speaks of this circumstance, namely, the feeding of 5000, yet says[3] nothing about the lad, or the affront that was offered to Jesus; and that, instead of his disciples toiling in a boat at sea, while he was alone on the mountain, they were with him, asking him certain questions.[1] Matthew differs from John concerning the lad and the treason; and from Luke, respecting the situation of his disciples.

This miracle, I find, then, like the rest, destroys its own credibility, if carefully examined. There is nothing contained therein, worthy a good and benevolent being to interest himself with; or what might not have been done much better. Surely, you must acknowledge, that it would have been far better, if he had fed this multitude on the first day, instead of keeping them fasting and fainting till the third day. Also, that it would have shewn more compassion, if he had gone to their streets and cities, and done his charitable deeds, instead of seducing them, with their families, from their homes and occupations. But of this, the priests, in all ages, have been aware. Therefore, they tell us, as Victor Antiochenus did those in the fifth century, that whenever we read of such miracles, that appear to be void of truth and justice, we ought not curiously to inquire whether they were justly or wisely done, but contemplate and admire the miracle! This advice might do for those who consider that "ignorance is bliss," and are therefore willing to remain in ignorance: but will not do for those who desire to receive the instruction of wisdom, justice, judgment, and equity.[112]

Having thus taken into consideration the jack-ass story (for it appears that it was a male, by Jesus sending for *him*,) with the fig-tree, and the enormous loaves and fishes, (it being contrary to sense and reason to suppose that they were at all like our common bakers' loaves and herrings,) I will now take my leave of those

Christian "night entertainments," till next month; when it is most likely, if I do not hear from you in the mean time, I shall resume the subject. Till then, I remain,

Your humble Servant,
JOHN CLARKE.

NOTES TO THE FOREGOING LETTER.

1 John xii. 12.
2 Matthew xxi. 1, 2.
3 Mark xi. 1—7.
  Luke xix. 30.
4 John xii. 14.
5 James ii. 10.
6 Deuteronomy xxii. 8.
7 Judges x. 4.
8   „   xii. 14.
9 Numbers xvi. 2—15.
10 Matthew xxi. 4, 5.
11 Ezra vi. 14.
12 Zechariah 1—18.
     „   v. 2—9.
     „   vi. 1, 2.
13   „   vii. 3.
14   „   viii. 8.
15   „   vi. 11—13.
16 John xviii. 36.
17 Luke xix. 39, 40.
18 Genesis xlix. 10—12.
19 John xi. 54.
20 Matthew xxi. 23.
21 Luke xix. 47.
22 John xi. 57.
23   „   xii. 13.
24   „   xi. 18.
25 Matthew xi. 19.
26 Luke xxiv. 42.
27 Exodus xii. 2—6.
28 Luke xxi. 30.
29 Mark xi. 21.
30 Romans xii. 14.
31 James iii. 10.
32 Micah iv. 4.

66 Genesis iv. 4.
67 — viii. 21.
68 Numbers xxv. 8—13.
69 Judges v. 24—26.
70 Romans xiii. 1.
71 Proverbs xxi. 1.
72 Phillipians ii. 13.
73 Matthew xix. 12.
74 1 Corinthians vii. 1.
75 Matthew v. 34.
76 2 Timothy ii. 4.
77 Luke xiv. 26.
78 2 Timothy ii. 24—26.
79 Habakkuk ii. 14.
80 Matthew xxvii. 8.
81 „ xxviii. 15.
82 Acts i. 19.
83 Matthew xi. 12.
84 Luke ii. 32.
85 Acts xv. 10.
86 Jeremiah xxxii. 39.
87 Acts vi. 9.
88 „ xxiv. 5.
89 „ xi. 26.
90 John i. 45.

LETTER X.

TO DR. ADAM CLARKE.

Sir,

I feel great pleasure in announcing to you, that this day completes the first of those three years, which the Christian Judge, Newman Knowlys, has allotted me to remain in "durance vile:" and, I trust, that before the other two years have expired, he will be made fully sensible, if he be not already, of the imprudence, as well as of the injustice, of persecuting and consigning to a gloomy prison honest men for matters of opinion. If not, let him beware of the "day of retribution." Think not, Sir, that an honest, undaunted, and injured man, who fears neither death, nor imaginary punishment, will ever submit to bear such wrongs without indulging a hope of REVENGE. It is only this pleasing hope, I do assure you, Sir, that enables me to bear my imprisonment with any degree of fortitude, and stimulates within me a desire to prolong my existence, in this state of wretchedness and misery. Jesus said, *love your enemies;* but as this precept is not observed by his followers, it cannot be expected that I, who am no follower of his, should render to it any obedience. No, Sir, nature forbids it. I must, therefore, declare myself an irreconcileable enemy, not only to Newman Knowlys, my Christian Judge, but likewise to George Maule, my Christian persecutor; he being the known agent of an unknown power. The soldier receives honour and reward for taking away the lives of men who have never done him the least injury. Surely, man will at least be justified, in avenging himself on those who have done him the greatest possible injury that one man can do towards another, namely, unjustly depriving him of his liberty.

v

Had not the pretended believers in those fabulous tales, persecuted me into a prison, I doubt whether you would have been ever troubled with these my observations: a prison being the most convenient place that a *mechanic* can have for propagating his opinions. Hence, the production of almost all those works, which fools and interested men, have proclaimed so obnoxious; they having been either composed or translated within the walls of a prison.

The men who are persecuted, without being convinced, in general you find to be more pertinacious in maintaining their opinions, than those who are treated with contempt. Though neither the one nor the other are proper means to convince them of their error, or to instruct their ignorance. Nothing but fair argument and free discussion can, or ever will, distinguish truth from error. And to quarrel with a man because he does not think as you think, is as ridiculous, as one man wrangling with and ill-treating another, because his opponent is something shorter or taller than himself: neither case being at the discretion, nor under the controul of any man, as I have already shown you in my last letter. Man must think as his own ideas, notions, or sensations, resulting from his peculiar organization compel him.

We find that the age has now arrived, when the minds of men, being expanded, are become more susceptible to the finer feelings of humanity, than to deprive a fellow-creature of the use of pen, ink, and paper; although he may be incarcerated in a dungeon for the most detestable or atrocious crime: which privilege cannot be ascribed to the principles of Christianity, but to the rise and progress of the Arts and Sciences. For, prior to the knowledge and growth of these, when Christianity was in the plentitude of its power, we are informed from authenticated history, that nothing less than burning, or the most excruciating tortures were employed, to compel a man to say he believed in that which his reasoning faculties assured him was false. You may reply, that those cruelties were only practised by that sect of persons called

Catholics, which I acknowledge to be the prevailing opinion. But, have you not read of that monster of blood and sensuality, called Charles the Second? whose restoration to the crown of England, is commemorated every year by public thanksgivings, prayers, and tokens of rejoicing among the Protestant priests. He had the cruelty, as well as the ingratitude to oppress, and persecute, not only to a prison, but to the most cruel deaths, those men you call Catholics: notwithstanding the many obligations he was under to them, for preserving his life at the hazard of their own, during his concealment. Look at the fate of Edward Coleman, Ireland, Pickering, Grove, &c., who were led to an ignominious death, merely because they were *Papists*. And many others were charged with some fictitious crime or other, by the emissaries of this *Protestant monarch*; and, notwithstanding the palpable falsehoods of their accusers, and the undeniable evidence of their innocence, yet, because they were *Papists*, no law nor justice could they obtain; suffer they must. Witness the fate of Hill, Green, Berry, Whitbread, and a number of others, who suffered the most cruel deaths, in the reign of this Protestant monster.

That you may not think that I have no just ground for charging the Protestants with such cruelties towards the Catholics, I will take the liberty of digressing a little from the life of Jesus, by inserting a note which Samuel Butler, who was a contemporary of K. Charles II, has introduced into his historical Memoirs of the English Catholics; from Dr. Challoner's Memoirs of Missionary Priests, vol. xi. page 215, and which was copied into the *Dorset County Chronicle*, of May 19, 1825, as follows:—

" This note contains the account of a martydom that took place near the town of Dorchester, in the reign of Charles II.; a martyrdom that, in the horrors of cruelty outhorrors all the horrible executions which the lying Fox has recorded, to disgrace the Catholic religion, and equals, if not surpasses, the blood-chilling tortures inflicted by the Pagan tyrants of Rome, on the Primitive Saints of the most High God.

"Mr. Green, a secular clergyman, had laboured in the English mission for many years, his residence being at Chediock, in Dorsetshire, the seat of Lady Arundel. When King Charles sent forth his proclamation, commanding all priests to depart the nation by a certain day, at their utmost peril, Mr. Green took a resolution to withdraw upon this occasion as many others had done. The lady of the house opposed the thing, saying it was to no purpose, the time allowed in the proclamation being now elapsed. Mr. Green had not seen the proclamation, but said with some assurance, that there remained two or three days, and therefore he would make the best of his way to Lime, the next sea-port, not doubting but he had yet time sufficient to have the benefit of the proclamation.

"When he came to Lime, and was going on board a vessel bound for France, he was roughly accosted by a custom-house officer, inquiring his name and his business there. Mr. Green very freely told him he was a Catholic priest, and that, as such, he was leaving the kingdom, in obedience to his Majesty's late proclamation. The officer answered that he was mistaken in his account, the day fixed in the proclamation for the departure of the priests and jesuits being already past; and therefore he was not to be allowed the benefit of the proclamation; and as he had owned himself a priest in his hearing, he must be had before a justice of the peace. Accordingly a constable was called, and Mr. Green was carried before a justice; and notwithstanding his pleading his good intentions of obeying the king's orders, and that he hoped where the mistake was only of two or three days, advantage would not be taken of his unwary but candid discovery of his character, to the endangering of his life, he was by the justice committed to Dorchester gaol; and after five months' imprisonment, was tried and condemned to die, as in cases of high treason, barely for being a priest." The following account of his martyrdom is copied from Mrs. Elizabeth Willoughby's MSS. who was an eye-witness:

"Upon Wednesday before, the sentence of death being given against him by Judge Forester, he said,

Sit nomen Domini Jesu benedictum in secula. (May the name of the Lord Jesus be for ever blessed.) He should have died upon Thursday, and to that end the furze was carried to the hill, to make the fire, and a great multitude of people were in the streets, and at the gate and lanes, to see the execution; but our great martyr did desire to die on Friday; the which was, by a friend of his, procured of the sheriff, though with very much difficulty, being opposed by Millard, the master-keeper. And it was noted that after his sentence, he never went to bed, and ate but very little, scarce enough to sustain nature; yet was he very cheerful and full of courage to the last. * * *
Much admired was his devotion. He, kneeling on the hurdle, made his prayer, and kissed it before he laid down upon it, and continued his prayers until he came to the place of execution. Then he was taken from the hurdle, and stayed on the hill, a good distance from the gallows, until three poor women were hanged. * * * * Now is our martyr brought to the foot of the ladder by the sheriff, where, falling upon his knees, he remained in devout prayer about half an hour. Then he took his crucifix and *agnus dei* from his neck, and gave them to this devout gentlewoman, my assistant in this relation; and his beads he gave to another; also he gave the master-keeper his handkerchief; and last of all to me, most unworthy, he gave his book of litanies, &c.; also from the gallows he threw me down his band, spectacles, and priest's girdle. Then turning himself to the people, and blessing himself with the sign of the cross he began."—[the writer relates at some length the substance of his speech, and the conclusion of it in the following words]:—

'I am brought hither for a priest and a traitor; that I am a priest I have confessed, and as such, I thought to have left this my country, in obedience to his Majesty's proclamation. I went to receive that benefit for my passage, but was refused, and taken upon pretence of my being some few days past beyond the limitation of the aforesaid proclamation, and brought to Dorchester prison; and am now for no other cause, I thank God, than for being a priest, to die, and not for any treason to my king or country. For I protest before Almighty God, I never wished hurt to my king or country in my life; but I prayed for his Majesty; and every day in my memento at the holy mass, I offered and remembered him to God. But there were laws made in Queen Elizabeth's days, by which it was made treason to be a priest. By this law I am condemned for a traitor; but surely the ancient laws of this kingdom would never have done it as the modern doth. And now judge you, whether the laws so lately made by men be sufficient to overthrow the authority of God's Church, and to condemn the professors of it? Nevertheless, I forgive all the world from my heart, and those who have had a hand in my death; and I beseech you all, if I have offended you in any thing, that you will every one forgive me. I have not had a purpose to give offence to any of you; and I pray God give you all his grace to seek him, so as you may be made able to attain his mercy and eternal glory.'

"Then he called to me, and desired me to commend him heartily to all his fellow-prisoners, and to all his friends. I told him I would, and that some of them were gone before him, and with joy expected him. Then, on my knees, I humbly begged his benediction; so did five more of ours, and he cheerfully gave us his blessing, making the sign of the holy cross over our heads. Then one Gilbert Loder, an attorney, asked him 'If he did not deserve death, and believe his death to be just?' To which he replied, 'My death is unjust;' so pulling his cap over his face, his hands joined before his breast, in silent prayer, he expected almost half an hour his happy passage, by the turning of the ladder, for not any one would put a hand to turn it, although the sheriff had spoken to many. I heard one bid him do it himself. A length he got a country clown, who presently, with the help of the hangman, (who sat astride on the gallows,) turned the ladder, which being done, he was noted by myself and others, to cross himself three times with his right hand as he hanged; but instantly the hangman was commanded to cut him down with a knife, which the constable held up to him, stuck in a long stick, although I and others did our uttermost to have hindered him. Now the fall which he had from the gallows, not his hanging, did a little astonish him; for that they had willed the hangman to put the knot of the rope at his poll, and not under his ear, as it is usual. The man that was to quarter him, was a timorous, unskilful man, by trade a barber, and his name was Barefoot, whose mother, sisters, and brothers, are devout Catholics; he was so long a dismembering him, that he came to his perfect senses, and sate upright, and took Barefoot by the hand, to show (as I believe,) that he forgave him; but the people pulled him down with a rope, which was about his neck; then did this butcher cut his belly on both sides, and turned the flap upon his breast, which the holy man feeling, put his left hand upon his bowels, and looking on his bloody hand, laid it down by his side; and lifting up his right hand, he crossed himself, saying three times, '*Jesu, Jesu, Jesu, mercy!*' The which, although I am unworthy, I was witness of, for my hand was on his forehead, and many Protestants heard him, and took great notice of it; for all the Catholics were pressed away by the unruly multitude, except myself, who never left him, till his head was severed from his body. While he was thus calling upon Jesus, the butcher did pull a piece of his liver out, instead of his heart, and tumbling his guts out every way to see if his heart were not amongst them; then with his knife, he raked the body of this most blessed martyr,—who even then called on Jesus, and his forehead sweat; then was it cold, and presently again it burned; his eyes, nose, and mouth, ran over with blood and water. His patience was admirable, and when his tongue could no longer pronounce that life-giving name Jesus, his lips moved, and his inward groans gave signs of those lamentable torments which for more than half an hour he suffered. Methought my heart was pulled out of my body to see him in such cruel pains, lifting up his eyes to heaven, and yet not dead: then I could no longer hold, but cried '*Out upon them that did so torment him !'* upon which a devout gentlewoman, understanding he did yet live, went to Cancola the sheriff, who was her uncle's steward, and on her knees besought him to see justice done, and to put him out of his pain, who at her request, commanded to cut off his head; then with a knife, they did cut his throat, and with a cleaver chopped off his head: and so this thrice most blessed martyr died. Then was his heart found and put upon a spear, and showed to the people, and so thrown into the fire, which was on the side of a hill. They say the heart did roll from the fire, and that a woman did take it up and carry it away. This I speak not of my knowledge, but what is here reported to be true ; and it may be very probable, because the hill is steep and uneven, and the heart not thrown as usually, but from the point of a long spear. Then did this gentlewoman and myself go to the sheriff and beg his body, the which he freely gave unto us.

"Now did the devil roar, and his instruments, the blinded Dorcestrians (whom with my soul I deplored) did fret and chafe ; and told the sheriff that he could not dispose of his quarters to Papists, neither should we have them. And truly, I believe, that if we should have offered to carry them away, they would have thrown both the body and us into the fire, for our number was but small, and they many thousands. Their fury did so rage against us, that we were forced to withdraw ourselves, and had I not procured the master-keeper's wife to have gone back with us to the town, they had stoned us or done us worse harm, as I was told by many credible people ; so great is their malice to Catholics ! God in his mercy pardon and convert them ! From the town we sent a shroud by a Protestant woman to wrap his quarters in ; whom it seems God did send to us on purpose to do this last office unto his servant ; for to us all she was a stranger, and lives twelve miles from the town. And when she heard us mourn that not any of us durst appear, she, with a courage, went and saw his quarters put into the shroud, and buried them near to the gallows, although she suffered many affronts from the ungodly multitude, who from ten o'clock in the morning till four in the afternoon, stayed on the hill, and sported themselves at football with his head, and put sticks in his eyes, ears, nose, and mouth, and then they buried it near the body!"

It is now [very probable that you may say, Christianity did not authorize them to act in this outrageous and cruel manner. But, Sir, have you not read, as one instance only, the parable of Jesus, wherein he makes the Nobleman to say,[1] —Bring hither those mine enemies, who would not have me to reign over them and slay them before me,—intimating, by the same parable, that such will be his conduct, when he shall came in glory to judge the nations.[2] And you know that Paul advises and exhorts the Christians to follow Christ in all things. However, as I have alluded to this parable I shall make bold to examine it, according to the statements given of it by Matthew and Luke; for neither Mark nor John make the least mention of such a parable having been spoken by Jesus.

Luke says,[3] that Jesus spake a parable, because he was nigh to Jerusalem, saying, "A certain nobleman went into a far country, to receive for himself a kingdom and to return. And he called his ten servants, and delivered unto them ten pounds, and said unto them, occupy till I come." If such a circumstance as this really never did occur, you must acknowledge that Jesus was telling them lies. But, he says further, "his citizens hated him, and sent a message after him, saying, we will not have this man to reign over us. And when he was returned, he commanded those servants to be called unto him, to whom he had given the money, that he might know how much every man had gained by trading. Then came the first, and said, Lord, thy pound hath gained ten pounds: and he said unto him, Well, thou good servant, because thou hast been faithful in a very little, have thou authority over ten cities. And the second came, saying, Lord, thy pound hath gained five pounds: and he said likewise to him, be thou also over five cities. And another came, saying, Lord, behold, here is thy pound, which I have kept laid up in a napkin; for I feared thee, because thou art an austere man; thou taketh up that thou layedst not down; and reapest that thou didst not sow. And he saith, out of thine own mouth will I judge thee, thou wicked servant; thou knewest that I was an austere man, taking up that I laid not down, and reaping that I did not sow, wherefore then gavest thou not my money into the bank, that at my coming, I might have required mine own with usury. And he said unto them that stood by, take from him the pound, and give it to him that hath ten pounds. For, I say unto you, that unto every one which hath shall be given; and from him that hath not, even that he hath shall be taken away from him. But these mine enemies which would not that I should reign over them, bring hither, and slay them before me." And when Jesus had thus spoken, he went up to Jerusalem, previous to his entry therein upon the jack-ass.

Matthew relates this parable, as having been spoken by Jesus, sometime after his entry into Jerusalem upon the ass, when he drove the buyers and sellers out of the temple.⁴ And instead of the nobleman giving to each of his servants one pound, Matthew says, that he gave unto one five talents; to another two; and to another one talent. That instead of the poor simple, but honest man, laying his money up in a napkin, he went and digged in the earth, and hid his Lord's money; for which, he is doomed, according to Matthew, to be cast into outer darkness, where there would be weeping and gnashing of teeth. But, passing by the discordance, which prevails throughout their several statements, let us examine whether this judgment was consistent with the principles of honour and justice? For Jesus likens this parable to the kingdom of heaven, and his coming to judge the world: consequently, we may expect, that his conduct and decision will be the same as was the nobleman's towards his servants.

If this nobleman's conduct were such as it is described to have been, namely, that of an austere and hard man, taking up that he laid not down, and reaping of that which he did not sow, his citizens were justified in hating him, and saying that they would not have such a man to reign over them; there being no law of nature that could compel a whole nation, perhaps consisting of several millions of human beings, to submit themselves to *one* individual, possessing no greater physical or mental powers than themselves, who would oppress and tyrannize over them. Kings, or Rulers, are, or ought to be, appointed or chosen by the persons over whom they are to rule; excepting in such cases where the people have ocular demonstration that they are appointed by a being superior to themselves in wisdom and understanding : else it would not be just to force any man to exercise authority over another. But instead of this, we find, that there are millions of persons in every nation, who never see the man that rules and governs them; who know not his power, his abilities, nor even his personal form. How can those persons be satisfied, that their ruler is better qualified for this office, than some one among themselves? Besides, how ridiculous must that nation appear, which suffers one individual to rule and govern it against its will? Such low-minded slaves, one would think, were not worthy of being called men, much less *free men!* Yet there are many nations, even in the nineteenth century, which submit to a most degrading rule or custom, because it has been practised and enforced upon their ignoble and ignorant ancestors ; such as the admission of the son, or nearest relative of their ruler, to succeed in the magistracy. We know that many a wise man is father to a foolish child, and many an honest man's son turns out a great rogue. Therefore, this hereditary succession must be contrary to common sense as well as to the laws of nature : for if it be just for the son to succeed to the father's prerogatives in one case, why not admit, with equal justice, this privilege in another? But no; they would call it incest, unnatural, and wicked, if the son were to succeed to his father's prerogatives with his mother. Men do not punish the son for the crimes of their father ; then why should the son be admitted to the same honour of which his father was found worthy, unless his virtues and abilities equally deserve it?

This hereditary succession, is not only inconsistent with the general principle of things, but it is contrary to the will of the Christian's God. For if God ever willed that the son should succeed the father, in the government of any nation, he surely would have enjoined it as a necessary and *ever*-lasting rule among his own peculiar people. Instead thereof, we find that neither the circumcised son of Moses, nor any of his relations, ever succeeded Moses in his official capacity of legislator or leader, but a stranger named Joshua, the son of Nun. Neither did the son of Joshua succeed his father. And among all the Judges who ruled over his chosen people afterwards, not one of their sons succeeded their father. Even when the Lord gave them a King to rule over them, he would not permit Jonathan to succeed Saul his father, although it appears that he was a very good and valiant man. But as soon as they began to admit hereditary succession, so soon did they fall into idolatry; which was first exemplified by Solomon, and afterwards by those that succeeded him.

Besides, if it be just that the son should succeed his father, in ruling over the bodies of men, why not the son of the priest likewise succeed his father in ruling the minds and opinions of men; one requiring equal talent and abilities with the other? But no; this also was never ordained by their God; for though a priest may sometimes have the character of being a good man, yet his son may practice that which is evil; as was the case with Eli and his sons.[5] Neither can we learn that the Apostles or any of the disciples of Jesus, were ever succeeded in their ecclesiastical duties by their children. This hereditary succession, then, cannot be legal; it being contrary to the will of God, as well as injurious to the peace and welfare of the nation. Read the bloody wars of England; in which, millions of human beings have been butchered in consequence of the disturbances created through hereditary succession. So that whenever a ruler betrays his trust, or exercises authority with which he was never empowered, by those he governs, they are justified in saying, that they *will not have this man to reign over them.*

And why should Jesus seem to condemn the conduct of that man, who had so carefully preserved the money of his master? Suppose that this man, like the rest, had put this money out to usury, or traded with it, and some unforeseen misfortune had occurred, like unto that which befel the usurers or money-changers in the temple, whose tables were upset by Jesus and his gang, whereby he might have lost it, would not this austere lord have had more reason to punish him for his breach of trust? Surely he ought to have been commended for insuring the best possible means of rendering to every man his due; not like the rest, who were only anxious about the morrow, *laying up treasures upon earth*,[6] which *thieves* might have sought for and stolen. Besides, how inconsistent is this commendation of those men who put their money out to usury, with his conduct in the temple against the usurers. In this latter place, he is exasperated with them: in the former, he approves of their practice; although David says, that the man is blessed who doth not put out his money to usury.[7] Yet Jesus speaks of this omission, as a crime, deserving the most severe punishment; no less than that of being cast into outer darkness, where there should be weeping and gnashing of teeth.

The conclusion, also, which Jesus has drawn from this parable, is most extraordinary. He says, that to every one that hath shall be given, and he shall have abundance; but from him that hath not, shall be taken away even that which he hath. Setting aside the absurdity of taking away that which a man hath not, it is most unjust to deprive a man of the little he possesses, let it be either in property or knowledge, only because he has but little. If this be just, why should we attempt to instruct the ignorant or relieve the distressed, when their poverty and ignorance are considered such enormous crimes? But the priests say, that his alludes only to the use they make of this little. How can any man make great use of little means? Can a poor ignorant man, instruct his fellow creature, or a beggar relieve the distressed? Yet these appear, to be the duties required by Jesus, according to this

w

saying. The poor must cast their all into the treasury, though it should consist of only two mites; or feed the hungry, clothe the naked, and visit the sick : while the rich, such as Abraham, Solomon, and others, should have presents given to them, and gifts year by year.[8]

This parable, he moreover, likens to the kingdom of heaven; when the son of man shall come to judge the nations, and separate them one from the other, as a shepherd divideth his sheep from the goats; setting the sheep on the right hand and the goats on the left. Then shall he say unto those on his right hand, come ye blessed and inherit the kingdom prepared for you from the foundation of the world; while those that are on his left, he will send into *everlasting punishment!* Whence, it appears, there will be but two separate places for all nations, let their crimes or virtues be whatever they may; which I consider an unjust division: there being many atrocious and abominable characters who believe in Jesus, and all the supposed messengers of God; and many a virtuous man who feeds the hungry, clothes the naked, and visits those who are in prison, yet, believes in neither God, Jesus, angel, nor spirit.

Besides, it is not possible to divide the nations in this manner, consistent with justice; for as Paine says, "the moral world, like the physical world, is composed of numerous degrees of character, running imperceptibly one into the other, in such a manner, that no fixed point of division can be found in either. That point is no where, or it is every where. The world might be divided into two parts numerically, but not as to moral character; therefore, the metaphor of dividing them as sheep and goats are divided, whose difference is marked by their external figures, is absurd. All sheep are still sheep, all goats are still goats; it is their physical nature to be so. But one part of the world are not all good alike, nor the other part all wicked alike. There are some exceedingly good; others exceedingly wicked. There is another description of men, who cannot be ranked with either one or the other. They belong to neither sheep nor goats: and there is still another description of them, who are so very insignificant, both in character and conduct, as not to be worth the trouble of damning or saving, or of raising from the dead."

This, then, is another instance of the intolerant spirit of Jesus, who would slay, or consign to everlasting punishment, all those who would not have him to reign over them; thrusting down Capernaum into hell,[10] and damning all those that could not believe in him[11] whom they had never seen. Even those that did see him, could not believe that he was any being superior to themselves, there being nothing in his countenance more than in any other man, that denoted him a superhuman being; or why should the woman of Samaria treat him with so little respect, when he asked her to give him some water to drink? If he were the express image of the person and brightness of the glory of some being superior to man,[12] he need not to have said unto the woman, "if thou knewest who it is that asketh thee." She surely would have known it, by seeing something extraordinary either in his countenance or his external figure. Even John the Baptist, although he saw the heavens opened, and heard a voice from thence, proclaiming him to the Son of God, yet he was not convinced; or why should he send messengers to him, inquiring whether he was really the *Messiah* or not?[13]

But, as this adventure with the woman of Samaria, is considered a proof of the omniscience of Jesus, by his telling the woman her fortune, let us examine into it, and see whether in consideration thereof, we ought to ascribe this knowledge of past events to a divine attribute, more than the foretelling of future events to which strolling gipsies and judicial astrologers make such pretensions.

John says, that when Jesus was going from Judea to Galilee, he must needs go through Samaria; and when he came to the city called Sychar, he sat down upon a well, because he was wearied with his journey. (What reason could any person have to respect him as being superior to themselves, who was continually subject to the same infirmities of hunger, thirst, and weariness?) And a woman came there to draw water, and Jesus asked her to give him some to drink, when she replied, "How is it that thou, being a Jew, should ask drink of me, who am a woman of Samaria? for the Jews have no dealing with the Samaritans." Yet, in the preceding verse, we are told that his disciples were gone into the city to buy meat! Then Jesus preached to her about some living water that he had got, which, very naturally, set the woman longing for some; therefore, she very civilly asked him to give her some of this living water: but Jesus, instead of granting her request, bade her to go and call her husband. The poor simple woman, astonished at his unintelligible jargon, told him that she had got no husband. Jesus said unto her, thou hast well said, for thou hast had five husbands, and he whom thou hast is not thine husband.[14] If Jesus knew this before, why did he bid her go and call her husband, when he knew she had none? Indeed, it appears by this and many other passages, that he treated adultery with great levity. For we find that even when a woman was brought before him charged with this crime, having been taken in the very act, he first artfully got rid of all her accusers, until he was left alone with her; and although all is not related what took place between him and this woman, yet we find that he acquitted her,[15] contrary to the decree of God; which strictly commanded the Jews to put both the *man* and *woman* to death, who were convicted of this crime.[16] This story carries evidence throughout of its not being fact; for Jesus being no magistrate nor ruler among the Jews, could neither acquit nor condemn any person charged with such a crime; neither would the scribes and pharisees apply to him for his judgment, on a matter of life and death; much less abide by his decision, so contrary to their own law, in letting the guilty woman escape. Neither Matthew, Mark, nor Luke give any account of this adventure.

This then is a proof, the priests say, of the omniscience of Jesus; he being an entire stranger to this woman, could search into the secrets of her heart, and tell her of things past. Really one cannot forbear moaning over the simplicity and credulity of the major portion of mankind. 'In the first place, we have no direct proof that such a person as Jesus ever existed. In the next, if he did, there is no certainty that he ever said those words to the woman, not one of his disciples being present to hear him. Then how should John know what he said? Jesus never wrote any thing himself; and if he had told them of it when they returned from the city, surely Matthew, Mark, or Luke, would have written something concerning such an extraordinary adventure. Besides, how could John tell but that he had pumped it out of her during his conversation, as an artful, strolling gipsy, will sometimes do, when practising on a poor simple thoughtless woman? I will not say that he had any previous knowledge of the circumstances of this woman, though it was not improbable, from his strolling about in all their cities, towns, and villages; but, this I will say, that if Jesus could tell the thoughts of the people, and needed not the information from any one, as John says,[17] he certainly could have known what the people said of himself, without his being obliged to ask that question of his disciples.[18]

And why should Jesus be so forward in acquainting the Samaritans of his Messiahship,[19] when, upon other occasions, he forbids his own countrymen, even charges his own disciples, to tell it to no man?[20] Or why should he even go into Samaria at all with his disciples, after he had given them such strict orders not to enter into any city belonging to the Samaritans?[21] Yet John informs us, that he must needs go there, where he staid two days with them.[22]

If Jesus had obtained any money from the woman, by this fortune-telling trick, I should have certainly declared that he ought to have been punished for it as much as our present fortune-tellers, who impose on the credulity of weak-minded persons. It would, moreover, have been some authority, as a precedent, for priests to squeeze money out of the people for their divinations. For what are priests but fortune-tellers, who pretend to tell the fortune of a man in a future state of existence? But no, as the common saying is,

" give the devil his due." Jesus never seems to covet money. All that he wanted was power: perhaps he thought, that when that was once obtained, money would, as a matter of course, soon follow; which induced him to promise his followers, that they should have houses and lands an hundred fold.[23]

Admitting that this story was even true, I cannot see any thing wonderful in it, to deserve even a supposition that he was gifted with any divine attribute. We know that there have been, and are now, many persons who pretend to tell fortunes, recover stolen property, and bring to light many hidden things of darkness. And many a woman will take her bible oath that she was told the first letter of her husband's name, many years before she had even seen him ! which is, truly, more wonderful than a man merely saying to a woman, thou hast had five husbands; the one relating to past, and the other to future, events.

But there is another thing connected with this story, for which I cannot account; that is, why should his disciples marvel at Jesus talking with a woman ?[24] It could not be, because she was a Samaritan, for they themselves had just been in the city to buy meat of her countrymen. Were they astonished at his condescension to speak to a woman, as though the sex were beneath his notice ? Or was it in consequence of his supposed bashfulness, that made them marvel at his courage in speaking to the sex? They surely were not under any apprehension of his falling into temptation by this whore ; yet one or other of these reasons must certainly have caused his disciples to marvel at his conversation with her. For my own part, I should think, that it was in consequence of his condescension ; because we never find him over complaisant to the female sex; but, on the contrary, he treats them, in general, in a very uncourteous or impolite manner.

When the woman of Canaan,[25] though Mark will have it that she was a Greek,[26] came to him, begging and praying, even worshipping him, entreating him to come and heal her daughter, see in what a surly and disdainful manner he received her : he, for some time, would not answer her a word; and when he did so, it was in no very respectful manner.

Even to his own mother he behaved in the most disrespectful manner: when a boy of twelve years old, he returned her, what would be called in the present day, by most parents, a very saucy answer.[28] At the marriage feast, even before company, he spake to her in the most contemptible manner possible,[29] saying, "Woman, what have I to do with thee?" And several times, while he was strolling about, when she came to look for him, he regarded her not, nor even so much as owned her.[30] If he therefore treated his own mother in such a distant manner, it would have been a matter of surprise, if his disciples had not marvelled at his conversation with this woman, knowing his aversion to the sex. Indeed, his approbation of eunuchs,[31] and his persuading and enticing men to leave their mothers, wives, and sisters, merely to follow him,[32] is sufficient proof of his ungenial disposition towards the female sex.

The next thing that attracts my notice, in this said book of John, is in the chapter following the fortune-telling story, wherein he speaks of a wonderful pool at Bethesda, near the sheep-market in Jerusalem. And as Peter has declared, that they had not followed cunningly devised fables,[33] let us examine this story, and see whether he has spoken the truth or not; agreeable to the doctrine of Paul, who advises us to prove all things, and hold fast that which is good.[34]

It is recorded by John, for no other historian mentions it, that this pool had five porches; wherein lay a great multitude of impotent folk, halt, and withered, waiting for the moving of the water. For an angel went down at a certain season into the pool, and troubled the water; whosoever, then, first, after the troubling of the water, stepped in, was made whole, of whatsoever disease he had. And a certain man was there who had an infirmity thirty and eight years. When Jesus saw him lie, and knew that he had been a long time in that case, he saith unto him, wilt thou be made whole? The impotent man replied, Sir, I have no man, when the water is troubled, to put me into the pool: but while I am coming, another steppeth down before me. Jesus saith unto him, rise, take up thy bed and walk. And immediately the man was made whole.[35]

Now we cannot, in the first place, tell whether the cure of this *impotent* man ought to be considered as miraculous or not, since we are not told what was his infirmity, which is a general name for all distempers. How can we be assured that he was miraculously cured, unless we knew that his disease was incurable by art? which none can have the presumption to affirm, from this statement of the case. Many instances may be given of the infirmities, which in time, especially in old age, wear off, although they may have been of long duration. However, as I find that Woolston has largely commented on this supposed miracle, I will here insert his observations.

He begins by stating, "that this whole story is what our Saviour would call a *camel* of a monstrous size, for absurdities, improbabilities, and incredibilities; which our divines and their implicit followers of these last ages, have swallowed without chewing; whilst they have been straining at gnats in theology, and hesitating at frivolous and indifferent things of the church, which are of no consequence.

"As to Jesus's miracle in this story, which consisted in his healing a man of nobody knows what infirmity, there neither is nor can be proved any thing supernatural in it, or there had been an express description of the disease, without which, it is impossible to say that there was a miraculous cure wrought. As far as one may reasonably guess, this man's infirmity was more laziness than lameness, and Jesus only shamed him out of his pretended illness, by bidding him to take up his stool and walk off, and not lie any longer like a lazy lubber and dissembler among the diseased, who were real objects of pity and compassion: or if he were no dissembler, he was only fancifully sick, and Jesus, by some proper and seasonable talk, touched his heart to his relief; and so, by the help of his own imagination, he was cured and went his way. This is the worst that can be made of this infirm man's case; and the best that can be said of Jesus's power in the cure of him, as will appear, by and bye, upon examination into it. But the other parts of the story, of the healing virtue of the waters upon the descent of an angel into them, is not only void of all good foundation in history, but is a contradiction to common sense and reason, as will be manifest, after an inquiry into the particulars of it.

"St. John was the beloved disciple of our Lord, and I hope he loved his master, or he was worse than an heathen, who loves those who love him. But this story and some others that are peculiar to his gospel; such as Jesus telling the Samaritan woman her fortune: his healing the blind man with eye-salve made of clay and spittle: his turning water into wine for the use of men, who had before well drunk; and his raising Lazarus from the dead, are enough to tempt us to think that he wilfully designed either to blast the reputation of his master, or to try how far the credulity of men, who through blind love were running apace into Christianity, might be imposed on; or he had never related such idle tales, which, had not the priesthood, who should be the philosophical part of mankind, been amply hired into the belief of, would certainly have been rejected with indignation and scorn before now.

"St. John wrote his gospel many years after the other Evangelists: what then should have been his peculiar business? certainly nothing more than to add some remarkable passage of his life, to the honour of Jesus, which they had omitted; and to confirm the truths which they had before reported of him. But, St. John is so far from doing this, that the stories he has particularly added, are not only derogatory to the honour of Jesus, but spoil his fame for a worker of maracles, to which the other Evangelists would raise him. By reading the other Evangelists, one would think that Jesus was a healer of all manner of diseases, however incurable by art or nature; and that, wherever he came, all the sick and the maimed (excepting a few infidels) were perfectly cured by him. But this story before us will be like a demonstration, that Jesus was

no such worker of miracles and healer of diseases, as
he is commonly believed to have been; and that he
wrought not near the number of cures he is supposed to
have done, much less any greater ones. The best conception that an impartial reader of the gospel can form
of Jesus, is, that he was a good natured *Orator*, and
could handsomely harangue the people off hand, and
was according to the philosophy of the times, a good
Cabalist: his admirers finding him endowed with the
gifts of utterance, which was thought by them more
than human, they fancied, that he must have the gift
of healing too, so would have him to exercise it; which
he did with success, working upon the fanciful imaginations of many, who magnified his divine power for it. The
apostles afterwards, to help forward the credulity and
delusions of the people, amplified his fame with extravagant assertions, and strange stories of miracles passing the belief of all considerate men. Whether this
representation of the case, according to the letter of
the gospels, be false and improbable, let my readers
judge by the story before us, which I come now to
dissect, and make a particular examination of its several parts. *First.*—Let it be observed, that this story of
the pool of Bethesda, abstractedly considered from the
cure of an infirm man at it by Jesus, has no good foundation in history: it merits no man's credit, nor will
any reasonable person give any heed to it. St. John
is the only author that has made any mention of this
story; and though his authority may be good, and
better than another man's, in relation to the words
and actions of Jesus, inasmuch, as he was most familiar
and conversant with him, yet, for foreign matters that
have no immediate respect to the life of Jesus, he is no
more to be regarded than any other historian; who, if
he palm upon his readers, an improbable tale of senseless and absurd circumstances, will have his authority
questioned, and his story pryed into, by the rules of
criticism, and rejected or received, as it is found worthy
of belief and credit. If there had been any truth in
this story before us, I cannot think but that Josephus,
or some other Jewish writer, would have spoken of it;

as it is an instance so remarkable, and peculiarly astonishing, of the angelical care and love of the distressed of Jerusalem.

"Josephus has, professedly, written the history of the Jewish nation, in which he seems to omit nothing that makes for the honour of his country, or for the manifestation of the providence of God over it. He tells us of the conversation of angels with the patriarchs and prophets, and intermixes extra-scriptural traditions, as he thought them fit to be transmitted to posterity. How came he then, and all other *Jewish* writers, to forget this story of the *pool of Bethesda?* I think we may as well suppose, that the writer of the natural history of Somersetshire, would neglect to speak of the medicinal waters of Bath, as that Josephus should omit that story, which, if true, was a singular proof of God's distinguishing care of his peculiar people, or an angel had never been so frequently sent, as we suppose, to the relief of the diseased among them.

"Is then St. John's single authority enough to convey this story down to us, without the assistance of another to corroborate it? Some may say, that there are several prodigies, as well as political events of ancient times, which, though they are reported but by one historian, meet with credit, and why may not St. John's testimony be equal to another writer's? I grant it; and though it is hardly probable but that this story, if true, before us, must have had the fortune to be told by others, yet, St. John's single authority shall pass sooner than another man's, if the matter be in itself credible and well circumstanced. But where it is blindly, imperfectly, and with monstrously incredible circumstances, related, like this before us, it ought to be rejected.

"*Secondly.*—What was the true occasion of the angel's descent into this pool? was it to wash and bathe himself? or was it to impart an healing quality to the waters for some one diseased person? The reason that I ask the first of these two questions, is, because some ancient readings of *verse* 4, say,* the angel ELOUETO, was washed; which supposes some bodily defilement or

---

* Vid. Milli. Nov. Test. *In Loc.*

heat contracted in the celestial regions, that wanted refrigerating or purgating in these waters : but how absurd is such a thought, needs no proof. To impart, then, compassionately, an healing power to the waters, for the benefit of the diseased, was the sole design of the angel's descent into them. And God forbid that any should philosophically debate the matter, and inquire, how naturally the waters derived that virtue from the angel's corporeal presence. The thing was providential and miraculous, our divines will say, so let it pass. But, I may fairly ask, why one diseased person only at a time reaped the benefit? or why the whole number of impotent folk were not at once healed? I wish our divines would give a satisfactory answer to these questions; and, when their hands are in, I wish that, for the sake of orthodoxy, they would determine whether the angel descended with his head or his heels foremost, or whether he might not come swap upon his breast into the waters, like a goose into a horse-pond?

"*Thirdly.*—How often in the week, the month, or the year, did the angel vouchsafe to descend into this pool? And for how many ages before the advent of Jesus was this gracious and angelical favour granted? and why not since, and even now? St. John should have been particular as to these points, which, he might have reasonably expected, philosophers would be curious enough to inquire about. If it were but once in the year, little thanks are due to him for his courtesy. One would think, sometimes, that his descent was frequent, or such a multitude of impotent folk, variously disordered, had never attended on it. At other times, one would think, that his descent was seldom, or the diseased, as fast as they came, which could not be faster than the angel could dabble himself in the waters, had been charitably dismissed with restored health.

Fourthly.—How came it to pass, that there was not better care taken either by the providence of God, or by the civil magistrates of Jerusalem, about the disposal of the angelic favour to this or that poor man, according to his necessities or deserts? Instead of which, he who could fortunately catch the favour was to have it. As he who runs the fastest obtains the prize, so, in this case, he who was most nimble and watchful of the angel's descent, and could first plunge himself into the pool, carried off the gift of sanation. Truly, an odd and a merry way of conferring a *divine* mercy! One would think that the angels of God did this more for their own diversion, than for the good of mankind. Just as some throw a bone among a kennel of hounds for the pleasure of seeing them quarrel for it, or as others cast a piece of money among a company of boys for the sport of seeing them scramble for it, so was the pastime of the angels at the pool of Bethesda. It was the opinion of some heathens that *Homines sunt Lusus Deorum*, the Gods sport themselves with the miseries of mankind; but I never thought, before I considered this story, that the angels of the God of the Jews did so too. If they delighted in it, rare sport it was for them; as much as it could have been for a *town mob*: for as the poor and distressed wretches cannot be supposed to have been of such a polite conversation as complaisantly to give place to their betters, or, out of compassion, make way for the most miserable, they, upon the sight or sound of the angel's fall into the pool, would, without respect of persons, strive who should be first; so those who were behind, and unlikely to be cured, would, like an uncivilized *rabble*, push and press all before them into it. What a number then, perhaps some hundreds, of poor creatures, were at once tumbled into the waters, to the diversion of the *city mob*, as well as of God's angels! And if one arose out of it, with the cure of his disease, the rest came forth like drowned *rats*, to the laughter of the spectators: and it was well if there were not sometimes more mischief done, than the healing of one could be of advantage to those people. Let him believe this part of the story who can, I cannot. Were an angel employed in this work, it must have been an angel of *Satan*, who delights in mischief. And if he healed one upon such an occasion, he did it by way of bait, to draw others into danger of life and limb. But as our *divines* will not, I suppose, bear the thought of this being a bad angel, I will leave them to consider upon our reasonings, whether it was credible, that either a good or bad angel was concerned therein, and desire them to give me a better reason, why there was but one at a time healed?

"If any pool or cistern of water, in or about this city of London, was so blessed with the descent of an angel to such an end, the Magistrates, such is their wisdom, would, if God did not direct, take care of the prudent disposal of the mercy, to the best advantage of the diseased. And if they sold it to an infirm Lord or Merchant, who could give for it most money, to be distributed amongst the poor and distressed people, would it not be more wisely done of them? To suppose that they would leave the angelic favour to the struggle of a multitude, is absurd and incredible. Why then should we think otherwise of the Magistrates of Jerusalem?

"*Fifthly.*—Let us consider who and what were the impotent folk that lay in the porches of Bethesda, waiting the troubling of the waters? John says that they were blind, halt, withered, and as some manuscripts have it, paralytics. What did any of these do there? How could any of them be supposed to be nimble enough to step down first into the waters, and carry off the prize of sanation, before many others of various diseases? Though the troubled waters might have been of such medicinal power, as to heal a man of whatever disease he had, yet none of the aforesaid persons, for want of good feet and eyes, could expect the benefit of it. The ears of the blind might serve him to hear when the angel soused like a stone into the waters; yet, through want of sight, he could not direct his way to the steps, but must expect to be jostled out of the right way by others, before he could reach them. And if the lame had good eyes to discern the descent of the angel, yet feet were all in all to his purpose. Consequently, these impotent folk might as well have staid at home, as resorted to Bethesda for a cure. I know not what fools the diseased of Jerusalem might have been, but if there were such a prize of health to be striven for by the distempered of this city, I appeal to any man of common sense, whether the blind, the lame, or the withered, would offer to engage in it. John, then, either forgot himself, or blundered most egregiously; unless he put this banter upon us, to try how far an absurd tale would pass upon the world with credit.

Sixthly, it is said that a certain man had an infirmity thirty and eight years. Though these thirty and eight years are, in our English translation, predicative of this man's infirmity, yet more truly, according to the original, they are spoken of as the time which he lay at the pool, waiting for an opportunity to be cured at it. What this man's infirmity was, we are uncertain, for infirmity is a general name for all distempers, and may be equally applied to one as well as to another; therefore, though we cannot certainly say, from this man's infirmity, that he was a fool to lay there so long, expecting a cure which it seems was impossible for him to obtain, yet what he says to Jesus does certainly imply folly in his conduct, or rather, destroys the credibility of the whole story. For he says that *he had no man to put him into the pool, when the waters were troubled;* that when he attempted to go, *another came and stepped down before him.* What then did he do at this pool, if he had neither legs of his own good enough, nor a friend to assist him in the attainment of sanation? Would he not have exhibited as much wisdom, had he waited in the fields as long, for the falling of the sky, that he might then catch larks? Our divines may, if they please, commend this man for his patience, but after a few years, or rather, the experience of a few days, another man would have been convinced of the folly and vanity of his hopes, and have returned home. And if he could not meet with success in his more youthful days, how much less reason had he to expect it in his old age, after *thirty and eight years'* affliction? Whatever, then, our divines may think of this man and his patience, I will not believe that there ever was such a fool: and for this reason, will not believe that John could literally so romance, unless he meant to cheat mankind into the belief of the greatest absurdity. A man that lies with sufficient grace to deceive others,

makes his story so hang together as to carry the face
and appearance of truth along with it; but this story of
St. John's, that for so many ages has been swallowed,
does not possess one common feature of plausibility.
But what militates the most against this story is,

Seventhly, that which follows, and absolutely destroys
the fame and credit of Jesus as a worker of miracles.
For if they were such a multitude of impotent folk at
this pool, why did not Jesus heal them all? Here was
a rare opportunity for the display of his healing and
Almighty power. Why then did he not exercise it to
the relief of that multitude of impotent folk? If he
could not cure them, there is an end of his power in
working miracles; if he would not, he was deficient of
mercy and compassion. Therefore, which ever way we
view this case, it turns to the dishonour of the holy
Jesus. What, then, could have been his reason, that out
of so great a multitude of diseased people he should
only exert his power, and extend his mercy, to this one
poor paralytic?

The Evangelists Matthew, Mark, and Luke, tell such
stories of the healing power of Jesus, that one would
suppose he cured all the diseased wherever he came.
He healed, they say, all manner of sickness and disease
among the people: and they make mention of particular times and places, where all the diseased came and
were healed by him: which assertions imply, that his
healing power was most extensive, and (excepting to a
hard-hearted and unbelieving pharisee, now and then)
universal; indeed, so effective, that it might be questioned whether any died during the time of his ministry,
in the places where he came. But this passage of St.
John's is a flat contradiction to their assertions, or Jesus
had never let such a multitude of poor innocent wretches
pass, without the exercise of his power and pity on
them. Some good reason, then, must be given for his
conduct here, and such a one as will adjust it to the
reports of the other Evangelists; or *Infidels* will think,
that either they romanced for the honour of their master,
or that St. John told this story to the degradation of
the character of Jesus through spite or envy.

" If Jesus had healed the whole multitude of impotent folk, without inquiring how many there were, I should have thought that he wrought a great many miracles, for in such a multitude, there must needs be, in all probability, many incurable, by either art or nature ; but since he only cured this *one* man, it affords matter of speculation, whether he was the *most* or *least* diseased among them.　Our *divines*, for the sake of the miracle, may possibly suppose him to be the most grievously afflicted man of them all ; but *Infidels*, on the other hand, will say, not so : and will, with their cavils, urge that this man was either a dissembler, whom Jesus shamed out of his pretended disease, or that he was only hippish, and fancied himself distempered so long a time ; and that Jesus, by suitable exhortations and admonitions, worked upon his imagination so effectually, as to persuade him into a belief that he was cured ; so bade him take up his bed and walk off.　Certain it is, that Infidels will say that it was not the miraculous power of Jesus that healed him, or he had used it then and there, for the sanation of others also.

" And thus have I finished my invective against the letter of this story.　If any are offended thereat, they enjoy what is the most reasonable thing in the world, the same liberty to write *for* the letter, which I have used *against* it."

Thus much, has Mr. Woolston said on the subject, which I think is quite sufficient to destroy the credibility of the whole story, without any further comment from me.　I will only just observe, that if what Matthew says be true, concerning the multitudes that followed him from Galilee, Decapolis, Jerusalem, Judea, and from beyond Jordan,[36] it was impossible for Jesus to have gone among such a multitude of impotent folk, in the heart of Jerusalem, without some one among them knowing him.　John acknowledges himself, that prior to this miracle, Jesus was well know at Jerusalem, as a worker of miracles, even among the rulers.[37]　And if so well known to them, is it likely that he should be unknown to the multitudes of impotent folk, who, one might be well assured, would have been the foremost to have inquired for him? Yet it appears by this account, that none of those impotent folk knew any thing of him; even the man himself, who was so miraculously healed, wist not who it was that healed him;[3][8] neither did he seem to think his cure as any thing miraculous, or he would certainly have recognised Jesus in it, if his fame was so noised abroad, through all the country of Judea and Jerusalem.

In my next I shall most probably examine the transfiguration of Jesus, and, at the same time, make a few observations on the soul, and future state of the existence of man. Also, if time will permit, I intend to speak of the paralytic, for whom the roof of the house was forcibly broken up, that he might be let down into the room, wherein sat Jesus. In the meantime, I trust, you will take into consideration that which I have already written. And that the word of truth may have free course, run, and be respected, is the sincere wish of

Your humble Servant,

JOHN CLARKE.

NOTES TO THE FOREGOING LETTER.

1. Luke xix, 27.
2. Matthew xxv, 31.
3. Luke xix, 11—28.
4. Matthew xxi, 12.
   „   xxv, 14.
5. 1 Samuel ii, 12.
6. Matthew vi, 19.
7. Psalm xv, 5.
8. Genesis xiii, 2.
   „   xx, 14—16
   1 Kings x, 25.
9. Matthew xxv, 31—46.
10. "   xi, 23.
11. Mark xvi, 16,
12. Hebrews i, 3.
13. Matthew xi, 3.
14. John iv, 3—18.
15. „   viii, 4—11.
16. Deuteronomy xxii, 22.
17. John ii, 25.
18. Matthew xvi, 13.

„

Mark vii, 26.

...

„   ,
32. „   „
33. 2 Peter i, 16.
34. 1 Thessalonians v, 21.
35. John v, 2—9.
36. Matthew iv, 25.
37. John iii, 2.
38. „   v, 13.

LETTER XI.

TO DR. ADAM CLARKE.

In my last, among other things, I promised to take into consideration the transfiguration of Jesus; which our priests say was only of itself a most surprising phenomena; but, the circumstances attending it prove the immortality of the human race.

Previous to commencing this subject, it will be necessary to remind you, that there has been a time when many persons sucked in supernatural nourishment, from their superstitious and credulous mother's breast, as they did their natural aliment; and ever after considered, that all things they saw were supernatural, if the cause of them was unknown. Thus, the rainbow was attributed to a supernatural cause, until increasing knowledge, in after ages, discovered that it was nothing more than the result of causes, quite natural, which could be imitated by art at pleasure. Thunder, lightning, &c., were considered as tokens of the displeasure of some supernatural being: the whole of which, you are well convinced, from practical knowledge, proceed from natural causes. It is, therefore, not to be wondered at, if those persons credited the transfiguration of a man's clothes and countenance, and ascribed it to a supernatural agency, when they considered the elements were transfigured by supernatural means.

This story of the transfiguration of Jesus I find related in the books attributed to Matthew, Mark, and Luke only; not a syllable of it is alluded to by John; although he is represented as being present during the transfiguration, while all the others were absent. Peter, in his epistle says, that he was an eye-witness thereof; consequently, what Peter saw with his own eyes, he had good reason for believing; though a man's eye-sight may be imposed upon by a crafty and dexterous juggler. But as neither you nor I were eye-witnesses of it, I cannot think that we have such good reasons for setting our seal to the truth thereof: especially, as Paul said, every man is or may be a liar.[2] Do not imagine that I am so ill-mannered as to say that Peter lied, when he said that he was an eye-witness of it, I only intend to hint, which, I trust I may do without giving any offence, that, possibly, his eye-sight deceived him; especially as I find it recorded in the story, that he, and those that were with him, were heavy with sleep.[3]

There are many men, even in our own days, who possess most astonishing powers and abilities, inasmuch if it were possible, they would seem to deceive the very *elect*.[4] Such as they who are called Ventriloquists; men who can change their voice so as to represent one from a different person, afar off, although spoken by the same person close beside the hearer. Others there are, who can, like Grimaldi the clown, throw themselves into such forms and attitudes, that if one were not well convinced to the contrary, one would really believe that they were differently organized from the generality of the human species. Yet, none of these persons lay claim to *supernatural* powers, or any thing beyond their own natural abilities; knowing too well, that the present generation, are become too enlightened to swallow such a suspicious looking bait.

Luke says (ix. 27.) that after Jesus had fed the multitude he, among other things, told his disciples that there were some standing with him who should not taste of death till they saw the kingdom of God; and that about *eight* days after this saying he took Peter, James, and John with him up into a mountain to pray. It appears, as I said before, very strange that this Jesus should be always praying, when the priests tell us that he was "very God of very God." But both Matthew and Mark contradict Mr. Luke, by saying that it was only *six* days after this saying.[5] These contradictions, I grant, are of no great consequence, being nothing more than we might reasonably expect to find in an

INSPIRED book! However, while Jesus was praying, we are told that the fashion of his countenance was altered, and shone, Matthew says, like the sun; his raiment also became white as the light: "and, behold, there talked with him two men, which were Moses and Elias." Luke further informs us that the, purport of this visit was to speak of his decease, the which he should accomplish at Jerusalem; a point upon which the other evangelists appear to be entirely ignorant, not having made the slightest allusion to it. "But Peter, and they that were with him, were heavy with sleep, and when they awoke, they saw his glory, and the two men that were with him."

Here we are told, that both James and John were with Peter, and saw these two men, and this strange phenomena; yet neither of them, in their writings, take the least notice of it. Perhaps you will say, that one historian is quite sufficient to relate a fact; then why should it be related by three, especially those three out of the four, in particular, who were not eye-witnesses of it, as was John? Other matters of much less importance, we find they all notice; such as the inscription upon the cross of Jesus; yet in this simple instance, they all differ one from the other, concerning the title. [6] However, we will admit that a circumstance is entitled to more credit by being related by those who did not see it, than by those who were eye-witnesses thereof; yet, how should Peter himself know what was their mission or confabulation, if he and they that were with him were heavy with sleep? Supposing that Jesus might have acquainted them with it, after they awoke, still, I think, it would have been more to his honour and credit, besides shewing more kindness to his disciples, if he had awakened them, as soon as the two illustrious personages made their appearance. He surely did not intend the meeting to be private, or he would never have taken Peter, James, and John with him up into the mount. Besides, the conversation of three such eminent characters as Jesus, Moses, and Elias, must have been such as would have ministered grace unto the hearers. It cannot be supposed that these two messengers would be sent from their gay and heavenly city merely to inform Jesus of what he already knew, namely, *his decease.* Perhaps they spoke unspeakable words, as Paul says, that were not lawful for a man to hear or utter?[7] If so, the Jews were justified, in suspecting Jesus of treasonable designs, as this private manner of receiving and holding consultations with the ambassadors of another world, in an unknown tongue, must have had a very suspicious look.

It may be said that these two men were sent to encourage and strengthen Jesus, in order that he might meet his fate with becoming fortitude and resignation, because it is written,[8] that "he made many prayers and supplications, with strong crying and tears, *unto him that was able to save him from death;*" (Whom could this mean, that is able to save the "Very God" from death?) and that "he was heard in that he feared." Then why should they seek such a solitary and obscure place for that purpose? Would it not have been far better, if they had made their appearance while he was surrounded by the Sadducees, who believed in neither angel, spirit, or resurrection? This would have convinced those unbelieving wretches, and so probably have saved them from damnation; as it is written that *he that believeth not shall be damned.* But it appears that they kept out of sight, purposely to keep them in ignorance and unbelief. I am fully persuaded that if those two men (Moses and Elias) had made their appearance when Jesus was carrying his cross, and assisted him with his burden, there would not have been an unbelieving Jew in existence, from that day to this. Moreover, it would have had a greater tendency to fill the earth with those *glad tidings,* which are so much and so highly spoken of, than all the teaching and preaching of Jesus, or any of his followers. It would have been acknowledged by all the historians of that age, and transmitted down to us with unquestionable authority.

Another thing which much surprises me, is, how Peter should know even before Jesus spake to him, that those two men were Moses and Elias? He had never seen them before; yet ere he was properly awake, he

could call them by their names! And why did they
disappear as soon as Peter and the rest awoke? This
behaviour was, surely, very unpolite. But, perhaps,
you will say, that they were naked; consequently they
were ashamed of being seen; for if they had any
clothes, it is most likely, some one would give us a
description of them, as well as of the garments of Jesus.

It is further stated, that after they had disappeared,
a cloud covered them: whence proceeded a voice saying,
"this is my beloved son, hear him." If the hill was so
high as it is described, it certainly could not have been
an uncommon thing for a cloud to overspread it. But,
the voice; aye, whose voice was that? I have already
noticed how artful some ventriloquists are in deceiving
a byestander; and no doubt but there were men in those
days, who possessed the same natural powers, as those
in our own. If so, why may we not give the same
honour to Jesus as to another? But what did this
voice say? Why—"Hear him!" Hear what? Jesus
was not saying anything extraordinary; he only told
them that they should tell no man of those things which
they had seen. Surely, to hear this, did not require
the aid of a supernatural injunction! If you conceive
that the voice proceeded from a God, in order that Peter
and the rest might be convinced, it must have had some
good effect; as a celebrated writer once said, that IF
GOD SPOKE, THE UNIVERSE WOULD BE CONVINCED.
But neither Peter nor those that were with him seem
to have paid any regard to this voice, or they would
never have deserted and denied him, and afterwards
treat the account of his resurrection as an "idle tale!"[9]

But, why should this change in his countenance be
called a transfiguration? By looking into my diction-
ary, I find that the word transfiguration signifies a
change of form or figure. We are not told that the
form or figure of Jesus was ever changed. If he had
been transformed into the shape of a baboon, a goat, a
calf, or the likeness of any thing different from the human form, we may be assured they would not have
failed to have made mention of it. Instead of which,
they merely say that his face shone! I have seen your

face shine, even in a pulpit, when the sun shone upon it; yet I never considered that you were transfigured; and no doubt, if you had had a white surplice on, or some light coloured robe, instead of a black one, you also would have appeared equally transfigured!

This story of the transfiguration, as it is called, instead of being the brightest, as the priests would fain make us believe, appears to me, to be one of the darkest and blindest tales of the whole book. I can make neither head nor tail of any part of it. For what purpose was he so transfigured? What good effect had it, even upon those who were eye-witnesses to such an event? Peter afterwards denied him altogether! Where was the necessity of sending those two men out of their comfortable place, (for I suppose that you imagine they came all the way from heaven,) merely to inform Jesus of what he already knew? A most important message truly! But the story altogether is only on a par with the rest of the blundering nonsense which designing men or ignorant dreamers have ever been noted for foisting upon the world.

There are not wanting those who contend that the appearance of these two men from heaven proves not only the existence of another world beyond the skies, but also the existence and immortality of the soul; and in order to frighten mankind into a belief of their abstruse doctrines, they have contrived to persuade almost every man that his soul will be punished in hell, or rewarded in heaven, according to the deeds done in the body and the tenacity wherewith he clings to the orthodox creeds of the day.

In addition, also, to this testimony of holy writ, there is no sophistry which the priests have left unused to maintain their assumption. When their stock of argument, such as it is, has been exhausted, the enquirer has generally been put off with the following supposition: that if God, who made the world, and infused life into every animate being, thinks proper, he can continue that existence after we have departed from this state of being. Upon this point I offer you a little comment.

If we admit that an almighty and intelligent being
fashions and frames our several bodies, and that in him
we *live*, and *move*, and *have our being*, we certainly must
acknowledge, that he may possess equal power, to re-animate these same bodies, if he thinks proper, after they
have become defunct ; just as easily as a man can renew the flame of a candle, immediately after the light
has been blown out ; provided the body remains entire,
and free from disorganization.   Or he might, if he
thought proper, change this *vile* body, and mould and
fashion it to whatever shape his fancy directed.   But,
if we find, by experimental knowledge, that this body,
in process of time, constitutes many other *human* bodies,
we leave him no power, however omnipotent he may be,
of raising two or more bodies out of the materials
with which one is formed.   To prove this, let us
consider the following observations, drawn from daily
experience.

When a body is bereft of life, some parts of it engender worms.   These worms become food for fish and
fowl ; thereby forming a part of their bodies.   Other
parts of this body evaporate into the atmospheric air,
by which all animals exist ; and are afterwards inter-
mingled with the waters of the great deep ; which,
also, is necessary to the production and support of all
animals.   While this transmigration is going forward,
other parts of this body, the nature of which will not
admit of animal production or evaporation, crumble to
atoms ; which, being converted to dust, produce that
which is called the vegetable creation ; which, likewise,
is essential to the maintenance and conservation of the
animal world.

If this peregrination of the human body terminated
here, we might suppose, that if an almighty and ingenious being did exist, he might be able to resolve those
animals and the elements, whence he might replace every
individual atom to its primitive state, and fashion them
again to whatever shape *he pleased.*[14]   Though, for my
part, I should think that it would scarcely be worth his
labour, to take so much trouble to collect the broken,
battered, and scattered particles, out of the elements

and the numerous bodies into which they have inter-mingled and commixed, and then to arrange, unite, organize, and colour them again, merely to put them out of his sight for ever after, (which, I suppose, must be the case, if they are doomed to dwell in *hell fire*, throughout eternity) unless *the continual wailing and gnashing of teeth* of those miserable beings afford him an extraordinary and exquisite degree of *supernatural* pleasure!

But, we find, by experience, that the human body is in a continual state of intermigration, through its inde-structible particles continually and incessantly emi-grating from one body to another; that it is formed again from the various particles of the decomposed bodies of other animals which have been produced from a former human body. Thus, man eats the fish and fowl, which have fed upon the worm generated from the body of man; also, of the beast that hath fed upon the grass produced and nourished from the decomposed parts of the human body, crumbled to dust. Man like-wise breathes and inhales the same atmospheric part-icles which have evaporated from the dead body of a former man: even the very particles of gas, thrown off by respiration and perspiration from one, while living, contribute towards the existence of another. There are even some men called cannibals, who derive their sus-tenance directly from the flesh and blood of other men. All sorts of food are turned into flesh and blood, as natu-ral as all sorts of wood are turned into fire, flames, and gas. In consequence of this continual and incessant routine of combining and dissolving action, the men of all generations are but as one body, undergoing many changes and variations of shape and figure; conse-quently cannot rise again, identified with their several bodies. The particles of matter which constitute my present body have contributed towards the formation of many former bodies; and will again form many future bodies without end, through the indestructibility of its atomical parts. As Shelly very justly observed—

" There is not one atom of yon earth
But once was living man,

> Nor the minutest drop of rain,
> That hangeth in its thinnest cloud,
> But flowed in human veins."

How, then, I ask, can all those different identical bodies rise out of the materials of one, they being, in fact, but the same body renewed?

There are some persons so well convinced of the impossiblity of those same bodies ever rising again, after life once becomes extinct, that they adopt the doctrine of Paul, in opposition to that of Jesus, by saying, that there is an indescribable something, called a SOUL, that exists within the body during life, and departs from it when the body becomes defunct: which *soul* will be furnished with a fresh body by God, and transported to another world. I grant that there is not much difficulty in the assertion; but can the fact be as easily proved? And, if we do not find the thing for which we are told to search in some particular spot, we certainly are justified in concluding that no such thing exists there. In former ages many persons employed their whole lives in searching for what was called the *philosopher's stone*, upon the mere assertion of some persons who had said that such a thing was in existence; but, after ages of fruitless inquiry, the search was abandoned and the assertion proved false

By this doctrine of Paul, it appears, that there is a kind of diminutive person, of a peculiar nature, enclosed within the body of man; which little person, or *inward man*, is placed there as a kind of director or superintendent of all the actions of the body, or *outward man*, for all of which it must be accountable when the body ceases to act; and according to the deeds done by the body will this little man be either punished or rewarded after it is *clothed upon* with another body.

If this doctrine be correct, does it not evince a deficiency of skill and judgment in the Creator of this human body? For what mechanic would put two springs to a work which might be made perfect with one? Could not this creator re-animate the same body again without having recourse to an agent? Why multiply beings without necessity ? Was it impossible for this creator to give unto this body the faculty of thought, without being necessitated to form another body? Besides, would it not be far more just by preserving this body from dissolution, to punish or reward it according to its own works, instead of making a new body which had neither done good nor harm, to enjoy the blessings it never had merited, or suffer the punishment it had never deserved? The priests, to extricate themselves from this difficulty, say no, because it is written that flesh and blood cannot inherit the kingdom of God.[15] How, then, I ask, could Jesus get there, when they say that he carried there flesh and blood, with all the apurtenances of the human body?[16] Elijah even took all his clothes with him excepting his mantle, into heaven![17] However, let them excuse it how they will, it certainly cannot be just to clothe[18] this little man with a new body, and then to punish or reward this new-made body, which had neither merited the one nor deserved the other; while the old body, however good it might have been, is left to perish in the general conflagration.[19]

Before I proceed further, let me ask, what is a soul? The priests say that it is a spirit. If I ask them what is a spirit? they will reply that it is a soul! This is all the definition of the word soul that I can get from any man. If I search the bible, I find that the spirit and soul are two distinct things, and both different from the body.[20] Some passages seem to insinuate that the soul is the principle of life, by saying that the soul of every living thing is in the hand of God.[21] If this be true, every rat, pig, sprat, fly, and flea, with every living thing, must be in possession of a soul; notwithstanding the unwillingness of the priests to admit such a levelling doctrine. Neither can I imagine how a soul can do wrong, or act contrary to the will of God, if he holds all the souls in his own hand, and directs the ways of man himself.[22] Surely, it must be his own fault if the soul doeth evil.

The priests further tell us that this soul is immortal, which means that it can never die. Is it not strange, that the Attorney-General, or some of his *vice* agents,

do not prosecute those priests for blasphemy, when the
bible so positively asserts the contrary? Did not God
say,[23] that the soul that sinneth shall die? Yet those
priests have the presumption to say that it cannot die!
What use is the bible to us if we are not to believe
what is therein written? Does it not say that God
removed man from the tree of life,[24] lest he might become immortal like himself? Zechariah, who was one
of the Lord's prophets, consequently knew all the
secrets of the Lord;[25] yet he asks, in a satirical manner,[26] whether their fathers or the prophets live for
ever? All are of the dust, as Soloman says, and all
turn to dust again, like the beasts that perish—man
having no pre-eminence above a beast.[27] Surely, if
man had an immortal soul, or was in any manner superior to a beast, such a wise man as Soloman, who had
all his wisdom given to him from God himself,[28] would
never have made use of such an assertion. Moses, also,
the chosen favourite of God, knew nothing of this immortal soul, or he would never have confined his rewards and punishments to things only pertaining to
this life.[29] David says likewise, that man abideth not
in honour; he is like the beasts that perish—the wise
men die, likewise the fool and the brutish person perish
—he shall go to the generation of his fathers; they
shall never see light [30] In the very day that his
breath goeth forth he returneth to his earth, and all his
thoughts perish.[31] But Job leaves this matter indisputable, by saying, that all flesh shall perish together.[32]
Surely nothing can be more opposed to a future state of
existence than those passages which I have here selected out many of the kind that are to be found in the
bible. Then what authority have priests to preach
such a strange and unaccountable doctrine, so contrary
to reason, philosophy, analogy, and the bible? Paul,
in one of his bombastical speeches says, that this mortal
must put on immortality, which is certainly an acknow-
ledgment, that the thing of which he speaks, whether
it be of the body or the soul, is at present but mortal.[33]
If the soul were immortal and invisible as some tell us,
it must be free from wound or trouble, being free from

touch. How then can it feel pain, or enjoy pleasure? Yet the bible says that the spirit is wounded,[34] and the soul oftentimes in trouble.[35]

And when was this soul put into the body? Whence did it come? You say that it comes from God. Should it be proved, what some persons say, that the soul consists of the ideas, memory, passions, and faculties, we must admit that this definition of soul applies to all animals, and to every living thing which he holds in his hand.[36] For, like men, the beasts of the field, and fowls of the air have ideas, memory, faculties, and pasions. And if they were possessed of the organs of speech, I doubt not, but they would, in process of time, so exercise their reasoning faculties, from the experience handed down to them from one generation to the other, as to equal, in a certain degree, many of those human beings called christians! This is not merely an hypothesis; it is founded upon daily experience. Do we not see the foolish puppy increase in knowledge, like the foolish infant, until he acquires the character of a sagacious hound? The full-grown horse is more cunning than the new born colt. "The ox knoweth his owner and the ass his master's crib."[37] All kinds of beasts, as well as birds, may be taught that of which they were before entirely ignorant. But not having the organ of speech to communicate their ideas to each other, their experience is confined to themselves, individually, consequently perishes with the body. Therefore, if the soul consists of the ideas, &c., God must be always employed in making souls, seeing that every animal is possessed of them in some degree or other.— The bible, moreover, seems to hint, that even the fields and forests have souls as well as bodies![38] And should science discover a plurality of worlds, which the bible also seems to acknowledge, (Heb. xi. 3.) what rest can this soul manufacturer have?—his very existence must be intolerable.

Besides, we are told that many persons have sinful souls. How came they by them? Did God put sinful souls into pure and holy bodies? or did he put a pure and holy soul into a sinful and corrupt body, to be polluted by the union? To answer this they contradict themselves, by saying, that God does not make every individual soul, but that we receive all our souls by traduction from Adam, in like manner, as one thought begets another, or, as the flame of one taper lights many others: it being as easy for God to make all the souls of men from one active thought and ardent desire, as to make all the bodies of men from one blood;[39] thought and desire, they say, having as great an affinity to the soul as blood to the body, By this account, it appears that God has nothing to do with the making of either our individual soul or body; but, that while the body is begetting a body, the soul is also begetting a soul! Then why instruct children, when interrogated who made them, to reply, that it was God? But will the bible support such an opinion? No, it evidently contradicts it. Did not God tell Jeremiah,[40] that he formed him in the belly? And David assures us that God has a book wherein all his members were written, when God covered him in his mother's womb, and made him in secret.[41] Moreover, it says that it is God himself who fashioneth the hearts of all men, and taketh them out of the womb.[42] And many more passages declare that God is the creator of every man. How then can it be said that we receive all our souls by traduction from Adam? It is then evident that, if God be the creator of souls, he must either put sinful souls into our bodies, or put a pure and holy soul into a sinful body to be polluted by the union; else how do they become sinful?

But whether we receive our souls by traduction or not, they maintain that God is the author of all things; consequently he must be the author of souls. Then may we not demand for what purpose were those souls made? For, according to the conditions which we are told are so essentially necessary for our salvation, very few souls have reason to anticipate a life of greater happiness than the present; but many, very many, have reason to expect much worse. Then if man be in danger of meeting such a deplorable fate, would it not have been better to have made him without this soul? Surely no one will presume to say that God was compelled to make souls. And if the clay feels itself hurt in its formation it certainly is justified in demanding of the potter, (admitting the ridiculous idea of pots and pans speaking) "Why hast thou made me thus?[42] If thou couldst have made me otherwise would it not have been more to thine own glory, as well as to my own peace and happiness, to have made me a vessel of honour, instead of thus making me a vessel to dishonour both thou and myself?" Paine says, that Paul seems to make this potter to represent God, and the lump of clay the whole human race: the vessels unto honour, those souls "on whom he hath mercy, because he *will* have mercy;" and the vessels unto dishonour, those souls "whom he hardeneth, (for damnation) because he *will* harden them." Let us see, then, what are the conclusions which Paine has drawn from this metaphor?

He says, "in the first place, a potter doth not, because he cannot, make vessels of different qualities from the same lump of clay; he cannot make a fine china bowl, intended to ornament a side-board, from the same lump of clay that he makes a coarse pan, intended for a close stool. The potter selects his clay for different uses according to their different qualities and degrees of fineness and goodness. Paul might as well talk of making gun flints from the same stick of wood of which the gun-stock is made, as of making china bowls from the same lump of clay of which are made common earthen pots and pans. Paul could not have hit upon a more unfortunate metaphor for his purpose than this of the potter and the clay; for if any inference is to follow from it, as a metaphor, it is, that, as a potter selects his clay for different kinds of vessels according to the different qualities and degrees of fineness and goodness in the clay, so God selects for future happiness those among mankind who excel in purity and goodness; which is the reverse of predestination!

"In the second place, there is no comparison between the souls of men and vessels made of clay; and therefore, to put one to represent the other is a false position. The vessels, or the clay they are made from,

are insensible of honour or dishonour. They neither
suffer nor enjoy. The clay is not punished that serves
the purpose of a close stool, nor is the finer sort rendered happy that is made up into a punch bowl. The
potter violates no principle of justice in the different
uses to which he puts his different clays; for he selects
as an artist, not as a moral judge; and the materials
he works upon know nothing, and feel nothing, of his
mercy or his wrath. Mercy or wrath would make a
potter appear ridiculous when bestowed upon his clay
—he might kick some of his pots to pieces!

" But the case is quite different with man, either in
this world or in the next. He is a being sensible of
misery as well as of happiness; and, therefore, Paul
argues like an unfeeling idiot when he compares men
to clay on a potter's wheel, or to vessels made therefrom; and with respect to God, it is an offence to his
attributes of justice, goodness, and wisdom, to suppose
that he would treat the choicest work of creation like
inanimate and insensible clay. If Paul believed that
God made man in his own image, he dishonours it by
making that image and a brick-bat to be alike."

Again, if this doctrine of Paul be true, namely, that
man is composed of two separate and distinct parts, a
soul and a body, *when*, I ask, doth this soul quit the body? The priests say, when the body ceases to perform
its functions; because it is written, " that when " her
soul was in departing (for she died.") I have watched
the mouth of a dying person, supposing that would have
been the cavity by which the soul would escape, but I
never could perceive anything proceed therefrom. Oh,
but they say it is invisible and cannot be seen. Then
how should any man know that there is such a thing if
it cannot be seen, much less presume to enforce a belief
of its future existence? The only answer that I can
get to this reasonable question is, that the bible says so!
In former days when all people were forbidden to read
a bible, excepting gentlefolks who were interested in
keeping the poor ignorant of their equal claim to gen-
tility, the priests, or monks and friars, could easily gull
them with such an absurdity; but since we, who are not

interested in anything that is contrary to truth and justice, have the bible forced upon us to read, we certainly
have an undoubted right to inquire of them where in
this bible do they find their authority for propagating
such a doctrine? I have already shewn that the bible
contradicts a future state of conscious existence, by saying that when the breath of man goeth forth he returneth to his earth; in that very day his thoughts perish.[45]
That all flesh perish together.[46] And that when God
was particularly attached to any of his creatures, he
took them away before death, flesh and blood, bones and
all, as was the case of Enoch and Elijah.[47]

Admitting that there even was a solitary passage to
be found in the bible, which seemed to insinuate something like a state of future existence, though I cannot
find a single one throughout the bible that will bear
such a construction to be put upon it by an unprejudiced mind, if there were, surely, the Sadducees would
have discovered it;[48] still, what dependence can be
placed upon a book like the bible, written by such ignorant men as our daily experience in the Arts and
Sciences prove them to have been? First, we find
that the persons who wrote this book imagined that
the earth had ends and corners to it,[49] consequently
was a level plane with foundations, corner-stones, &c.;
that the part which they inhabited, with the adjacent
countries, constituted the whole earth, which could
easily be covered with water; that the firmament or
sky were as a canopy spread out over the earth,[50]
in which the stars were fixed like so many lamps, that
would, some time or other, fall to the earth, as the figs
fall from a fig tree that is shaken by the wind;[51] that
the earth was the centre of the solar system, round
which the sun and starry host revolved;[52] that light
and darkness had each a separate place appointed for
their dwelling, as if, while one of them was engaged in
performing its functions, the other was refreshing itself![53] that the place called heaven was above, and
that called hell, beneath. Indeed, so superstitious were
they, that they thought with Milton, that

"Millions of spiritual creatures walk the earth
Unseen, both when we wake and when we sleep." (54)

But you, Sir, whose knowledge in those matters ranks you among the most learned of the age, assure us that the stars are many times larger than our earth, which renders it impossible for them to fall towards this globe, it being contrary to the well known laws of nature for a large body to gravitate towards a lesser: even if God were so pleased to alter those laws, still those stars being so much larger than this earth and so numerous, would, were they to fall upon it, inevitably crush it to atoms. As to the earth having ends and corners, I, myself, have had occular demonstration that the earth is of a spherical or globular form, consequently can have neither ends nor corners, foundations nor corner-stones. You, moreover, assure us that it revolves every 24 hours round upon its own axis; then how can any place be said to be either above or below, when it must, unavoidably, have an opposite position every 12 hours? Besides, it is evident from your own observations that the sun is the centre of the universe, round which the earth and planets are incessantly revolving; and that instead of light and darkness being, as it were, shut up in a bag and let out when wanted, every school-boy in the present age knows that darkness is nothing more than the absence of light; consequently, the inquiry of Job's God concerning the place thereof, may be easily answered.

There are many other things which are spoken of in this book that prove the writers thereof to have been far more ignorant of the nature of things than ourselves. Then what credit can be given to their bare assertions when we find that their account of things pretended to have been demonstrated to their senses, is proved to be erroneous? As a proof that this book is considered to be a thing of no value by the learned, we never find any one referring to it for corroboration, or consulting it for instruction, in any one thing relating to the Arts and Sciences, or in that which is really beneficial or necessary to the interests of mankind. Even our legislators never consult this book when enacting laws for the preservation of good order and for the defence of the country, any more than those who have never seen them. Then of what use are they?

To proceed further with this soul; I would ask those soul-mongers how doth it grow? Is it as big in the body of the infant as in the full grown man? If they they say that it increases and grows with the body, what just grounds have they for concluding that it will not likewise perish with the body? Can this soul exist without the body, and dispense its vital powers? If so, it must also be possessed of the same faculties as the body, or what consciousness can it have of its existence? Of its deficiency we have indisputable proofs; for why cannot this soul inform the body when deprived of the visionary organs, how to distinguish one colour from another, or why cannot it do that which is assumed to be of immense importance, namely, wrest the true word of God from the many spurious writings which make pretensions thereto. The same also, if the auricular organs are imperfect, the soul is as ignorant of sound as is the body; and so with respect to every other faculty with which the body is endowed. What kind of a thing must this soul be when separated from the body? It can neither give nor receive either pain or pleasure, if it doth not possess the necessary organs of sensations for so doing. Then what utility can there be in dressing it again in a fresh body? A girl may change the dress of her doll many times, yet the doll receives neither pain nor pleasure thereby, though the mind of the girl may change ever so often; because it perceives not the change, not being conscious of existence.

Where, I would likewise ask, is this soul lodged? Some persons have thought that it was fixed in the great toe, to point out the way in which the body should move! Were this the case, the body would lose its soul when the toe was cut off. Others have thought that the soul was knit with every nerve, and vein, and artery. Then, again, some portion of the soul would be lost whenever the body was mutilated. It cannot be lodged in the brain, or it would correct the judgment of the idiot and insane; unless it likewise becomes infected with insanity. Peter speaks of a hidden man of the heart![55] but the bible assures us that the heart and soul are two distinct and separate things.[56] Then where is it? What is it? These are reasonable questions, which demand and deserve a satisfactory and rational answer, before we can bear witness to the truth of its existence.

If the soul be life, then every animal possesses a soul. Indeed I cannot see why Christians in particular, should deny other animals the privilege of having a soul! Many other sects, more numerous than the Christians, believe in the doctrine of transmigration : even the bible seems to acknowledge that there are four-footed beasts, and wild beasts, fowls of the air, and creeping things of the earth, in heaven, or how could Peter see them descend therefrom?[57] And many passages declare that there are beasts in heaven resembling our *lions, oxen, eagles, &c.*[58] If Christians will still persist in their uncharitable opinions, and monopolize the soul for their own species, exclusive of all others, then, I say that the beasts, if they possess not a soul, are far more happy than the human race ; being exempted from that dread of punishment in everlasting torments, which the souls of mankind, for the most part, are doomed to suffer : the dismal prospect of which embitters their whole lives, through a *certain fearful looking for of judgement.*[59]

It may be asked, what is my opinion of a soul? This I cannot answer, until I can learn what is meant by the word, soul. If any person can give me any information upon the subject, I will most willingly and gratefully receive it. Until then I am compelled to reply by demanding, how an opinion can be given of that, the meaning of which cannot be defined? I know that the human body possosses the power of locomotion, while the several parts of the said body are in perfect order ; and this may be called, if they please, the soul or principle of life, it being the main-spring of all our actions. If the body cease to act or perform its several functions, it is then evident that this soul or principle of life is broken or deranged, as it is with a watch when the main-spring is either broken or dislodged ; and until some artist or ingenious person can discover the seat of action, or main-spring of life, it will be impossible, as it has been hitherto, to renew its motion. But, as knowledge is making such rapid strides among men of all professions, I doubt not but in process of time some one will be enabled to renew this locomotion or principle of life, as easily as the watchmaker can repair wind-up and set his watch in motion : though, if the materials of the watch were all deranged and destroyed, how absurd it would be for any man to assert, and endeavour to enforce the belief on others, that the motion of the watch still existed! Yet this would be not more ridiculous than for some persons to suppose, that life, which is only the result of a peculiar organization, continued and upheld by the peculiar properties of its constituent parts attracting and repelling each other, should exist, after those organized parts were separated and decomposed!

The word soul I consider to have been originally made use of as an image to represent life to the sense of man, as being distinct from the material body; which some subtle and ingenious person afterwards personified: probably Homer, as he is the first person on record who speaks of a life after death. But what man in Christendom believes in the wild, fantastical, though beautiful, imaginations of this Grecian heathen Poet? They all acknowledge his writings to be fabulous, though they represent a future state for the life of man, after it and the body are separated. And if his Odyssey be correctly translated, he speaks (Book iii. line 580.) of bullocks having souls!

I have heard many persons, who did not themselves believe in the existence of this soul, or in any future state, contend that a belief thereof was absolutely necessary to curb and bridle the passions and appetites of the vicious and licentious; to deter men in every station of life from vice, and to restrain crime universally. If we found that the result of this belief produced such effects, we might be inclined to prefer fiction or falsehood to truth; but instead thereof, we find that those persons who have been taught from their infancy, and are, or pretend to be, thoroughly persuaded of a future state of punishment, exhibit more wickedness in general, than those who discredit every thing of the kind. There are some persons, I grant, who are firm believers of this doctrine, whose reputation is fair to the world; but remove them from their present comfortable situation in life, to one attended with more difficulties, and then see whether all the terrors of hell and damnation, fire and brimstone, devils and pitchforks, will prevent them from taking advantage of some unlawful means, to extricate themselves out of their embarrassments, notwithstanding they are so well convinced of the dreadful consequences resulting from such conduct.

> "To know men's souls, and what they are,
> View them beset with dangers and with care ;
> For then their words will with their thoughts agree,
> And as the mask falls off, show what they be."

I grant, also, that the belief of a future state of punishment may, in some instances, restrain a timorous man, sometimes, from doing that which he has been taught to believe as criminal. But if this crime as it is called, would not injure his fellow creature, it is depriving a man of the enjoyment of his own will and pleasure to restrain him; consequently becomes an evil to that man.

Suppose we were to admit that with some weak-minded persons, this belief operated so powerfully as to subdue even some of their evil propensities; yet will this trifling good upon a few individuals, counterbalance the many and great evils which have arisen through this belief? What persecutions, wars, and horrid cruelties have ensued through a difference in opinion concerning this doctrine! What a life of misery and want do millions of our poor, oppressed, and wretched fellow beings endure, with degrading patience and base submission to their lordly tyrants, merely through the vain and delusive hope of leading a more easy and comfortable one in another world!

Besides, if those persons' minds could be so easily wrought upon by this doctrine, would they not have been as capable of receiving an impression from a strictly moral preceptor, unaccompanied by those dogmas which only tend to fill the mind with gloomy apprehensions of a *fearful looking for of judgment*, even among the most virtuous, lest they should seem to come short of the promise?[60]   And, although there may be a few who are naturally kind, benevolent, and well-disposed persons among those who do believe in this doctrine, yet their good qualities ought not to be ascribed to their mere opinions concerning this or that, but to their temperament or organization, which renders them incapable of acting and feeling otherwise.   This is clearly demonstrated, by observing the conduct of many of those who treat the idea of a future state of conscious existence with contempt; yet is their moral conduct equal to that of the most accomplished believer : also by those who have been educated in the strictest rules of morality, and are moreover, firm believers in a state of punishment, after the dissolution of the body; yet, nevertheless, lead the most profligate and abandoned of lives : a proof that the organization of man is more powerful than all the terrors which the imagination of man can invent.   The moral actions of men, as well as their religious opinions, depend on circumstances, and not upon their own *free-will*, as has been erroneously supposed.·   Many examples might be given to prove that all men are guided in their actions, some way or other, by circumstances, depending chiefly upon their temperament, though their education may act powerfully in preventing its developement.   Thieves and highwaymen oftentimes discover some good qualities belonging to them, notwithstanding the vicious and immoral education they have received.   Kings and Priests though we may suppose they are, or ought to be, always instructed in the strictest rules of virtue and morality, are nevertheless, oftentimes found capable of committing the most wicked and detestable crimes.   Whence it appears plainly, that man cannot act otherwise than he does, let his opinions or belief be whatever they may; consequently, no good can be derived from a belief in a future state, but much evil may be produced by a difference of opinion concerning it; therefore, the best method of preventing the evil, is to destroy the cause, seeing that it cannot be productive of any good, sufficient to counter-balance the many evils arising therefrom.

Having shown that the conduct and actions of men arise principally through their temperament, and are determined by circumstances over which they can have no control, it may be asked whether it is just and reasonable to punish men for doing those things which they could not possibly avoid? To this I reply that it must certainly be both just and reasonable to remove every obstacle that would tend to destroy or injure the interests of society. Thus fire and water, though very useful in themselves, become, as soon as they exceed the boundaries of utility, the most dangerous enemies to society, consequently are treated as such. So with respect to those unfortunately organized beings whose temperament and circumstances, induce them to prey upon, or otherwise injure, their fellow creatures : when such propensities become manifest, it is both just and reasonable that such characters should be deprived of that liberty by which they commit their depredations, in order to secure the peace and harmony of the commonwealth ; which may be effectually accomplished, by imprisonment only.

The punishment of death I conceive to be neither politic nor just, excepting it be inflicted on a criminal convicted of murder. It can render no benefit to the injured person, neither does it prevent the crime. It is no where authorised by the scriptures. The Mosaic law enforced the exaction of an eye for an eye ; a tooth for a tooth ;[61] a double restitution of stolen property. In no case of theft was the life of the offender taken away ; even the man, convicted of arson, was only required to make restitution for the loss sustained.[62] And the christian doctrine teaches that instead of seeking redress for an insult, or restitution of property stolen, we must not resist evil, nor refuse to give unto him that asketh.[63] Moreover, Jesus commanded that whosoever shall smite thee on one cheek, turn the other to him also. And whosoever shall compel thee to go a mile, go with him twain. This is a clear proof that the laws of England are not founded on those books, supposed to be the word of God.

The taking away the life of a man convicted of forgery or of theft, not only prevents the criminal making restitution to the injured person, but actually prevents many tender hearted persons seeking redress from that law which enforces such a severe and unnecessary punishment. The consequence of which is, that the offender is oftentimes permitted to continue his depredations with impunity. This is actually the case with a young man now in Newgate, waiting to take his trial at the ensuing sessions, charged with picking pockets, who has been six times before confined under similar charges, but always acquitted through the non-attendance of the prosecutor! If men are to be found so unwilling to prosecute their fellow creatures for these trifling offences, how much more reluctantly will they come forward to prosecute in matters of life and death?

Besides if the doctrine of *eternal* punishment be true, how cruel and merciless must that law be which sends the man to it before there is a necessity? The following observations, taken from a Glasgow paper, will not be inapplicable to the subject :—

"Some people delight in assuring us of the general conversion of condemned criminals, and their most pious behaviour on the scaffold ; nay, to such an extent is this carried, that we scarcely hear of an execution without an account of the criminals' perfect assurance of a blessed immortality: and we are almost made to believe, that the gallows is a sort of railroad to the skies, carried on by a joint-stock company of judges, priests, and hangmen. But only giving credence to one half of these stories, and believing that in one half of these cases, the criminals are indeed *sincere converts :* What is the deduction? Why, if a few days could reform them, not only from vice to virtue, but to such virtue as was meet for the society of "just men made perfect," then a proper course of discipline might have made them good members of society, and preserved their lives to the advantage of the community. This argument appears to cut two ways. We either believe that condemned criminals are converted, or that they are not. If we believe that they are, where then is the necessity of taking away their lives? If we believe that they are not, we are sentencing them, not only to death here, but to everlasting punishment hereafter. Under which of these heads will the advocates for capital punishment enlist themselves?"

But the doctrine of eternal punishment, is contrary to reason and justice; it can only proceed from the most cruel and revengeful feelings, the opposite to goodness and mercy, which are supposed to be the attribute of the divine Judge. The glory of God does not require it. What advantage will he derive from the misery of the damned? The most implacable vindictive savage monster becomes satiated with the tortures of his most inveterate enemy, and concludes by giving the death blow. Is this God less merciful than the savage? And is there no difference in the degrees of punishment? No proportion whatever between the the crime and the punishment? Must the poor distressed man who steals a sheep from his wealthy neighbour in order to support his starving family, endure the same eternal punishment as the turtle-fed Bishop of Clogher, who commits the most detestable offence? or the merciless Yeoman of Manchester, who thrusts his sword into the breast of a defenceless and innocent woman? The scriptures themselves refute this doctrine. Every man shall be rewarded according to his work, it says.[64] And although this God, may award to the labourer who only works one hour, the same proportion of kindness as to those who have borne the burden and heat of the day,[65] (which, by the bye, is not consistent with justice,) yet he cannot inflict the same portion of punishment, on the man who only covets his neighbour's ass, as on the man who commits murder; for according to James, " Whosoever shall keep the whole law, and yet offend in one point, is guilty of all."[66]

Before I conclude this subject, I will again revert to the several dispositions and propensities, which are found in the human race, arising from the peculiar and diversified organization of their bodies; being aware that the idea thereof is treated by the inattentive observer of things as ridiculous and absurd. But, if we study with attention the works of nature, we shall find that it is not a mere chimera of the brain, but founded on truth and experience. The philosopher can perceive from a puddle an inch deep, the vast distance between earth and sky. Observe the timidity of the cold hearted deer; the fury of the ferocious tiger; the subtilty of the crafty fox; the inoffensiveness of the lamb; the faithfulness of the dog; the lasciviousness of the goat; the stupidity of the hog; the sagacity of the elephant; with many others, both of birds and beasts, whose different propensities result alone from their peculiar construction of parts. If the tiger was organized like the deer, or the hawk like the dove, they could not act in a ferocious manner; neither would the fox display so much cunning, if formed like the hog: and as we perceive that these propensities and qualities differ in each species, as in the greyhound and mastiff, the draught horse and the race horse, &c.; so we perceive a variation in the human species, not only in their size, colour and physical powers, but in their dispositions and intellectual faculties: for the arrangement of the organs, says a writer, with the disposition of the fibres, and a certain motion of the fluids, engender the passions, and those degrees of heat with which they actuate us, and direct our will oftentimes contrary to reason. How then can we be free to determine our actions, when we cannot withstand those craving appetites, and headstrong passions?

The inference to be drawn from this, proves that the cruel and passionate man; the weak and tenderhearted; the lascivious and crafty person; the sage and the idiot; derive all their different propensities and qualities from the variation and peculiar construction of their organized parts, and not from any peculiar creed or doctrine, which they may have received or adopted. This is exemplified within the walls of Newgate, where, during the last twelve months, nearly two thousand persons have been accused of various crimes, some of them the most abominable, cruel, and detestable; yet they have all been instructed in the doctrine of the Christian religion, by priests who enforce upon them a

belief of future punishment, and which they, no doubt,
sincerely believe as, they seem struck with astonishment
and horror at the man who entertains a doubt thereof.
Even those who have suffered an ignominious death for
their crimes and vices, professed to believe to the last
moment, in a future state of existence. While, on the
other hand, out of the many thousands that inhabit
London alone, who professedly disbelieve in a future
state, not two persons have been convicted of any
flagitious crime.

I have now examined the doctrine of eternal rewards
and punishments, and the nature of this imaginary thing
called a soul, and cannot find the least benefit arising to
society from a belief therein. It certainly is the only
method which priests could take to exculpate their God
from the charge of shewing partiality to his creatures
during their state of probation in this life, which is
everywhere evinced by the favours shown to the idle,
the voluptuous, and the wealthy; while the industrious,
the diseased, and the indigent, are wanting the common
necessaries of life. As Malachi said (iii. 15) *the proud
are happy, and they that work wickedness are set up;
yea, they that tempt the Lord are even delivered.* But,
in order to justify the providence of this God, he further
adds, that the Lord has a book of remembrance, wherein
is written the names of those who fear him, and think
upon his name, lest in that day when he *maketh up his
jewels*, he should not be able to discern between the
sheep and the goats !

I conclude by summing up the aforesaid observations. Of what utility is this soul? When sleep
overtakes us, will this soul guard or warn the body of
danger? If the soul is born with the body and enlarges
and strengthens itself, in the same progression as the
body, partaking of its pleasures and sharing of its pains,
in health and sickness, subject to the like vicissitudes
in infancy and old age; what just reason have we to
conclude, that it will not share the same fate with the
body in the hour of death? If the soul and body be distinct things, which are separated the moment the body
ceases to perform its several functions, how do they

meet again in those persons who are recovered from drowning, suffocation, and many other apparent deaths?

If the soul receives its motion from the body, must it not remain dead and useless when separated from it? If it be capable of moving itself, must it not be material? If the soul or spirit be not the result of matter, how can matter proceed from a soul or spirit? Is it absolutely necessary for God to make a fresh body for this soul, in order that vice may be punished, and virtue rewarded? Will it be just to punish or reward a body, that hath neither done good nor harm? Cannot God punish vice, and reward virtue, in this life, without deferring it to a future? Will it be just and equitable to punish equally, the lesser and greater faults? Has man the power of committing a crime so horrible, as to deserve eternal punishment? What benefit will the "just men made perfect," or even God, derive from the continual and never-ceasing howlings, groans, weeping, and gnashing of teeth, of those unfortunate and miserable beings, that are burning in fire and brimstone? Is it in this manner that we are to *love our enemies?* Is it not more noble to forgive an injury than to revenge an insult? Can eternal punishment be reconciled with infinite justice, and infinite goodness, the perfections which are so essentially necessary to a devine nature? In short, a belief in the immortality or even existence of a soul, cannot be visually, nor orally demonstrated: nor can we determine that to be departed which we have never known to be created or begotten, nor seen to exist. And if men are enjoined to *love their enemies,* and *do good to those that ill-treat them,* by this God, is it not blasphemy to think that he, himself, will act contrariwise?

Trusting that you will not fail to send me answers to the foregoing questions; or should you receive any communication respecting a future state, and the immorality of the soul, from Messieurs *Jesus, Moses, or Elijah,* you will not neglect sending me word thereof immediately.

I remain,
Your humble Servant,
JOHN CLARKE.

NOTES TO THE FOREGOING LETTER.

1 2 Peter i. 16, 17.
2 Romans iii. 4.
3 Luke ix. 32.
4 Matthew xxiv. 24.
5   „   xvii. 1.
  Mark ix. 2.
6 Matthew xxvii. 37.
  Mark xv. 26.
  Luke xxiii. 38.
  John xix. 19.
7 2 Corinthians xii. 4.
8 Hebrews v. 7.
9 Luke xxiv. 11.
10 1 Corinthians xv. 14.
11   „   „   51.
12 Matthew x. 28.
13   „   v. 29.
14 1 Corinthians xv. 38.
15   „   „   50.
16 Luke xxiv. 39, 51.
17 2 Kings ii. 11, 13.
18 2 Corinthians v. 2.
19 2 Peter iii. 10.
20 1 Thessalonians v. 23.
21 Job xii. 10.
  Psalm lxvi. 9.
22 Proverbs xvi. 9.
23 Ezekiel xviii. 4.
24 Genesis iii. 22, 23.
25 Amos iii. 7.
26 Zechariah i. 5.
27 Ecclesiastes iii. 19, 20.
28 1 Kings iv. 29.
29 Deuteronomy xxviii. 29.
30 Psalm xlix. 10, 19.
31   „   cxlvi. 4.
32 Job xxxiv. 15.
33 1 Corinthians xv. 53.
34 Proverbs xviii. 14.

LETTER XII.

TO DR. ADAM CLARKE.

~~~~~~~~~~~~~~~~~~~~~~~~~~

Sir,

In a former letter I promised to take a review of
that absurd and incredible story, related of Jesus, when
he cured a sick man of the palsy, after the roof of the
house had been broken up, to let him down into the
room wherein he sat; because his bearers could not
enter in at the door for the press of the people.[1]   This
story seems to me so unaccountably strange, that I must
have recourse to my old friend Woolston again, for his
opinion concerning it.   For me to suppose that Jesus,
who could drive his thousands before him out of the
temple, and draw as many after him into the wilderness;
whose very looks could strike down to the ground a
multitude of soldiers,[2] yet could not, by either force or
persuasion, cause the people to retreat or make way for
this poor man to come to him, and be healed, without
causing so much trouble to the sick man and his bearers,
besides unnecessarily injuring the house of his friend,
cannot, by me, be reconciled to either truth or reason.

Woolston says that "this story, (without excepting
that of the pool of Bethesda) is the most monstrously
absurd, improbable, and incredible of any.   There is
not one miracle related of Jesus, that does not labour
under more or less absurdities, either in substance or
circumstance; but this for number and greatness of
absurdities, I think, surpasses them all; they actually
stare a man in the face, and are so obvious that I
wonder they have hitherto been overlooked; and that
some considerate and intelligent person has not, before
now, hesitated and boggled at them.   If interest had
not blinded the eyes of our learned clergy, they would

A a

easily have descried the incredibilities and absurdities of this story, and in any other impostor's case, soon have pointed them out to the ridicule of his admirers and adorers.

" If a man were to torture his brains for the invention of a romantic tale of improbable and surprising circumstances, that he might withal hope to palm for a truth, were it but for a week or a day, upon the faith and understanding of the credulous; he could never have presumed I think, so far upon the weakness of their intellects, as to imagine that anything so gross or contradictory to sense and reason, would have gone down with them as this story of the paralytic. Yet it has passed currently through many ages of the church; has been read with attention by the learned, and revered by all Christians, without exception, hesitation, or doubt. In short, so palpable is the falsity of the story of this miracle, that it requires no extraordinary degree of sagacity to detect the falsity thereof.

" The people, it seems, so pressed and thronged about the house where Jesus was, that the paralytic and his bearers could not get near the door. For what did they so throng and press ? Was it to see Jesus who, according to the prophet Isaiah, was without form and comliness? Even were he one of the most graceful of all men, as Painters and Publius Lentulus have described him, yet this could be no reason for such a crowd. I will grant that an extraordinary person, either for beauty or deformity, may attract the eyes of the people, and occasion too great a throng about him; still this will not account for the press about the person of Jesus at Capernaum, the place where he dwelt, and where he was most commonly seen and well known. Neither could it have been to hear him preach. Though an excellent preacher does sometimes, and a very indifferent one does oftener, draw multitudes after him; yet Jesus as a prophet, was without honour at Capernaum, his own country; consequently it is not to be supposed that for his doctrine he was so much followed there, though we read that he preached the word unto them.

" Was it then to behold him working miracles, and

curing the diseased? This is the likeliest reason of the crowd pressing round the door of the house. And perhaps it was a day appointed beforehand, for his healing of the diseased, which might occasion a more than ordinary concourse of the people. But then this reason would have induced the people to make way for the lame, blind, and paralytics, to come to Jesus, or they frustrated their own hopes and expectations of seeing the miracles wrought; and acted more unreasonably than ever any mob can be supposed to have done, either before or since this miracle.

"But whatever was the reason of this tumultuous crowding, for it is hard to be accounted for, it is said that the poor paralytic with his bearers could not get to the door of the house for the press, and therefore in all haste is he hauled up to the top of the house, and let down through a breach of the roof into the room wherein sat Jesus. What need was there for such haste and pains to get to Jesus for a cure? If they had waited a few hours, at furthest, in all probability, the tumult would have ceased and access easily been had to him. But that the bearers of the poor man should enterprise a trouble and difficulty, that could not require less time than the tumult could be supposed to last, is a little strange and somewhat incredible.

"St. Chrysostom says, that the paralytic saw that the market place or street was thronged with people, who had obstructed all passage to the house where Jesus was, yet did he not so much as say to his friends and bearers, 'What is the reason of this tumult? let us stay till it is appeased, and the house cleared of the people, who ere long will depart; and then we shall privately and quitely get admittance to Jesus.' Then why did he not say so? Any one besides himself and his bearers, if they had any reason or sense about them, would have so argued. St. Chrysostom says, that it was their faith that made them in such haste to get to Jesus; but I should have thought that their faith might have worked a little patience, and disposed them to stay until Jesus came out to them, or they more easily get unto him. And it is an addition to the strangeness and incredibility of this story that it did not.

"Supposing the haste of this paralytic to proceed from his dangerous state so much, that he could not wait for the dispersion of the crowd; but, for want of a free entrance by the door, must, cost what it will, be raised up to the top of the house, and a breach therein made for him. Yet, the question is, whether such an enterprise was or could be feasible and practicable? For my part I can have no conception of the possibility of it. If they could not get to the door of the house for the press, how should they come near the sides of it? It cannot be imagined that the bearers walked over the heads of the people with the sick man! This is certainly another difficulty in this story, which renders it yet more strange and incredible.

"But without questioning the possibility and easy conveyance of the sick man and his couch, over the heads of the mob, to the sides of the house, we will imagine that he is now brought thither, where we behold him and his bearers with their pullies, ropes, and ladders, (that were not at hand, neither could they be suddenly procured) hauling and heaving him to the top of the house. Of what height the house was is not of much consequence. Some, for the credit of the story, say, that it was a very low one; though ancient and modern commentators are pretty well agreed that it was an upper room where Jesus was; consequently the house was, at least, two stories high. But if it were much higher, I will admit that art and pullies, (which they wanted for the present) would raise the man and his bed to the top of it, so we will not dispute nor differ upon this matter. On the top of the house then we are about to behold the sick man, his bed, and his bearers, with their hatchets and their hammers, &c. (which they certainly could not have brought with them, not knowing that they would have any occasion for their use) uncovering the roof of the house, breaking up tiles, spars, and rafters, and making a hole capacious enough to admit the man with his bed through. An odd, strange, and unaccountable work this, which, if they had not been cunning fellows, would hardly have entered into their heads to project. But at work they are, when it is well if Jesus and his disciples escape with only a

broken pate, by the falling of tiles; and if the rest
are not almost smothered with the dust; for it appears
that the breach was made just over their heads. Where
was the good man of the house all this while? Would
he suffer his house to be thus broken up, without endeavouring to prevent their foolish and needless attempt,
until the mob was dispersed, and free liberty to his
door might be obtained? which could not be long first.
Is there nothing in all this of difficulty and obstruction
in the way of the belief of this story?

"Some modern commentators, being aware of these
difficulties in the story, and willing to reconcile men to
the easier belief of it, say, as Drusius did, that the
houses in Judea were flat roofed and not ridged. And
Doctors Lightfoot and Whitby say that there was a
door on their flat roofs, by which the Jews used to
ascend to the top of their houses, where they discoursed
on law and religious matters; and that it was through
such a door, by a little widening of the sides of it, that
the sick man was let down in the presence of Jesus;
to which opinion I would yield, if it were not liable to
these objections, viz, that it is not reconcileable to what
Luke says of their letting the paralytic down through
the tiling with his couch, in the midst where Jesus was;
nor hardly consistent with what Mark says of their
uncovering and breaking-up the roof of the house:
which expressions the Evangalists had never used if
there had been a door, by which he might have descended. If we indulge Lightfoot and Whitby in their
notions, I ask, what occasion was there to widen the
door way, and break down its sides? They may say,
because the passage otherwise was too narrow for the
man's couch to get through. Why then did they not
take him out of his couch, and let him down in a
blanket, a chair, or a basket? Or rather, why did not
Jesus to prevent this trouble and damage to the house,
ascend himself through the door to the top, and there
speak the healing word to this poor man? To say that
Jesus could not or would not go up to this sick man, I
would not, for fear of an imputation of blasphemy
against me. Our divines are, therefore, to look for

A a 2

what they will hardly find, an answer to these said
questions, which will comport with the wisdom, the
goodness, and honour of Jesus; or here will be another
nd insuperable bar to the credibility of this story.

"In short there are more and greater difficulties
affecting the credit of this miracle, on the side of Jesus,
than any before urged. Could not he have made the
access to himself more easy? Could not he, to prevent
all this trouble and pains of getting to the top of the
house, and of breaking up the roof, have desired or even
forced the people to make way for the sick man and his
bearers? This, surely, was not impossible for him to do.
If it were hard for another it could not have been so
for him, who was omnipotent. He that could drive his
thousands before him out of the temple, and draw as
many after him into the wilderness, might surely, by
force or persuasion, have made the people, however
unreasonable and mobbish, to retreat. Then why did
he not? Without a good and satisfactory answer,
which I cannot conceive, to this question, here is the
most unaccountable and incredible part of the whole
story, that reflects on the wisdom, the power and goodness of Jesus. If there had been no other absurd
circumstances about it, this is enough to spoil its credit
so far, as that I believe it impossible for our clergy, with
all their wit, penetration, and sagacity, to get over.

"Believe then this story, thus taken to pieces, who
can? It is such an accumulation of absurdities, improbabilities, and incredibilities, that a man of the most
easy faith, if he at all think, cannot digest. It is not
credible, I say, to suppose that the people of Capernaum,
where Jesus dwelt and was so well known and little
admired, would at all *press* to see or hear him. And if
the occasion of their concourse was to behold his
miracles, it is unreasonable to think they would so
tumultuate to their own disappointment. They would
rather make way for the diseased, for the satisfaction
of their own curiosity, to come to Jesus. And if they
did mob-it to their own disappointment about the door
of the house, it was next to an impossibility for the
poor man and his couch to be heaved over their heads
is we.

and raised to the top of the house. More unreasonable yet to think that the master of the house would suffer the roof of it to be so broken up for the admission of the sick man, when by an appeal to the authorities, he might have procured assistance to clear away every obstacle to an entrance by the door. But most of all against reason, to suppose that Jesus would not give forth the healing word, and so prevent all this labour; or by his divine power have dispersed the mob, in order that the sick man might have had free and easy access to him.

" Whether all this be not absolutely shocking to the credit of this story, let my readers judge. In my opinion, no tale more monstrously romantic can be told. I do not here question the power of Jesus to heal this paralytic, nor the miraculousness of the cure. The trouble of that question is saved by the many other incredible circumstances of the story, which is such a contradiction to sense and reason as is not to be equalled in any thing that is commonly received and believed by mankind. Cicero says that there is nothing so absurd which some of the philosophers have not held. And they might, and did, some of them, hold very gross absurdities; but this story before us, which is the object of the faith of our learned priesthood at this day, is a match for the worst of them.

" But as absurd as this story is, I expect that our clergy will be disgusted with my ludicrous display of it; and that Archdeacon Stubbs, in particular, will again be ready to exclaim against me, and say that this is turning a miraculous fact, and a divine testimony of our religion into ridicule. Whereupon it is to be wished, that the Archdeacon would write, what would be a pleasure to see, a vindication of this story. If he can account for the possibility and credibility of it, he shall have my leave to make another dull speech in convocation against me. And it is not unlikely but he may say as much for it as any other man; for as the story is senseless, it is the better suited to his head and brains. If he do not, I much question whether any other Clergyman of more wit, will appear in its defence."

These are the objections which Mr. Woolston makes against believing in the letter of this story; a man, who, like myself, digested every subject before he gave it full credit; without which, there can be no true faith. We judge by effects; we believe by analogy; we trust by faith: which credulity, oftentimes proves deceitful. What binds one friend to another, but faith? yet how often is this faith, only in this simple matter, proved to be fallacious? Can the most skilful mathematician calculate on what is passing in the mind, by the sight of the countenance, or by the sound of words uttered? Are we not perpetually duped, deceived and betrayed by trusting to faith upon appearances, instead of certainty? What evidence can we have then of things *not seen?* Yet religion of every kind is nothing more than a system of faith! Faith to credit what? Matters of fact? No: but matters of faith! By faith we understand the worlds were framed.[3] By faith, we are told, that men subdued kingdoms—stopped the mouths of lions—quenched the violence of fire—escaped the edge of the sword—passed the red sea as by dry land[4]—and many other wonderful things, which are said to have been done by faith; and which also requires faith to believe them.

In the chapter of Matthew, which we have just examined, we find that a woman who was diseased with an issue of blood twelve years,[5] was cured of her disease through faith; to believe which, we are also required to have faith. Without faith there can be no religion. With faith, any thing may be religion, however ridiculous and absurd. But as we should never condemn unheard, let us examine this story of blood and faith, as it is recorded by Matthew, Mark, and Luke:[6] for John seems to have been a faithless being, or he never would have omited noticing such a wonderful display of faith, as was exhibited by this woman.

Those three historians all agree in saying that it was done while Jesus was journeying towards the house wherein the daughter of Jarius was laid; but they all differ respecting the time when he undertook this journey; but of this I shall speak hereafter, when I examine the result of the journey. Therefore, we will pass by the contradictions, and treat only of the subject, which I find too delicate for me to handle, so must again fly to my old friend Woolston, for his assistance.

He says that " as there is a particular narration of this miracle, among the few others, that are specified, so reason should tell us that this is one of the greatest that Jesus wrought, or it would not be related of itself, but thrown into the lump of all manner of diseases which he healed. And how then shall we come to the knowledge of the greatness of this miracle? Why, there are but two ways to it, and they are :—

" First, by considering the nature of the disease, or the lamentable condition of the patient before cure; and

" Secondly, by considering the manner or means by which the cure was performed.

" If one or both of these considerations do not manifest the certainty of a miracle, Infidels may conclude that there was none in it.

" First. As to the nature of the disease of this woman we are much in the dark; and very uncertain of what kind and degree it was. St. Matthew, writing of it, says the woman was *aimosoyousa*, that is obnoxious to bleeding. Mark and Luke say that *ousa, en seomati aimatos*, she was in an efflux, or running of blood. But neither the one nor the other of the Evangelists signify of what degree her hemorrhage was, nor from what part of the body it proceeded, nor how often or seldom she was addicted to it. It might be, for aught we know, only a little bleeding at the nose to which now and then she was subject. Or it might be an obnoxiousness to an evacuation of blood, by siege or urine. Or it was not improbably of the menstruous kind. Any of these might be the case of this woman, for what is written; and I do not find that any of our divines have determined of what sort it was. But a great miracle is wrought, they think, in her cure, without knowing the disease, which Infidels will say is asserted at random and without reason : inasmuch as it is necessary to know the nature of the distemper, or none can truly say that there was a great, much less a miraculous cure wrought.

"Supposing this hemorrhage proceeded from what part of the body our divines think fit, how will they make a grievous distemper of it, in order to constitute it a miracle? The woman subsisted too long under her issue of blood, and bore it too well for any one to suppose her case very grievous. Beza will have it that it that it was a constant and incessant effusion of blood that the woman laboured with. But this could not be, nor was it possible, as I suppose physicians will agree, that nature could endure it so long, for the woman to live twelve days under it, much less twelve years.

"No more then, than some slight indisposition can reasonably and naturally be made of this woman's distemper. And it would be well, if Infidels would rest here with their objections against it. But what if they should say that this hemorrhage was rather of advantage to the health of the patient, than of danger to her; and that the woman was more nice than wise, or she never would have sought so much for help and cure of it. Some hemorrhages are better kept open than stopped and dried up. And if Infidels should say that this was a preservative of the life of the woman, like an issue at which nature discharges itself of bad humours, who can contradict them? Nay, if they should say that the cure of this woman's hemorrhage by Jesus, was a precipitation of her death, (for she died a short time after it,) rather than a promulgation of her life, (for she lived twelve years under it, and was of good strength when she applied to Jesus for a cure, or she could never have borne the press of the people to come at him,) who can gainsay them? It is true she was solicitous for a cure, and uneasy under her distemper, or she would never have spent all she had on the physicians, which is a sign, some may say, that her disease was grievous, irksome, and dangerous, as well as incurable by art. But Infidels will say, not so; for there are some slight cutaneous distempers sometimes, issuing with a little purulent and bloody matter, that nice women will be at a great expense to remove, and are always tampering and often advising about them, though to no purpose. And if they should say that this was the worst of the case of this woman, who can disprove it?

"In short here is an uncertain distemper both in nature and degree; how then can there be any certainty of a miracle in the cure of it? Mr. Moore, the apothecary, accurately describes the diseases he pretends to have cured; and he is in the right on it, so to do or he could not recommend his art, nor aggrandize his own fame. So the bodily disease of this woman should have been clearly and fully represented to our understanding, or we can form no conception of the power of Jesus in the cure thereof. And I cannot but think that the Evangelists, especially Luke, who, they say, was a physician, had made a better story of this woman's case if the power and authority of Jesus were to be urged from the letter of the story. It is enough to make us think that he cured no extraordinary or grievous maladies, or the Evangelists would never, in particular, have instanced- this, against which so many objections may be raised. Therefore, reasonably speaking, there could not have been anything extraordinary in the disease of this woman; consequently, no great miracle wrought in her cure. Let us now,

"Secondly, consider the manner of her cure, and whether any miracle is to be thence proved. The woman said within herself, that if she could *but touch the hem of his garment*, she would be made whole. And I cannot but commend her, at this distance of time, for the power of her faith, persuasion, or imagination, in the case, which was a good preparative for relief; without which it is certain she must have continued under her disease. The power of imagination, it is well known, will work wonders, see visions, produce monsters, and heal diseases; as experience and history both testify. There being many instances, which may be given of cures performed by frivolous applications, charms, and spells; which are unaccountable any other way than by the imagination of the patient. Against the reason and judgment of a physician, sometimes the diseased will take his own medicines and find benefit therefrom. And I do not doubt but stories may be told of cures wrought, the imagination of the patient helping, by as mean a trifle as the touch of the garment of Jesus, and yet may not be considered miraculous! Even in the ordinary, natural, and rational use of physic, it is requisite that the patient should have a good opinion of his physician and his medicines. A good heart in the sick, tends not only to his support, but helps the operation of prescriptions: as despair and dejection of spirits sometimes kill, where, otherwise reasonably speaking, proper medicines would cure. So a good conceit in the patient at other times, whether the medicines be pertinent or not, is almost all in all towards the cure. And if Infidels should say that this was the case with the woman in the gospel; if they should say as St. John of Jerusalem did, that her own imagination cured herself;* and should urge the probability of it, because Jesus could do no cures and miracles against unbelief, (Matt. xiii. 58.) who can help it? In this case our divines must prove that this woman's hemorrhage was of that kind that no faith nor fancy in herself could help her, without divine power. But this is impossible for them to do, without there had been a more certain description given of her disease than that which is given by the Evangelists.

" Our divines will indeed tell us, that it was the divine power, co-operating with the faith and imagination of the woman that cured her; because Jesus said that virtue had gone out of him, to the healing of her. And I wish that Infidels would acquiesce here, and not say that the virtue of Jesus hung very loose upon him, or the woman's faith, like a fascination, could never have extracted it, against his will and knowledge. But what if they should say that Jesus being secretly apprised of the woman's faith and intention, took the hint, and to comfort and confirm her in her conceit, and to help the cure forward, said that virtue had gone out

---

* Non autem fimbria Jesu, sed ejus cogitatio eam salvam fecit.—*In loc. Merci.*

of him? This would be an untoward suggestion, to which, if Infidels should make, our divines must look out for a reply.

"It is said of the Pope, when he was last at Benevento, that he wrought three miracles, which our Protestant Clergy, I dare say, will not believe. But for all that it is not improbable but that some diseased people, considering their superstitious veneration for the Pope, and their opinion of the sanctity of the *present*, might be persuaded of his gift of miracles, and desirous of his exercise thereof; and if they fancifully or actually received benefit by his touch, it is no wonder, without considering it a miracle. Suppose we had been told that the Pope cured a woman of an hemorrhage, like this in the gospel, what would Protestants have said to it? Why, 'that a foolish, credulous, and superstitious woman, had fancied herself cured of some slight indisposition; and the crafty Pope and his adherents, aspiring after popular applause, magnified the presumed cure into a miracle! If they would have us Protestants to believe the miracle, they should have given us an exact description of her disease, and then we could better have judged of it.' The application of such a supposed story, of a miracle wrought by the Pope, is easy; and if Infidels, Jews, and Mahomedans, who have no better opinion of Jesus than Protestants have of the Pope, should make it, there is no help for it."

Thus far has Mr. Woolston assisted me in reviewing this pretended miracle; and although he has left room for further criticism still I think it would be both needless and tiresome, until a reasonable and rational answer be given to that already written. For me to handle all the pretended miracles of Jesus in this manner, would be a long and tedious task; and probably you yourself will acknowledge it to be unnecessary. I shall, therefore, as I see that Mr. Woolston has been beforehand with me in this also, just copy a few of his observations on that most silly and absurd action of Jesus, when he made clay of dirt and spittle, and put it to the eyes of a man born blind, by which means, it is said, the blind man received sight.

B b

After which I shall take into consideration the stories of his raising the widow's son, and the daughter of Jairus, with the resurrection of Lazarus, with which I shall conclude my observations on his miracles; for if those three miracles are found to be credibly reported, they themselves are sufficient to silence all unbelievers; unless you, sir, or any of your Christian friends, have a particular desire to know my opinions upon any other miracle which I may have neglected to notice : though I trust you will admit that I have selected those that are considered to be the most remarkable and stupendous, among the number that are transmitted down to this generation. John said[7] that the world itself would not contain the books that must have been written, if all the things that Jesus did were related! After which John said no more, well knowing that he had said enough! I shall, therefore, imitate him, by concluding my introduction to the examination of this miracle.

John, we find, nearly occupies the whole of the ninth Chapter in relating the most wonderful miracle performed by Jesus, in giving sight to a man born blind, by only using a little dirt and spittle, which I should have thought would have been the principal ingredients to deprive a man of sight! This story is confined to the authority of John, as not one of the other historians take the least notice of it; consequently there can be no contradictions concerning it among them.

John says, " that as Jesus was passing by, he saw a man that was blind from his birth—and he spat upon the ground, and made clay of the spittle, and he anointed the eyes of the blind man with the clay; and said unto him, go, wash in the pool of Siloam : and the man went, and washed, and came seeing. And this was on the sabbath day." Here we are informed, that this man was blind from his birth; consequently, must have been wandering about in darkness, while Jesus was working with his father in a carpenter's shop so many years. As Jesus is described as being a person of so much compassion, why did he not, upon some holiday, or sabbath day, if he could find no other time to leave his father's business, go and seek this poor blind man, and relieve him from his deplorable condition, instead of deferring it till he was upwards of thirty years of age? Surely no good and compassionate man would have spent his time in a carpenter's shop, chipping and chopping pieces of wood, which might have been as well done by others, if he had the power of rendering to his fellow creatures such an important service, as that of giving sight to the blind! And if he were sent to destroy the works of the devil,[8] he could not begin about it too early. But what does Woolston say to this miracle?

He says, that, "blindness, as far as one may guess, by the Evangelical history, was the distemper on which Jesus frequently exercised his power. And there is no doubt to be made but he might have healed many of some weakness, defect, and imperfection or other in their eyes: but whether he wrought any miracle upon any that he is supposed to have cured is uncertain. It is notorious that there are many kinds of blindness that are incurable by art or nature; and there are other kinds from which a man may be relieved through nature and art. And unless we knew of a certainty that the sore or blind eyes which Jesus cured, were absolutely out of the reach of art or nature, infidels will imagine that he was only master of a good ointment for sore eyes, and being successful in the use of it, ignorant people would needs think that he had wrought miracles!

"The world is often blessed with excellent Oculists, who, through study and practice, have attained to wonderful skill in eye-maladies; which, though they are of various sorts, yet, by custom of speech, all pass under the general name of blindness. And sometimes we hear of famous chance doctors, like Jesus, who, by some gift of nature or fortune, without any skill in the structure of the eyes, have been very successful in the cure of one distemper or other, incident to them. Such as Sir William Read, who, though no scholar, nor of acquired abilities in physic and surgery, yet cured his thousands of sore or blind eyes; and many of them too, to the surprise and astonishment of professed surgeons and physicians. Whether he or Jesus cured the greatest number of blind eyes, cannot be precisely known; but to please our divines, it shall be granted that Jesus cured the greatest number; but that he cured worse or more difficult distempers, cannot be at all admitted. It is true that Sir William met with many cases of blind or sore eyes that were above his power of healing; and so did Jesus, or he would never have suffered such multitudes of the blind and otherwise distempered people to have gone away unhealed. Our divines will here say that it was never through a deficiency of power in Jesus, but through want of faith in the diseased, that he did not heal them; but in other surgeons and physicians, it is confessedly their own insufficiency. To which I have only this answer, that our physicians and surgeons are to be commended for their ingenuity and honesty, in imputing it to their own defect of power, instead of laying the blame to their patients, when they perceive they cannot cure them. Thus our divines find unbelief necessary sometimes, if for no other purpose than supporting the credit of the healing power of Jesus.

"But to come to the particular consideration of the miracle before us. Jesus restored, it seems, a blind man to his eye-sight, by the use of a peculiar ointment, and washing of his eyes, as directed, in the pool of Siloam. Where lies the miracle? I cannot see it; therefore hope our divines will take their opportunity to point it out to me. Our surgeons, with their ointments and washings, can cure sore and blind eyes of one sort or other; and Jesus did no more here; yet he must be reckoned a worker of miracles, and our surgeons but artificial operators! Where is the sense and reason of this distinction being made between them? If Mr. Moor, the apothecary, for the notable cures which he performs by the means of his medicines, should write himself, and be accounted by his admirers, a *miracle-worker*, he and they would be laughed at for it. Yet Jesus, for his curing the sore eyes of a poor man with an ointment, must be held in veneration for a divine and miraculous operator, as much as if by the breath of his mouth, he had removed some huge mountain or other !

" A miracle, if I mistake not the notion of our divines about it, is a supernatural event, or a work out of the power of nature or of art to effect. And when it is spoken of as the cure of a disease, as of blindness or lameness, it ought to be so represented as that skilful and experienced surgeons and physicians, who can themselves do strange and surprising cures by art, may give it, upon their judgement, that no skill of man could reach the operation without the aid and assistance of a divine and almighty hand. But there is no such care taken in the description of any of the diseases which Jesus cured, much less of this before us ; against the miraculousness of which, consequently, there are two exceptions to be made.

" *First*, that we know nothing of the nature of this poor man's blindness ; nor what was the defect of his eyes ; nor whether it was curable by art or not : without the knowledge of which it is impossible and unreasonable to assert, that there was a miracle wrought in the cure of him. If his blindness or weakness of eyesight, was curable by human means, there is an end of the miracle. If the Evangelist had given us an accurate description of the condition of this man's eyes before cure, we could have judged better. But this is their constant neglect in all the distempers which Jesus healed, and is enough to induce us to doubt of his miraculous power. There are, as I have said, some sorts of sore and blind eyes curable by art, as experience doth testify ; and there are others incurable, as physicians and patients do lament. Of which sort was this man's, we know not. The worst that we know of this case is, that he was blind from his birth or infancy, which might be ; and yet time, nature, and art, might give relief to him. As a man advances in years, the diseases of childhood and youth, oftentimes wear off. What we call the King's-evil, or an inflamation in the eyes, in time will abate of its malignity. Nature will not only by degrees work the cure itself, but the seasonable help of a good Oculist will soon expedite it ; though in time of infancy he could be of no use. And who knows but this might have been the case of this blind man, whose cure Jesus, by his art, did only hasten and help forward? However, there are grounds enough to suspect that it was not divine power that healed this man, or Jesus had never prepared and ordered an ointment and wash for him.

"Should our divines suppose, or describe for the Evangelist, a state of blindness in this man, incurable by art, that would be begging the question; which no unbeliever will grant. But to please them I will yield, without enquiring into the nature of this man's blindness, that if Jesus had used no medicines, if with only a word of his mouth he had cured the man, and he had instantaneously recovered as the word was spoken, here would have been a real and great miracle wrought, let the blindness or imperfection be of what kind or degree soever; but for Jesus to use ointments and washings absolutely spoils the credit of the miracle, and we ought by no means to ascribe that to the immediate hand and power of God, which medicines and balsams are applied to effect. And this brings me to the

" *Second* exception, against the miraculousness of the cure of this blind man; which is, that Jesus used human means to cure him; which means, whether they were at all proper and effectual in themselves, do affect the credit of the miracle, and give occasion of suspicion that it was art and not divine power that healed him; or Jesus, for his honour, had never had recourse to the use of them. And what were those means, or that medicine, which Jesus made use of? Why 'he spat upon the ground, and made a balsam of dirt and spittle, with which he annointed the eyes of the poor man, and restored his eye-sight.' A strange and odd sort of an ointment that I believe was never used before, nor since, for sore and blind eyes! I am not student enough in physic and surgery, to account for the natural and rational use of this balsam, but wish that skilful professors of those sciences would help me out of this difficulty. If they could rationally account for the use of this eye-salve, though it was by supposing that Jesus, imperceptibly had in his mouth a proper unctious and balsamic substance, which he dissolved into spittle, they would do great service to a certain cause : and I wonder that none of them, whether well or ill affected to religion, have not yet bent their thoughts towards framing a reason for his so doing.

"In the practice of physic and surgery, there are, sometimes very odd and unaccountable medicaments made use of; and now and then, very whimsical and seemingly ridiculous ones, by old women, to good purpose : though none of them are to be compared to Jesus's balsam for sore eyes! I have heard of a merry mountebank of distinction, whose catholic medicine was hasty-pudding, which, indeed, is a notable remedy againt the *esuriency* of the stomach, under which the poor often labour. But the eye-salve of Jesus, for absurdity, whim, and incongruity, was never equalled, either in jest or in earnest, by any mountebank or quack-doctor in existence! Whether infidels think of this ointment of the holy Jesus with a smile, or reflect on it with disdain, I cannot guess. As to myself, I should think that this eye-salve of Jesus would sooner put out a man's eyes than restore a blind man to sight. And I believe that our divines, for the credit of the miracle, and our surgeons, for the honour of their science, will agree that it could not be naturally operative and effective of the cure of this blind man.

"What then could be the reason for Jesus using this strange eye-salve, when for the sake of the miracle, and for the honour of his own power, he should have cured the man with a word speaking? I am puzzled to think how our divines will extricate themselves from this strait, and account for the use of this eye-salve. Surely they will not say that Jesus used this senseless and insignificant ointment, merely to put a *slur* upon the practice of physic and surgery, as if other medicines were of no more avail than his dirt and spittle. They have more wit than to say so, lest it should incense a noble and most useful profession, not so much against themselves, as against Jesus, and provoke them to a nicer and stricter inquiry, than I can make into his miracles, the diseases he cured, and his manner of operation; whence they might infer, that he could be no miraculous healer of diseases, by his using medicines and ointments; nor his Evangelists orthodox at theology, who are so inexpert at anatomy and the description of bodily distempers. This might be of bad consequence to religion; and yet I wonder that none of those who are supposed to be a little disaffected with Christianity, have not taken the hint from this pretended miracle, and some others of a similar nature, to endeavour to prove that Jesus was but little better than a quack-doctor.

"For my own part, I should think that Jesus was some juggling impostor, who wished to pass for a miraculous healer of diseases, though he used underhand proper medicines. The clay and the spittle he made an open show of, as what, to appearance, he would cure the blind man with; but in reserve he had a more sanative balsam which he subtilely slipped in the stead of the clay, with which by repeatedly annointing the eyes of the man, and afterwards thoroughly washing and cleansing them effected his cure. If our divines will not admit this to have been the case, it certainly is incumbent on them to answer seriously these questions, viz. what reason had Jesus for making use of this eye-salve, made of clay and spittle? Whether, if it were of service towards accomplishing the cure of this blind man, it does not destroy the miracle? And if it had no effect in the cure of him, whether Jesus was not a vain and trifling operator, in making use of such insignificant and impotent medicines, to the dimunition of his divine power? These questions are not ridiculous but calm and sedate reasoning, which our divines require. Therefore, a grave, rational, and substantial answer is expected to them, without any dimunition of the miracle."

As I have a particular desire to close this work with the present year, I shall be under the necessity of passing by the parables, which for the most part, are both ridiculous and unintelligible; such as no man wishing to instruct the ignorant, would attempt to put forth.

That they are unintelligible is evident, from the many different interpretations which are given to them. And as such is the case, would it not have been better for him, as Paul says,[9] to have spoke only five words with the understanding, so that others might receive instructions therefrom, than ten thousand words in an unknown tongue, which none can understand? Moreover, of what use are these parables? When they were spoken, they who it is said heard them, even his own disciples,[10] could not comprehend their signification. How then can we be expected to understand their meaning or purpose? It is written, that he spake nothing but parables; that without a parable spake he not unto them.[11] How then, can any doctrine be formed upon anything which he is supposed to have said? Solomon, the wisest of all men seems to insinuate that none but fools make use of parables.[12] And surely, no wise man would assert, that he and his father were one;[13] or, that while eating and drinking a little bread and wine,[14] he was eating and drinking his own flesh and blood! But who would not think that the man was deserving a place in Bedlam, who should assert that all men should be damned, who would not believe in such ridiculous nonsense? Yet there are many, even in this enlightened nineteenth century, who do, I really believe, actually and sincerely credit such absurdities, yet are suffered to go at large! But shall you and I, who are so well acquainted with the tricks and artifices which are made use of, to enslave the minds of the credulous, by men of all ages, and in every nation, give credit to such tales? You, Sir, well know, that the means made use of, are nothing but incomprehensible mysteries, secret decrees, and oracles holding forth unintelligible enigmas, which are hid from the wise and prudent[15] because they have too much sense to credit, or attempt to interpret them; but are always revealed to babes and sucklings, the emblems of ignorance. Then why, Sir, suffer yourself to be damned out of your reason? The man who will permit that, will easily be damned into any opinion. As Peter Annett says "nothing can be too monstrous to his pliable timidity; or too shocking to his easy credulity, if it be well pointed with damnation." Let us then, Sir, be always careful to preserve this intellectual light of reason, by supplying our lamps with sufficient oil, lest we should be likened to the foolish Virgins,[16] of whom Jesus speaks, that suffered their lamps of reason to go out, through carelessness; when, being involved in the darkness of mysteries, they were shut out of the kingdom of truth, and exposed to every minister of falsehood and iniquity.

I am, Sir,

Your humble Servant,

JOHN CLARKE.

NOTES TO THE FOREGOING LETTER.

1 Mark ii. 4.
2 John xviii, 16.
3 Hebrews xi, 3.
4   „   „   29   36.
5 Matthew ix. 20.
6 Matthew v. 20.
  Luke viii. 20,
7 John xxi. 25.
8 1 John iii. 8.
9 1 Corinthians xiv. 19.

10

...

„

LETTER XIII.

TO DR. ADAM CLARKE.

SIR,

According to promise, I intend now to take into consideration those three most extraordinary miracles as performed, it is said, by Jesus, viz, his first raising the daughter of Jairus;[1] then the son of a widow at Naim;[2] and lastly, his restoring Lazarus to life, after he had lain in the grave four days.[3]

In this examination, I shall not attempt to deny the possibility of restoring persons to life who to all appearance have become defunct, we having so many proofs of its practicability in our own days: but I will prove, from the circumstances connected with the means employed, in restoring those supposed aforesaid dead bodies to life, that nothing miraculous transpired, in their resuscitation, admitting the truth of the relation, above the power and abilities of an ordinary juggler to accomplish. Likewise, that the stories themselves, by the absurdities, improbabilities, and incredibilities contained therein, evince nothing more than fiction.

We are not informed that he raised any more persons from the dead besides those three already named. If he did, we may rest assured that none of them were attended with more extraordinary circumstances than those three, which are so particularly recorded; which I will grant, are quite sufficient to convince all those who read them, that Jesus must have possessed more than human power and abilities to have accomplished in that surprising and unnatural manner, provided the accounts given of them are well circumstanced and credibly reported. It must, therefore, be presumed, that those three miracles were reputed to have been the greatest, if not the only ones of the kind, that Jesus wrought, or his historians would not have selected them from others, which he might have done, in this especial manner.

Although I have just admitted, that if the accounts of Jesus raising those three persons to life, were credibly reported and transmitted to us, with unquestionable authority, they were enough to conciliate the confidence of all mankind, that Jesus was something more than human, or he could not have done those things, yet, I do not mean to assert, that, were the like things done in our days, they would be entitled to the same merit, or deserve the like praise. I wish this to be particularly understood, lest some gentlemen or other belonging to the "Humane Society, for recovering drowned persons," or of any other society whose merit lies in restoring those who have been suffocated, or strangled, to life, should accuse me of blasphemy, in ascribing to them powers which alone belong to a superhuman being. Because in the age that these three persons are supposed to have been raised, we are well informed that the Jews in particular were entirely ignorant of the means which are employed in our days for resuscitating dead bodies. So that if any person in that age were ever restored to life again, after they had been apparently dead, it must have been a miracle indeed, to perform which was then beyond the power of the human species. Let us now examine the account given, and judge accordingly,

These three miracles we find differ greatly in their degree. The most surprising and stupendous, is that of restoring to life a man that had been laid in the grave four days. The next, in magnitude, is that of the widow's son, at Naim, who was restored to life while on his passage to the grave. The least, and most objectionable of the three, is the raising the daughter of Jairus, who was not dead, according to the confession of Jesus, but only sleeping;[4] or more probably had been frightened out of her senses, by the noise and ado that were made,[5] and so had fainted. However, we will sift them as they are related, and by their own words, they shall be either justified or condemned.

Matthew says, that while Jesus was eating meat in the house of Matthew, the custom-house officer, and conversing with the disciples of John, "a certain ruler came and worshipped him, saying, my daughter is even now dead, but come thou and lay thine hand upon her, and she shall live." Whence it is evident, that this ruler confessedly believed in the power of Jesus, or he would not have demeaned himself so far as to worship him, and en treat him so earnestly. But this story will not harmo nize with the Gospel according to John, wherein it states that none of the Pharisees nor rulers of the synagogues believed on him:[6] and we are quite certain that the Sadducees could not, if they believed in neither angel, spirit, nor resurrection.[7] Here then, we find a stumbling block, at the very threshold of the story!

Mark says, that the name of this ruler was Jairus; whose name, we may suppose, was unknown to Matthew, or why did he not mention it in his relation? Mark, moreover, says that this ruler did not tell Jesus that his daughter was *dead*; for according to Mark and Luke, the ruler did not himself know that she was dead, until he met some one in his way home, who acquainted him with the news of her death; but only that she was lying at the point of death, and that he besought Jesus to come and heal her, instead of restoring her to life, as Matthew states. Another circumstance in which Mark differs from Matthew greatly, is the time and place in which this ruler came to solicit the aid of Jesus. According to Mark, it was a long time after the feast with Matthew, whom Mark called Levi[8] And the place where the ruler met with Jesus, seems to have been on the beach, nigh unto the sea,[9] instead of being in the house of Matthew.

Luke tells us a little more than this, for he informs us that the girl was the only daughter of Jairus, and about twelve years of age; but *he* does not say that she was dead, but only that she lay a dying, the ruler not knowing to the contrary, before he met his neighbour as he was returning with Jesus to the house wherein his daughter lay. So much for the harmony existing between the narrators of this tale.

c c

The story of the widow's son is only related by Luke; and that of Lazarus is noted by none but John. Is not it strange, that Matthew, Mark, and Luke, should all have considered it so necessary to relate that which unquestionably is the most trifling of the three, namely, the raising the daughter of Jairus, who was not dead, Jesus said, but only sleeping, or probably fainting; yet, of that which, if ever performed by Jesus, must have been a most astonishing and stupendous miracle, namely, the raising of Lazarus after he had laid in the grave four days, not one of them take the least notice, beside John? Surely we will not suppose that they were ignorant of it, Luke in particular, who had such perfect understanding of all things, from the very first.[10] Neither can we suppose that they had forgotten it, because Jesus promised them before he died that he would send to them the Holy Ghost, who would teach them all things, and bring all things to their remembrance.[11] If you say that the testimony of John was quite sufficient to establish the truth of Jesus raising Lazarus from the dead, why should not the testimony of Matthew be equally sufficient to warrant the truth of Jesus raising the daughter of Jairus, without the aid of Mark and Luke to bear witness thereof?

The writer of the life of any celebrated personage always takes care to mention every remarkable and important occurrence which may be particularly and closely connected with the life of his hero; so that no biographer, afterward, should have occasion to add anything thereto, or enlarge upon what he had written. If a third or fourth biographer, fifty or sixty years after the first historian, (the supposed difference of time between the writings of Matthew and John) should attempt to add a more remarkable and notorious transaction to the life of the hero, than any that the first had related, it would be rejected as spurious; because the readers thereof would say, if this transaction were actually true, the first historian, or at any rate, the second or third, must have been acquainted with it; and they certainly would not all have neglected to notice such a remarkable and important circumstance, as the raising a dead carcase again to life, after it had lain in the grave four days! And if upon these very natural and reasonable considerations, they should disbelieve the story, will a good and merciful being damn them all to all eternity for their unbelief? Why then did not Matthew, Mark, or Luke make mention of this miracle of all miracles, namely, the raising of Lazarus? And why, again, I ask, did not Matthew or Mark relate the story of the widow's son, as they certainly must have known more of it than Luke, if it ever did actually occur, as Luke was no disciple of Jesus nor eye-witness of his actions? We do not even know whether he ever so much as saw Jesus, he being only, it is supposed, a companion or follower of Paul, several years after the supposed death of Jesus. Of this I shall speak hereafter.

Some think that Matthew and Mark were content with giving an account of one instance only, of this miraculous kind; supposing, that Christians would judge of the power of Jesus, in others, by it. Granting this; yet who would not relate that which was the most remarkable and miraculous of the three? Instead of which, they have related only that which is scarcely entitled to the name of a miracle, even were we certain of its authenticity; seeing, that we cannot be assured, that the daughter of Jairus was actually dead; at least, you must confess, that it is disputable, by the account given of it being so imperfect, in comparison with the other two.

If, as Woolston says, "Matthew, the first writer, had recorded only the story of Lazarus, whose resurrection was the greatest miracle; and Luke had added thereto, that of the widow's son; and John had, lastly, remembered us of the ruler's daughter, which the other Evangelists, not through ignorance or forgetfulness, but studying brevity, had omitted, then all had been well, and no objection could be made, of this nature, against the credit of any of them. But this unnatural and preposterous order of time, in which these three miracles are recorded, the greatest being postponed to the last, and that fifty or sixty years after the first, administers just occasion, to suspect the truth and credibility of them all."

Might not the Infidels join with the Jews, in saying, that by reason of this preposterous narration, it is evident, that Jesus raised not the dead at all? The only person that Christians can reasonably pretend that he did raise, was the daughter of Jairus, of whom Matthew speaks; and she, according to the story and confession of Jesus, was only asleep, or in an extacy, when Jesus revived her. But the Nazarenes or Galileans, who were, after a time, called Christians, finding their account in a resurrection-miracle, for the further advantage of the cause, devised another story, of better circumstances, in the widow's son, by Luke. This, again, not being so great a miracle as the Church wanted, John, when nobody was alive to contradict and expostulate with him for it, trumps up a long story of a thumping miracle in the case of Lazarus; who, he makes appear, had been dead so long, that he stunk again. If there were nothing else objectionable in these stories, this one circumstance, of placing the least first, and the greatest last, is quite sufficient to prove them all fabulous.

I do not suppose that Christians are willing to subscribe to this decision, because of their prejudices; but if those three miracles had been reported of Mahomet, instead of Jesus, in the same disorder of time, by three or four different historians, would they not have quickly discovered the forgery and imposture? I am sure that you yourself, and very justly, would have affirmed, that the three stories were, apparently, three fables and falsehoods; and that the three historians visibly strove to outstretch each other: the first, being modest and sparing in his romance; the second, made sensible of the insufficiency of the former tale, devises a miracle of larger size; and this proving insufficient to the end designed, a third writer, rather than the honour of the hero should sink for the want of a resurrection-miracle, forges a huge story of a monstrous size: against which it is, and always will be, objection enough, that it was not related by the first historian. Whether you, or any other Christian, would not have argued in this manner, if the story had been reported of Mahomet, instead of Jesus, I will leave to the opinion of every unprejudiced and reasonable man. Nay, I will come a little nearer home to you : suppose, that John, who was, it is supposed, nearly a hundred years of age when he˙wrote this story of Lazarus, consequently in his dotage, had not reported it, but that Clement, instead of him, had joined it to his incredible tale of the resurrection of a Phœnix ; or if Ignatius, Polycarp, or any other of the apostolical fathers, had related such a tale, attended with such circumstances, and in the same disordered state, would not our Christian critics have set their heads to work, in order to explode it ? Should the Jews, and infidels draw such conclusions from these stories, I cannot for the life of me imagine what answer our right reverend fathers in God, and very reverend divines, would make to them !

Again : Let us now inquire who were those persons so miraculously raised ? What station in life did they fill, that they, in particular, above all the rest of mankind, should receive this honour, and enjoy such a privilege ? Were they the most fit and proper persons that could be found, upon whom Jesus ought to manifest his divine power ? for, surely, if Jesus, who was it is said, the wisdom of God, had not considered them more worthy and better qualified than their neighbours and countrymen to receive this honour, he would never have selected them from amongst all the Jews in such an especial and extraordinary manner. Indeed, if God be no respecter of persons, I cannot see why Jesus should have singled any out in particular, but have raised again all that died, whether Greek, or Jew, Barbarian or Scythian, bond or free, circumcised or not, if Christ be all, and in all ! [12]

But to the first question : who were they that were thus raised by Jesus ? Why it appears that one was an insignificant girl ; another an unknown youth ; and the other an obscure old man ! I grant that in the case of the boy and girl there might have been some reason for Jesus restoring them to life, because they might, in process of time, have become fruitful, and multiplied their species according to the law of God.[13] And no doubt their resuscitation was the means of chasing away sorrow from the hearts, and tears from the eyes, of their disconsolate parents; but were there not many more widows and parents in Judea who were placed in similar circumstances during the ministry of Jesus? Then why did he not give to them also, the oil of joy for mourning, and the garments of praise for heaviness, that by them also the Lord might have been glorified?[14] I cannot find anything in the history either of them or their parents that should entitle them to this honour, above the rest. There were many others of riper years and of more worth, whose loss were, no doubt, more severely felt by perhaps the whole nation, than that of this boy and girl. We do not even find, after they were again restored to life, that they were more serviceable to the cause of Jesus than if they had been in their graves: neither were their parents, even the ruler, who had such opportunities of befriending Jesus during the frequent consultations of the rulers respecting his conduct, yet he is never once mentioned afterwards, either for good or bad! Is it not reasonable to expect that if two such miracles as these had been wrought upon the children, the parents in particular would have become the followers and disciples of Jesus? But no; we hear no more of the ruler, the widow, nor their children.

In the case of Lazarus there does appear some grounds for believing that Jesus would, if he could raise any body, raise him from the dead, because it seems that he was a man greatly beloved by Jesus;[15] and his affection for him might have induced him to exert his power in restoring him again to life and friendship; though I think that he would have shewn more friendship towards his friends, if he had gone, when first entreated, while he was sick, and healed him:[16] he would then have saved him from enduring the pangs of death, and prevented all that anguish and sorrow with which his sisters and friends were afflicted. But if Jesus were so affectionately attached to his friends, why did he not raise John the Baptist, who was a man of greater merit, and more worthy of this favour and his protection than this useless old man, Lazarus? We never read that Lazarus, either before or after his resurrection, was of any utility to Jesus or his cause : while John, who we find was the forerunner, and most useful assistant that Jesus ever had, is overlooked and neglected, being suffered to undergo a most cruel death without any help or resurrection. If Jesus could so easily raise the dead to life, he would undoubtedly have raised him whose life was so essential to the propagation of the Gospel, by his preparing the way of the Lord, and making the rough and crooked places smooth and straight for the people. You will not, surely, reply that it was out of the power of Jesus to raise him, because his head was separated from his body, when we are told that all power was given to him: for, although with men this might seem impossible, yet with God it is written that all things are possible. So that this can be no excuse for his neglect of John the Baptist. And I am sure that Jesus never had a better opportunity of manifesting his divine power, than that of tacking on the head of John to his body, and then breathing into his nostrils the breath of life : in doing which there could be no more difficulty than in resuscitating a stinking carcase ! As we find that he did it not, I much question whether he could raise any.

It may be said that the power of Jesus in reanimating dead bodies was limited to three persons only, or he would have willingly raised all that died, considering that if men would not believe Moses nor the Prophets, they would not believe, though one rose from the dead.[17] Then where was the utility of his raising any if he knew they would not believe? But admittting this ridiculous idea, could he not have found three other persons more eligible, whose lives were of more importance to the nation than those three useless, insignificant, and obscure individuals? Suppose that instead of this girl and boy, and old man, whose lives were of no consequence to the community either before or after their resurrection, he had chosen some worthy and judicious ruler or magistrate that might have died in those days; or some moral and industrious merchant, mechanic, or artist, whose death might have been a public loss; or some poor honest man, the father of a numerous family that derived all their support from the industry of their parent, as there are always in every age, and in every city such objects offering themselves, would he not have merited more applause, and obtained a greater number of followers by publicly raising them to life, than by raising such unworthy and insignificant characters as those that he is reported to have raised? Indeed if Lazarus had arrived, and was safely lodged snug within the bosom of Abraham, I cannot see wherein lay the friendship of Jesus in recalling him hence again, to bear the pangs of death a second time; for I suppose you will admit that he died again some time or other. These considerations lead me to expect that I shall find the whole of these resurrection stories to be nothing more than fictitious tales. We will now inquire in what manner those persons were raised by Jesus?

First, Were those persons dead long enough to justify us in maintaining, that they were actually dead, irrecoverably dead, beyond the power of art or nature to restore; and not judged as being so, hastily and rashly, as many others have been who have fallen into a trance, or continued so long in a lethargetic state that they have been deemed irrecoverable, and buried accordingly? The daughter of Jairus could be but just expired, admitting that Jesus was mistaken when he said that she only slept. And we know that there have been instances of persons of weak intellect, so overcome with the force of imagination, that they have actually imagined themselves dead; others, having fainted through fear or some other cause, have been judged by the spectators as absolutely dead, till their re-animation convinced them of their error. It may be likewise necessary to bear in mind, that even the medical gentlemen, in those days, were less skilful in their profession than what they are in the present day: consequently, more liable to be imposed upon, or of falling into an error. It is therefore not improbable, but that this girl was only frightened out of her wits by the weeping, wailing, and, perhaps, passionate screams of her female attendants, when she had, as is often the case with a sick person, the appearance of death only on her countenance! If this were not the case, why did Jesus, as soon as he entered, turn these inordinate weepers out of the house, before that he could bring her to her senses again?[18] If he did those things that men might believe, he should, if he did not choose to send for the chief priests and principal men of the city, together with all the unbelieving Sadducees, to witness this grand miracle, have admitted, at any rate, her friends, to remain and bear witness thereof, in order that they might believe and be saved, which would have prevented every suspicion of fraud in the miracle. Besides to constitute a miracle, she should have been dead, at least some days, if not weeks, or months.

Next; the widow's son at Nain. Although there was somewhat more the appearance of death in him, than in the daughter of Jairus, yet there is much room for suspecting that some fraud or imposition was practiced in this transaction. We have, besides, many examples in history, of persons having been unfortunately buried alive, through the ignorance of their friends respecting the power of lethargy: and of others who have only just revived in time to prevent a premature interment. And as Jesus was often accused by the Jews, with being an impostor and a deceiver of the people, who certainly must have had some indisputable evidence of his guilt, or they would never have so often charged him therewith, in such a public manner; we are, therefore, not sure that Jesus did not concert a plan with the widow and her son, in order to aggrandize his fame as a worker of miracles. Some women, we well know, have tears at command, especially widows! And some lads are very crafty and subtle. This casual meeting of Jesus with the body on the road, looks very suspicious, as though it had been a contrivance, between the parties to put a better face upon the matter. I do not say that it was really so; but that it were possible, and even very probable, that such a plan might have been contrived and adopted, between the widow and Jesus. And where there is the least room for doubt or suspicion of fraud, it is all nonsense to talk of a real and certain miracle; especially as we have so often detected the like imposition in the former miracles, ascribed to Jesus. This, like the former, would have looked much more like a miracle, if Jesus had permitted the bearers to have carried the body to the place of interment, and there, after securing the body in the grave, certified to the people, that he would come in so many days, or weeks, and restore him again to life, in the presence of the whole city. This would have made it a miracle indeed, at which, neither Jew nor Infidel could have cavilled, excepting at the preference given by Jesus to this young man, instead of raising up some husband, or father of a family, and restoring him to his disconsolate wife and children.

Some persons have been bold enough to ask, why Jesus, if he had so much compassion for this poor widow, did not raise her husband as well as her son? But they should remember, that if Jesus had done such a notorious miracle as that, the whole nation would have been convinced of his divine power, and so all become converted. There would have been none left to be damned : neither would he have had occasion to weep over the city, in consequence of their unbelief! And although it is written that this rumour of raising the widow's son was noised throughout all Judea, and throughout all the region round about;[19] yet neither Josephus, nor any other Jewish historian, not even the other evangelists, take the least notice of this most extraordinary and wonderful miracle !

Last, though not least, is the case of Lazarus; which, though it is said that he had lain in the grave four days, consequently is not liable to some of the objections urged against the former two, yet there are other circumstances connected with this story, that evince more likelihood of fraud and imposition than in either of the others.

Lazarus it seems was a particular friend of Jesus;

insomuch that the love which Jesus bore to Lazarus excited astonishment among the Jews. If, then, there were so much love and friendship existing between them, what was it that one would not have done to have assisted the other? If Jesus thought that his credit rested upon the performance of such a miracle as that of raising a dead man to life, can we doubt that Lazarus, to serve him, would have hesitated a moment in complying with the wish of his friend; which was nothing more than a temporary confinement within a hollow cave, the entrance of which was only closed by a stone,[20] during the space of four days? You may possibly say that four days were too long for any man to fast, without endangering his health, but you will please to remember that inspired arithmeticians did not compute time in the same manner as our vulgar arithmeticians do, who reckon that two and two are equal to four. Not so with holy arithmeticians; for when Jesus was laid in the sepulchre on the Friday evening, being the eve before the Sabbath,[21] in which he remained no longer than till daylight on the Sunday morning following, the first day of the week,[22] they nevertheless reckon it as being three days that he was entombed in the heart of the earth:[23] whereas, if our *unholy* and *vulgar* arithmeticians had had to calculate the time, they would have said that he had only been two nights and one day, or a day and a half, in the sepulchre!

Besides, we are not certain that he lay there so long, as it is unknown when he did rise; only, that the body was missing at the time they went to look for it, on the Sunday morning, before day-light, while it was yet dark.[24] It might have been gone during the sabbath, as Jesus was Lord of the sabbath, consequently could do as he pleased on that day, while the people were devoting themselves to religious exercises. It is therefore evident, by this method of reckoning three days, for a day and a half, that those four days which Lazarus is said to have lain in the grave, could not have been more than two of our present duration; during which time it was possible for him to have lived without food; supposing that none were even secretly conveyed to him by his sisters, who we may imagine were acquainted with the plot, when they went under pretence of weeping over his grave.

As to his stinking, we have only the bare assertion of his sister, who only mentioned it as being possible that such was the case. We do not read that any of the bye-standers said a word about his stinking beside his sister. And the weeping and lamentations of Jesus and the sisters of Lazarus might have been, for aught we know to the contrary, all sham and counterfeited; the better to carry on the juggle of a feigned resurrection. Though for my part I cannot see what occasion there was for Jesus to weep if he knew that Lazarus would rise again. He had just before told his disciples that he was glad for their sakes, well knowing what he was about to do.

It is also stated that Jesus called Lazarus with a *loud voice*.[25] If Lazarus were dead in reality, he could no more hear a *loud* voice than he could a whisper; but if he had been asleep, or dull of hearing, perhaps in consequence of the napkin being bound round his head, or if he had, just at the critical moment when Jesus called him, been at the further end of the cave, then I will grant that a *loud voice* was necessary. Unless some one or other of these reasons be assigned, I cannot see why Jesus should have been obliged to holla to him in that manner.

Another circumstance which justifies us in suspecting that knavery and fraud was practised between the parties is that the face of Lazarus was bound about with a napkin,[26] so that the spectators could not discern that visible change in his countenance which naturally must have occurred, if he were really dead, by the sudden transition from death to life. All these things being considered, it is evident that this story of raising Lazarus will no more bear the test of examination than the other marvellous tales which have fallen under our notice.

Should you think that all these objections will not affect the credit of these miracles, yet you must acknowledge that if Jesus had the power of raising the dead, it would have been more to his honour and glory, besides preventing those doubts of infidels, if he had made choice of some persons, who were well known to have been unquestionably dead, having lain so long in their graves that their putrified state might have been visible to all around. Moreover, if the raising of dead bodies were to be the evidences of his divine power, he should have invited the principal magistrates and rulers of the city to bear witness thereof. And further, to prevent all suspicion of fraud and imposture, they, or some persons appointed by them, should first have carefully examined the body, in order to discover whether or not the body was actually dead. There should have been no napkins before faces; but the putrified and ghastly visage, resuming the similitude of its pristine form, as when in health and strength, should have been made manifest to all the spectators. Finding that none of these things were done, my reasoning faculties will not permit me to place any more confidence in these tales, than in the exploits of "Baron Munchausen!"

Respecting the soul of Lazurus I cannot expect that you can positively declare where it had been, during the four days that his body had been lying in the grave, because John himself does not appear to have known, or surely he would have given us some information thereof: perhaps you may suppose, that it was wrapt up in a napkin, and deposited in one corner of the cave, waiting for the *loud voice* of Jesus: and this, I think, is the best answer that can be given, were you asked for your opinion; because it cannot be presumed that the soul of Lazarus, the beloved friend of Jesus, should have been billetted among the black soldiers of hell; supposing that Jesus himself choose to descend there, he had no doubt very particular reasons for his journey; though there are some persons, so very precise in all things, who consider that Jesus would have done much better, and behaved more honourable, if he had kept his word with the penitent thief on the cross, whom he promised to meet the same day in paradise.[27] However, if Jesus had a fellow feeling that induced him to visit his old friend, the devil, though he were in hell, we must not suppose that Jesus would enjoin the same pilgrimage to all his friends, as being necessary to their salvation; else, we should frighten all our archbishops and priests out of their livings! And what would the laity do with all their money if they had no priests to support? We should then find them so *irreligious* and *profane* as to feed and clothe themselves and their children, better then they are able to do at present, which certainly would be very criminal in the sight of a God of Love! Neither can we suppose that the soul of Lazarus was in Paradise, or among the general assembly of the first born, or Jesus would never have recalled his friend hence again, to a wicked world, so full of misery and trouble! But wherever his soul was, the place thereof did not seem to be very agreeable to Lazarus, or he had never so much dreaded being put to death a second time, as to abscond for fear of the Jews. This clearly showed his unwillingness to return to the place from whence he came!

John, moreover, states that when this miracle was performed, many of the Jews, who had seen these things which Jesus did, believed on him; but some of them did not believe; for they went their ways to the Pharisees, and told them what Jesus had done,[28] in this pretended miracle: which proves that this miracle was not manifested to every one alike; but that some among them more cunning than the rest, had discovered the cheat, upon which they went immediately and gave information to the chief Priests and Pharisees how this business had been transacted, who, upon this intelligence, took council together how they should put both Jesus and Lazarus to death, from that day forth: which as soon as Jesus and Lazarus heard, they took to their heels and scampered away; for it is written, that from that time Jesus walked no more openly among the Jews, but went thence into a country, near to the wilderness, (a very convenient hiding place) and there continued with his disciples, or they all, probably, would have met with that punishment which they so justly merited for their imposition.

But as I have a copy of a letter by me, supposed to

have been written by a Jewish Rabbi, to my old friend Woolston, upon this subject, I will here submit it to your inspection : trusting that you will not find it altogether unworthy of notice.

"Sir,—When we last discoursed on the miracles of Jesus, I promised to send you my thoughts on the resurrection of Lazarus, which I look upon as a notorious imposture; and for proof, need go no further than to the circumstance of its story, as related by your Evangelists.

"If there had been an indisputable miracle wrought in the resurrection of Lazarus, why should the Chief Priests and Pharisees have been so incensed as to take counsel from that day forth, to put both Jesus and Lazarus to death for it? Where was the provocation? I can conceive none. Though the Jews were ever so cankered with malice and hatred to Jesus before, yet, such a most stupendous miracle was enough to stop their mouths and turn their hearts. Or, if their prejudices against Jesus were insuperable, and they hated him the more for the number and greatness of his miracles, why was poor Lazarus, inoffensive Lazarus, upon whom this good and great work was wrought, an object of their hatred too? Your divines are to give a credible and probable account of this matter, such an one as will comport with reason and sense, or we shall conclude that it was fraud detected in this pretended miracle, that justly provoked the indignation of our ancestors.

"To say, what is all you can say, that it was downright inhumanity, barbarity, and brutality in the Jews to hate Lazarus as well as Jesus, will not do for us. Though this may, with many Christians, who are ready to swallow, without chewing, any evil report of our nation; yet it cannot go down with reasonable and unprejudiced men, who must have other conceptions of human nature, in all ages and nations, than to think it possible that a man in the case of Lazarus, could be hated and persecuted, for having had such a good and wonderful work done on him. Then why was he so hated and persecuted? Why, for this I say, and no other reason can be assigned, than because he was a confederate with Jesus, in the wicked imposture, which he was putting upon mankind.

" But, supposing what never can be granted, that the Jews of old were so inhuman, brutish, and barbarous, as to hate and persecute Lazarus, as well as Jesus, for this miracle, yet, why did Jesus and his disciples, with Lazarus, run away and abscond? Is not here a plain sign of guilt and of fraud? Men, that have the cause of God, truth, and power on their side, never want courage and resolution to stand in defence thereof. And however your Christian Priests may palliate the cowardly and timorous conduct of Jesus and his confederates, in this case, yet with us it is like demonstration, that there was a discovered cheat in the miracle, or they would have undauntedly faced their enemies, without any fear or apprehension of danger from them.

" Our ancestors then, who unquestionably detected the fraud, were in the right of it, to persecute with severity the whole party concerned therein. And if they had avenged themselves upon Lazarus for his part, as well as they did upon Jesus, they were to be commended. Whether such a monstrous imposture, as was this pretended miracle, happily discovered, did not call aloud for vengeance, and most exemplary punishment; and whether any nation in the world, would suffer the like with impunity, let any impartial man judge!

" For all the reports of your Gospels, it is unnatural to hate a miraculous healer of diseases; and there must be something suppressed about the inveteracy of the Jews to Jesus; or his healing power, if it were so great as is imagined, must have reconciled them to him. But that they should not only hate Jesus, for raising the dead, but the person raised by him, is improbable, incredible, and impossible.

" If historians can parallel this story of the malignity of the Jews towards Jesus and Lazarus, upon such a real miracle, with anything equally barbarous and inhuman, in any other sect or nation, then we will acknowledge the truth of it, against our ancient nation. Or if such inhumanity, abstractedly considered, be at all agreeable to the conceptions that any one can form of human nature, in the most uncivilised and brutish nation, then we will allow our ancestors, in that case, to have been that people.*

"Was such a real and indisputable miracle, as this of Lazarus is supposed to be, wrought at this day, in confirmation of the truth of Christianity, I have no doubt but that it would bring all us Jews to a man, into the belief thereof. And I cannot think it possible for any sect of persons, to be so bigoted, biassed, and prejudiced, as not to be wrought upon by it; or if they would not part with their interest and prejudices for it, they would have more wit and temper than to break forth into a rage against all or any of the persons concerned therein. And, for my life, I can entertain no worse thoughts of our old nation.

"Suppose that God should sent an ambassador at this day, who, to convince Christians of the mischief and inconvenience of an hireling priesthood, should work such a miracle as was this of the resurrection of Lazarus, in the presence of a multitude of people; how would your Bishops and Clergy behave themselves? Why they would be mute as fishes: or if they did fret and grieve inwardly for the loss of their interest, they would have more prudence (ask them else) than to shew their anger openly, and persecute both agent and patient. Wherefore then are they so censorious and uncharitable as to preach and believe another notion and doctrine of our ancestors? But if a false prophet, for the subversion of an hireling priesthood, should, in spite of the clergy, counterfeit such a miracle, and be detected in the operation, how then would priests and people, magistrates and subjects behave? Why, they would be full of indignation, and from that day forth, take counsel how they might put both the impostor and his confederate to death, of which they would be most

---

* If our Jewish friend had any faith in the miracle which Paul is said to have wrought upon the barbarians (Acts, xxviii. 6.) he, no doubt, would have advanced that as a proof, that even the barbarians, instead of persecuting a man for working a miracle, though of no advantage to any of them, looked upon such a man as a God!—J. C.

deserving: and if they did not abscond and fly for it, like Jesus and his disciples, into a wilderness in the country or some such place and there hide themselves, the rage of the populace would hardly wait the leisure of Justice to dispatch and make terrible examples of them. Was not this exactly the case with this imposture of Jesus in the resurrection of Lazarus, and of the punishment with which they were threatened, and which he afterwards so justly suffered?

"Mankind may, in some cases, be very obdurate, and so hard of belief as to stand out against sense, reason, and demonstration. But I will not think worse of our ancestors than of the rest of mankind; or that they, more than others, would have withstood a clear and indisputable miracle, such as the raising of a dead body to life. Such a manifest and surprising miracle, let it be wrought for what end or purpose we can possibly imagine, would strike men with awe and reverence; and none could hate and persecute the author of the miracle, lest HE who could raise the dead, should exert His power against themselves, and either wound or smite them dead for their wickedness. For which reason, the resurrection of Lazarus, to the certain knowledge of our ancestors, was all fraud, or they would have reverenced the power of him that rose him.

"It may be true what John says, that many of the Jews, who had seen the things that Jesus did, believed on him, that is, believed that he had wrought here a great miracle. But who were these? Why, the ignorant and credulous, upon whom a much less juggler than Mr. Fawkes could have easily imposed. But on the other hand, it is certain, according to Christian commentators, that some of them did not believe the miracle, but went their ways to the Pharisees, and told them what things Jesus had done; that is, told them after what manner the intrigue was managed, and complained of the fraud therein. How they came to discover the fraud was not the business of John to relate; and for want of other ancient memorials, we can only guess thereat. Perhaps they discerned some motion in the body of Lazarus, before the word of command to *come forth* was given; or perhaps they discovered some fragment of the food in the cave, upon which he had been subsisting during those four days. However they could not but take notice of the napkin about his face all the while; which, to have prevented all suspicion of fraud, Jesus should have removed, in order that his mortified countenance might be seen before the miraculous change of it was wrought. This neglect of Jesus (at which I wonder that John had no more wit than to notice) will be a lasting objection to the miracle. Jesus was not so foolish but that he was aware of the objection, which he would have obviated, if he durst, by a removal of the napkin, to the satisfaction of all spectators there present. But this he could not do without endangering an exposure of the whole. Therefore, as this was not done, we Jews now deny that there was any miracle wrought; and whether our unbelief, upon this circumstance, be not well grounded, we appeal to Christian priests themselves, who must own that if there were a miracle wrought here, the matter was ill conducted by Jesus, or related foolishly by the Evangelists.

"It is a sad misfortune that attends our modern inquiry after truth, that there are no other memorials extant of the life and miracles of Jesus than what are written by his own disciples. Not only has old time devoured, but Christians themselves, (which in the opinion of the impartial, make for us) when they got power into their hands, wilfully destroyed many writings of our ancestors, as well as those of Porphyry, Celsus, and others, whose writings the Christians could never answer; otherwise I doubt not but they would have given us clear light into the imposture, that was manifested at the resurrection of Lazarus. But, if Jesus, according to his own Evangelists, was arraigned for a deceiver and a blasphemer, in pretending to the son-ship and power of God by his miracles, in all probability this piece of fraud, in the resurrection of Lazarus, was one article in the indictment against him. And what makes it very likely, is, that the chief Priests and Pharisees, from the date of this pretended miracle, took council together, to put him to death; not clandestinely nor tumultously to murder him, but judicially to punish him with death ; of which, if they proved their indictment by credible and sufficient witnessess, he surely was worthy of suffering.

" As it is plain, from the story in John, that there was a dispute among the bye-standers, at the resurrection of Lazarus, whether it was a real miracle or not, so it is the opinion of us Jews, which is of the nature of a tradition, that the chief Priests and civil magistrates of Bethany, for the better determination of the dispute, and quieting the minds of the people, requested that Jesus should re-act the miracle upon another person, there lately dead and buried. But Jesus declining the test of his power, the whole multitude of believers, as well as the unbelievers before, questioned the resurrection of Lazarus ; and were highly incensed against both him and Jesus, for the deceit manifested in this supposed miracle. This was one reason, among others, of that vehement and violent outcry, and demand, at the trial of Jesus, for his crucifixion. I will not answer for the truth of this tradition, but as the expedient was obvious, so it has the face of truth and credibility ; and for the proof of it, I need only apply to Christian Priests and Magistrates, whether, under such circumstances, in a dispute of a miracle of such importance, they would not require for full satisfaction, that it should be acted over again ? And if the juggler refused, whether there would not be a general clamour among the people, of all ranks, for his execution ? .

" Matthew, Mark, and Luke, who knew as much of this sham miracle as John, had not the confidence to report it ; because when they wrote, many eye-witnesses of the fraud were alive to disprove and contradict them : therefore they confined their narratives to those less juggling tricks of Jesus, that had passed more current. But after the Jewish state was dissolved, and their judicial records were destroyed, and every body dead that could confute him, then John ventures abroad the story of this miracle ! And if the good providence of God had not infatuated him, in the insertion of the circumstances here observed, it might have passed through all generations to come, as well as it has done for many past, as a grand miracle!

"Thus, Sir, you have a few of my thoughts on the pretended miracle of the resurrection of Lazarus. I have more to bestow on it, but that I would not be thought to be too tedious. There is no need to argue against the other two resurrection stories; you know, *omne majus includit minus*, if the greatest of the three miracles be an imposture, the two lesser ones, of consequence, are artifice and fraud. And although these arguments may not be convincing to your Christian Clergy, who are hired to believe these stories, yet, they cannot, in consequence, deny, that the arguments above are not a sufficient justification of our Jewish disbelief.

"Should you, Sir, at any time, take into consideration the story of the resurrection of Jesus, I beg of you to accept of a few of my conceptions on that head; which, I promise you, shall be out of the common road of thinking. Your divines think that they have exhausted that subject, and absolutely confuted all objections that can be made against it, but they are greatly mistaken. Sometimes we Jews dip into their writings on this head, and always smile with indignation, at their foolish invectives, against the blindness of the eyes and hardness of the hearts of our ancestors. If they would but favour us with the liberty of writing for ourselves, which is only just and reasonable, we would cut them out some more work, of which they are not aware. In the mean time, I remain your assured friend.—N. N."

Thus ends the letter of a supposed Jewish Rabbi, which I should not have noticed, if I had not found contained therein, such calm and sedate reasoning as is seldom to be found in the writings of Christians. I therefore hope, that you will send me your opinion, after you have given it due consideration, as I should very much like to see an answer thereto. I intend also, forwarding to you his conceptions concerning the resurrection of Jesus, as soon as I take that subject into consideration, which I do assure you, are, as he says, out of the common road of thinking; and such as I trust, will afford you ample scope for speculation.

Before I close these resurrection stories, I intend to inquire what became of these three persons, after their resurrection? How long did they live? And of what utility were their restored lives to Jesus and the community? Upon this subject the evangelical, as well as the ecclesiastical writers, are silent; which is quite enough to convince us, without further argument, that there is no truth in any of these tales; and that no such persons were ever raised from the dead, or we should certainly have had some account transmitted to us of their description of, and communication, respecting that

> " Undiscovered country, from whose bourne,
> No traveller returns !"

Woolston says, " it is true that Epiphanius says,[*] (what he found among traditions) that Lazarus lived thirty years after his resurrection." But how did he spend his time all that while? Was it to the honour of Jesus, the service of the church, and propagation of the gospel? Of that we know nothing, though, in reason and gratitude to Jesus, his benefactor, it ought to have been so spent. And surely history would have informed us thereof, if it had been so employed.

According to the opinion of Grotius, Lazarus, for the rest of his life, absconded, and skulked about the country, in dread of the Jews, who were laying in wait for him: which is a suggestion, not only dishonourable to Jesus, as though the same power that raised him from the dead could not protect him against his enemies, but reproachful to Lazarus himself; who should have chosen to suffer death again, rather than refuse to bear an open testimony of the power of Jesus, the author of his resurrection. Which ever way it was, we hear no more of Lazarus, than that he lived thirty years afterwards: which tradition, without any other memorial of his life, brings the miracle more under the appearance of a fable, than if he had died soon after his resurrection. And is it not, moreover astonishing, that we hear nothing

---

[*] Quin & illud inter traditiones reperimus trigintatum annos natum fuisse Lazarum, cum a mortuis excitatus est ; atq ; Idem ille postea triginta aliis annis vixit.—*In Haeres, lxvi, Sect.* 34,

afterwards of the daughter of Jairus, nor of the widow's son at Naim? Does not this silence in history, about these most extraordinary persons, make their miracles questionable, and more like *Gulliverian tales* of persons and things, which, out of the romance, never had any being?

Jesus did but call a little child,[29] and sat him in the midst of his disciples, and that act was remembered, in the piety and zeal of Ignatius,* who made a renowned Bishop. But the blessing and favour conferred on those three raised persons were exceedingly greater; and one might have expected that Lazarus and the widow's son would have been eminent ministers of the gospel, if not Bishops of Rome and Jerusalem! Instead of which, we find that their lives were afterwards passed in obscurity; or what is as bad, Ecclesiastical history has neglected to notice them. What can any one, hereupon, think less than that the favour of these miracles were lost upon underserving and ungrateful wretches: consequently, the friendship of Jesus was misplaced, which clearly proves that he did not know all things! Neither did Paul seem to know any thing concerning those three persons rising from the dead, or surely he would never have had the impudence to tell King Agrippa, that Christ was the first that rose from the dead.[30]

It is likewise strange that we hear no more of the after fame and life of any of the multitude of deceased persons, whom Jesus so miraculously cured, excepting of the woman who was healed of an issue of blood; who, although she had spent ALL *she had*, even ALL *her living* upon physicians,[31] yet, out of the remains, erected, Eusebius says, (Ecclesiastical History, Book vii. Chap. 18,) two most costly statues of brass, at Cesarea Philippi, to the memory of Jesus, and of the miracle wrought upon her by him; with the exception, then, of this women and Mary Magdalene, out of whom he cast seven devils,[32] I cannot find that mention is made of any other person, afterwards, whom Jesus

---

* In Nicephor, Callist, Eccl. Hist. Lib. ii, Chap. 35

cured : which, of itself, is sufficient to shake the credit of all his miraculous cures.

Thus have I concluded my observations, with the assistance of Woolston, upon these three resurrection stories. Whether I have fulfilled my promise in proving them to be three fictitious tales, I will leave you to determine. Should you think that I have failed in so doing, you will, no doubt, send me word thereof; at the same time, giving good and substantial reasons for your opinion to the contrary: for you know it is required of every one always to give a reason for the hope that is within them.[33] Your silence on the subject will be an admission that my arguments are unanswerable.

I have now no further observation to make that I consider necessary on the miracles of Jesus, until I come to treat upon the story of his own resurrection, upon which the Christian Church is built: when, I have not the least doubt, I shall be able to prove to you, that Christ is not risen; consequently, as Paul says, if such be the case, then is all our preaching vain, and your faith is also vain.[34] If I do this, I trust that you will acknowledge that the community should no longer be forced to maintain the swarm of idle and ignorant Ecclesiastical vermin that now infest the land; but that every honest man should enjoy the fruits of his labour; and that he, as Paul says, who is able and will not work, should have nothing to eat.[35]

This, Sir, was, in the beginning, ought to be now, and soon will be, the language of every good and virtuous man, possessing "Common Sense." Already do we begin to see the scales of bigotry falling from the eyes of reason ; and those, who were before blinded by superstition, looking up now in this "Age of Reason," and discerning men, not as trees walking,[36] but walking as men should walk. That the "Crisis" may soon arrive when the "Rights of Man" will be clearly seen, understood, and enjoyed, by every human being, is the sincere and ardent wish of

Your humble Servant,

JOHN CLARKE.

NOTES TO THE FOREGOING LETTER.

1 Matthew ix. 18.
— Mark v. 22.
— Luke viii. 41.
2   „   vii. 11.
3 John xi. 17.
4 Matthew 9, 24.
5 Mark v. 38. 39.
6 John vii. 48.
7 Acts xxiii. 8.
8 Mark ii. 14.
9   „   „   13.
10 Luke i. 3.
11 John xiv. 26.
12 Colossians iii. 11.
13 Genesis i. 28.
14 Isaiah lxi. 3.
15 John xi. 36.
16   „   „   6.
17 Luke xxi. 31.
18   „   viii. 51.

Luke vii. 17.
John xi. 38.
Mark xv. 42.

32
33
34
35
39 Mark viii. 24.

LETTER XIV

TO DR. ADAM CLARKE.

SIR

I intend to occupy this letter with those little incidents recorded of Jesus, which I may deem necessary to notice, prior to his resurrection; with an examination of which I shall commence my next. My intention for so doing, is merely to point out the discordance which subsists between the narrators, and to compare it with our ideas of consistency and harmony.

John informs us, that after Jesus had raised Lazarus, he walked no more openly among the Jews, because the Chief Priests and Pharisees had given a commandment, that if any man knew where he were, he should shew it, that they might take him.[1] Notwithstanding this declaration, John immediately after states, that he came again to Bethany, where Lazarus was, who had been dead six days before the passover: and that while they were supping together, Mary, the sister of Lazarus,[2] took a pound of ointment of *spikenard*, and anointed the feet of Jesus, and *wiped his feet with her hair*:[3] (a nasty creature!) This was done, according to John, previous to his riding into Jerusalem upon his Jack-ass, in the midst of the Jews.[4] Here then we find that John was plagued with a bad memory, for he had just before told us, that Jesus walked no more openly among the Jews, after he knew that the intention of the Chief Priests was to take him and put him to death. Indeed the whole of this letter, will point out to you such a string of contradictions and inconsistencies, as to make it appear like ocular demonstration, that none of the historians of Jesus knew anything concerning the persons of whom they were writing; or they would never have given such contradictory accounts of those most remarkable and notorious transactions, if they ever did occur, as are related of him, at this period of his life.

Matthew and Mark say, it was not until after his public exhibition of Assmanship, in Jerusalem, when he drove the buyers and sellers out of the temple,[5] (which, by-the-bye, John relates as having been performed long before, even the first thing he did after his transforming the water at Cana,[6]) that he came to Bethany;[7] and instead of finding Lazarus there, and raising him from the dead, neither Matthew nor Mark so much as mention the names of either he or his sisters. Is not this strange that they should neglect to notice the man whom Jesus loved and honoured in such an extraordinary manner, admitting that the miracle wrought upon him, by Jesus raising him from the dead, was too trifling and unimportant for them to relate? Luke mentions the name of Mary and her sister Martha, who belonged to some village that Jesus entered, where they made a feast for him,[8] but says nothing of their relationship to Lazarus, his death and resurrection, or her anointing Jesus.

The person in Bethany, of whom Matthew speaks, as being acquainted with Jesus, was called Simon the leper, with whom Jesus was sitting at meat, when a woman came and poured a box of alabaster ointment on his head, instead of his feet, as described by John. *Query;* did she likewise wipe his head with her hair as Mary did his feet? If so their heads and faces must have been most conveniently placed, to answer other purposes! Now, observe the difference of time between these two historians. John says, that it was six days before the passover commenced, to which Jesus rode upon the ass. But Matthew says, that it was not till sometime after his stately ride into Jerusalem; where he staid driving the buyers and sellers out of the temple, cursing the fig-tree, and disputing with the chief Priests and Elders of the people in the temple:[9] the very persons whom John says had given a commandment that if any man knew where he were, he was to shew it, that they might take him! After which, Matthew says, he staid and spake many parables publicly and

openly, to whole multitudes of people before this
mony of anointing was performed, which occurred
two days, instead of six, as John says, before the
over, in the house of Simon the leper, instead of that
Lazarus. Now, Sir, I appeal to any man possessing
common sense, whether it be possible to reconcile these
contradictions, or decide upon which to believe? Yet
the Priests tell us that we must believe them both, and
many more such contrarieties, or we shall surely be
damned! But, as though those two different accounts
were not sufficient to try our credulity, we have a third
to perplex us still more in reconciling to truth and
reason; for Luke says that this anointing was performed
in the early part of his ministry, about two years, it is
supposed, before the passover, at which he was betrayed;
and that, moreover, it was in the house of a Pharisee
named Simon,[10] (not a leper, nor yet Lazarus) in the
city of Naim, instead of Bethany!

Matthew likewise informs us, that when his disciples
saw it, they were indignant Mark says only some of
them. And John says only one, namely, Judas Iscariot.
While Luke says, that it was Simon himself that
noticed it, but not with indignation. You may, probably, suppose that these were all different women that
annointed Jesus, some his head and some his feet, at
different places; one at Bethany, in the house of Lazarus; another in that of Simon the leper; and the other
at Naim, in the house of Simon the Pharisee. But if
you will cast out the beam of prejudice from the eye of
reason, while you read these several accounts, you will
find, notwithstanding their contradictions, respecting the
time, place, and persons, by the observations made upon
the act, and their concomitant circumstances, that they
all refer to one and the same transaction, without my
further enlarging upon them: being convinced that you
are not like unto some who read and do not understand,
or I would demonstrate it beyond a doubt.

As I have nearly arrived to his apprehension and
death, and wishing to treat his resurrection more
elaborately, I shall pass by many other absurdities,
improbabilities, and contradictions, which are to be

in various parts that I have not noticed, lest I
be accused of prolixity : though I believe your-
d many others beside, have written more largely
his subject, though not exactly in the same man-
I have done. For you know that it is written,
ere are diversities of gifts, and diversities of
ions[11]—every man hath his proper gift of God,
er this manner, and another after that![12]
thew and Mark both say that as soon as the
had anointed Jesus, Judas Iscariot went and
nted with the chief priests to deliver to them
for thirty pieces of silver.[13] This to me appears
, that the chief priests should be necessitated to
ecourse to such a clandestine measure, in order to
end a man against whom the whole nation,
ing a few poor ignorant and defenceless mortals,
t variance. Had not they the same power to
him as they had to escort him through the town,
erwards crucify? The people, John says, were
for stoning him themselves. And who were
ager for his death, in preference to a robber and
rer, than the people? Then why should the
riests fear to arrest him in a judicial and public
r? It could not have been through their ignorance
hiding place, for it appears that he came publicly
e city, and ate the passover! yet, concerning this
occurrence, we have very different reports.
thew says, that Judas brought back the thirty
of silver to the chief priests, and cast them down
temple; after which he went out and hanged
[:14 and the chief priests took the silver pieces,
ught with them the potter's field, to bury strang-
: which they called the field of blood. Peter
' that instead of taking the money back, and
it into the temple, he went himself and purchased
with the reward of iniquity, meaning the money
he received for betraying his master, in which
fell head-long, when he burst asunder, and all
vels gushed out! And this, moreover, Peter says,
nown unto all the dwellers at Jerusalem! yet
· Mark, Luke, nor John knew a word of it, or

surely they would have noticed, in some way or other, such an extraordinary circumstance, while they were speaking of Judas.

Again, both Peter and Matthew assign different reasons for the fate of Judas. Matthew says that it was to fulfil a prophecy, spoken by Jeremy the prophet, saying, "And they took the thirty pieces of silver, the price of him that was valued, whom they of the children of Israel did value, and gave them for the potter's field as the Lord appointed me."[16] But Peter says, that it was to fulfil that which the holy Ghost spake, by the mouth of David, concerning Judas. "For [he says] it is written in the book of Psalms, let his habitation be desolate, and let no man dwell therein; and his bishoprick let another take."

First let us inquire how could the Holy Ghost, of whom no mention is made throughout the Old Testament, speak by the mouth of David, when John says that the Holy Ghost was not given till after Jesus was glorified?[18] Indeed, we find, that many years after his death, there were many of his disciples who did not know that there was such a thing in existence, as a Holy Ghost![19] Neither is there any allusion whatever made in the book of Psalms, nor yet indeed, throughout the whole Bible, prior to these words of Peter, concerning a bishop or a bishoprick; they being things unknown to the Jews in those days. The only similar expression to be found in the book of Psalms, is where David is offering up prayers for the destruction of his enemies; which conduct was quite contrary to the will of the Holy Ghost, if it were he who spoke by the mouth of Jesus, for he commanded them to love their enemies, to do good to those who hated them, and to pray for those who despitefully used and persecuted them.[20] Instead of which we find that David uttered the most horrid imprecations against them: the 109th Psalm, to which Peter alluded, being one instance, in which he says, "let his days be few, and let another take his office; let his children be fatherless, and his wife a widow; let his children be continually vagabonds and beg; and let them seek their bread also out of their desolate places;

let the extortioner catch all that he hath; and let the stranger spoil his labour; let there be none to extend mercy unto him; neither let there be any to favour his fatherless children; let his posterity be cut off, and in the generation following, let their name be blotted out;* let the iniquity of his fathers be remembered with the Lord; and let not the sins of his mother be blotted out." And in the 69th Psalm, he says, "let their table become a snare before them, and that which should have been for their welfare, let it become a trap. Let their eyes be darkened, that they see not; and make their loins continually to shake. Pour out thine indignation upon them, and let thy wrathful anger take hold of them. Let their habitation be desolate, and let none dwell in their tents." These are the prayers and supplications that are appointed for Christians to offer up, either by singing or reading, every 13th and 22nd evenings of the month, to a throne of grace, whereon sits a God of love and mercy!

Thus we find, that out of these two vengeful and bloody-minded Psalms, Peter has selected a few words from each, in order to form a prophetical passage for Judas. I remember that when I first began to address my letters to you, a fanatic, with whom I had formerly been acquainted, sent me word that I did not treat the holy Scriptures fairly, by selecting a passage from one place and one from another, and then connecting them together, as though they had the same meaning, while they treated upon quite different subjects. I, not deeming it impossible that such an error might have been made, through ignorance or inattention, having no claim to infallability, directly sent to him entreating him to point me out a passage in which I had done so, that I might correct it as early as possible. But for reasons, I suppose, best known to himself, I have since neither seen nor heard from him, nor from any other person, that such is the manner in which I have conducted this review of the life of Jesus. If my old acquaintance had

---

* We do not read that Judas Iscariot had either wife or children, so that this cannot apply to him. Neither is his name yet blotted out of the book of the Lord!

but noticed the above mentioned quotations by Peter, and a number of others that I could point out to him, he would have found that the inspired writers of these holy Scriptures, were guilty of that fault, of which he only supposed that I had been. Here you find that Peter takes part of one verse from one Psalm, and connects it with part of another from a different Psalm;[21] in the same manner as Mark did when he selected one verse from Isaiah, (xl. 3.) and joined it to part of another from Malachi, (iii. 1.) in order to form a prophecy for John the Baptist.[22] But what has this prophecy, as Peter calls it, to do with the bowels of Judas tumbling out, or the field of blood? I can perceive no analogy between the two cases.

Again, what has Judas and his thirty pieces of Silver to do with Jeremiah and his field, which he bought of his cousin, Hanameel, for seventeen shekels of silver?[23] If those thirty pieces of Silver, were those which they called Drachms, they did not amount to half the value of seventeen shekels. And if they were those called Staters, they would be more in value than double the number of seventeen shekels: take which you will, neither will assimilate. Then what has this field to do with Judas betraying his master? I wonder that Matthew did not quote the thirty changes of garments, that Samson betted with his friends;[24] or the thirty ass-colts, upon which the sons of Jair rode,[25] and make of them a prophecy for Judas, the one being as applicable as the other! O, but perhaps you will say, that Saint Matthew made a mistake when he quoted Jeremy, it being Zachariah that he meant; wherein I shall find that thirty pieces of Silver are mentioned. If this be the case, I must confess that this is a very hazardous book for us to rest our "eternal states" upon, if holy men write one thing while they mean another! However, let us see what Zechariah says upon the subject?

He says, while deploring the destruction of Jerusalem, that the Lord had commanded him to feed the flocks of the slaughter; which literally implies, to teach or preach the law to the miserable inhabitants of Jerusalem. To this, it seems, he agreed, for he says "I will feed the flock of slaughter, even you, O poor of the flock." Then he says, he took two staves, the one he called Beauty, and the other he called Bands, which probably, alluded to the two men which he had taken to assist him in his work of teaching, for then he says I fed the flock. The word staff, being often applied, by holy men, to symbolize aid and assistance in public matters.[26] After which it appears, that he quarrelled with three other shepherds, or priests, whom he was obliged to cut off in one month; which induced him to say that he would no longer feed them, but that they might die, and be cut off, or eat the flesh of one another, if they choose. He then took his staff, even Beauty, and cut it asunder, or discharged him from his office; (as Samuel did Saul, when he told him that the Lord had rent the kingdom from him,[27]) in order that he might break his covenant which he had made with all the people. After which he demanded his price, or the arrears that were due to him for his services, according to the covenant which he had made with the people. But knowing that in consequence of his first breaking the covenant, he could have no legal claim upon them, he leaves it to their own generosity, by saying if ye think good, give me my price, and if not, forbear. However, it seems that they weighed him out thirty pieces of silver for his price or wages, which he took and cast unto the potter, in the house of the Lord. He then cut asunder his other staff, even Bands, having no further occasion for him, by which means the brotherhood between Judah and Israel was broken.[28] After this we read no more of Zechariah; the three remaining chapters in the book, that bears his name were evidently not written by him, but added thereto in after ages.

Now prithee inform me, what has all this to do with either Judas or Jesus? "There is," as Paine observed, "no part that has the least relation to the case, stated in Matthew; on the contrary, it is the reverse of it. Here the thirty pieces of Silver, whatever they were for, is called a goodly price; they were as much as the thing was worth; and, according to the language of the day, was approved of by the Lord, and the money given to the potter in his house. In the case of Jesus and Judas, as stated by Matthew, the thirty pieces of silver were the price of blood; the transaction was condemned by the Lord, and the money, when refunded, was refused admittance into the treasury. Everything in the two cases is the reverse of each other." Luke and Mark, though they speak of a covenant being made between Judas and the chief Priests, yet say not a word about the prophecy, or the fate of Judas. And John disregards it altogether!

We are next told by Mark and Luke, that after Judas had bargained with the chief Priests, Jesus bade them go into the city, where they should meet a man bearing a pitcher of water, whom they were to follow, and in whatsoever house he went there they were to bespeak a place wherein they might eat the passover.[29] Matthew says not a word about the man and the pitcher; but instead thereof, says that Jesus told them to go at once to such a man and bespeak the place.[30] And John says, not a word about either. However, in the evening when all was prepared, Jesus went there and sat down with his disciples. Is it not strange that the master of the house did not go and give information of him, agreeable to the commandment of the chief Priests and Rulers? But as they were eating, Matthew and Mark say, that Jesus told them that one of them should betray him:[31] while Luke and John say that he did not tell them this until supper was ended.[32] If we examine the questions and answers, with the manner in which they were given, we shall find much inconsistency in the several reports.

Matthew and Mark say that when Jesus had told them that one of them should betray him, they began to say unto him one by one, is it I? To which, Jesus answered, according to Matthew, it is he that dippeth his hand with me in the dish. Judas immediately inquired of Jesus whether it was him? and Jesus answered thou hast said. Mark speaks of the dipping in the dish, but says nothing about the question put by Judas to Jesus, nor his answer thereto. Luke says that when Jesus told them that the hand of the men that should betray him was with him on the table, they began to inquire among themselves who should do this thing; and immediately fell a wrangling as to which of them should be accounted the greatest, without making any further inquiry concerning the person that should betray him. John says that when Jesus spoke of it they began to look at one another, doubting of whom he spake; until Peter beckoned to one that was leaning on the breast of Jesus, to inquire of him who was meant? To whom Jesus answered, he it is to whom I shall give a sop when I have dipped it. He then dipped the sop and gave it to Judas.

Again, during supper, we are told by Matthew and Mark, that as they were eating, "Jesus took bread and blessed it, and brake it, and gave it to his disciples, and said take, eat; this is my body. And he took the cup; and when he had given thanks, he gave it to them, and they all drank of it. And he said unto them, this is my blood of the new Testament, which is shed for many." Luke says that he took the cup after supper: and John says not a word about the bread and wine; although, according to his own account,[33] he was there present, leaning on the bosom of Jesus. But John considered, no doubt, that men would sooner believe that Jesus bit his own nose off and ate it, than that he should give his own flesh and blood for another to eat: and although he himself was not backward in spinning a "tough yarn," yet he had the prudence to substitute, for the body and blood, a bason of water and a towel, with which, he tells us, that Jesus washed his disciples feet; when after so doing, he entered into a long discourse with them; not a word of which is related by either Matthew, Mark- or Luke! Is not this very strange, that not one of them should have noticed such an important discourse as this, contained in the 14th, 15th, 16th and 17th Chapters of John, but leave it for a man to report fifty or sixty years after them? But what is still more wonderful, is, that John should have omitted to speak of that ceremony which forms such a conspicuous and important article in the Christian Religion, namely, " the Sacrament of the Lord's Supper!" Surely, he could not have been ignorant of it, when he was present at the supper. Then why should he suppress a thing of such vast importance? It is true that he reports a saying of Jesus, to the same effect, when Jesus said "except ye eat of my flesh, and drink of my blood, ye have no life in you."[3 4] But this was spoken a long time before the supper, in another place, upon a different occasion, and attended with different circumstances; and if not spoken as a metaphor, must have had some reference to the fate which he might either wish or expect his body would meet, after his death. I cannot find, in all the writings ascribed to John, that Jesus ever had a thought about instituting such a nonsensical and absurd ceremony, as to make a belief that while they were eating a little bread and wine, they were eating his flesh and blood. I have often seen children playing at "make believe" with their toy cups and saucers, in which they "make believe" to drink tea, coffee, &c. Surely, this "make believe" story of eating flesh and drinking blood, while eating bread and drinking wine, is children's play altogether!

Matthew, Luke, and John report, that prior to their departing from the supper table, Jesus told Peter that before the cock crowed he should deny him thrice. Mark says that it was after they went out into the mount of Olives, when Jesus told Peter that before the cock crowed twice he should thrice deny him. What inconsistencies are here reported by inspired men who wrote, you say, as they were moven by the Holy Ghost! It is needless for me to dwell upon his discourse, during the supper, as related by John, seeing that the whole account is so evidently a most glaring fabrication.

Matthew, Mark, and Luke say that after they had supped, and sung an hymn, they went out into the Mount of Olives; where, according to Luke, Jesus withdrew himself from them about a stone's cast, and kneeled down and prayed.[3 5] But Matthew and Mark say, that he went from the Mount of Olives to a place called Gethsemane,[3 6] where he separated his disciples, taking Peter, James, and John, with him to watch, while he went a little further off, where he "fell down upon his face, and prayed, saying, O my father, if it be possible let this cup pass from me; nevertheless, not as I. will, but as thou wilt." Of these places and this prayer, John takes not the least notice, although Matthew states that he was one of the three witnesses or watchmen, that was present while Jesus was praying! Instead thereof, John informs us, that after Jesus had finished his discourse at the supper, "he went forth with his disciples over the brook Cedron, where was a garden, into which he and his disciples entered.[37] (It was well for them that there were no spring-guns, man-traps, nor garden fellonies, in those days!) Surely you will acknowledge, that it was something stronger than a *ghost* that inspired these men to write in this manner!

But what could he mean by this prayer? He had previously said that no man could take away his life, without his own consent.[38] Then could he not, if he repented of his bargain, relinquish his design, and so escape the death he so much feared,[39] without asking the will of any being? If he came down from heaven to do the will of God,[40] which was that he should be delivered into the hands of wicked men, and be by them slain, according to the determinate counsel and foreknowledge of God,[41] why should he pray to an unchangeable God to alter his will and determinate counsel? Besides if his prayer had been granted, how would the scriptures have been fulfilled? which, he said, testified of those things relating to himself, namely, his death and resurrection.[42] If this were not the intent of his prayer, namely, for God to revoke his decree which he had made from the foundation of the world, and render his word which he had spoken to the fathers by the prophets, vain and void, what did it mean? Surely, he did not make this mockery to shew us the insufficiency and absurdity of prayer; proving thereby, that if the well beloved son of God, with whom the father was well pleased, could not prevail upon this unchangeable God to pass this bitter cup from such an obedient Son,[43] although he prayed as never man prayed; for it is written that he prayed till his sweat were as it were great drops of blood falling down to the ground,[44] what folly it must be for sinful and disobedient worms to offer up their luke-warm and senseless petitions to a being with whom there is no variableness nor shaddow of turning![45]

Besides, what presumption it is for man to request of, or dictate to, a God of infinite wisdom, what he should do, and what he must give! Who art thou, O man, that presumeth to teach and instruct the Lord? Surely, he knows best, and if he be a compassionate and benevolent being, will give what is most needful and necessary to his creatures. Moreover, if he be acquainted with the secrets of our hearts,[46] what occasion is there to plague and disturb him in relating them? Does he derive any pleasure, do you think, in listening to our continual and multifarious complaints? Or must we compare him to the unjust judge, of whom Jesus speaks;[47] who, before he would grant a request, must be continually teased with solicitations? If so, what man can exceed, or even equal, the earnestness and importunity of Jesus? yet we find he could not prevail. Then where is the utility of our praying, if he will not heed his own well beloved Son? Indeed, if the prayers of men could prevail with him, he would be the most changeable of all beings! though I cannot see how it is possible for him to answer all prayers to the satisfaction of all men; for while one is praying for rain, another is praying for a continuance of dry weather! If two armies are preparing for battle against each other, they both pray for victory. The Protestants pray him to convert the Catholics; and the Catholics pray him to convert the Protestants. One man prays that his life may be prolonged; while probably there may be many of his relatives, at the same time, praying for his death!

We are told by James, that if any man lack wisdom, let him ask of God, that giveth to all men liberally, and upbraideth not, and it shall be given him.[48] But Paul says that it is written, God will destroy the wisdom of the wise, and bring to nothing the understanding of the prudent.[49] And Jesus himself, thanks God that those things which were of the utmost importance to be made known, were hid from the wise and prudent.[50]   Then where is the utility of praying for wisdom? especially, as Solomon says, that in much wisdom there is much grief; and he that increaseth knowledge, increaseth sorrow.[51]   Besides, did you ever hear tell of any man obtaining wisdom by prayer alone? If you yourself, had spent your time in praying, instead of reading and conversation, by which you made your observations and gathered your experience, besides employing much labour of the mind, attended with much cogitation and care, could you have arrived to that degree of eminence, to which your attainments have raised you? No, surely; the farmer might as well expect his ground to yield him an abundant harvest, without manuring, cultivating, or sowing, alone by prayers, as a man to obtain wisdom by only asking for it.

You may reply, that we must not expect things natural, but in a natural way; it being only supernatural grace, that can be obtained in a supernatural manner. But what do we know of supernatural things? or of what benefit are they to us? Will supernatural grace feed the hungry, clothe the naked, or ·heal the sick? James says that the prayer of faith will save the sick:[52] but did you ever hear of one being healed by prayer alone? I know that you cannot credit those absurd tales related of Prince Hohenlohe in your own days: then how can you believe that such things were done in former times? the one having as much claim to your belief as the other. Perhaps you will say that James was not speaking of the natural infirmities of the body, but of supernatural or spiritual sickness. But what authority have you or any man to put such a construction on his words? He evidently was speaking of natural things, or why should he illustrate his declaration by a reference to the case of Elias? who, he says, was a man subject to like passions as we are, yet obtained, first, a very great drought, and then afterwards a plentiful supply of rain, by prayer only. Besides, Jesus says expressly, that whatsoever ye shall ask the father in his name, shall be given you.[53]   He, certainly, was not speaking of supernatural things, of which all men are ignorant, consequently cannot ask for that of which we know nothing, else his promises were both vain and ridiculous.   If by supernatural grace, you mean that saving grace, whereby we are saved through faith in Jesus Christ,[54] I remember that when I first took the "Age of Reason" in my hand to read, I went upon my knees, and prayed to Almighty God most fervently that he would keep me steadfast in the faith, and not suffer me to fall by the hand of the adversary, for the sake of his *dear* son Jesus; and in this posture did I spend the whole night, reading a little, and then praying!   Whether you will say of him, as Elijah did of Baal, that he was asleep, or peradventure on a journey, [55] I cannot tell; but certain I am, that he could not have heard me, or he would never have rejected my most sincere and earnest entreaties, that night in particular, unless he were the most hard-hearted and merciless being in existence.

Prayer, then, I consider to be a useless and degrading ceremony, especially public prayers, for which there is no authority whatever, to be found in these books.   The first public prayer meeting of which we read in the Bible, was only accidental, not enjoined; and that by a ships company of Idolaters.[56] Surely, the Christians will not make this their precedent!   But Jesus, in a special manner, forbade it, when he told the people that when they prayed, they should not stand in the streets and synagogues, praying like hypocrites, but go into their closet and shut the door, and pray in secret.[57] Yet in spite of his admonition and injunction, to the contrary, we find that men are every where desiring to wear long robes, and for a show make long prayers; although Jesus said that for these things they shall receive greater damnation![58]

I myself have oftentimes spouted at Love Feasts, Class and Band meetings, &c., concerning the necessity and efficacy of prayer.   But since the glorious Sun of Reason has dispersed all those dark and gloomy clouds of Superstition which then hovered over my mind, I have discovered that I never received any thing, by merely praying for it, but that which I was sure of obtaining if I had not prayed. We are taught to pray for our daily bread; but unless we clap our "shoulders to the wheel" will God supply us with it? And if we do not pray for it, shall we not obtain it equally the same as though we prayed? Then what utility can there be in spending our time and breath in prayers? There are many things you know, for which all men have prayed at one time or other, yet have never received; when this is the case, you say that we ask and have not, because we ask amiss.[59] Did Jesus ask amiss when he prayed? If not, why was not that for which he so earnestly entreated, granted? You cannot say that his prayer was lukewarm, or that he was so perfectly resigned to the will of God, as to submit to it quietly, or he never would have prayed till he sweated great drops of blood; insomuch that it was found necessary to send an angel to him from heaven, in order to strengthen him.[60] Of this angelic visit, no one but Luke, who was not present, takes any notice. Peter, James, and John, who were present, according to Mark, say not a word about the angel! Let us now review the manner in which Jesus was apprehended.

Matthew and Mark say that when Jesus had made an end of praying, he came to his disciples, and said to them, sleep on now, and take your rest—rise and let us be going.[61] What fickle-mindedness! Luke says that he reprimanded them for sleeping, by saying to them, Why sleep you? rise and pray. As John knew nothing of the place, the prayer, the watch, nor the angel, he could say nothing of their sleeping or rising; yet it is strange, when we are told that he was one of the watch! However, he goes on to relate that as soon as Judas made his appearance, with a band of men and officers, Jesus went forth to meet him, and demanded of them whom they were seeking? They answered him, Jesus of Nazareth, Jesus said unto them, I am he. And Judas was standing with them. As soon as he had said to them, I am he, they went backward and fell to the ground. The other historians, all say, that while

Jesus was speaking, Judas came with a multude armed
with swords and staves, and kissed him; that being the
sign agreed upon between Judas and the multitude.
Now I cannot see what occasion there was for any sign.
If Jesus were such a conspicuous and popular character
as he is described, through his preaching and teaching
in every city, town, and village, he must have been well
known to the multitude, without their employing an
informer. But which of these accounts are we to believe? John says, that instead of Judas betraying
Jesus with a kiss, he stood by while Jesus went forth
and betrayed himself! One, moreover, would have
thought, that if the majesty of his countenance, or the
terror of his voice, could strike to the ground, such a
multitude of men and officers, it would have been a
sufficient sign to them of his divine power; which would
have induced them to have fallen down again, as soon
as they were up, and worship him, instead of laying
violent hands upon him; at least they might have gone
away quietly, if they were not so frightened as to run
away, and leave him alone!

They all make mention of a noble and gallant exploit
that was done with one who was with Jesus, at the
time of his apprehension, in drawing a sword, and cutting off the ear of a servant belonging to the High
Priest. Luke and John say that it was his right ear;
and John tells us still more, by saying that his name
was Malchus, and the one who did it was Peter. Here
is something uncommonly strange in this adventure. If
Peter, who it appears, was a good marksman, had committed an assault upon an officer, no less than the
servant of the high Priest, would they not have taken
him to prison as well as Jesus? And why should Jesus
reprimand Peter for so doing, when he had previously
ordered them to get swords and take with them? Surely
he did not intend them to carry swords, like some of our
dandy nobles, merely for show, without making use of
them when required! Whence it is evident that he
had a design of defending himself, or why should he
charge them to sell their garments, in order to buy
swords, if they had not happened to find two among

them? But seeing so great a multitude armed with swords and staves coming against him, he thought it most prudent to relinquish his intention, and submit quietly. I cannot see for what other occasion the *meek and lowly* Jesus could keep swords among his disciples, while going about preaching peace and good will to the people! Luke says that he touched the ear of the man and healed him: that is, I suppose, he picked up the ear which Peter had so neatly cut off, and clapped it on again; though none of the rest say a word about this miraculous cure. Neither is any mention made of it at the trial of Jesus, though it might have convinced the high Priest of his divine power, more than all his preaching or hear-say miracles.

Matthew tells us something, also, of twelve legions of angels, which none of the others notice. And Mark relates a strange tale, concerning a young man who followed Jesus, with only a linen cloth cast about his naked body;[62] on whom they laid hold, but he escaped from them, leaving the linen cloth, and fled naked! Surely we may suppose that they were all mad together. Who was this young man? What did he among them naked at that time of the night? for it appears that they had lanterns and torches. For what purpose did holy men of God write this story? What instruction can we receive by it, in the way of righteousness? Is it not surprising to see what absurd and ridiculous tales some men can easily swallow?

After this, Matthew informs us that they led Jesus away to Caiaphas the high Priest; but John says that they led him away to Annas first, the father-in-law of Caiaphas. And that Peter, with another disciple, who was known to the high Priest, followed Jesus into the palace. But the others all say that Peter only followed Jesus, the rest having all fled. Here follow a string of contradictions among them all, concerning the conversation of Peter with the servant girl; his swearing, cock crowing, &c. which we will pass, as matter of no importance, and confine ourselves now to Jesus; only I would here just observe, that it is upon this bloody-minded, faithless, lying, cursing, swearing Peter, the church of Christ is built![63]

Jesus being now brought before the high Priest, we are told by Matthew and Mark, that they sought for false witnesses, but found none; yea, though many false witnesses came, yet found they none. (This verse[64] is truly sublime, and passeth all understanding!) At the last came two false witnesses, and said, this fellow said I am able to destroy the temple of God, and to build it in three days. Now these were not false witnesses, for according to John,[65] Jesus did make use of such an expression. But what need had they to search for false witnesses, when so many true ones were to be found? If they had sent for the money-changers, the swine-herds, the owners of the Jack-ass and the fig-tree, with all those who might have detected him in his juggling tricks, they would not have required false witnesses. neither Luke nor John say a word about these false witnesses.

We are next informed that Jesus was led away to Pilate, where the questions that were put to him, and his answers thereto, are all differently reported by his historians. Matthew and Mark say that he answered them nothing; but John informs us of a great deal that passed between Jesus and Pilate; while Luke says that Pilate sent Jesus to Herod, who questioned him with many words, but he answered him nothing. This, also, is very strange, that none of the others should take notice of such a remarkable and national occurrence as this: for by it, Luke says, Pilate and Herod, who were before at enmity with each other, were made friends!

Pilate, it seems, had a great desire to save Jesus, but the people were so greatly incensed against him, that nothing less than his death would appease them; yet we have just been told that the chief priests were afraid to arrest him because they feared the people.[66] However, when Pilate found that his power and authority were too feeble to contend against the voice of the people, he delivered to them Jesus to be crucified, after he had scourged him. What need had Pilate, who it appears was his friend, to inflict this additional punishment, if he were going to crucify him, especially to a man in whom he could find no fault? This additional punishment was not prescribed in the Jewish law, by which law it appears he was condemned to die.[67] Then Matthew says, they stripped him, and put on him a scarlet robe: but Mark and John both say, that it was a purple robe. I am not much acquainted with either purple or scarlet robes, but I think that there is some difference, not only in the colour, but in the dignity which they confer upon the wearer.

They all give some account of the insults that were offered to Jesus; but they all differ respecting the time and place, or manner in which those insults were given. Matthew, Mark, and Luke, likewise say that as they led Jesus away to the place of execution, they met a man of Cyrene, Simon by name, him they compelled to bear his cross. But John says nothing about this man; instead of whom, he says, that Jesus bore the cross himself. Again, Matthew, Mark, and John say that he was crucified at Golgotha; while Luke says that it was at Calvary.

John informs us that it was about the sixth hour when Pilate delivered Jesus to the Jews to be crucified. But Mark says expressly, that it was the third hour when they crucified him. Matthew, Mark, and Luke, say, that from the sixth to the ninth hour, there was darkness over all the earth.[68] But John, instead of darkness, says that after the sixth hour, the soldiers could see to cast lots for his garments; and Jesus could see his mother and Mary Magdalene, &c, who were standing by the cross, seemingly so close that he could speak to them. In this account they not only contradict each other, but are inconsistent with themselves; for although none besides John makes mention of the mother of Jesus, yet they all mention Mary Magdalene and other women, who, instead of standing by the cross, as John says, all declare that they were looking on, afar off. How could they see afar off, those things which they say were done while he was on the cross, if there were such a total darkness as is here described, over the whole earth?

Matthew says, that before they crucified him, they gave him to drink, vinegar mingled with gall. Mark says, that it was wine mingled with myrrh. While Luke and John say, that they gave him nothing to drink until after he was upon the cross, when they gave him some vinegar to drink.

Mark and Matthew state that both the thieves, who were crucified with Jesus, reviled him; as also did those who were passing by. But Luke positively affirms that only one of the thieves reviled him, the other rebuking him for so doing. While John takes no notice of any person, thieves or passengers, reviling or railing him!

According to Luke, Jesus told the penitent thief, that on the same day he would be with him in Paradise. But how could Jesus meet him in Paradise, that same day, if what the priests say be true, who tell us that Jesus decended into Hell when he died? According to Mark, we find that Jesus was alive at the ninth hour, or three o'clock in the afternoon. Was there sufficient time after that, for him to descend into Hell, and there preach to the spirits in prison,[69] and thence to Paradise, that same day? Surely, you will not say, that Hell and Paradise are one and the same place! neither can Paradise be in Heaven, because we are told that Jesus did not ascend there until forty days after his resurrection. But to whatever place Jesus went, by Solomon's account, we shall all go likewise: for he sayeth that all go unto one place![70]

The inscription, likewise, which was written over the head of Jesus, upon the cross, is differently reported by those inspired men: although many a school-boy would have remembered it word for word, if only accidently passing by at the time.

Matthew.	Mark.	Luke.	John.
THIS IS JESUS THE KING OF THE JEWS,	THE KING OF THE JEWS.	THIS IS THE KING OF THE JEWS.	JESUS OF NAZARETH THE KING OF THE JEWS.

It is absolutely impossible that these copies are all correct; for two sides of a contrary proposition cannot be both true; one must be erroneous, if not both And if you ascribe these different reports, to the negligence or inattention of the historians or copyists, to what credit are they entitled when they relate things of a more complicated and incredible nature, seeing that they cannot agree with each other, concerning this most simple occurrence? You may conclude, that the testimony of John, is best deserving our confidence, because he was there present, standing by the cross;[71] while the rest being absent, or looking on afar of, could only write by hearsay. If so, then, I ask, did Matthew write by hearsay likewise, that which the angel of the Lord spoke to Joseph in a dream, concerning the conception of Mary? No, you will reply, the Holy Ghost communicated that intelligence to Matthew. Then why did he not likewise communicate the precise words of this inscription, in order to prevent mankind from laying hold of such discordance, as a ground for their unbelief; which he must certainly have known would be the consequence, if all things were known to him from the beginning? Besides, how is it possible for us to ascertain, infallibly, which is hearsay evidence, and which Holy Ghost communication? The objection to this inscription, though unimportant, is, nevertheless, not frivolous. It proves to us the absurdity of placing our confidence in that which may be only hearsay evidence, and the danger in resting our " eternal states" upon such uncertainties; there being no infallible rule laid down, for us to distinguish between the erring reports of men and the communications of a Ghost!

When Jesus came into this world, it appears, by Luke, that the heavens were opened, when a multitude of the heavenly host was seen by some shepherds: who, moreover, saw the glory of the Lord shine round them.[72] This seems to have been the acme, or utmost stretch of the marvellous, that Luke could possibly imagine. But Matthew, whose mind was more groveling, owing probably to his former occupation in the custom house, confines his *chef d'œuvre* to the rending of rocks and

opening of graves, which he says occurred at the death
or departure of Jesus out of the world : when the dead
bodies of the saints "came out of the graves after his
resurrection, and went into the holy city and appeared
unto many." Although this story may be esteemed less
sublime than the story of Luke, it is, notwithstanding,
no less marvellous in our eyes. And yet, extraordinary
as it may seem, neither Mark, Luke, nor John, nor any
other historians, sacred nor profane, of that age, take
the least notice of it! This omission on the part of
every other writer, is enough to overthrow the credibility of the whole story : for these unnatural and
surprising things could not, as Mr. Fletcher says, have
been done in a corner; they must have been " as notorious as the sun at noon day" throughout the empire.
Moreover, if such an occurrence did transpire, it were
impossible, for not only the Jews, but even the Romans
themselves, to withstand such evidence. Instead of
which, we are told that the next day the chief priests
and pharisees, went to Pilate and spoke of Jesus as
still having been a deceiver?[73] although the graves, at
the same time, were open with the dead bodies staring
them in the face! for it seems they did not come out of
their graves until after his resurrection on the third
day; though the rocks rent, and the graves opened, as
soon as he had given up the ghost. Matthew has not
informed us of any one of their names; nor of the
persons to whom they made their appearance : neither
of the length of time which they had lain in their
graves; so that we cannot tell whether they rose as a
mass of living worms, or whether they only stunk like
Lazarus.

Eusebius, Pamphilus, Bishop of Cesarea, in Palestine,
who flourished in the early part of the fourth century,
informs us that there were some records in the City of
Edessa, in Mesopotamia, which contained the corres-
pondence between Abgarus, King of Edessa, and Jesus
Christ; to which he says is added, in the Syraic language, an account of the visit which Thaddaeus the
apostle, made to Abgarus, after the death of Jesus : to
whom he told, among many other things, that when

Jesus rose from the dead, others who had lain buried many ages rose again with him. (Euseb. lib. i. chap. 13.) The same author likewise informs us, (lib. iv. chap. 3.) that Quadratus dedicated and presented a book to Adrian, the Roman Emperor, about the year 120, A.D. in which he reports that those who were raised from the dead, "did not only appear after they were healed and raised, but also were afterwards seen of all; and that not only while our Saviour was conversant upon earth, but also after he was gone, they continued alive a great while, insomuch, that some of them survived even to our times." Is it not strange that those old fashioned men, who had lain buried so many ages should only have made themselves known to Mr. Matthew, Thaddæus, and Quadratus, during an interval of eighty years, from the reign of Tiberus, when they rose, to the reign of Adrian, when they were known to Mr. Quadratus? it being evident, from the silence of every other Jewish and Greek writer, concerning those men, that they were entirely unknown to them. Even the Apostle Paul must have been entirely ignorant, not only of their existence, but likewise of their resurrection; or what need had he to argue with the Corinthians concerning the resurrection of the body;[74] when he could so easily, if not produce the living witnesses, have referred them to the event, which must have been well known to all the nation, by the total darkness, earthquake, rending of the rocks, and opening of graves. Here would have been evidence undeniable and indisputable, concerning the resurrection of the body, which must have convinced and silenced the Sadducees in spite of all their prejudices and scepticism; but as I find he did not even so much as notice these things, I can neither believe the report of Mr. Matthew, nor yet the evidence of Eusebius.

Then for what purpose was all this ado, of rending of rocks, and opening of graves? Why should their "canonised bones, hearsed in death, burst their cerements? Why should the sepulchres, wherein we saw them quietly in-urned, open their ponderous and marble jaws to cast them up again? What may this mean?"

The nature of man still remained the same; their hearts were not rent, though the rocks were; neither did their understanding appear to have been opened, though the graves opened. Perhaps, you will say that it was the will of God that it should be so, in order that the scriptures might be fulfilled, which says, that they seeing, might see and not perceive; and hearing, might hear and not understand, lest they should see with their eyes, and hear with their ears, and understand with their hearts, and should be converted.[15] But will this accord with your opinion of Him, whose tender mercies are over all his works; who delighteth not in the death of a sinner, but willeth that all men should be saved, and come to the knowledge of the truth? In truth, if so, it was an odd and unaccountable way of calling sinners to repentance; of seeking and saving the lost sheep of Israel, by exhibiting such signs and wonders, that could neither be seen, heard, nor understood!

Concerning these dead bodies which rose out of their graves and appeared unto many, Mr. Matthew has made a complete bungling story altogether. He should have written, for our information and instruction, the intelligence which, undoubtedly, these dead bodies gave to their friends, respecting "the other world" from which they came. Also of their future circumstances; whether they entangled themselves again with the affairs of this world, marrying and multiplying their species, till death discovered the fugitives and arrested them the second time; or whether they returned back again to their graves immediately and buried themselves, or suffered others to do it for them again? Such information would have been much more acceptable and instructive, than a vast number of other idle and unimportant tales, with which the holy Evangelists have taken the trouble of filling up their books. I cannot forbear smiling sometimes when I read this story,—(though the appearance of so many,—not a few,—naked putrified bodies,—not spirits,—must have been truly a disgusting sight,)—at the motley group of naked men and women,—for I suppose there were some of both sexes,—running about the city! Matthew says they were saints; so that it is no

ler they were void of shame. A modest man or
an would rather hide themselves in a grave, than
se their nakedness to public view. And if they only
to stare and look about, being as mute as ghosts,
might as well have staid in their graves for what
they did! This, I suppose you will not admit,
God should send a parcel of saints back into this
l, attended with such extraordinary circumstances,
ly to say and do nothing. Therefore, my imagina-
represents to my view a ghastly putrified man,
ing after a lovely young woman, whom he wishes
aim as his wife, that buried him a few years back,
) she is endeavouring to escape from the embraces
is horrible spectre, having, perpaps, given her hand
his death to some vigorous and *lively* person : and
versa. How this matter could be settled I know
for throughout the whole Mosaic law, I cannot
out whose wife the woman should be, if her first
and was, after having been dead and buried, to take
enefit of the act, or gaol delivery from purgatory,
return to life again, and find that she had married
s absence.

hen Matthew wrote this story, it seems that he
r but little of the scriptures, which says that "he
goeth down to the grave shall come up no more;
all return no more to his house; neither shall his
know him any more."[76] "For man lieth down, and
l not till the heavens be no more; they shall not
e, nor be raised out of their sleep."[77] Even if they
, we are told that a dead body is so obnoxious in
sight of God, that he would never suffer a Jew
uch one, without purifying himself.[78] Therefore,
cannot find that any of the chief Priests, Pharisees,
Sadducees, believed these things, the truth of which
must have known if they ever did transpire, I
ot see any just ground for me to give them credit.
l Paul did not believe in this story, which must
been known to all the dwellers at Jerusalem; or
ever would have said that Christ was the first fruits
em that slept;[79] it being foretold that he should
e first that should rise from the dead.[80]

Having now arranged the several reports of the principal events which are said to have occurred between his apprehension and death, I conclude this letter by saying, that if four men, though *uninspired*, wished to obtain credit, they never would have written such contrary accounts of one and the same thing. Whence it is evident, that the writers of these books had no knowledge whatever, of the persons or things of which they were writing, and which I will make manifest at the conclusion of this work. It being utterly impossible for one and the self same action to take place at different times, and in different places, and still occurring at one place at the same time, attended with so many contradicting circumstances. Yet, notwithstanding this palpable and evident display of error and falsehood, what volumes have been written; what pains, what labour have been employed in endeavouring to reconcile these contradictions! which being found to be totally impossible, the advocates thereof have been obliged to seek the aid of sophistry, in saying that the holy men who wrote these books agreed to disagree among themselves, in order to prevent any suspicion of its being a concerted plot to impose upon the credulity of mankind! Admitting this to have been their design, does it not prove their ignorance by the contrary effects which it has produced? The tree, we are told, is known by its fruits. What jury would condemn a dog on the evidence of four men who all contradicted each other? Yet the Priests would have us to believe that their contradictory evidence is a sure sign of truth! Therefore, to say that their contradictory reports are a proof that the reporters did not act in concert, is all that can be said: which is an admission of their ignorance, concerning the things related, or there would not have been any disagreement in their several reports; especially among *inspired* men!

To make straight a highway for the advancement of truth and knowledge, through this desert of ignorance and imposture, is the intention of

Your humble Servant,

JOHN CLARKE.

NOTES TO THE FOREGOING LETTER.

1 John xi. 54. 57.
2 "   "   2.
3 "   xii. 3.
4 "   "   12.
5 Matthew xxi. 12.
—   "   xxvi. 7.
— Mark xv. 7.
—   "   xiv. 3.
6 John ii. 15.
7 Matthew xxi. 17.
8 Luke x. 38.
9 Matthew xxi. 23.
10 Luke vii. 36.
11 1 Corinthians xii. 4. 6.
12   "   vii. 7.
13 Matthew xxvi. 15.
— Mark xiv. 10.
14 Matthew xxvii. 3.
15 Acts i. 18.
16 Matthew xxvii. 9.
17 Acts 1. 20.
18 John vii. 39.
19 Acts xix. 2.
20 Matthew v. 44.
21 Psalm lxix. 25.
    "   cix. 8.
22 Mark i. 2, 3.
23 Jeremiah xxiii. 9.
24 Judges xiv. 12.
25   "   x. 4.
26 Isaiah iii. 1.
    Psalm xxiii. 4.
27 1 Samuel xv. 28.
28 Zechariah xi. 4, 14.
29 Mark xiv. 13.
— Luke xxii. 10.
30 Matthew xxvi. 18.
31   "   "   21.
    Mark xiv. 18.
32 Luke xxii. 20, 21.
— John xiii. 2. 21.
33   "   xxi. 20.
34   "   vi. 53.
35 Luke xxii. 41.
36 Matthew xxvi. 36.
— Mark xiv. 32.

Ecclesiastes iii. 20.

TO DR. ADAM CLARKE.

~~~~~~~~~~~~~~~~~~~~~~~~~~~

Sir,

I am now about to commence an inquiry into that article of faith called the Resurrection of Christ, which being considered the chief corner stone of the Christian fabric, will require more than ordinary care and circumspection in its examination; and I trust that it will be no more criminal to inquire *why* and *wherefore*, than it is *what* we are to believe; seeing that it is only by inquiry that mankind have attained the knowledge of many useful and important truths, and detected many errors and falsehoods, which in former ages were received and held forth as so many infallible truisms. Some persons no doubt, may shudder now, as well as then, at the presumption of such an inquiry, and say that it is a subject not adapted to our finite faculties, therefore not proper to be examined. But if it be not proper to examine into its merits, it cannot be a fit subject to propagate; neither would an all-wise and benevolent being propose that to our finite faculties which they were incapable of comprehending. Besides, are not the deeds of truth made more manifest by being brought to light? It is only he that doeth evil that hateth the light, lest his deeds be reproved.[1] Let us, then, bring this deed to the light of reason, that the truth thereof may appear: so that the trial of your faith, being much more precious than that of gold which perishes, though it be tried in the fire,[2] may be found worthy of honour and credit. For as the gold that cannot stand fire is thereby proved counterfeit, so that doctrine which cannot bear the test of examination, but shuns the light of reason, cannot be true. Let us see, then, on what grounds this faith is built. If on fact, let the truth of the fact appear; but if on faith only, that is, one faith upon the faith of another, let those whose business and interest it is to support and defend that faith, and who hold fast the traditions which they have been taught,[3] contend earnestly for that faith[4] and give us a reason for the hope that is within them, with meekness and fear.[5]

After the crucifixion of Jesus, we are informed by John, that a man named Joseph of Arimathea, besought Pilate that he might be allowed to take away the body; which being granted, he, and another named Nicodemus, took the body and wound it in linen clothes, with about an hundred weight of myrrh and aloes; when they laid it in a new sepulchre, which was in a garden in the place where he was crucified.[6] Yet, strange as it may appear, neither Matthew, Mark, nor Luke, take the least notice of Nicodemus nor his spices; but merely say that Joseph took the body, and after wrapping it in a linen cloth, laid it in his own new tomb which he had hewn out of a rock; when after rolling a great stone to the door of the sepulchre he departed.[7]

Matthew next informs us, of that which seemingly none of the other historians knew, as no one besides himself makes mention thereof; namely, that the next day the Chief Priests and Pharisees went to Pilate, "saying, Sir, we remember that that deceiver said, while he was yet alive, after three days, I will rise again."[8]

Now these words we remember, certainly imply that the Chief Priests and Pharisees must have heard him say, that after three days he would rise again. But none of his historians say, nor give the least hint of Jesus uttering such an expression in their hearing; nor of any such declaration, whereby they could possibly expect or imagine such an unnatural and out-of-the-way event. Even if he had, can it be supposed, that they, who would not believe his miracles, nor give any credit to his sayings on other occasions, should feel so alarmed at this wild and extravagant prediction? Whenever Jesus spoke of his rising the third day, it was always spoken in private, to his disciples only, apart from the rest; and who when he did speak of it, did not understand his meaning. Then if they who heard him did not understand nor remember this saying, how should those understand and remember that which they had never heard?

Matthew informs us, on a former occasion, that certain of the Scribes and Pharisees came and asked Jesus to give them a sign; though I cannot see what occasion they had to ask for a sign, if he had given them so many as are recorded. And Jesus answered them, and said, "an evil and adulterous generation seeketh after a sign; and there shall no sign be given to it but the sign of the prophet Jonas; for, as Jonas was three days and three nights in the whale's belly, so shall the son of man be three days and three nights in the heart of the earth."[9] But what could the Scribes and Pharisees learn by these words? Jesus did not say that after those three days and three nights, he would rise again. Surely, you will not presume to say that the unbelieving Scribes and Pharisees had more faith and understanding in the sayings of Jesus than his own disciples? for they never understood this saying, nor expected him to rise again, although to them at other times he had spoken of it plainly; and had, moreover, shewed them a token of its practicability in the case of the widow's son, and Lazarus; yet, when they were told of his resurrection, by the women, they received the intelligence thereof as an idle tale.[10] Suppose we were to admit that this was the prediction, upon which the Chief Priests and Pharisees grounded their fears, how was it fulfilled? In the first place, he was to have lain three days and three nights in the heart of the earth: whereas, we find that he only laid in a tomb, hewn in stone out of a rock, wherein he remained but two nights and one day, admitting that he laid there so long: for it seems not to have been exactly known when he did rise, only that the body could not be found at the end of the second night. Now according to common computation and common sense, two nights and one day can never be three nights and three days; nor can any man make them so, though he were to preach three days and three nights about it!

Moreover the sign was not given to those to whom it was promised : for if his rising on the third day were to be the sign of the Prophet Jonas to which he alluded, and which he promised to give, and no other, to that evil and adulterous generation, they certainly never had that sign : for we do not read that he was ever seen by any one of that evil generation after he was risen, only by his own disciples and particular friends, who did not belong to that evil and adulterous generation, Jesus having chosen them out of it before his death.[11] Besides there is no similarity between the two cases. Jonah was not dead while he was in the belly of the whale ; but Jesus is said to have given up the ghost before he was taken down from the cross. Jonah was a false prophet, insomuch that what he foretold did not occur according to his prediction ; but Jesus, you say, was a true prophet. Jonah was angry with the Lord because he would not destroy 120,000 persons to please him ;[12] but Jesus, we are told, ever liveth to make intercession for us,[13] being willing that all men should be saved.

Another expression which Jesus is said to have made publicly is related by John, who says, that after Jesus had been manifesting more than human power, in driving out of the temple whole multitudes of people, the Jews came and demanded a sign of him, to convince them that he had authority for so doing ! To this demand, instead of complying, he said, destroy this temple and in three days I will rise it up again.[14] But the observation which the Jews made on this saying, convinces us that they understood him to speak of their temple, which had been forty six years in building, and not of the temple of his body ; and which saying, they moreover brought forward as a charge against him, when apprehended.[15]

Another time, Matthew says, that the Pharisees and Sadducees came and desired him to show them a sign ; when Jesus told them that no sign should be given, but the sign of the prophet Jonas, and he left them and departed,[16] without so much as telling them what was that sign. Though Mark when speaking of the same circumstance, says, that he told them that no sign should be given to them at all, without mentioning either Jonas or the sign ![17] How then could Mr. Peter have the assurance to affirm, that he was continually working miracles, wonders, and signs, in the midst of them ?[18] Then, when, or where, or how, could the Chief Priests hear him say, that after three days he would rise again? You cannot suppose that any of his disciples could have told them of it. No, not even Judas; because it is written, that this saying, when he spoke it, was hid from them, and they perceived it not:[19] yet Matthew says, that, when he told them of these things they were exceeding sorry.[20] This appears very strange that they should be exceeding sorry because they could not understand! This prediction, of rising again the third day, I find, was, according to the several accounts given, told by Jesus to his disciples in a private manner on five different occasions; yet never once understood nor remembered by them, till after his resurrection![21] Then where was the utility of his foretelling his resurrection at all, if the saying was hid from them, and if he did not intend to appear publicly? It would surely have been as easy for him to have made his grand *entré*, into the senate or council chamber, as it was for him to appear after his resurrection, to his own disciples, in a private room were the doors were kept shut. However, as I have by me, the copy of a letter, supposed to have been written by a Jewish Rabbi concerning this part of the resurrection story, which I have already promised to send you, I will now insert it for your consideration and instruction.

"Sir,—According to promise, I here send you my thoughts on the resurrection of Jesus, in which I shall be shorter than I otherwise would be, because of the customary bounds of your discourse.

"The controversy between us Jews and you Christians about the Messiah, has hitherto been of a diffusive nature; but as the subject of this is the Resurrection of your Jesus, so by my consent we will now reduce the controversy to a narrow compass, and let it turn entirely on this grand miracle and article of your faith. If your divines can prove his resurrection against the following objections, then I will acknowledge him to have been the Messiah and will turn Christian; otherwise, he must still pass with us for an impostor and false prophet.

"I have often lamented the loss of such writings, as unquestionably, our ancestors dispersed against Jesus, because of the clear light they would have given us of this cheat and imposture. But I rejoice and thank God that there is little or no want of them to the point in hand; for I had not long meditated on the story of this resurrection, as it is related by your Evangelists, before I plainly discerned it to be the most notorious and barefaced imposture that ever was palmed upon mankind; and if you please to attend to the following arguments, I am persuaded that you, and every one else, will be in the same mind, if equally disinterested.

"To overthrow and confute the story of this monstrous and incredible miracle, I was thinking once to premise an argument of the justice of the sentence denounced against, and executed upon, Jesus; who was so far from being the innocent person you Christians would make of him, that, as may easily be proved, he was such an impostor, deceiver, and malefactor, that no punishment could be too great for him. But this argument, which I reserve against a day of perfect liberty to publish by itself, in defence of the honour and justice of our ancestors, would be too long for the compass of this letter; and therefore I pass it by: though it would give much force to the following objections: it being hard, and even impossible, to imagine that God would vouchsafe the favour of a miraculous resurrection to one, who for his crimes, deservedly suffered and underwent an ignominious death. But waiving, I say, that argument for the present, which of itself would be enough to prejudice a reasonable man against the belief of his resurrection, I will allow Jesus to have been a much better man than I believe him to have been, or as good a one in morals as your divines would have me to believe, and will only consider the circumstances of the story of his resurrection, as reported by the Evangelists: from which, if I do not prove it to be the most bare-

faced imposture that ever was put upon the world, I
deserve for the vanity of the attempt, a much worse
punishment, than he, for his fraud, endured.

"I have sometimes wondered, considering the nature
and heinousness of the faults for which he died, that our
Chief Priests and Pharisees had any regard to his prediction of rising again the third day, it being so much
like a bamboozlement of the people. There is no other
nation in the world that would not have slighted such a
vain prognostication of a known impostor, let him
foretell with ever so much confidence, his own resurrection. I dare say that any other magistrate of ordinary
prudence, would have despised him for a presumptuous
enthusiast. But when I reflected on the imposture
manifested in the resuscitation of Lazarus, and the pernicious consequence which nearly ensued through it,
against the peace and welfare of our nation, if it had
not been happily discovered, my wonder ceased; and I
now admire the wisdom, caution, and circumspection
which our Chief Priests exhibited, against all possible
fraud and deception, in the foretold resurrection of
Jesus. Though Jesus himself was cut off, who was the
head of the conspiracy and prime projector of the
designed fraud in the case of Lazarus, yet his associates
were still numerous; and it was not impossible but that
they might concert a project, of a pretended resurrection
of him, in accomplishment of his prediction; which
might have been of more fatal consequence, and tended
to such confusion and distraction among the people, as
would not have been so easily quelled and quieted.
Whereupon our chief Priests very prudently considered
of precautions against an imposition here; and wisely
made application to Pilate the Governor, that proper
and effectual measures might be taken against a counterfeited resurrection, and so prevent the evils which
might ensue through a belief thereof. Therefore one of
them, as spokesman for the rest, seems to have made
the following speech:—

"'Sir, we remember that this deceiver and impostor
'Jesus, who was yesterday crucified, and justly suffered
'death for his blasphemy, and many delusions of the

'people, that were of bad consequence, and might have
'been much worse if he had not been timely brought to
'condign punishment, said repeatedly before that, not-
'withstanding the death he was to undergo, he would
'rise again to life on the third day after. It is not
'that we are at all apprehensive of such an unnatural
'and incredible event, knowing him to have been a
'false prophet as well as a deceitful juggler; of that we
'can have no fear nor belief : but as it is not long since
'that the inhabitants in and about Bethany, had like
'to have been fatally deluded and imposed upon by him,
'in a pretended resuscitation of Lazarus, one of his
'disciples and confederates in iniquity, so it is not
'altogether impossible but that his disciples and accom-
'plices, who are many, may project a feigned resurrec-
'tion of this Jesus, to accomplish his prediction, by
'stealing away his body, and then pretend that he is
'indeed truly risen from the dead. Should such a sham
'miracle be contrived among them, and cunningly
'executed, it would be πλανη (not an error, but an
'imposture,) of worse consequence to our nation and
'religion than the former, in the case of Lazarus, could
'have been, if it had never been detected. We crave,
'therefore, the favour of your Excellency to give orders
'for securing his sepulchre till the third day be past ;
'that neither his *dead* body may be taken away, and a
'resurrection pretended, nor a *living* one slipped in its
'place, and a miracle be counterfeited ; when we will
'be present on that day at the opening of the sepulchre,
'and give satisfaction to the people of his being a false
'prophet.'

"Whether Pilate was at all intent on the prevention
of fraud in this case, or would not willingly have con-
nived at it to increase the divisions and distractions
of our unhappy nation, may be questioned. But the
request of our chief priests was so reasonable, and
their importunities so urgent, that he could not resist
them ; therefore ordered them a watch for the sepulchre, which they might make as sure as they could
against fraud and imposture, till the third day.

"Whereupon our chief priests deliberated what measures were most fit to be taken upon this occasion. And as I cannot, and do not, believe that any man else can devise any thing better for the security of the sepulchre against fraud, than the method which they took, so I admire and applaud their prudence, circumspection, and precaution in the case. They sealed the stone at the mouth of the sepulchre, and placed a guard of soldiers about it; which were two such certain means for the prevention and detection of cheat in the resurrection, as are not to be equalled in any other.

"They sealed the stone of the sepulchre, which, though it was no security against violence, yet was an absolute one against fraud. I shall not attempt to describe in what manner the stone fitted the mouth of the sepulchre, as a door does the entrance of a room, nor how it was sealed. The use and manner of sealing doors of closets, of chests, and of papers, are well known and common; and as it is an obvious expedient for the satisfaction of the signators against deceit, so it has been an ancient as well as modern practice. Nebuchadnezzar, (Daniel vi, 17,) sealed the door of the den of lions into which Daniel was cast, with his own signet. And wherefore did he seal it? Why, for the satisfaction of himself and courtiers, that when he came to open and compare the signature with his own signet, no art nor artifice had been used for the preservation of Daniel. So our chief priests sealed the sepulchre of Jesus, at which they designed to be present when opened the third day; that being the time appointed by Jesus for his resurrection: and then give ample satisfaction to the people that there was a real, or there could be no resurrection. Wherefore else did they seal the stone of the sepulchre?

" Your Grotius thinks,* that the seal of Pilate was affixed to the stone; but as I believe Pilate did not concern himself much about the matter, so I much question, whether this was the case. It is more reasonable to suppose, that the Chief Priests and other civil

---

* Adducor ut credam Pilati annulo et hunc Lapidem signatum. *In Loc, Matt.*

magistrates of Jerusalem signed or sealed the stone with their several signets, which could not be opened unless they were all present, without suspicion of fraud: this being their intention on the day appointed, not doubting, what no person could question, but Jesus would wait their coming, and arise, if he could, in their sight, and that of the vast numbers of people who would be sure to have attended on the occasion, in order to bear witness to such an extraordinary miracle. Such a resurrection would have been satisfactory to the whole nation! and such a resurrection, reasonably speaking, Jesus would, if he could, have vouchsafed, in accommodation to the sealing of the stone.

" But, notwithstanding the precaution, in sealing the stone, which was the best thing that could be done to prevent fraud, the body of Jesus was privately withdrawn early in the morning of the day before the appointed time, and a resurrection pretended by his disciples; while you would have us and our ancestors to believe that there was no deceit in the case, though, confessedly, none of the sealers of the stone were present! Who can believe it? Was there ever, or can there be, any imposture, more contrary to sense and reason, palmed upon the understanding of a rational being, than this story of his resurrection?

"A question here arises, which is, on what day, and what time of the day, did our chief priests, the sealers of the stone, expect what they could never think would occur, the resurrection of Jesus? Or what was the extent of the time meant by Jesus, when he said that after three days, or on the third after his passion, he should rise again? If any impostor or prophet, like Jesus, should in this age, so predict his resurrection, and be executed on a Friday, the day for his resurrection would be presumed to be on the Monday following, and not on the Sunday before day. And I humbly conceive, that former ages and nations, did so compute time after this fashion. Accordingly, on Monday our chief priests, I do not doubt, intended to have been present at the opening of the seals of the sepulchre, and to behold the miracle. But the body of Jesus was clandestinely moved off early on the Sunday, the day before that signified and predicted for his rising, to the diversion, more than surprise of our ancestors, at the notoriety of the fraud committed, and at the vanity of the pretence of a resurrection. Now I appeal, even to your chief priests of the church, whether here is not another note of cheat and imposture; and whether the disciples of Jesus were not afraid to trust his body the full time in the grave, because of the greater difficulty they would have to carry it off afterwards, in order to frame a resurrection?

"Yet, because your divines, who have a singular method in making two nights and one day, the time that Jesus was buried, equal to three days and three nights, and at whose various ways of computation I always smile, do assert that Sunday was the third day, I will suppose so with them; and will, if they please, grant that our chief priests, the sealers of the stone, expected his resurrection on that day, therefore intended to repair to the sepulchre in order to open the seals, on the Sunday; still at what time of the day were they to come, or could be expected to arrive at the sepulchre? Surely not before noon! But the body of Jesus was gone before day-light! before our chief priests could reasonably be expected out of their beds! and a bare-faced infringement of the seals was made, against the laws of honour and honesty. And this your Christian priesthood would have us to believe, in the present day, is proof sufficient that there was a real resurrection. O! most monstrous!

"If our chief priests had trespassed upon the patience of Jesus, by not attending at the appointed time to open the seals, then his resurrection without their presence would have been excusable; or if they had endeavoured to confine him in the grave longer than was meet to fulfil his prediction, he would be justified in escaping as soon as he possibly could. But this, his pretended rising, a day before the chief priests could imagine he would, and earlier in the morning than he should, for the sake of their requisite presence, together with the fracture of the seals against the law of security, is such a manifest and indisputable mark and indication of fraud, as is not to be equalled in all or any of the impostures that ever were attempted to be put upon the world! In short, by the sealing of the stone we are to understand that nothing less than a covenant was entered into between our chief priests and his followers, by which the veracity of Jesus, his power and Messiahship, were to be tried. It is true that we do not read of the apostles giving their consent to such a covenant, but if it had been demanded we may presume that they could not have reasonably refused. The condition, then, of this covenant would be, that if Jesus rose from the dead in the presence of the chief priests, when the seals were opened at the appointed time, then he should be acknowledged to be the true Messiah. But if he continued in a corrupt and putrified state of mortality, it should then be granted by all that he was only an impostor. Very wisely and rightly agreed. And if the disciples had stood to this covenant, Christianity would have been nipped in the bud, and suppressed in its birth. But they had other views and another game to play at all adventures; the body must be removed, and a resurrection pretended, to delude, if possible, all mankind! in which they have been more successful than could have been possibly imagined, upon a project that had so little sense or reason, colour of truth, or artifice, in its contrivance and execution.

"Our chief priests were apprehensive, at first, of their stealing away the body and pretending a resurrection; but after the sealing of the stone those fears vanished: because upon the stealing the body away, against such security and precaution, the fraud would be self-evident and no further proof would be required. Yet, notwithstanding this security, the body was removed and a resurrection pretended: which, to the amazement of every one who can think freely, has been believed by some through all ages of the church ever since! Upon the whole I think you may as well say, that when a sealed closet is broken open and the treasure it contained stolen or taken without the knowledge of the signators, there is no fraud nor knavery in the conveyance, as to say, that there was none in the resurrection of Jesus. The cases are equal and parallel! What then can your Christian priests say to this demonstrative argument of a manifest fraud in this resurrection story? Why, I have being thinking what they will or can say; and upon the maturest consideration, I do not find that they can make any other than one or more of these shuffling answers: viz.

" '1. That it was impossible for the disciples to steal away the body of Jesus, because of the vigilance of the guards; therefore there was a real resurrection, not-withstanding the absence of the chief priests and sealers.

" ' 2. That, though the chief priests and sealers of the stone were not present, as I say they ought to have been, to witness the miracle, his resurrection was made manifest to them afterwards, the same as though they had been present.

" '3. That if Jesus did not actually arise from the dead, the belief of his resurrection would never have been so propagated at first, nor would have been retained in the world for so many ages ever since.'

" I can think of no other answers, and I conceive it impossible for your Christian priests to form any other to the aforesaid arguments of fraud in the resurrection. But how weak, frivolous, and insufficient they all are, will appear upon an examination of them.

" To the first I reply, and confess that if it were im-possible to evade the vigilance of the guards, then there must have been a real resurrection. But if there were but a bare possibility of deceiving them, then this answer is of no force. And I am of opinion that the thing was not only possible, but easy, feasible and practicable. Though the Roman soldiers were of as much fidelity and integrity as any of their profession, yet it is well known such creatures are subject to bribery and cor-ruption, if the disciples had any money wherewith they could tempt them. Or if their faithfulness to their trust was untainted, yet it is not improbable but their officers, at the direction of Pilate, who found his account in the distractions of our nation, might have given the hint to wink hard at the contrivance and commission of such a fraud. But not to insist on either of these ways in evading the watch, our ancestors said what your Evangelist has recorded, that the disciples, taking the opportunity of the guards slumbering, carried off the body of Jesus; which was a thing not only possible but very probable.

"Of what number the watch consisted is uncertain. Your Whitly says that they were sixty in number; but he has no reason nor authority to think that there were so many. If they had been a guard against violence, I should easily have believed that there had been more than sixty, instead of less. But, inasmuch as they were only a watch against fraud, and against any casual defacing of the seals on the stone before the chief priests came to open the sepulcure, three or four soldiers were quite sufficient for this purpose. And I cannot think that any more constituted that watch.

"It is not then at all improbable, that a few soldiers should be fast asleep at that time of night, or so early in the morning when the clandestine work was done; especially after keeping such a gaudy day as was the feast of the passover; which like the festivals of all other nations, was celebrated with excess and intemperance. Foot soldiers then you may be sure upon the bounty of one or other, did not want; neither would they scruple to take their fill, which like an opiate, locked up their senses for that night, not suspecting such a bold and impudent transaction: when the disciples being aware of the lucky moment, carried off the body of Jesus in safety!

"And where is the absurdity in supposing that the disciples themselves might not contrive to intoxicate the guards? Herodotus tells us a story of a dead body being carried away by such an artifice. And I do not think that the disciples of Jesus were either so foolish or conscientious as not to take the hint, and enterprize the like fraud. Peter, who upon occasion, could swear and curse and lie like a trooper, would hardly scruple to fuddle a few foot soldiers. But which ever way it it came to pass the watch was asleep, which is neither hard to conceive, nor difficult to believe; and then the disciples executed that fraud, which has for ages since been the delusion of so many nations!

"Your Evangelist would hint that the chief priests gave money to the soldiers, to say that they were asleep, when the disciples stole away the body of Jesus; as if they were bribed to a false testimony; but there never was nor can be such a thing. If there had been a real resurrection, to their astonishment and amazement, as represented by Matthew, no money could so soon have corrupted them, as to cause them to perjure themselves, being under such fears of God and of Jesus. I do not doubt but our chief priests rewarded the soldiers for speaking the truth, with a promise to secure them from the anger of Pilate for their sleeping and neglect of duty. Here then is no answer to my objections against the resurrection of Jesus; seeing that it was not at all impossible for the disciples to steal the body away by evading the watch, who were, we may reasonably suppose lulled asleep when the disciples did it. Neither is their any more force in the second answer, viz. That though the chief priests who sealed the stone, were not present to open the seals, yet his resurrection was afterwards manifested to them, as though they had been there.

"This is something like an answer, if there be any truth in it. A manifestation of Christ risen afterwards to our chief priests, would have been equivalent to their presence at, and sight of, the miracle. But how, and when was this resurrection manifested to them? Did Jesus ever appear personally to them afterwards, and satisfy them that he was the same person whom they had crucified for being a deceiver and false prophet? No; this is not once asserted by any of your Evangelists, nor even insinuated by any other writer, either ancient or modern. How, then, was his resurrection made manifest to the chief priests? Why your divines say, which is all that can be said, that the words of the disciples, who being men of honesty, simplicity and integrity would not lie, are to be taken for it. Very fine, indeed! Our chief priests are to take the word of those disciples for the truth of his resurrection; and look upon them as men of veracity whom they knew by experience to be a gang of impostors, especially in the pretended resurrection of Lazarus! When deceivers will not lie nor thieves dissemble, then will I believe these disciples, and acknowledge from their bare assertions, that the resurrection of Jesus was made manifest to our chief priests.

"This was always a ground of objection with us Jews, against the truth of the resurrection of Jesus, that he did not appear personally afterwards, to our chief priests, to Pilate, and to others of his crucifiers and insulters, and upbraid them for their ill treatment of him; likewise to convince them of their infidelity. Whether Jesus would not have done so if he really rose from the dead, and whether he ought not in reason, for the conviction and conversion of unbelievers, with me is no question. Celsus, of old, in the name of the Jews, made the objection;* and Olibio, a late Rabbi, has repeated it. But in all my reading and conversation with men and books, I have never yet met with a tolerable answer. Origin and Limborch, the writers against Celsus and Olibio, gently slide over the objection as if it were too hot or too weighty for them to touch or handle! To recite the poor short and insufficient answers made by these two great authors, would be not only exposing their weakness, but giving such strength to the objection, as would be needless and superfluous. Therefore I will leave the objection, which Origen owns to be a considerable one,† to the meditation of your modern advocates for Christianity. And when they can prove that Jesus, after his resurrection, did manifest himself to his crucifiers, the chief priests and sealers of the stone, or that according to the law of

---

* Si Jesus volebat revera declarare suam divinam Potentiam debuerat suis insultatoribus, ipsiq; Præsidi qui capitalem sententiam contra se tulerat, denique cæteris omnibus se ostendere.—*In Orig.* lib. ii, *Contra Celsum.*

† Magna sane Res et miranda occurrit hoc loco, quæ non solum aliquem ex vulgo credentium exercere posset, sed perfectiores etiam: cur non dominus post resurrectionem æque ac superioribus temporibus conspiciendum se præbuerit.—*In Orig.* lib. ii, *Contra Celsum.*

reason he ought not to have appeared personally to their confutation, then I will turn Christian and grant them all they desire. In the mean time, I must believe that the non-appearance of Jesus to the Chief Priests is a confirmation that he did not rise from the dead, but that his body was stolen away, or he would have waited in the sepulchre for the coming of the sealers of the stone, and their regularly opening of the grave, to the conviction and conversion of all present, and confirmation of the faith in all ages since.

"The third answer to the aforesaid arguments of fraud in the resurrection, drawn from the nature, use, and design of sealing the stone, is, that though the sealers were not present to open the seals, yet Jesus did, nevertheless, rise from the dead, or the belief thereof could never have been at first propagated by the apostles; nor would for so many ages of the church since have stood its ground.

"There is as little reason in this answer as in either of the two former. Who knows not, that many errors in philosophy, and as many frauds in religion, have been sometimes accidently, sometimes designedly, espoused and palmed upon mankind? who, in process of time, became so wedded to them, through prejucice or interest, that they would not give themselves leave to inquire into their rise and foundation. False miracles have been common things among Christians; and as the resurrection of Jesus is their grand and fundamental one, so it is not at all difficult to account for the rise, propagation, and continuance of the belief therein.

" Why it has been believed through these latter ages of the Church, is nowise wonderful. The priests had therein an interest; and the ignorant and superstitious their comfort; so the wise and considerate, for fear of persecution, dare not inquire into its grounds.

"The only difficulty here, is to know upon what principle the project and story of the resurrection was at first devised? Whether it was ambition, or revenge upon our ancient and pharisaical priesthood, that first prompted the disciples to it, is not material to the question. We know that such bad principles too often put men upon desperate attempts. However, an imposture it was, which is evidently shewn by the above arguments. To say that the disciples and confederates in the fraud would not have stood and died by it, if the resurrection had not taken place, is no argument in its favour; many cheats and criminals, beside them, have asserted their innocence, and denied their guilt, in the utmost extremity of death without the like views of fame and honour. The only thing that is surprising and astonishing in this sham miracle, is, that though it was the most manifest, barefaced, and self-evident imposture, that was ever put upon the world, it has been the most fortunate and successful: having passed through so many ages and nations with reputation and renown; and might have continued for many ages to come, but for the above argument, which clearly overthrows its credit.

"Some may say here, where was the wisdom or providence of God all this while, to suffer so many ages and nations to labour under such a delusion? Why, I will tell you. The providence of God in it, certainly was to humble mankind, in the end, for their vain ostentation of wisdom, learning, and science, falsely so called: to shame them for their madness and wickedness in persecuting one another, for differing in opinion concerning that of which they were alike ignorant. To caution them against a blind and implicit faith for the future, in believing anything out of the sight and reach of their understandings. To convince them of the necessity that there is for liberty to think, speak, and write freely, about any religion; in order that error may be corrected and truth discovered. And, lastly, to reduce the world, whenever it shall become ripe, to the golden religion of nature; which, upon the testimony of our old cabalistical Doctors, and of your Jesus himself, is the end of the law and the prophets!

"Thus have I spoken to the answers which your Christian priesthood may be presumed to make, against the aforesaid argument of fraud in the resurrection of Jesus, drawn from the design of our chief priests in sealing of the stone of his sepulchre. I should not have concorned myself to speak to these, their supposed, answers, but to save the trouble of their making them, and the imagination that there might have been some force in them.

"As to the stories of the several appearances of Jesus after his pretended resurrection, sometimes to the women, and at others to his disciples, I am not at all obliged to refute them. For if these appearances had been more frequent, better circumstanced, and more solemnly averred, they would have required no confutation. There is no doubt but his disciples, who unquestionably stole away the body in order to pretend a resurrection, would talk much about his appearance, and his conversation with them afterwards. And if they had told better and more plausible tales of him, it would be nothing to the purpose. I say better and more plausible tales than those upon record; which carry their own confutation along with them, through their incoherence, nonsense, and absurdity.

" Whoever blends together the various stories of his appearances, as related by his historians, will find himself not only perplexed how to make an intelligible, consistent, and sensible story out of them, but must, with Celsus,* needs think, if he thinks at all of what he reads, that it is like some of those old wives' confused and incredible fables of apparitions, ghosts and witches with which the Christian world in particular has, in former ages, abounded. The ghosts of the dead, in the present age, and especially in this Protestant country, have long since ceased to appear; and we, now-a-days, hardly ever hear of such a thing as an apparition. What can be the reason of this silence? Why, the belief of these stories being banished from the minds of the people, the crafty and vaporous forbear to trump them upon us; because there has been so much fraud detected in many of these stories, that the wise and considerate part of mankind have re-

---

* Quamy is Celsus has Jesu post Resurrectionem apparitiones conferre conetur cum vulgaribus spectris and visionibus. *In Orig. Lib ii. Contra Celsum.*

jected them altogether, excepting this of Jesus; which, to a degree of admiration, has stood its ground. It is therefore no wonder that the clergy, who are less credulous than other folks concerning the stories of apparitions, do stick so close to this of Jesus, the only one accepted out of all the others; it being such a sweet morsel of faith that they willingly swallow and digest it, because by it they are enabled to live in idleness and luxury: otherwise it would never have escaped the fate of all other apparition stories: nay it is more probable that it would have been rejected the first of them, there being scarcely one, I dare to say it, among all the stories of apparitions, ghosts, and such like visionary beings, were they all to be collected together, that is more absurd, and ridiculous, than this one of Jesus!

"I have not room here to make any remarks on your Evangelical stories concerning the apparition of Jesus after his death; and if I had, I dare not, for fear of transgressing the rules of decency, sobriety, and sedateness of argument. I cannot read the story without smiling, there being two or three passages therein that remind me of Robinson Crusoe filling his pockets with biscuits, when he had on neither coat, waistcoat, nor breeches! Sometimes I think that your Evangelists wanted wit to adapt their tale to sense, and to accommodate the transaction to the laws of nature. Sometimes I think them crafty; and minded, like Daniel de Foe in his aforesaid romance, to put the banter upon the credulity of mankind with some disguised and latent absurdities, that, in the conclusion and discovery thereof, they might be heartily laughed at for their belief! I dare not then I say, so much as hint at one of these absurdities, lest I should unwarily be tempted to crack a jest thereon. But the time I hope is coming when I shall be permitted to use more freedom of speech. And should your priesthood, in proof of the resurrection, urge any of these stories of his corporeal presence and appearances after death, I trust that they will permit me to make as many merry descants on them, as your bishops, when academical jesters, used to do on other men's bulls and blunders.

" In the mean time I depend on the foregoing simple, sober, and sedate argument, founded upon the nature and design of sealing the stone of the sepulchre, which demonstrates fraud in this grand miracle. And, for confirmation thereof, I will close this letter with a parallel case and story.

" Not many years since, **Dr.** Emms, one of the society of French prophets, who were in their inspirations like Jesus and his disciples of old, declaimers against the pharisaical priesthood of this age, did himself, or some of his fraternity for him, predict his resurrection on a certain day; on which day there assembled a great concourse of people about his grave to behold the miracle, as there would have been about the sepulchre of Jesus if he had lain in it his full time. But this gathering was all in vain; no resurrection took place. Now suppose that in this case, the magistrates and priesthood of the city, to prevent a cheat and delusion of the people, had interred the doctor in a church vault, and sealed the door thereof against the day appointed for his resurrection, commanding likewise a night watch to look to the vault that no deceit nor violence were used, would you not say that this was done wisely on their part to guard against fraud and imposition, as it was in the case of Jesus? But if after all this precaution, some of his followers had drawn aside the watch to a gin shop whilst the others carried of the body, and then pretended a resurrection had taken place, what would all reasonable men have said? Why, that it was a most barefaced and impudent imposture! And suppose that the Doctor's fraternity had afterwards affirmed, that they had not only seen, but ate and conversed with him several times after his death: and likewise, told us some particular stories concerning him; such as, how he appeared to some of their women, who were admonished of the certainty of his resurrection, by a youth, or an angel, or two,—they could not tell which, but they were as like to angels, (which they had never seen before) as could be ! Then that he appeared to two men, as a traveller, who knew him, not by his countenance, for their eyes were holden, but by his talk on scripture, his usual cant, before his death, and an habitual motion which he had of breaking of bread. Then another time he was corporeally present among his old acquaintance, but they thought they saw a spirit. And a few days after he again appeared among them; but some of them doubted, whether it was the doctor, or not! And sometimes, he would slip into their company when the doors were all shut, either from behind a curtain, or miraculously creep through the key hole! · That he would, moreover, change his form and shape, so that his most intimate friend would not believe it was him till he discovered a sore in his side, which the power of God did not heal in his resurrection!— And after that he vanished out of sight, and was taken up to heaven. Suppose all this, I say, that the French prophets had told such like stories of the resurrection of Dr. Emms, and of such appearances to them, what would your priests and all other wise men have said to them? Why that they were all idle tales, manifest lies, sham, and imposture. For, they would say, if the Doctor had truly risen, God, by whose power he must have been raised, would have kept him his full time in the grave, and have raised him in the presence of the priests, magistrates, and people, in order to prevent every suspicion and appearance of fraud. Moreover he would have walked publicly afterwards in the streets without any fear or danger, to the satisfaction of all who had known Dr. Emms, as being the man whom they had seen dead and buried. Without danger I say from the populace; who would have been so far from affronting him, that they would almost have adored him for the miraculous favour which God had conferred upon him in raising him again to life. And instead of sculking about and absconding himself during the forty days he chose to remain here, he would have presented himself at every public meeting and assembly throughout the country. As none of these things were done, it is plain that the whole is a complete fabrication.

"I need not make the application of this case and story of Dr. Emms, as your priests know well enough how to do this for me. To say that there were none who would be found so desperate as to engage in such a fraud and imposition, as in the supposed case of Dr. Emms, is a mistake; many thousands for their diversion would engage in such a plot. And the stories of ghosts and apparitions, which are mostly the result of fraud and deception in the crafty to delude the ignorant, is a proof thereof. I myself would be most forward to concert and join in such an intrigue; if it were only to banter the clergy, ruffle their tempers, and secretly laugh at them. Nothing would deter me from it, but the dread of the civil power, from which danger the disciples of Jesus were secured. So the disciples stood to the fraud; told the story of Jesus *risen* so often, till they believed it themselves and drew multitudes besides into a belief thereof!

" Before I conclude this letter I think it my duty to give you my opinion of the religion, which Jesus and his followers were for introducing into the world; notwithstanding the artifice and fraud practised in his pretended miracles. And though our Chief Priests and ancient nation were justified in passing sentence and executing it upon Jesus, yet I must do him the justice to own that the doctrine which he and his disciples taught, was, for the most part, useful and popular; being no other than the *law of nature;* which, all nations, being wearied with their own superstitions, and sick of the burden of the priests, were running into apace. One of your ancient fathers (Justin Martyr, in Apol. 2) says, that they who lived according to the law of nature, were true Christians. But in process of time, Christians most shamefully adulterated Jesus's doctrine. If they had not sophisticated the primitive religion of Jesus; if they had not built their systematical divinity upon him, and brought strange inventions of men into his worship; if they had not again subjugated and entangled themselves in another and much worse yoke of bondage to an intolerable and tyrannical priesthood, the world might have enjoyed much happiness under his religion, as it was at first promulgated: or more truly speaking, the state of nature and liberty which may be looked for upon the coming of our Messiah, the allegorical accomplisher of the law and the prophets.

"Thus, sir, have I finished my letter on the resurrection of Jesus; and whether I have not said enough to justify our Jewish disbelief of that miracle, let your chief priests judge and determine. They have a potent reason I know for their belief, at which we Jews cannot come, or may be we might believe with them.

"Though I have here shewn that Christ is not risen, yet I have more wit than to say, with Paul, that the preaching of your priesthood is in vain. Their oratory is still useful, if it be but to tickle the ears and amuse the understandings of the people about doctrines they do not understand, whether true of false. And such an order of men as are your priesthood, must, by their habit of long robes, be an ornament to society: therefore it is an honour to the country to have them well fed and clad! Had I room for it, I could write a curious encomium in praise of them, and tell the world of what use and advantage they have been in all ages. O! what wars and persecutions might have been raised in the world, but for their pacific tempers! How would sin and immorality have broken loose upon mankind, like a deluge, but for the goodness of their lives, and excellency of their precepts! How has the increase and multitude of their warm sermons, been the ruin of Satan's hot and divided kingdom of darkness and error! Is it not owing to their pains and labour that every age, for many past, has been improving in virtue?! And is not the present, for piety and good morals, that perfection of time which is not to be equalled, but by the restitution of the golden age?!

"I am, your friend,

"N. N."

In this letter, you may perceive, what great stress the Jew has laid upon the use and design of the watch, and of the sealing of the stone at the mouth of the sepulchre: likewise upon those remarkable words spoken by the chief priests, when they besought Pilate to grant them a watch; saying, that the last *error*, or as he interprets it, *deceit* or *imposture*, will be worse than the first; evidently alluding to the fraud practised in the pretended resuscitation of Lazarus; which shows plainly that the fraud therein was detected and well known to the chief priests, or they never could have had the assurance to assert as much before Pilate. This appears to have been so glaring, and self-evident, that the cunning translators of this book, artfully substituted the word *error*, for πλανη, *planh*, or imposition.

No man of common sense would believe it possible for the chief priests, who always considered Jesus to be an impostor and deceiver of the people when living, to be anywise alarmed about his resurrection, in consequence of anything which he might have said to that effect, much less to watch for it, when his own disciples had not the least idea of such a thing. These latter did not entertain such an idea, or why should the women have put themselves to so much trouble and expense in preparing spices and ointments, if they expected him to rise again the same day on which they were applied? I must confess that this account perplexes me much, to imagine why these women, who had seen Nicodemus lay out the body of Jesus with an hundred weight of spices, should think of bringing more! for Luke says, expressly, that these women beheld the sepulchre, and how his body was laid;[2 2] and, it appears by all the historians, they did not quit it until after the stone was rolled to the door. Then what need had they to bring more spices? Was not an hundred weight sufficient for one body?

Again, if the chief priests and pharisees went the next day to seal the stone, as a matter of course they would look into the sepulchre to see if the body was there, before they clapped on their seals: else the body, for what they knew, might have been taken away the first night, before the watch was appointed! And if they saw the body thus spiced and preserved, they surely would have considered it unnecessary and ridiculous to set a watch for the keeping of that which his own disciples had been so forward in preserving: by which they would be well assured that his disciples had no thoughts of his rising again, nor any intention of stealing away the body in order to propagate such a report; or they would never have gone to the expense of spicing it in that sumptuous manner. They did not spice the body of Lazarus. Why? because they expected Lazarus would be - raised again, according to agreement, before he counterfeited death. But Jesus they knew was actually dead; and seeing him crucified, so spiced his body, not expecting nor supposing it possible for him to rise again to life in this world.

The advocates of this resurrection story say that the chief priests and pharasees did not expect a real resurrection, but was only afraid that such a report might be raised could the disciples but obtain the body. How could they think of such a thing, when they knew that the disciples had run away and left Jesus as soon as he was apprehended, and were moreover fearful of discovering themselves,[2][3] lest they should be recognized and punished accordingly? Besides the body being left there in safety the first night, without a watch, would convince them that the disciples had seemingly no such design, or they would have taken it away before the next day. Yet supposing that they did make such a report, what then? Without some proof of his resurrection, could they imagine that the people would be such credulous fools as to believe such an unnatural and unheard of prodigy, as that of the revivification of a man after he had been crucified, dead, and buried for three days, without stronger proof than a mere report propagated by his own party, who were already known to the people as deceivers and impostors? Although the chief priests might have known that many of the people had suffered themselves to be deceived by reports of this kind, still in the present instance they would naturally premise that the people would expect ocular demonstration : curiosity would excite them to inquire where he was, and how he looked after his revival? To have shewn them a dead body, would have only discovered the vilainy attempted on them; and surely, they could have been under no apprehensions of his disciples restoring the dead body to life again, after they had got it in their possession in order to make of him a king! What then could they suppose that the disciples could do with the body if they obtained it? You certainly must acknowledge that the chief priests and pharisees were capable of reasoning in this manner, upon the effect which such a report of a resurrection, being made by his own disciples, would have upon the minds of the people, before they would set a watch. And if so, what ground had they to fear such a report, without corresponding evidence? If they dreaded a real resurrection, they surely were not so ignorant as to imagine that they could conceal the consequences which they must naturally expect from such an event; nor so impious as to suppose that the puny efforts and resistance of their watch could withstand the power of that being who was to raise him? Then where was the necessity of a watch? I can see none. Besides what occasion had the chief priests and rulers of the people to go and ask Pilate for a watch? Could they not themselves have employed some persons to watch for those three days, without going to ask a man of whom, above all men in office, one would think they would have been most mistrustful, knowing his recent partiality towards Jesus? If you suppose that they were fearful of trusting men to watch the body without being armed, it clearly proves the character which those disciples must have had among the people; whom they must consider, by their requiring armed men to resist their dishonest designs, as a race of bloody-minded monsters, capable of murdering an un-armed watch, so that they might but procure the body to enable them to carry on their imposition. Neither is this supposition groundless, when we remember how ready Peter was to smite with the sword; and the desire of James and John on a former occasion, to see a whole village with all its inhabitants burned with fire.[24] But if such had been their fears and reasons for an armed guard, they must certainly have had a whole band or strong guard of soldiers; which, if such had been the case, must have been publicly known to all the dwellers at Jerusalem; at least it could not have escaped the observation of those who were most concerned about the body; such as they who were preparing spices and ointments to carry with them the following morning. Yet we find that they knew nothing of this watch, or they never would have inquired among themselves as they were going, who shall roll away the stone for us.[25] Neither can we suppose that a party of modest women would have gone among a company of soldiers at that time of the morning, in such an obscure place, if they had known that the soldiers were there!

I have dwelt thus largely upon this story of the watch and seals, because it seems to have been written, and is often advanced, as a proof that no fraud was committed in the resurrection of Jesus; it being impossible for any of his disciples to steal away the body were they so inclined, while it was thus guarded and secured by a watch. We sometimes, however, do read of such things as watchmen themselves stealing that which they were appointed to protect.

Although this story of guarding the sepulchre is of such importance to the Priests, in their endeavours to prove that no fraud could have been practised in the resurrection of Jesus, yet neither Mark, Luke, nor John take the least notice of it. How they could possibly avoid noticing it, if it really did occur, I cannot tell; for their account of the resurrection is rendered incomplete without a watch to secure the body: because it appears to have been deposited in an insecure place, where any *resurrection man* could easily have got at it; else how could a few poor feeble women think of going to it, with so much confidence, at that time of the morning? It was not buried in the heart of the earth, but only laid, *for the present*, in a tomb, or cave, hewn out of a rock, close by where he was crucified; because the sabbath drawing near, they had no time to bury him according to their religious rites and ceremonies. Therefore a watch appointed by his friends would have been necessary, to secure his interment on a future day, they having no thoughts of a resurrection. But a watch appointed by the chief priests, who, after he was dead, had no reason to concern themselves as to what became of the body, was entirely unnecessary; and it is moreover incredible that those men who were so remarkably strict in the observance of their sabbath, should on that day assemble together, proceed in a body to Pilate, procure a watch, and move and seal a stone, when they were forbidden even to speak their own words.[27]

Let us now examine the result of this watching the body, as it is reported by Matthew. He says that while the watch was there, behold there was a great earthquake. Strange that no other historian, either holy or unholy, should hear or know of this earthquake; but that all should suffer it to "pass by, unheeded like a summer cloud!"

" And the angel of the Lord descended from heaven, and came and rolled back the stone from the door, and sat upon it, and his countenance was like lightning, and his raiment white as snow." In this account, we discover the ignorance of the writer, who could frame such an absurd story. The angel is here described as having descended from heaven. What became of him afterwards? Did he again ascend to the heaven from which he descended? If so, the earth must have stood still, waiting for his ascent, excepting he waited till the next morn, when the earth would have been in the same position under his heaven as when he descended; otherwise the earth would have carried him round to the opposite side of his heaven; for it must not be supposed that this heaven revolves round with the earth; for Job seems to signify that heaven is a fixture, by its having pillars![28] And if the earth had waited for him but one single minute, it would have been shattered to pieces by the shock, and the whole system of the universe deranged. Besides this descending, rolling the stone, and sitting upon it, prove that an angel must be a material being; for nothing that is immaterial can be said to ascend or descend: because immateriality implies being without form or substance; and if there be no form nor substance, what is there to ascend or descend? or what force or power can a thing of no substance have to remove a great stone; or diversity of shape to exhibit a sitting posture; much less to be clothed upon with raiment, either white or black? But for what purpose did the angel undertake such a journey ? Did Jesus require his immediate assistance before he could get out ? Could not he, unto whom all power was given, remove this stone, however great it might have been, without troubling his angels ? for certainly it could have been no pleasant job for this angel to leave his comfortable seat in heaven, to come and sit upon this nasty cold stone ; or was his terrific presence deemed necessary to frighten away the watch that Jesus might be enabled to rise without any molestation ? Surely not, for we are told that Jesus when living could by a look strike down to the ground, backward, a whole band of armed soldiers :[29] how much more would his looks have terrified them had they seen him rising from the dead ! Neither can I perceive the policy in frightening away the watch ; who if they had but seen him rise would have been far better witnesses of his resurrection than those of his own party, who were already regarded as impostors and deceivers of the people. And had not those men immortal souls that required saving ? Then why did he not rise quietly while they were there, and convince them that he was indeed risen, without making such a fuss to frighten them away ? But it appears no one saw him rise ; for the angel frightened the watch away *before*, and the women did not come until *after* he was risen !

Again, Matthew says that for fear of him (the angel) the keepers did shake, and became as dead men ; yet it appears they had life enough to run into the city and acquaint the chief priests of all these unaccountable things. And what was the consequence of all this ado with the angel and the earthquake ? Was the whole city converted thereby ? No, not even the watch ; for we are told that these men, who had just before been quaking with fear and had become as dead men through fright and terror, at the sight of a superhuman being, and the danger to which they were exposed by the earthquake, became now the most barefaced liars and perjured villains in existence, for the sake of a paltry bribe, by saying that the disciples came by night and stole away the body while they slept !

This story is not only unreasonable and improbable,

but is actually impossible. In the first place these men were Roman soldiers. To have slept upon duty, according to the Roman discipline, would have been punished with death. It cannot, therefore, be supposed, that they would sign their own death-warrant, by saying that they had slept on their watch. Neither can we imagine that a company of men could, all of them, so easily and so soon resume so much hardihood, as to brave the danger to which they must naturally expect that they would expose themselves; which was the judgment and vengeance of that power they were belying, and of which they had so lately felt the effects. These occurrences must have left such an impression upon their minds, that no earthly bribe whatever could so soon have obliterated. I ask you, whether you think it possible for the greatest sceptic in existence, if he had such ocular demonstration as this watch is reported to have had, could have the effrontery and temerity to fly in the face, as it were, of this awful power, after having so recently felt its effects? How much less, then, shall we suppose that the chief priests and Elders of the people, whose dogmas taught them to believe that God did sometimes visit his creatures in this manner, as in the case of Abraham, Moses, Elijah, &c., should concur with the watch in thus withstanding the power of God; for they must reasonably suppose that no other power could raise the dead. Moreover they must naturally expect that after such an extraordinary and awful visitation, some great and notable thing was about to transpire; they would be expecting every minute a visible display of his power and presence. Could they possibly imagine that Jesus would rise in that manner, only to disappear again like "a bottle of smoke?" Surely they had every reason in the world to expect that he would make his appearance, if not to punish, at least to upbraid them for their unbelief? We have no right nor authority to suppose that they in particular, any more than ourselves, were so hardened as to deny the evidence of facts, so awful and evident, if they believed the story told by the watch. They promised Jesus very fairly while he was upon the cross, that if he would but come down they would believe in him;[30] which Jesus might as well have done at once, if he could, as to take such a round-about way of convincing them as he did, which after all proved fruitless! For who believed him besides his own immediate followers? Besides where was Jairus, and Nicodemus, and Joseph, and Gamaliel, all rulers and honourable counsellers? Did they also agree in bribing the watch to tell such a lie? or did they receive a bribe themselves to wink at the proceedings? No, surely, they were honourable men. Instead therefore of the chief priests and elders taking counsel together to bribe the watch, we may be well assured that at least they would have remained silent, and waited the issue of this awful event, lest haply they should be found fighting against God.[31]

Should you say that miracles produce no effect upon the mind of an unbeliever, or as Jesus said, though one rise from the dead, yet they will not believe;[32] then for what purpose were those miracles wrought? Or what utility could there be in Jesus rising from the dead, if he knew none would believe it? Those who did believe in him needed no such miracles. Indeed he seems to signify that those are more blessed who believe without seeing anything.[33] Whence it appears that these miracles were wrought in vain; consequently discover a want of knowledge and foresight in their author or operator.

In my next I intend to examine the evidence of those who are said to have been eye witnesses of the appearance of Jesus after he was risen, and judge, from their several reports, whether they are deserving of credit. Till then, I remain,

Your humble Servant,

JOHN CLARKE.

NOTES TO THE FOREGOING LETTER.

1 John iii. 20, 21.	"
2 I Peter i. 7.	20
3 2 Thessalonians ii. 15.	21 "
4 Jude 3.	"
5 1 Peter iii. 15.	"
6 John xix. 38. 41.	"
7 Mark xv. 46.	
Matthew xxvii. 60.	
8 " " 62, 63.	22
9 " xii. 39, 40.	23
10 Luke xxiv. 11.	24
11 John xvii. 14.	25 Mark xvi. 3.
12 Jonah iv. 1. 11.	
13 Hebrew vii. 25.	
1 Timothy ii. 4.	
14 John ii. 19. 21.	
15 Mark xiv. 58.	
16 Matthew xvi. 4.	
17 Mark viii. 12.	
18 Acts ii. 22.	
19 Luke xviii. 34.	

LETTER XVI.

TO DR. ADAM CLARKE.

Sir,

We next come to criticise the accounts given us of the appearance and ascension of Jesus Christ, after his resurrection; but before we enter fully upon the consideration of that question, let us re-examine the manner of his death, in order to ascertain, if possible, whether he was most assuredly dead, irrecoverably dead, when taken down from the cross; or whether it were not possible for him to deceive with a pretended death, in order to frame a pretended resurrection?

We are informed by John, that Jesus was on his trial before the judgment seat of Pilate, on Friday, about the sixth hour, or twelve o'clock according to our computation of the day: whence he had to carry his cross to the place of execution, which was up a mount to the westward of the town, as described in the map of the holy land. This journey, together with the ceremony of fixing the apparatus and nailing him to the cross, must have occupied one hour at least; so that before he could have been raised it must have been one o'clock. Then the Jews, being so remarkably precise in observing their sabbath, which commenced at six o'clock, would not defer the taking of him down, breaking of legs, and clearing all away to the last minute. This we may reasonably conclude occupied them another hour; after which it appears there was time enough for Joseph to go to Pilate, and wait until the centurion came to corroborate his report of the death of Jesus: and if he had not to go and purchase, he had to lug an hundred weight of spices to the mount : which, with the spicing of his body and the laying it in the tomb, must have occupied another hour, all which being done before the sabbath commenced, at six o'clock, leaves but three hours for the time which Jesus was suspended on the cross.

Crucifixion is a lingering and starving death; invented purposely for the lengthening the time of the unfortunate culprit's sufferings; there being a bracket or block fixed to the cross for him to stand upon, which bears up the body and to which the two feet are nailed; the arms only being extended to the extremities of the cross-board, to which the hands are nailed through the palm. This, then, being the amount of suffering that Jesus endured, it is not reasonable to suppose that such would cause his death in the short space of three hours; especially when we read of persons remaining alive under such circumstances for several days. We have ourselves known many instances of men suffering much more than Jesus did, and for a greater length of time, and yet afterwards survive. Besides the thieves who were crucified with him, were not dead in this short time; for that reason their legs were broken although they had undergone the same suffering as Jesus. These things being considered, we have no just reason to believe that Jesus, a strong healthy young man, was actually dead when taken down from the cross; especially as we find that he was able to converse with those that were standing by him, and to cry out at the ninth hour, or three o'clock, with such a loud voice. Neither can we imagine that this short time would starve a hearty young man to death; although he might not have had any food since the preceeding evening; for we are told, that at other times he could fast for forty days together! It is then more probable that he had only fainted away, or pretended death, by hanging down his head and remaining silent, after ·he had spoken with a loud voice; he well knowing into whose hands he would be placed; and this might have been all agreed upon before he surrendered himself; by which deception he preserved his legs from being broken. As to the story of a soldier piercing him in the side it is self-evidently false. The Roman soldiers being under such strict discipline, dare not attempt such a wanton thing without the command of the centurion; and he, we may be assured, would not give such an order, he being the friend of Jesus. Neither dare he give that order if so inclined; for if Jesus had been pronounced not dead, like the two thieves, he must have acted agreeably to their law, which was to break his legs: and no other means dare he or his soldiers use than those prescribed by the law, any more than the sheriff of London dare give orders to cut a man's throat while he is hanging.

We find also that as soon as Jesus was taken down, he was immediately placed in the hands of his friends: among whom was Joseph, who, with Nicodemus, wrapped the body in linen, so that no signs of life might be discerned. We do not read of any one feeling his pulse or endeavouring by any other means to ascertain whether he was really dead; though we are told that the report of his death, in that short time, was even a matter of astonishment to Pilate.[1] There were none but chosen friends around him; who seemingly took care that strangers should not come too near his body; and he was immediately deposited in a tomb belonging to his friend Joseph, who rolled a stone to its mouth, (mind! a *rolling* stone which could easily be moved or rolled away.) When, therefore, the mob was dispersed, and all things quiet in the evening, after dark might he not be safely conveyed away? and, with proper care and attention, he might soon recover; even admitting that his side had been pierced by the spear of the soldier. Many a man, you know, has been run through the body and afterwards recovered.

What certainty, then, can we have of his death when such a probable scheme as this might have been laid and so easily performed? I do not say that such was the case; but where there is a bare possibility of its being so, it cannot be accounted incredible.

I come now to speak of his appearances after his supposed or pretended death, as they are related by the inspired historians: and to save you the trouble of turning over the leaves of your Testament, I will quote their precise words as reported by them severally; shewing. by a blank space, what one or other have omitted; and calling your attention to their discrepances.

Matthew xxviii.	Mark xvi.	Luke xxiv.	John xx.
Verse 1. In the end of the Sabbath, as it began to dawn, toward the first day of the week, came Mary Magdalene, and the other Mary to see the sepulchre.	Verse 1. And when the Sabbath was past, Mary Magdalene, and Mary the mother of James and Salone, had brought sweet spices, that they might come and anoint him. 2. And very early in the morning, the first day of the week, they came unto the sepulchre, at the rising of the sun.		Verse 1. The first day of the week, cometh Mary Magdalene, early, when it was yet dark, unto the sepulchre,
2. And, behold, there was a great earthquake; for the angel of the Lord descended from heaven, and came and rolled back the stone from the door, and sat upon it. 4. His countenance was like lightning, and his raiment white as snow. 4. And for fear of him, the keepers did shake, and became as dead men.			
	3. And they said among themselves who shall roll us away the stone from the door of the sepulchre. 4. And when they looked they saw that the stone was rolled away; for it was very great. 5. And entering into the sepulchre	2. And they found the stone rolled away from the sepulchre. 3. And they entered in, and found not the body of the Lord Jesus. 4. And it came to pass, as they were much perplexed thereabout	and seeth the stone taken away from the sepulchre.
	they saw a young man sitting on the right side, clothed in a long white garment, and they were affrighted.	behold, two men stood by them in shining garments. 5. And as they were afraid, and bowed down their	
5. And the angel	6. And he saith	faces to the earth,	

Matthew xxviii.	Mark xvi.	Luke xxiv.	John xx.
answered and said unto them, fear not ye; for I know that ye seek Jesus which was crucified.	unto them, be not affrighted. Ye seek Jesus of Nazareth, which was crucified;	they said unto them, why seek ye the living among the dead?	
6. He is not here; for he is risen, as he said come, see the place where the Lord lay.	he is risen; he is not here; behold the place where they laid him.	6. He is not here, but is risen;	
7. And go quickly, and tell his disciples that he is risen from the dead; and behold, he goeth before you into Galilee; there shall ye see him; lo, I have told you.	7. But go your way, tell his disciples, and Peter, that he goeth before you into Galilee; there shall ye see him, as he said unto you.		
8. And they departed quickly from the sepulchre with fear and great joy, and did run to bring his disciples word.	8. And they went out quickly, and fled from the sepulchre; for they trembled and were amazed; neither said they any thing to any man; for they were afraid.	9. And returned from the sepulchre,	
9. And as they went to tell his disciples, behold, Jesus met them saying, All hail, and they came and held him by the feet, and worshipped him.	9. Now when Jesus was risen, early the first day of the week, he appeared first to Mary Magdalene, out of whom he had cast seven devils.		
10. Then said Jesus unto them, be not afraid; go tell my brethren that they go into Galilee, and there shall they see me.			

Matthew xxviii.	Mark xvi.	Luke xxiv.	John xx.
11. Now when they were going, some of the watch came into the city, and shewed unto the chief priests, all the things that were done.	10. And she went and told them that had been with him, as they mourned and wept.	and told all these things unto the eleven, and to all the rest.	2. Then she runneth, and cometh to Simon Peter, and to the other disciple, whom Jesus loved, and saith unto them, they have taken away the Lord out of the sepulchre, and we know not where they have laid him.
	11. And they, when they had heard that he was alive, and had been seen of her, believed not.	10. It was Mary Magdalene, and Joanna and Mary the mother of James, and other women that were with them, which told these things unto the Apostles. 11. And their words seemed to them as idle tales; and they believed them not.	
		12. Then arose Peter and ran unto the sepulchre,	
		and stooping down he beheld the linen clothes laid by themselves,	

Matthew xxviii.	Mark xvi.	Luke xxiv.	John xx.
		and departed wondering in himself at that which had come to pass.	10. Then the disciples went away again unto their own home. 11. But Mary stood without, at the sepulchre, weeping; and, as she wept, she stooped down and looked into the sepulchre. 12. And seeth two angels in white, sitting, the one at the head, and the other at the feet, where the body of Jesus had lain. 13. And they say unto her, woman, why weepest thou? She saith unto them, because they have
			why weepest thou? whom seek-

Matthew xxviii.	Mark xvi.	Luke xxiv.	John xx.
		*	not yet ascended to my father; but go unto my brethren, and say unto them, I ascend unto my father, and your father, and to my God and to your God. 18. Mary Magdalene came and told the disciples, that she had seen the Lord, and that he had spoken these things unto her.

These four different statements, we are told, were written by divine inspiration! Let us examine the discordance which subsists in these four several accounts concerning that which if we do not believe we shall all certainly be damned !

Matthew states that Mary Magdalene and the other Mary went only to see the sepulchre. (1) · Mark says, that they carried spices with them for the purpose of anointing him. (1) Luke speaks of several women going there. (10) And John mentions only Mary Magdalene. (1)

Matthew says, that they went at the end of the sabbath, as it began to dawn. (1) Mark says, the sabbath was past, at the rising of the sun. (1—2) But John says that Mary went there while it was yet dark. (1)

Matthew mentions only one angel. (2) Mark speaks of a young man. (5) Luke says there were two men ; (4) who were afterwards called angels by the women. (23) While John reports two angels. (12)

Matthew says that the angel was outside, sitting on the stone which he had rolled from the door. (2) Mark says the young man was inside of the sepulchre. (5) Luke tells us that the two men stood by them. (4) But John declares that the two angels were sitting. (12)

Mark and Luke say that the women entered into the sepulchre. Was not this impossible ? for if the angel was sitting on the stone at the door, as described by

Matthew, his looks would frighten them, and his information prevent them from entering. John says that Peter first entered therein. (6)

Luke says that the two men reminded the women of that which Jesus foretold prior to his death. (6—8) Not one of the others say a word concerning this prediction.

According to Matthew the two women met Jesus as they were returning from the sepulchre. Mark says that he was seen first by Mary Magdalene, but does not say how nor where! John says that Mary Magdalene saw neither Jesus nor angels, till her second visit to the sepulchre: and then we cannot be certain whether it was Jesus or the gardener that she saw, seeing that she herself did not rightly know, because he would not let her touch him! It you are still disposed to credit the words of this woman out of whom Jesus had already cast seven devils, say why did not Jesus shew himself to Peter and give his orders to him personally, instead of sending a message to him by the women, as Mark says, (7) especially as that other disciple whom Jesus loved was with him? But we read that although both of them ran as fast as they could to the supulchre, and examined everything very minutely, neither the angels nor yet Jesus would show themselves to either, but to this Mary Magdalene! But Luke will not admit that he was seen at all by her; for he says positively that the women saw him not, (24) but that his first appearance was made to Cleopas and another, on the road from Jerusalem to Emmaus. Paul, when speaking of his appearances, says that he was first seen of Cephas; then of the twelve:[2] making no mention whatever of Mary Magdalene or any other woman!

Matthew says, that when the two women saw him they held him by the feet. (9) John says that Jesus would not be touched. (17)

Matthew says, that not only the angel told the women where Jesus was going, but Jesus himself came and told them likewise. (7—10) Mark speaks of a young man telling them to go and tell his disciples and Peter, but says nothing of Jesus telling them so himself.

John, speaking of Mary Magdalene, says that the angels only asked her why she wept; (13) leaving Jesus to tell her himself where he was going. While Luke takes no notice of any message, sent by either Jesus or angels!

According to Luke, it appears that Peter went by himself to the sepulchre, after the angels were gone, into which he only stooped down, and saw the clothes lying. (12) But John says that another disciple ran with him, and they both went into the sepulchre (6—8) before the angel came. Some may suppose, that the angel who came first to roll away the stone had left his post, and gone to refresh himself in the neighbourhood; but I should rather imagine that he was only strolling about in the garden, gathering a nosegay or some earthly curiosity for his family in heaven! However it is evident, that if this angel were the same young man of whom Mark speaks, he could not have seen Peter, or he would not have sent a message by the women to Peter, in the special manner that Mark describes.

Now, with all this manifest confusion and contradiction in their several reports, which and what are we to believe? Did he appear first to Cephas, or to Mary Magdalene? Or was it to her only, or when with her companions? Was it the first or second time that she went to the sepulchre, when she or they saw him? Did they really hold him by the feet, or was he so ill-natured as not to let them touch him? yet afterwards we read of his telling them to handle him,[3] and inviting Thomas to thrust his hand into his side![4] Did he send word that he was going into Galilee, or to his father? Or did he send any message at all? Was it a young man, or an angel? or two, or only one, that was sitting or standing, inside or outside, of the sepulchre? Did Peter enter into the sepulchre or not? And was it before or after the women entered? Did he go by himself wondering? or did another run with him? Was it at the end of the sabbath, or was the sabbath past? Was it at the rising of the sun, or while it was yet dark, that she or they first went? Did they merely go to see the sepulchre, or was it for the purpose of anointing the body? Admitting that it were even possible to reconcile these contradictions, yet you must acknowledge that in the midst of so much confusion and seeming disagreement, the account is very difficult and hard to be understood by a way-faring man; which should not have been the case, if dictated by an all-wise and benevolent being that wished all men to gain a knowledge of the truth.

I now come to speak of his second appearance, (though, according to Luke, it was his first) when Jesus thrust himself into the company of two men, one of them named Cleopas, as they were travelling from Jerusalem to Emmaus, a distance of 60 furlongs, (between seven and eight miles) on the same day that he is supposed to have risen.[5] Here, we are told, that they chatted together along the road till they arrived at the village; when Jesus made as though he would have gone further:[6] but being constrained by the two men he went in with them, because the day was far spent: when, having refreshed himself with meat, he took some bread and brake it; and by the peculiar manner, I suppose, that he had in breaking of bread, the two disciples discovered him to be Jesus who had been crucified: upon which, Jesus, finding himself discovered, immediately vanished out of their sight like any other ghost!

Is not this a strange story altogether? Whoever this Cleopas and the other were, it is evident that Jesus before he was crucified was well known to them, or how could they so soon have recognized him when he vanished out of their sight? Indeed we have reason to suppose that Cleopas was uncle to Jesus; for John says, that Mary, his mother's sister, was the wife of Cleopas.[7] Then how was it possible for these two disciples, for so they are called, to forget their old acquaintance after an abscence of only three days? Luke says their eyes were holden, so that they should not know him.[8] But Mark informs us, that he appeared to them in another form.[9] If he appeared to them in another form, why should he spoil their eyesight? or if their eyes were holden, what need had he to change his form? But what form can you suppose that he assumed besides that of the human species? Surely he was not so bad as the devil, whom you suppose took the form of an *Orang Outang!* yet there is some similarity between the two cases; for the one deceived the woman, and the other deceived those two men. What motive he could have for thus disguising himself I cannot imagine, if he wished them to bear witness of his resurrection.

Luke further tells us that the two men, after Jesus had vanished out of their sight, rose up the same hour, and returned to Jerusalem, where they found the eleven gathered together, to whom they told all these things, " saying the Lord is risen indeed, and hath appeared unto Simon." Did he not appear likewise to Cleopas? And who could this Simon be? It could not be Simon Peter, because he must have been one of the eleven to whom they were speaking. One of the eleven would not believe the story, although he had heard it in the morning from Mary Magdalene and the other women!

John, when speaking of this meeting at Jerusalem, says that Thomas was not present;[10] therefore there could have been no more than ten: for Judas had hung himself, or burst his bowels, and Matthias was not chosen until after his ascension![11] However while these two were telling these ten or eleven, (for there is no knowing which to believe) in pops Jesus among them; and being fatigued with his journey back again, sat down and ate some broiled fish and honey comb:[12] though if I understand Matthew and Luke aright, they say that Jesus had promised neither to eat nor drink any more, till he arrived in his father's kingdom.[13] While they were thus feasting, Jesus took the opportunity to remind them of that which he had formerly told them; at the same time saying that all those things were written in the law of Moses, and in the prophets, and in the Psalms, concerning his suffering and his rising from the dead the third day.[14] But although the books to which he referred are still extant, no such prophecies are to be found therein; either of his, or of any one else, rising from the dead. Such an idea never could have entered the minds of Moses, David, nor of any of the prophets, or we should have had them dwelling largely upon it ; but they give not the most distant hint thereof !

In the heading of the xvi Psalm, we find it written thus :—" David is shewing the hope of his calling, of the resurrection, and life everlasting." But David never wrote these words. The headings of all the Psalms, and of all the Chapters, with the divisions thereof into verses, were the work, you know, of latter ages, and done according to the fancy and will of the transcriber : even you yourself have headed the Psalms and Chapters in the Bible that bears your name, according to the interpretation which you were pleased to put on them. Let us examine, then, the subject matter contained in this Psalm, and judge for ourselves whether David was therein speaking of Jesus rising the third day, or even of his own resurrection.

We find that David, like all fanatics of every denomination, is extolling the goodness of his own God, (2) and promising to delight himself with those of his own persuasion ; (3) at the same time condemning all those who hasten after other Gods. (4) Then he begins to speak, in figurative language, of the comforts which he supposes he derived from his God ; saying, that the Lord is the portion of his inheritance and of his cup : (5) that the lines had fallen unto him in pleasant places ; yea, he says, I have a goodly heritage, (6) for which he blesseth the Lord. (7) And being confident that he should not be moved, (8) that is, dethroned, nor overpowered by his enemies, (for he was always at war with some one or other,) he cries out, " my heart is glad, and my flesh shall rest in hope, (9) for thou wilt not leave my soul in hell ; neither wilt thou suffer thine holy one to see corruption. (10) Thou wilt shew me the path of life ; in thy presence is fulness of joy ; at thy right hand there are pleasures for evermore." (11)

Now wherein throughout this Psalm, does David speak of, or allude to, Jesus rising again the third day? Indeed I know not how he could speak of, or allude to, a person that was not then in existence! But wherein does he speak of his own resurrection? He is evidently speaking like a man in raptures, at the prospect which he had of securing this goodly heritage, or royal estate, of which he was then in possession; and in the hope of its permanency, he says, " my flesh shall rest in hope;" being confident that God would not leave his soul in hell, that is, in trouble, nor in the power of his enemies: this being a figure of speech which he often adopts, to signify sorrow, uneasiness of mind, or trials; as when just delivered from the hands of Saul, he says that the sorrows of hell had compassed him about;[15] and in another place he says, that when the pains of hell got hold of him he found trouble and sorrow.[16] It is evident that the world hell, as used by him, was a figure of speech to denote his trouble and sorrow. Like unto Jonah when in the belly of the fish, who cried out unto the Lord by reason of his affliction; " out of the belly of hell," he says, " cried I."[17] Likewise Isaiah, when speaking of the troubles and afflictions of the people, says that "hell hath enlarged herself, and opened her mouth without measure."[18] This word, which is rendered hell by the translators, from the Hebrew word *Cheol*, or Greek *Ades* or *Hades*, is applied to several things in the Hebrew and Greek Bibles; and in no one instance does it allude to any future place of punishment beyond the grave or death, as is foolishly believed by ignorant men, and wickedly taught by artful and interested priests.

As to the hell, hell-fire, everlasting fire, and everlasting punishment,[19] of which Jesus spoke, it is now generally admitted by all Christian divines who have any knowledge of the Greek language, that by these words we are to understand that Jesus was alluding to the fire of the valley of the son of Hinnom, or Tophet, as it is called by Isaiah and Jeremiah;[20] situated on the east side of Jerusalem, as described by Joshua and Jeremiah.[21] In this valley we are told, the idolatrous Israelites caused their sons and daughters to pass through a fire, in honour of their idol, Molech, which appears to have been set up therein; and which King

Josiah afterwards, removed.[22]   This valley, then, in consequence of the abhorrence which the Jews afterwards had to these practices of their idolatrous ancestors, was made a receptacle for all the filth and stinking carcases which were carried out of Jerusalem; and there was a continual fire kept up, to consume those impurities and prevent infection.   This fire might, very truly, be called the everlasting or age-lasting fire, as it burned night and day, and never went out through want of fuel.   Indeed it is probable that in this place the Israelites buried and burned the carcases of their enemies, whose numbers must have been prodigious; their battles being unlike our petty "Waterloo" squabbles!—for if they slew 500,000 men at once, of their own brethren,[23] how vast must be the numbers of their enemies whom they slew, when those numbers took them sometimes six months in destroying;[24] and at others, seven months in burying;[25] and whose carcases, Isaiah says, was "looked upon by all that went forth from Jerusalem, as "an abhorring unto all flesh" by reason of their worm, (which naturally breeds in putrified bodies,) never dying, and their fire never being quenched.[26]   To this place also the Jews were accustomed to throw the dead bodies of those malefactors who for their heinous offences were declared unworthy of the rites of burial.   And in some cases, men who had committed certain capital offences were burned alive in this valley.   It is therefore evident that Jesus, when he spoke of the Gehenna of fire, and the judgment of the Gehenna, (which our translators have rendered hell fire, but which in the original Greek signified the valley of Hinnom, from the Hebrew words, *gei ben Hinnom,*) alluded to those judgments and practices of the Jews and their Sanhedrin.

For some persons to suppose that David was alluding to that imaginary place of punishment which Christians call hell, is not only ridiculous, but impious.   Jesus having represented this hell as being at so great a distance from heaven, says, that it is impossible for a man when once in hell ever to get into heaven, because there is such a great gulph between the two places that none can pass from the one to the other.[27]

I did intend to make some inquiry respecting the local situation of this hell; but as I cannot find any account thereof in the Scriptures, it is not worth the trouble to regard the many different opinions and conjectures of ignorant and fallible men. Jesus only spoke of it in a parable, as a place of fiction, and not as a fact upon which any doctrine should be formed ; or he would not have treated the subject in the manner he did. For we may be assured, that if there was such a place to be dreaded, he would have made it the "theme and burden of his song :" instead of which, he never speaks of it, but in a parable or fable ! John, following the mystical and allegorical sayings of his master, says that this hell shall be destroyed, by being cast into a lake of fire, as soon as the dead have been delivered out of it.[28] And should it be in the bowels or centre of the earth, as some men imagine, Peter says that the earth and all contained therein shall be burned up.[29] So that this place of everlasting punishment, if in the position named, will then have an end, like all other earthly things !

Let us now return to David who, having confidence in God that he would not leave his soul in hell, or in trouble, says, "neither wilt thou suffer thine holy one to see corruption;" claiming, through his own holiness, he being the Lord's anointed,[30] a long life to enjoy this goodly heritage, for which he prays in some such figurative language in nearly fifty of the Psalms; especially in Ps. lxi. 5. Some suppose that David, by his saying "thine holy one," alluded to Jesus. Why should they imagine that, when David knew nothing of Jesus, he being not in existence till 1000 years after David was dead and buried ? David was, seemingly, always in trouble, either from his friends or his enemies, and had enough to do to think of himself. Does he not style himself, "the Holy one of Israel ?"[31] And in another place he says, "preserve my soul, for I am holy."[32] Indeed his language throughout the Psalms is principally figurative : for how is it possible that we can imagine that he is speaking literally, when he says "thou hast brought up my soul from the grave ?"[33] We must not suppose that his soul had literally been in the grave; for he says, in other places, that those that lie in the grave are remembered no more by God,[34] neither can they return him thanks, and praise him therein;[35] because "all their thoughts perish in that very day that they return to the earth."[36]

Is this, then, the Psalm to which Jesus alluded when he spoke to his disciples? What is there con- tained therein, that can in any wise apply to Jesus rising again the third day? Besides Jesus never said that he had been to such a place as hell; neither do his historians make mention of such a circumstance. There- fore finding that these historians have been guilty of advancing that for which they had no authority, such as referring to the law of Moses, the prophets, and the Psalms, for a prediction concerning Jesus rising again the third day, how can we rely or place any confidence in their other assertions, we having no other testimony thereof but their own words? And when we find them relating such unaccountable and unnatural things, and differing so much in their several reports, how is it possible for men, possessing common sense to give them any credit? The disciples themselves, it is said, could not believe that Mary had seen Jesus:[37] and as to the story of the angels it seemed to them like an idle tale! and even when those two men, Cleopas and Simon, came and told them that they had not only seen, but had walked and talked and supped with Jesus, still they would not believe.[38] Moreover so little faith had they among themselves, that Thomas would believe none of them until he had seen Jesus himself.[39] If he, then, who is supposed to have seen such a thing as rising from the dead before, in the cases of the widow's son and Lazurus, could not believe without occular demon- stration, how can we, who have never seen Jesus nor any of his miracles, believe the improbable tales written by persons entirely unknown to us nearly 2000 years back, and belonging to a nation now extinct, and whose descendants we treat with ignominy and contempt?

Again. John describes this feast to have been held on the first day of the week, the day of his ressurection:[40]

this Luke also admits, by saying that the two disciples went to Emmaus on the same day which he rose, and returned back to Jerusalem in the evening, the same hour that Jesus left them where they found the eleven gathered together, among whom Jesus made his appearance and ate his supper. But Luke makes it appear, that after supper, the same evening, Jesus led them out as far as Bethany, where he parted from them and was carried up into heaven.[41] And John informs us, that eight days after this supper Jesus came among them to convince Thomas of his infidelity.[42] John moreover speaks of another meeting which took place while Peter was fishing; at this meeting it seems Jesus stood cook: for John says that as soon as they came to land, they found a fire of coals there, and fish laid thereon, and bread, all ready for dinner![43] After this we hear no more of him from John, not even as to whether he went into heaven, or to lodge again at Bethany with his old friend and resurrection brother, Lazarus! Matthew, instead of all these appearances at Jerusalem, at Bethany and the sea side, only says that Jesus met the eleven in Galilee, according to his appointment with the women: and instead of recording that he was taken from them into heaven, avers that he promised never to leave them, but abide with them always, even unto the end of the world.[44]

Which of these accounts are we to believe? Did Jesus go to heaven from Bethany, which was only fifteen furlongs (about two miles) from Jerusalem,[45] or did he go to Galilee, the nearest part of which to Jerusalem was upwards of sixty miles, and there hide himself for fear that the Jews if they caught him would crucify him again? And if he did go to heaven, which place was it from, and when? For according to Luke it was the same day on which he rose; while the writer of the Acts says that it was not till forty days after, when he was taken up out of their sight from off the mount called *Olivet*, which was a sabbath-day's journey, or rather more than half a mile distant from Jerusalem.

Respecting the Ascension, not one of his disciples

say a word about it. It is only reported by Mark and Luke, who were not of his disciples : neither does it appear that they ever saw him, dead or alive. Matthew, John, Peter, James and Jude, who all wrote of him, and must have been eye-witnesses of his ascension if it ever did occur, take not the least notice of such a most extraordinary and important event. Indeed if we had no other account but those of his reputed disciples, we should never have known of his going to heaven! for in all his sayings and doings during life he never so much as once alluded to it.

Jesus, we are told, often upbraided the Jews for their unbelief; but throughout the whole of his life we do not find that the Jews had any reason for believing him to be more than a dextrous juggler, or an artful deceiver; or why did he not give them a sign which they were continually demanding and requesting? If he had particular reasons for not granting them one while living, surely he might have given them one while he was strolling about for forty days, like a ghost! Should you suppose that he was afraid of being apprehended and crucified again, yet when he was on the point of ascending into heaven, what could he fear? Why, then, did he not publicly ascend in the sight of all Jerusalem? He would then have prevented every doubt, and thereby saved the lost sheep of Israel much easier and sooner than his disciples could, by preaching to them such an incredible story upon their own credit only. For myself, I cannot think how it was possible for him to ascend from the earth, without being observed by some of the inhabitants of the place, as well as "the eleven," unless he went up at night in the dark; and then he might, probably, have deceived his own disciples!

In conclusion, I ask every reasonable man, what credit can be given to such an unnatural and incredible tale, told by Jesus's frends, and unsupported by any other historian of that age; abounding, too, with so many errors, imperfections, and contradictions? For what purpose did he rise again? Was it merely to catch fish, eat and drink, and play at hide and seek, with a few particular friends? We do not find that he was seen by any other person. Paul has stated that he was seen by five hundred brethren at once;[46] but this assertion is not corroborated by any other historian, not even by his own disciples, who certainly knew more of him than Paul did! We know nothing of Paul, but what he is pleased to say of himself. He should have told us when and where he was thus seen by the five hundred brethren; for we cannot discover that there were ever more than one hundred and twenty assembled together at one time; and this was not till after his supposed ascension;[47] yet they say nothing about it. It is, moreover, quite absurd to suppose that Jesus was forty days backwards and forwards with his disciples after his resurrection, and that they would know nothing of it. Surely, you will not pretend to say that they did not think it worth their notice! Then what authority had Paul for such an assertion, if not noticed by the other historians?

Having now carefully and strictly inquired into the probity of the life, character, and miracles said to have been done by Jesus, called the Christ, admitting the existence of such a person as recorded in the books said to have been written by *divine inspiration*, I find, that in consequence of the many improbable, incredible, and useless stories contained therein, besides the numerous errors and contradictions in their detail, it is absolutely impossible for any reasonable man to conclude, after such an examination, that such events ever occurred; or that the accounts thereof were ever written or dictated by any honest and sensible being, much less by one possessing superior wisdom and benevolence! For if the writers thereof had had the aid and assistance of a Ghost to bring all things to their remembrance, and the gift of tongues whereby they might have expressed them, surely these powers would at the same time have enlightened their understandings so as to enable them to express themselves in a plain and intelligible manner; and likewise have directed their pens consistently with each other. Besides, the necessity that exists to employ such a prodigious number of men at enormous salaries, to explain and defend those books, is another proof of their imperfection and want of veracity. If the men so employed in their defence and support, were no better fed and clad than these who they say were inspired to write these books, the books would long since have been treated like the fables of the heathen mythology. Indeed the necessity for their writing so many thousands of volumes in the defence and support of the Jewish and Christian oracles, ought to be a convincing proof to men of sense and judgment that they are destitute of truth : for truth is clear and plain, uniform and harmonious, and needs no advocate to defend its cause : and although custom may alter the face and fashion of things, and length of time in some cases may lay truth and falsehood on a level, because things which cannot be easily inquired into soon pass for truth with the careless and indolent, yet truth, thus debased, like the ever luminous orb which illumines our earth, though obscured sometimes from our vision by a passing cloud, must ultimately shine forth in all its native purity and splendour.

We are told, that the four gospels were written by Matthew, Mark, Luke, and John. But what authority is there for this assertion? Suppositions can never be admitted as demonstration without some portion of proof. In the books themselves, we cannot find the least intimation respecting their authors, nor when nor where they were first written? The most ancient records that we can find give no account thereof. All is doubt and conjecture! If we trace history back one thousand years, we discover that there were then con-continual wranglings, even among the bishops and priests themselves, concerning the authors and their time. It is therefore no wonder that there should be so many different conjectures concerning their genuineness in the present day.

In the first ages of Christianity, we find that many of the books, which now constitute the New Testament were considered spurious, even by those who were not accounted heretics. The Manicheans, once no inconsiderable sect of Christians, rejected as spurious all the miraculous events related in the New Testament : they having other Scriptures to show, which asserted that Christ was a mere man : and his pedigree is drawn at large by Epiphanius, in his *Advers. Manicheos*, page 617, &c. *(Edit. Patav.)* The Epistles of James and Jude ; the second and third of John ; and the second of Peter; together with the Revelations, were all considered doubtful by Eusebius, and rejected by many in his day ;* the latter book, the Revelations, he says was written by one Cerinthus, an arch heretic.† The Epistle also of Paul to the Hebrews was rejected by some,‡ although they were publicly read in most churches.|| Some there were, called the Ebionites, that rejected all the Epistles of Paul, considering him as an imposter and an apostate from the law.§ Indeed Eusebius says that they made but small account of the Gospels, excepting the Gospel according to the Hebrews, with which it appears many were delighted. Yet this Gospel according to the Hebrews has long since been deemed spurious, and too absurd to transmit to this generation ! Others there were who not only rejected the Epistles of Paul, but likewise the Acts of the Apostles; and who, also, as Eusebius says, "put together a confused heap of collections, extracted out of the four Gospels," which they entitled "a Gospel made up of the four Gospels;" being what was commonly called in his day, the Gospel of Tatianus.¶

Besides we find that in the first ages of Christianity they had a number of sacred books, such as the Gospels of Andrew, of Barnabas, of Peter, of Thomas, of Matthias, of Nicodemus, of Bartholomew, of Jude, of Mary, of Eve, of Philip, of Marcion, of Lucianus, of Cerinthus, of Hesychius, of Judas Iscariot, of Merinthus, of the twelve Apostles, of Apelles, of Basilides, of Titianus, of Scythianus, of Thaddaeus, of Valentinus, of Truth, of Perfection ; of the Ebionites, of the Encratites, of the Nazareens; of the Infancy of Christ, of the Egyptians, of the Hebrews, of the Manicheans; and the Gospel of Jesus Christ, with some others, a catalogue of which,

---

* Eusebius, Book iii, Chap. 25.   † Ibid, Book iii, Chap. 28.
‡ Ibid, Book iii, Chap. 3. || Ibid, Book iii, Chap. 23.
§ Ibid, Book iii, Chap. 25 and 27.   ¶ Eusebius, Book iv, Chap. 29.

may be seen in *Toland's Amyntor*. There were also numerous Epistles ascribed to Barnabas, to Jesus Christ, to Themison, to Clemens, to Polycarpe, to Ignatius; as well as the Manichean epistle of Christ with those of Paul to the Laodecians and Seneca. There were also the Revelations of Peter, of Cerinthus, of Paul, of Stephen, of Thomas, of Hermes; with the Acts of Andrew and John, of Thomas, of Philip, of Peter and of Paul; and besides these, there were Acts of the Apostles written by Leucius, by Leuthon, by Lentitus, by Seleucus; also others used by the Ebionites and the Manichees. There were likewise other books considered as sacred, such as the Doctrine of the Apostles, the Protevangelion of James; the Pastor of Hermes, the Preaching of Peter; the Preaching of Paul; the Traditions of Matthias; the Writings of Bartholomew; the Work of James; the Doctrine of Peter; the Judgment of Peter, and others which are referred to, or noticed, by some of the ancient Ecclesiastical writers, as having been received as sacred and acknowledged to contain the words and will of God, as much as those which are now called canonical. Why are not all these books received as sacred now, seeing that our fore-fathers believed in them? You reply because they were found to be spurious. But how was this discovered, unless they examined into them? And if by examination they were found to be forgeries, why may not those which are now received, upon the like examination be proved forgeries likewise? Shall we rest our faith upon the opinions of our fore-fathers who were so easily deceived? How can we know how they were right in some, while they were wrong in so many? We cannot surely be infallibly sure of the truth of any.

Again. The number and order of the books in the Old Testament, were also different from their present state. From the writings of Melito we find that Eusebius has extracted the following account. Melito, after having been requested to give an accurate account of the books of the Old Testament, how many they were, and in what order they were written, says, "I travelled into the East, and came into that country where these things were heretofore preached and done: when I made an accurate inquiry about the books of the Old Testament, a catalogue whereof I have herewith sent you. Their names are these: Genesis, Exodus, Leviticus, Numbers, Deuteronomy, Joshua, Judges, Ruth; the four books of the Kings; the two books of the Chronicles; the Psalms of David; the Proverbs of Solomon, which is called the book of wisdom; Ecclesiastes; the Song of Solomon; Job; the Prophecies of Isaiah, and Jeremiah; one book of the twelve (minor) prophets; Daniel, Ezekiel, and Esdras."[*]

Here we find not only a difference in their order to those received in the present day, such as Job after the Song of Solomon, and Daniel and Ezekiel after the minor prophets, but an omission of the books of Nehemiah and Esther, with the Lamentations of Jeremiah: admitting that Esdras means Ezra; and that two out of the four books of the Kings, are the same as those now called the two books of Samuel.

Against the authenticity and genuineness of the Jewish books we find that there were men who wrote volumes: such as Apion, Grammaticus, Apollinus, Molon and Lysimachus; but whose writings have been artfully destroyed, while some of the answers given to them have been as carefully preserved in the writings of Josephus. We do not usually find men starting up and writing volumes against well known and authenticated facts. It is only incredible, disputable, and unsupported tales, against which men write.

The Gospel ascribed to John, nowhere makes mention of the name of its author. It is only headed, "the Gospel according to John:" which, so far, may be correct; it being as likely to have been written by a man named John, as by one of any other name. But who was this John? Your saying that it was John the disciple of Jesus, who leaned on his breast during supper, will not do: because I believe that you know no more of John nor Jesus than any other man in this age. I must have some more substantial evidence, either from himself or his friends, before I can believe your report;

* Eusebius, Book iv, Chap. 26.

and this demand, you cannot but say, is reasonable.   In
the book of the Revelations the writer acknowledges his
name to be John: but no where, in either the Gospel
or the three Epistles ascribed to John, does the writer
make himself known; except in the second and third
Epistles where he styles himself the Elder.[48]   But
what Elder we know not.   Papias, a bishop of Hierapolis, who, according to Eusebius, flourished at the same
time with Polycarpe and Ignatius, in the reign of
Trajan, about the year 110. A. D, mentions one John
the Elder, besides John the Apostle.*   If it were the
same John that wrote the Revelations, why should he
be ashamed to make himself known in his Epistles and
Gospels ? seeing that in the Revelations he has confessed his name to be John no less than three times in
the first Chapter,[49] and acknowledged his name, as all
honest authors should do, at the conclusion of the
book.[50]   We may believe that John wrote the Revelations, because he affirms it; though it might be only a
fictitious name, if what Eusebius says be true who, as I
have already noticed, said it was written by one
Cerinthus.   But whatever John it was, of him we are
all alike ignorant; for he does no where acknowledge
himself to have been him that was present at the supper
with Jesus ; or even that he was ever personally known
to him, excepting in his dreams or revelations.   So
that we are left in the dark as much respecting the true
author, as we are about the meaning and utility of these
Revelations !

But, if we attend to the concluding article of the
gospel,[51] we shall find, by its own evidence, that it
was written, not by the disciple that leaned on the
bosom of Jesus, but by some of his acquaintance ; for,
after speaking of this disciple, it says : " this is the disciple which testifieth of these things, and wrote these
things; and we know that his testimony is true:"
evidently, implying, that some person or persons wrote
these things upon the testimony of this disciple with
whom they pretended to be acquainted, by their saying
" we know that his testimony is true."   Therefore, the

* Eusebius, Book iii, Chap. 39.

most that can be said in favour of this book, is, that it is a second hand report of things made by some unknown persons; for they do not themselves say that they had seen these things done, but only that they could depend upon the testimony of their relator: and so you and I must in like manner, depend upon their testimony! Was there ever any thing so monstrously absurd! Besides by whomsoever it was written, it has since undergone considerable alterations; for the eighth chapter containing the story of the adulterous woman, is not to be found in the old Syriac copy, nor yet in any of the ancient Greek manuscripts!

I grant that in the beginning of the first Epistle ascribed to John, he says: "that, which we have seen and heard, declare we unto you." But what does he say that he has seen and heard? Why, "the word of life, which, he says, he has seen and handled"![52] What he means by this word of life he does not say. He no where declares that he ever saw Jesus, or any of the wonderful things which are related of him: neither does he ever allude to his miraculous resurrection. If by the word of life he means Jesus, whom he had seen and handled, there were many more persons beside him who both saw and handled Jesus. Then how can we tell from among them all who is the identical person that is writing, seeing that he has not confessed his name?

Concerning the gospel ascribed to Matthew, it is as obscurely written as that by the supposed John. The author no where states his name to be Matthew; it being only headed, like the others, " *according* to Matthew." We find that Eusebius has quoted an extract from the writings of Irenaus, another bishop of Lyons, in France, who he supposed wrote in the reign of Commodus, or about the year 180, wherein he states that "Matthew published his gospel among the Hebrews, written in their own language, while Peter and Paul were preaching the gospel at Rome and founding the church."* But we cannot tell from this report what Matthew he meant. Many a man named Matthew has

* Eusebius, Book v. Chap. 8.

published books which he never wrote. Yet Eusebius takes it for granted that he must mean Matthew the publican, the disciple of Jesus; because Origen, an ordained priest, who employed a number of men and girls to write books for him,* about the year 240, says in one of them, that "it was written by one Matthew, formerly a publican, but afterwards an apostle of Jesus."† How did Origen know this two hundred years after it had occured? Why, at the commencement of his report he says: "I have understood by tradition." So this is all the proof that *he* had! and we are taught that we must believe his tradition, or we shall all be damned! Moreover, those very books which Mr. Origen and his girls wrote, were, within one hundred and fifty years after they were written, or about the latter end of the fourth century, condemned by Epiphanius, a bishop of Constantia, in Cyprus, as being blasphemous!‡

The gospel ascribed to Matthew has likewise since been discovered to have been originally written in Greek. And there are many persons who, tracing their authority back to Epiphanius, refuse to receive this gospel as it is thus written; in consequence of Epiphanius declaring, (in his *Haeres Ebion*,) that the Ebionites and Nazarenes, who were supposed to have been the first Christians, made use of a different gospel, said to be according to Matthew, than that which was afterwards received as genuine, being deficient of the first chapter; and who considered Jesus, according to Eusebius, as being "an ordinary man, and nothing more than man: justified only for his proficiency in virtue; and begotten by Mary accompanying with her husband."§

As a further proof how much this book has been altered and corrupted since it was originally written, by we know not who, nor when, nor where, nor for what purpose, we find at the end of the old Arabic version the following testimony annexed:—"The end

* Eusebius, Book vi, Chap. 23.　　† Ibid, Book vi, Chap. 25.
‡ Socrates Scholasticus, Book vi, Chap. 12.
§ Eusebius, Book iii. Chap. 27.

of the holy gospel of the preaching of St. Matthew, which he preached in Hebrew, in the land of Palestine, by the influence of the holy spirit, eight years after our Lord Christ ascended in his flesh to heaven, and the first year of the emperor Claudius." This could never have been written in the days of Irenaus in the latter end of the second century, or he never would have said that it was written while Peter and Paul were at Rome; as this must have been, according to the account given in the Acts of the Apostles of the perigrination of Paul, nearly thirty years after the ascension. It has been much questioned whether Peter or Paul ever were at Rome; for if such a novel and extraordinary circumstance as the preaching of this gospel and founding of churches, ever took place in Rome, it surely would have been noticed by some historian of the age: but not one of them has even so much as made any allusion to either them or their preaching. We have the more right to expect this corroborative testimony, especially if what Eusebius says be the truth, that "during the reign of Nero, Linus, of whom Paul speaks when writing to Timothy,[53] was made the bishop of Rome."* The above testimony of Irenaus, does not prove that this gospel was written by Matthew, but only signifies that he preached it to the Hebrews. Many a man, you know, preaches that which he never wrote.

The gospel according to Mark is also subject to the same objection; the writer thereof not having made himself known. Indeed we are at a loss even to guess who Mark could be, admitting the writer's name was Mark. Jesus had no disciple of that name, as we are informed; neither is there such a name mentioned in any of the four gospels. We first read of one John Mark, in the Acts of the Apostles,[54] a companion of Barnabas; and who it appears was his nephew.[55] Peter likewise makes mention of one Marcus, whom he calls his son.[56] But whether they were one and the same person or not, we do not read of their writing any gospel, or that they were ever personally known to

* Eusebius, Book iii, Chap. 2.

Jesus. Eusebius reports that Papias, the bishop of Hierapolis, says in the preface to one of his books, that "it shall not be tedious to me to set down in order, together with my interpretations, those things which I have well learnt from the Elders, and faithfully remembered, the truth whereof will be confirmed by me. For if at any time I met with any one that had conversed with the Elders, I made a diligent inquiry after their sayings; what Andrew, or what Peter said; or what Philip, or Thomas, or James, or John, or Matthew, or any other of the Lord's disciples were wont to say. And what Aristion and John the Elder (the disciples of our Lord) uttered. For I thought that those things contained in books could not profit me so much as what I heard from the mouths of men yet surviving." And further, he says "this also the Elder said, Mark, being the interpreter of Peter, accurately wrote whatever he remembered; but yet not in that order wherein Christ either spake or did them; for he was neither an hearer, nor yet a follower of the Lord."*

Now, what credit can be given to the writings of a man who only went gossiping about, making inquiries into old men's stories? He no where says that he had either heard or seen the Apostles himself; though Irenaus, seventy years after him, was pleased to say that he was an auditor of John! This Papias, whom Eusebius acknowledges in the same chapter to have been a man of ordinary wit and altogether ignorant and simple, seems to have had but little faith in the books extant in his days, by his saying that the things therein could not profit him much. Yet upon the testimony of such men, under such circumstances, who neither saw nor heard the men called the Apostles, christians build their faith, and advance this testimony as an evidence of its solidity! I cannot find one among all the Ecclesiastical writers, (and Papias was one of the earliest, according to their own account,) who represents himself to have seen or heard any one of the persons that are said to have written the gospels and epistles; but all confess that they were told so by this man, who heard

* Eusebius, Book iii, Chap. 39.

it from that man, and so on! Indeed Eusebius himself is acknowledged by all modern writers to have been a very credulous man: and one whose writings contain a number of contradictions. He not only contradicts himself in many places, but also the writings of the men to whom he refers for corroboration; and oftentimes perverts their meaning to suit his own purpose and strengthen his own argument. In speaking of Mark, he says, (Book ii. chap. xv.) that when Peter heard that his hearers had requested Mark to write a gospel, and that one had been written by Mark agreeable to their request, " he was much delighted with the ardent desire of the men: and confirmed that writing by his authority, that so, thenceforward, it might be read in the churches:" whereas Clemens, the school-master to Origen, who wrote nearly a century before Eusebius, and whose writings he quotes, (Book vi. chap. 14,) says that when Peter understood that Mark was imparting the gospel which he had composed, " he used no per-suasives, either to hinder or incite him to it." And this likewise Clemens confesseth he only learnt by tra-dition.

Again: observe what contrary reports this Eusebius gives of different writers. In Book v. Chap 8, he makes Irenaus to say that Mark wrote his gospel after the death of Peter. But in Book vi. Chap. 25, he makes Origen to say that he wrote it as Peter expounded to him! He moreover states that Mark, after he had written the Gospel, went into Egypt, in the second year of Claudius, according to his Chronic; but the author of the Alexandrian Chronic says that it was in the third year of Caligula! where Eusebius says he preached the Gospel, and settled churches at Alexandria: and that so great " a multitude of men and women embraced the faith of Christ, that even Philo in his writings vouch-safed to relate their conversation, their assemblies, their eating and drinking together, and their whole manner of living."* Who can find the least allusion made by Philo, in all his writings, to such a sect of persons as Christians? Philo speaks of the Ascetae, in Egypt;

* Eusebius, Book ii. Chap. 16.

the men of whom he says were called Therapeutae, and the women Therapeutriæ. But that these were not Christians is evident by the description which Philo gives of them; for, he says, they "were diffused far and wide over the whole world, and spent their intervals of time in meditations on philosophy: they having writings of some ancient persons, who had been famous leaders of their sect." These persons could never be Christians; for Christian writings, so far from being ancient were scarcely in existence in the days of Philo; neither could their leaders have been ancient persons. Philo moreover says concerning those persons, that "when they read the scriptures they philosophized after their own country way, and expounded them allegorically: for they supposed that the words were only notes and marks of some things of a mystical nature which were to be explained figuratively." What authority had Eusebius to assert that Philo was speaking of Christians? He could not even allude to the Essenes, as some suppose he did, because he says "they were diffused far and wide over the world, and had women among them:" whereas the Essenes, Philo himself says, in his "Apology for the Jews," were only in Judea and Palestine; and were moreover haters of women-kind.*

Eusebius says† moreover: "it is reported that this Philo, in the times of Claudius, came to be familiarly acquainted with Peter at Rome." But this report is no proof that such was the case. Rumour is painted as full of tongues, and is always, as Shakspeare says, "stuffing the ears of men with false reports." Indeed it almost appears to me, that this Philo has been made the foundation for the history of Paul. In the first place there is not much dissimilarity in their names, if transposed. Philo was a traveller; so was Paul: Philo wrote many books; so did Paul. Philo allegorised the book of Genesis; so did Paul.[57] Philo wrote of righteousness; of unwritten laws; of sacrifice; of the three

---

* Philo, *de Vita Contemplat*. And Josephus's "History of the Jewish Wars," Book ii. Chap. 12.
† Euseb. Book ii, Chap. 17.

virtues; of rewards and punishments; of the immutability of God; of nature and invention; of who is the heir of divine things: so did Paul. Philo pleaded his cause, before the Emperor Caligula. So Paul did, we are told, before King Agrippa. I incline to the opinion, that if all the writings of Philo were extant we should find that his life and writings were made the model for those of Paul.

I will speak now of the Gospel "according to Luke;" the author of which we know no more about than we do of the rest; his name not being once mentioned in all the four Gospels! Paul speaks of one Luke, a physician,[58] who, he tells Timothy, was with him;[59] but says nothing of his writing any Gospel or Epistle. Surely you will admit that a physician may attend a man troubled with a thorn in his flesh,[60] without being obliged to write Gospels! Eusebius reports that Irenaus said: "Luke compiled in a book, the Gospel preached by Paul, of whom he was a follower."[*] But what dependance can be placed on the sayings of Irenaus, when Eusebius acknowledges in the same Chapter that his authority for so saying was only tradition! That which was called the Gospel of Marcian was no other than this Gospel altered and interpolated. Irenaus, Tertullian, and Epiphanius, all say that Marcion left out the two first Chapters, and inserted many things of his own. But is it not as likely that others have since added those Chapters which he is accused of having left out, and which in his days he could never find in? You know it is very common for some persons to accuse others of that of which they themselves are alone guilty!

The Priests likewise tell us that the Acts of the Apostles were written by Luke. But how do they know by whom they were written? Whence do they obtain authority even for such a supposition? I know it is reported that Irenaus supposed they were written by Luke, because when Paul wrote to Timothy he informed him that Luke was with him. But were there not many others with him, beside his physician? Why

* Eusebius, Book v, Chap. 8.

must he be singled out in particular, to write histories and Gospels? Surely one would think that he had enough to do in attending to his patients. Paul no where alludes either to his writing or accompanying him in his travels. If we must draw conclusions from suppositions founded upon the book itself, it would seem that the Acts were written by Silas instead of Luke: for in chap. xv. 40, we find that Paul made choice of Silas to accompany him : and directly after, in the next chapter, (xvi. 10, 17,) we find the writer always making use of the plural number, *we* and *us*; which were never used before Silas was chosen his companion. Indeed the different reports of the writer of the Acts and the writer of the Gospel according to Luke, concerning the time which Jesus staid with his disciples after his resurrection, prove that they could never have been written by one and the same person. For one says that Jesus was forty days, and the other makes it appear that he was on earth only one day, as I have already shewn.

I have now gone through the principal events of both the Old and New Testaments; endeavouring, with as much brevity as possible, to descant upon every article of faith, which is considered of importance. Should there be any which I have left unnoticed, you must attribute it to my dread of being accused of prolixity, and not to an artful evasion; being ready and willing at any time to answer every disputant.

The principal foundation for faith in these books is, as I have always understood, their internal evidence, and the credibility and veracity of their authors; of all of which I think I have clearly proved, to every impartial and unprejudiced mind, that they are utterly deficient, as well as that their authors are entirely unknown to us, or to any historian of known integrity. Josephus, the historian, who was a priest of Jerusalem, we find to have been a most absurd, wild and extravagant writer; his massy gates and prodigious stones ; his cow bringing forth a lamb ; his gigantic ghosts ; his madmen, and armies running up and down the clouds; and many other of his incredible and ridiculous stories, destroy his credit as an honest writer. Therefore any testimony of his must be received with great suspicion. Besides, the few words which are found in his 18th and 20th Book of Antiquities, concerning Jesus and his brother James, are clearly proved to be none of his writing, but to have been interpolated since. The stratagems and sophistry which the priests in all ages have been under the necessity of employing, in order to obtain a degree of credit for their tales are, or ought to be, sufficient to satisfy every man of sound judgment, that they are destitute of truth and have no solid foundation. We do not find men disputing respecting the existence of Guy Fawkes, who attempted to blow up the Protestant parliament with gun-powder in the reign of James I., nor yet of the riots and confusion which took place in London and in all England, as soon as his Most Gracious Dutch Majesty, King William, (of ever blessed memory,) landed; when the protestants pulled down and destroyed every house and chapel belonging to the catholics, plundered and burned their goods. Why are not these things controverted? Because they were facts well known, and transmitted to us on unquestionable authority; therefore can admit of no disputation. Would not this have been the case with all the things related in these books, had they been facts well known? But though these things are, if true, of far greater importance to all mankind than the whole world besides, and if they ever did occur, must have been more notorious to the whole world, yet they have always been disputed from the earliest ages. Surely "something is rotten in the State of Denmark!"

Moreover how can we be assured that the book now called the "Word of God," are the identical words originally written? Do we not discover many alterations which have been made therein, through the necessity of translating them from one language into another by ignorant and fallible men, who, as Papias said when Matthew wrote his Gospel in the Hebrew tongue, "every one interpreted it as he was able?"

If I could believe that Jesus ever liveth, and has witnessed all the horrid tortures, the agonies, the sufferings and miseries of millions of human beings, through that infernal religious engine, the inquisition, and through the ambition of kings and the avarice of priests who committed their enormities in his name, I should think him to be the most cruel vindictive being that could be conceived by the mind of man : especially when we are told that all power is given to him, whereby he might have softened the hearts of the tyrants and persecutors ; or have wafted the innocent away in chariots of fire, and so have spared them the agonizing pains which they endured. Surely you will not say that it was absolutely necessary for these men to encounter these trials and undergo such tortures, before they could be found worthy of obtaining a seat in heaven ! If such be the only means of obtaining heaven, why do not the present christians suffer in like manner ? Why were the early Christians singled out in particular, to travel the rugged path, while those of the present day can ascend so easily from a bed of down ?

Before I conclude let me ask you wherein do the Christians excel in moral virtue the pagan Romans ? I find throughout the Roman history that the Romans in general, practised that which Jews and Christians only preach and prate about. The Old Testament itself, discovers that the chosen people of God were more de-- praved, and more ignorant, and less merciful, than those of any other nation. The New Testament likewise exhibits the christians, who were chosen before the foundation of the world, and predestinated unto the adoption of children, by Jesus Christ to himself,[61] as being the most immoral characters ; or what need were there for all those reproofs and admonitions of which we read in so many places ?[62]

Justin Martyr, who wrote a book about the middle of the second century, entitled " A Dialogue against the Jews," acknowledged that the christians were accused by Trypho, at Ephesus, as being a most impious and wicked set of persons that had just sprung up* (which by-the-bye is a complete contradiction to Peter, (1. 1.) who describe, them as being scattered throughout the

* Eusebius Book iv. chapter 18.

world, 100 years before Justin's days!) Constantine the Roman emperor, after the establishment of Christianity, acknowledged, in a rescript which he sent to Miltiades, bishop of Rome, that the people were more divided, and had become more degenerated and worse than before.[*]   I trust that you will excuse my describing the christian character at the present day, it being so notorious.   Witness the lives of their present bishops and priests!

Trusting that you will excuse the style, and pass by all grammatical errors which you may find in these, my letters, I conclude, wishing you as many days of health and strength as you have honesty to preach TRUTH and MORALITY among your less informed fellow creatures. And then the blessing of all mankind, men, women and children, will be upon you, and remain with you always.—Amen!

I am, Sir,

Your humble servant,

JOHN CLARKE.

---

[*] Eusebius Book x. Chap. 5.

NOTES TO THE FOREGOING LETTER.

1 Mark, xv. 44.
2 1 Corinthians xv. 5.
3 Luke, xxiv. 29.
4 John, xx. 27.
5 Luke, xxiv. 13.
6 "   "   28.
7 John xix. 25.
8 Luke, xxiv. 16.
9 Mark, xvi. 12.
10 John, xx. 24.
11 Acts, i. 26.
12 Luke, xxiv. 42.
13 "   xxii. 16, 18.
    Matthew, xxvi. 29.
14 Luke, xxiv. 44, 46.
15 Psalm xviii. 5.
16 "   cxvi. 3.
17 Jonah ii. 2.
18 Isaiah v. 14,
19 Matthew, v. 22.
     "   xxv. 41. 46.
    Luke xii. 5.
20 Isaiah xxx. 33.
    Jeremiah xix. 6.
21   "   " 2.
— Joshua xv. 8.
—   " xviii. 16.
22 2 Kings xxiii. 10.
23 2 Chronicles xiii. 17.
24 1 Kings xi. 16.
25 Ezekiel xxxix. 12.
26 Isaiah lxvi. 24.
27 Luke xvi. 26.
28 Revelations xx. 13, 14.
29 2 Peter iii. 10.
30 1 Samuel xvi. 13.
31 Psalm lxxxix. 19.
32 "   lxxxvi. 2.
33 "   xxx. 3.
34 "   lxxxviii. 5.
35 "   "   10, 11.
     "   vi. 5.
36 "   cxlvi. 4.
37 Mark xvi. 11.
38 "   "   13.
39 John xx. 25.
40 "   "   19.

INDEX TO THE MIRACLES EXAMINED.

JOSHUA HOBSON, PRINTER, 5, MARKET STREET, BRIGGATE, LEEDS.

Lightning Source UK Ltd.
Milton Keynes UK
UKOW06f2036080817

306953UK00011B/1030/P

9 781334 237171